MALAYAN
SPYMASTER

MALAYAN SPYMASTER

MEMOIRS OF A RUBBER PLANTER, BANDIT FIGHTER AND SPY

BORIS HEMBRY

monsoon

monsoonbooks

Published in 2019
by Monsoon Books Ltd
www.monsoonbooks.co.uk

No.1 Duke of Windsor Suite, Burrough Court,
Burrough on the Hill, Leics. LE14 2QS, UK.

First published in 2011 (Monsoon Books, Singapore).

ISBN (paperback): 978-981-08-5442-3
ISBN (ebook): 978-981-4358-30-9

National Library Board, Singapore Cataloguing-in-Publication Data
Hembry, Boris.
Malayan spymaster : memoirs of a rubber planter, bandit fighter and spy / Boris
Hembry. – Singapore : Monsoon Books, 2011.
p. cm.
Includes bibliographical references and index.
ISBN : 978-981-08-5442-3 (pbk.)
1. Hembry, Boris. 2. British – Malaysia – Malaya – Biography.
3. Plantation overseers – Malaysia – Malaya – Biography.
4. Intelligence officers – Great Britain – Biography. 5. Intelligence officers
– Malaysia – Malaya – Biography. 6. World War, 1939-1945 – Military
intelligence – Malaysia – Malaya. 7. Malaya – History – Malayan Emergency,
1948-1960. I. Title.
DS597.15
959.5104092 -- dc22   OCN697719574

MIX
Paper from
responsible sources
FSC® C018072

Printed and bound in Great Britain by Clays Ltd, Elcograf S.p.A.
21 20 19   5 6 7

Contents

Preface

Malayan Spymaster has been abridged from *In Lands Beyond the Sea*, memoirs written by Boris Hembry, my father, solely for his family and not for publication. However, we find his reminiscences of life as a planter in Malaya in the late heyday of the British Empire, his activities in clandestine forces in South East Asia during the Second World War, and subsequently his part in the fight against the terrorists during the Communist insurrection in the post-war Malayan Emergency, not only fascinating but a source of great pride.

His account of the events of June 16th, 1948, at Sungei Siput, Perak State, must be the definitive record of the very beginning of the Emergency. Twice mentioned in despatches, awarded the Netherlands Resistance Memorial Cross and the Colonial Police Medal, the recommendation for the DSO for his work with ISLD (SIS/MI6), during which he not only landed from a submarine on Japanese-occupied Sumatra and Malaya, but also, whilst Head of Malayan Country Section, ISLD, conceived, planned and activated what has been acknowledged as the most successful intelligence-gathering operation in the Malayan theatre of war, was rejected on the grounds that such awards were not made to field officers of the Secret Intelligence Service.

This book is published at the instigation of Boris Hembry's family who consider his story deserves a wider readership than first intended. We dedicate it to those expatriates of many generations whose devotion to that beautiful country and its peoples helped to lay the foundations of present-day peaceful and prosperous Malaysia.

My father died in September 1990.

John Hembry
Brillac, France

Foreword

During the past 25 years members of my family and several friends have suggested that I should write the story of my life. I have always opposed this suggestion on the grounds both that the events of the years of greatest interest, 1930–1955, have already been fully recorded by historians and professional writers and there was little I could add, and out of laziness.

Eventually I was persuaded by the argument that my family, and particularly my grandchildren Robin, Timothy and Annabel, in years to come, when they have children of their own, may like to have a first-hand record of the life of their Hembry grandparents.

It is now over 50 years since I travelled half way across the world to seek my fortune. I failed in that ambition, but found love, lasting friendships, happiness, adventure in times of peace and war, and, naturally, disappointments.

For over a quarter of a century Jean and I enjoyed a way of life that can never again be experienced. We were privileged to live in Malaya during the last three decades of the British Empire, finally leaving that beautiful country just before it achieved its rightful independence.

My story is that of an expatriate rubber planter, an ordinary man who was required on occasions, and like so many of my contemporaries, to do some less than ordinary things in extraordinary times.

I have made no attempt to romanticise or exaggerate. I have relied on memory, promptings from Jean and friends, documents I have retained and, for the period spent in the jungle behind the Japanese lines and my escape from Singapore in early 1942, the notes written during my enforced inactivity at Barrackpore, Calcutta, shortly after the events described. Where I am mistaken, no matter. These memoirs are not for publication.

After a somewhat reluctant start I found that the memories came flooding back, sometimes after having committed to paper other events of the same period. I have usually been disinclined to retrace my steps.

I can make no claim to having left any mark on the world. The only memorial to show that I have passed by will be my descendants. On reflection, however, and like countless thousands of my fellow countrymen, I think that I am entitled to feel some pride in having made a contribution, however small, to the victories over the Japanese in the Second World War, and the communist terrorists and their political masters during the equally real war known as the Malayan Emergency.

What little I have achieved has been with the unfailing love, friendship and encouragement of Jean. I dedicate this story to her, with all my love.

Boris Hembry
Canterbury, 1983

Note

Although the spellings of many names and places have been changed since Malaysia gained independence, those that were customary during the period described have been used throughout this book. A Glossary of the current spellings of Malay and other words, acronyms, initials, etc can be found at the end of the book in the Glossary.

Estates on which Boris Hembry worked in Malaya and Indonesia

KEY

1 Gajah Muntah Estate
2 Sungei Gettah Estate
   and Kong Moh Seng
   (KMS) Estate
3 Waterloo Estate

4 Kamuning Estate
5 Bukit Asahan Estate
6 Ulu Remis Estate
7 Sungei Plentong Rubber
   Estate

ESCAPE ROUTE OF THE STAY BEHIND PARTY

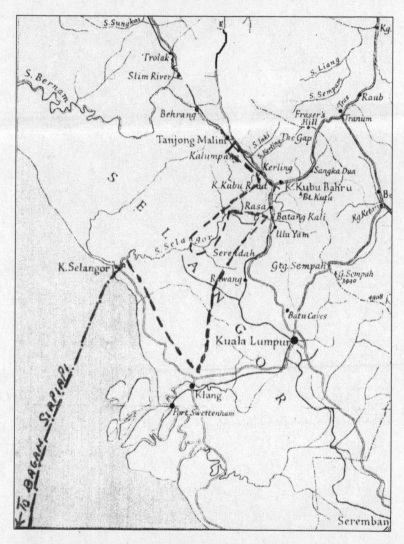

Source: Map and sketch from Boris Hembry's scrapbook.

Landfall in Malaya

March 1930

I stood on the deck of the old cargo ship *Achilles* one morning in March 1930, a callow, thoughtful youth of 19, watching the dim wet coastline of Cheshire and north Wales disappear. I would see the shores of Britain again only twice in the next 17 years.

My parents had accompanied me to Liverpool, where we were joined by my brother Bill, and, after dinner at the Adelphi, had found our way to the Blue Funnel Line ship lying in the docks. We arrived on board to be met by a steward who showed me to the twin-berthed cabin that was to be mine for the next 31 days. I was privileged – it was on the port side. Young planters on their way out East for the first time were not usually permitted to travel POSH.

I was the first passenger on board and was joined shortly by a mining engineer who turned out to be my cabin companion. The steward served us coffee, and soon afterwards I said my goodbyes, but not before my father had tipped the steward three pounds, bidding him to look after me well on the voyage. This the 'steward' promised to do. But I never saw him again; he was shore crew and had disembarked before we sailed.

How was it that I, Boris Hembry, not yet 20, should find myself on a cold March night on board this old tramp steamer bound for Singapore and a rubber estate in Johore state, southern Malaya?

At Brentwood School I had a friend called Mick Kitchener. By then I had also met the girl I was to marry, Jean Cuthbertson, who went to the nearby Ursuline Convent school. Jean coincidentally also happened to know the whole Kitchener family very well, including Mick's older brothers, Jack and Dick, who were rubber planting in the Straits Settlements – as Malaya was known then.

After I had matriculated and left school I had been articled to a firm of surveyors in London. My father had paid 100 guineas for my articles, against which I received a salary of 15 shillings a week – in effect my father's money very slowly coming back to me. As luck would have it my father had chosen a firm that was on its last legs, so my future was uncertain. However, I did pass the preliminary examination of the Surveyors Institution (now the Royal Institute of Chartered Surveyors) which was to be of great benefit in the years to come. But after 18 months of travelling up to London each day on this miserly wage, I began to doubt the wisdom of my chosen career and to listen with increasing interest to the news of the Kitchener boys in Malaya.

My father, who had gone out with the Imperial Yeomanry to fight in the Boer War and had stayed on afterwards to seek his fortune, had an old friend from his South African days named Ernest Ridsdell whom we visited from time to time. Ernest had become a very successful accountant in the City and was by then chairman of several Malayan rubber companies. During our conversations I had learned that the salary of a junior assistant on a rubber estate in Malaya was at least 30 pounds a month, with an additional allowance for servants, and free accommodation. Compared to 15 shillings a week that seemed a fortune.

So early in 1930 I took the plunge. With my father's encouragement, I approached Ernest and, after several interviews in the City with company secretaries and directors, I was appointed junior assistant on Sungei Plentong Rubber Estate, near Johore Bahru, managed by Ridsdell & Co.

Including myself there were six passengers on the *Achilles*: the mining engineer; a Doctor Reed, who was returning to his practice near Tapah; a young Scot, who, like me, was going out for the first time as a junior assistant on an estate; a young man on a round trip to Japan for health reasons; and a manager from the Blue Funnel Line's City office being transferred to Port Said.

I remember feeling desperately homesick for the first few days, and this lasted until we turned into the Mediterranean. Except for short visits to aunts in Wales, and a year at boarding school when I was eight, I had never been away from home.

The Bay of Biscay crossing was smooth. I have crossed the Bay 12 times and only once, in 1947, has that most turbulent of waters lived up to its reputation. My very first sight of Gibraltar to port, with the high sierra behind, and the snow-capped Atlas Mountains in Morocco to starboard, has always remained with me. It was the point in each subsequent voyage out to Malaya when I considered that I had finally left England behind.

Early one morning, about 10 days out of Liverpool, we arrived at Port Said, and I had my first experience of 'The East' – its sights, its sounds and, above all, its smells. The ship was besieged by bumboats, gully-gully men, souvenir sellers and vendors of all descriptions, shouting their wares and services from their boats which lay alongside the ship, whilst we stopped to pick up the pilot to take us to the coaling station.

Most interesting of all was the coaling of the ship. This was carried out by Tamil coolies, carrying baskets of coal on their head, jogging up the gangways and dumping their loads into the ship's bunkers. I had been told in London that Tamils were to be the main source of labour on a rubber estate so I watched them at work with great interest. I wondered how such apparently emaciated bodies could possibly lift the very heavy baskets of coal, carry them 50 yards or so, up a gangway and along the deck, with such dexterity, seeming ease, and above all else, such cheerfulness, for hours on end. I was, of course, later to realise that what I took for emaciation was in fact wiriness, and the cheerfulness was only appreciation for being employed at all, and thus being able to eat and to feed their families. After a quarter of a century of employing many nationalities I unhesitatingly place the Tamils, who originate from the Madras area of India, near the top of the list for reliability and loyalty.

We spent some time in Port Said so were able to stretch our legs on dry land, and to visit that great emporium Simon Artz, known to many generations of travellers going out East. It was Harrods set at one of the world's great crossroads. One could kit oneself out with anything and everything needed for the deserts of the Middle East, for Africa, India and the Far East and, for those returning from 'lands beyond the sea', for Europe. Many old Eastern hands would leave their winter-weight clothes in storage at Simon Artz for collection on their return journey.

We journeyed through the Suez Canal in convoy. It seemed very strange to be, quite literally, sailing along in the desert, passing palm trees, camels, Egyptians riding donkeys, villages, all only within a few yards of the ship. In Lake Timsah, about halfway down the canal, we stopped to allow a northbound convoy to pass. Looking over the rail and up at a great P&O liner, homeward bound, certainly made me realise the difference in our status. But, in retrospect, I would not have changed places for my first trip out to the Orient.

On leaving the canal we sailed into a sandstorm. Only those who have actually experienced this phenomenon can appreciate quite what this means. Sand penetrates everywhere and everything. There is no movement of air. It becomes unbearably hot, for there was no air conditioning in those days. The Chinese stokers were collapsing in the engine room and being brought up on deck to recover. The Captain did the only possible thing in the circumstances and reversed course, to sail into what little wind there was. After nearly two days the sandstorm abated and we resumed our southerly course and eventually, much to the relief of passengers and crew alike, turned into the Indian Ocean.

There was very little to do on board except to read and to play cards and deck games. These included the odd game of cricket, usually the passengers versus the crew. The balls were of rope, made by the bosun. My brother Bill had been presented with a cricket bat, bought from Jack Hobbs' shop in Fleet Street, and autographed by the Master. Bill had given up cricket in favour of golf (he was to play in the Amateur Championship on numerous occasions, and played off scratch when nearly 70 years of age!) and had passed on the bat to me. It was the only one on board. One day one of the officers took a mighty swipe at the ball and the bat slipped out of his sweaty hands and flew overboard. I hoped that it would eventually be washed up on Indian shores, where it would be appreciated for what it was, rather than on African or Arabian, where it would most probably be used as firewood.

Before leaving England I had been given a book of short

stories by W. Somerset Maugham, which I enjoyed very much as an introduction to the Far East, at least as seen through what I soon learned to be the author's somewhat jaundiced eyes. Probably his most famous story, 'The Letter', was based on fact, but concerned the wife of a schoolmaster in Kuala Lumpur and a mining engineer, not a planter. I read a lot as the ship had a very good library. I read Joseph Conrad's Far East stories with particular fascination and much enjoyment, although realising that they were set at the end of the previous century and that times had changed, at least on the Malay Peninsula.

The voyage across the Indian Ocean was uneventful, except for the loss of my precious cricket bat, and my first sightings of the ever-present flying fish, sharks and whales. I particularly remember the starry tropical nights, little realising that I was to experience the same sense of wonderment and awe, in these same waters, some 13 years later, from the conning tower of a submarine.

To arrive at Penang by sea in the early morning must be one of travel's most magical experiences. The coastline is rocky and the jungle comes down to the shore, until one rounds the point at Batu Feringgi and the beautiful beaches come into view. One catches sight of Penang Peak, shrouded in mist, rising to 2,000 feet, in the middle of the island. The mainland is on the port side, with Kedah Peak, over 4,000 feet high, silhouetted against the rising sun and the gathering rain clouds. As the ship makes its way slowly through the roads towards the anchorage opposite Georgetown, larger buildings appear – the E&O Hotel, the Penang Club, the Municipal Buildings, the station clock tower, and the Francis Light Memorial. Even today Penang is considered the 'Pearl of the Orient'. Just imagine what it must have been like 60 years ago.

The roads were full of shipping: liners belonging to P&O, Blue Funnel, BI (British India) and Orient Lines, large cargo vessels, the smaller Straits Steamship coasters and, of course, scores of junks and sampans; even dhows from Oman. Except for a Dutch liner bound for the Dutch East Indies and the monthly Portuguese ship to Macao, nearly all would be flying the Red Ensign.

The *Achilles* dropped anchor and we were taken ashore by

launch. The mining engineer departed for Ipoh and Dr Reed took charge of us remaining passengers, all first-timers to the East. My first call ashore was to Ridsdell's agents, McAuliffe, Davis & Hope – I was to learn later that they were known, with good reason, as McAwful, Davis & No Bloody Hope. Here I met Jock Reid, who ran the estates side of McAuliffes. McAuliffes were accountants. The firm was actually owned by the three Grummitt brothers, nicknamed, again with some justification, Grummitt, Grabbitt and Keepitt.

I should explain that the majority of European-owned rubber estates in Malaya at that time were individual companies, both private and public, and they employed agents – other companies such as Guthrie's, Sime Darby and Ridsdells – to manage them. They all had their own boards of directors and company secretaries in the City to whom the managing agents were responsible. Of course, the major tyre companies, for example Dunlop and Firestone, also owned estates, as did several Continental European companies, such as SOCFIN (Société Financière des Caoutchoucs).

In those days the Straits Settlements were divided into three kinds of territories. Singapore, Malacca, Penang and Province Wellesley were Crown Colonies. Perak, Selangor, Negri Sembilan and Pahang were Federated Malay States, whilst Johore, Kedah, Trengganu, Kelantan and Perlis were Unfederated Malay States. All the Malay States had sultans as titular rulers, each with a British-appointed mentri besar or adviser to the Sultan – in effect the prime minister.

It made little difference where one lived. Great Britain was the protecting power, and the Malayan Civil Service (MCS) provided administrators at all levels, the mentris besar, the management of the Public Works Department (PWD), the district officers, the magistrates (although some were Malays) and judges, and the police of lieutenant rank and above, throughout the country. The clubs, banks, agency houses, lawyers, veterinary surgeons, doctors and others were in all the major towns, and the system of British law generally prevailed. It was considered at the time that, after India, the Sudan and Malaya could always count on getting the best recruits into the Colonial Service. (I must say, knowing what I do now about the responses of the most senior officials to the events leading up the surrender to the Japanese in 1942, and my own experience when serving on the Federal War Council during the post-war Emergency, I find this difficult to believe.)

Jock Reid was a small, broad-shouldered, bow-legged Scot, with a Glaswegian accent one could cut with a knife, a fair-minded and extremely pleasant man whom I was to know for the rest of my time in Malaya. After welcoming me he confirmed that I was expected at Sungei Plentong Estate, Johore, but would probably be transferred in six months or so, soon after Barton, the manager, returned from his home leave which was due to begin shortly after my arrival.

Dr Reed took us to lunch at the Runnymede Hotel which along with the Raffles in Singapore was one of the two most prestigious hotels in Malaya. The Runnymede had magnificent views across the Penang Strait to the massive rock formation of Bukit Mertajam, Kedah Peak and the jungle-covered mountains in the background which formed the backbone of the Malay Peninsula. 'Malaya' is derived from a Hindustani word for mountain, and was first used by voyagers from India many centuries previously on seeing these mountains from the sea. Hence, too, the 'Himalayas'.

After lunch – henceforth I was to know it as tiffin – we hired a car and drove around the island, visiting the Snake Temple, the Chinese Temple and the Botanical Gardens, and I saw for the first time the padi fields, banana groves, rubber plantations and jungle, and the hustle and bustle, the noise and the smells, and the peoples of many races, all of which were to be so much part of my future life. We rejoined the ship late in the evening, but not before I had experienced for the first time the cacophony of a tropical night, the almost deafening sounds produced by every kind of bullfrog, lizard and insect imaginable.

We sailed that night for Port Swettenham, further down the coast and the port for Kuala Lumpur. Port Swettenham, named after one of the great early administrators of the Straits Settlements, had only one wooden jetty – a far cry from the Port Klang of today, which is a vast port complex. Here we bade farewell to Dr Reed and the few passengers who had boarded at Penang for the short trip down the coast, and after only a couple of hours set off on the final leg of the voyage to Singapore.

I got up well before dawn to watch our arrival. The final few miles into Singapore are dotted with islands, usually the home of Malay fishermen, many to be seen in colourful sarongs, busy on the beach repairing their nets, or fishing from sampans (wooden boats) or blahts (small huts built on stilts in quite deep water, and from which they could cast their nets). They also used the blahts to lay out their catch to dry. The smell of a typical blaht was indescribably awful, as I was to find out 12 years later when escaping to Sumatra. Like Penang, the approach to Singapore was full of shipping of all sizes and description, only more so. Then as now, Singapore was the major port and commercial centre for the whole region, the hub from which Malaya exported most of its rubber and tin production. Thus its importance to Great Britain, and the Royal Navy's 'impregnable' Singapore Naval Base.

The *Achilles* went alongside Collyer Quay to disembark passengers, before returning to the roads to discharge its cargo into lighters. I was met by a young assistant from Ridsdell's local agents, Sandilands Buttery, named Leighton, and driven to their offices to meet Mr Bromley-Davenport, the manager. After the usual pleasantries he remarked that he had no idea why I had been sent out because rubber was selling at only sixpence a pound, and the price was still falling, and that it was entirely possible that we would all be sent packing in a matter of months. Poor Bromley-Davenport. He correctly read his own future, but luckily both Leighton and I survived the slump and we continued to meet off and on for the next quarter of a century.

Leighton drove me to the Raffles where, after a beer in the Long Bar, he left me to wait for Barton, my new manager, who was driving in from Sungei Plentong, not only to meet me but also to discuss estate business with the agents. Barton arrived at about noon, a tall, stoutish man with a tremendous laugh, and we got on well from the start. We were to have very little time together before his departure on leave, but I must have created a reasonable impression because he specifically requested for me to act for him when he went home on leave again in 1934.

He took me to the Singapore Club for tiffin. It was then the most prestigious club on the island, situated in the Post Office building overlooking the Padang. I remember being most impressed at the sight of numerous tuans besar having their post-tiffin snooze in long planters' chairs, and the large number of servants in attendance. These were summoned by shouting 'boy!' – something I was to do many years later, in a fit of absentmindedness, at the Cumberland Hotel, in London, to the acute embarrassment of my party and myself, and to the equally acute annoyance of the waiter.

Tiffin over and business concluded, we set up off up the Bukit Timah Road towards mainland Malaya.

Creeping in Johore

April 1930 – December 1930

We crossed the causeway to Johore Bahru and arrived at the manager's bungalow at about tea time. The road from JB – as Johore Bahru was known throughout Malaya – to the village of Sungei Plentong passed through mile after mile of rubber plantations, which all seemed pretty dreary to me at first sight, but these rows upon rows of rubber trees, much disliked by journalists and authors down the years, soon became of absorbing interest to me as I began to learn my chosen profession.

The entrance to Sungei Plentong Estate was through the village, really little more than a collection of corrugated iron- and atap-roofed huts lining the main road, although the shops seemed to be well stocked with everything that one could want by way of tinned foodstuffs, dry stores and live chickens and ducks. My first impression, even as a new boy, was of rather weary-looking trees, much bracken, and rutted roads. Unfortunately, second impressions only confirmed the first. I was soon to realise that the Ridsdell group of companies was not known for the quality of its trees or the husbanding of resources. In the good times of high rubber prices and profits, during and just after the Great War, the Ridsdell companies had declared large dividends, so, unlike more soundly administered firms, most of them had little in reserve to fall back on when times were hard.

I liked the look of the manager's bungalow. Bungalow is a Hindustani word, used from Bombay to Shanghai to describe any house occupied by a European, no matter the size or the number of storeys. Barton's was single storey, built on brick piers, as was normal in Malaya, spacious, roofed with thatch laid on corrugated iron, and with a wide verandah on three sides. It looked out over to a jungle-covered bukit (hill) in the middle distance – of which more later. It also had electricity, something that I was not to have again until Jean and I moved to Kamuning Estate, Sungei Siput, in 1936.

Barton was expecting not only me that day, but also the visiting agent (VA). Most rubber companies employed senior planters to visit their estates every six months or so, to inspect, criticise and recommend changes. He brought with him not only the expertise of many years planting, but also an up-to-date knowledge of what was happening on other estates in the group, and also of planting and manufacturing innovations. On completion of his visit the VA would write his report, usually in the manager's office, which was then read by the manager, and the criticisms and recommendations fully discussed before submission to the local agents in KL and, eventually, the board in London.

This VA arrived in the evening and after supper he and Barton got down to talking shop, and what, in my naivety, I thought was heavy drinking. But being excluded from the shoptalk, I had but one whisky and water and went to bed early, feeling suddenly very homesick and not a little apprehensive of what the morrow would bring.

The most popular alcoholic drinks amongst Europeans were Tiger beer and a 'stengah', a long whisky with water or soda. Although stengah means 'half' in Malay, the normal proportions were about one third whisky to two thirds water, so that several stengahs could be downed before one exceeded a couple of English pub-sized doubles. Long drinks helped to replace the fluids lost through heavy sweating during the day.

At 5.30 the next morning I attended my first muster. Every morning the coolies mustered on the estate padang, an open space where people congregated for meetings or games; rather like the village green in England. I did not have to ask the way. I merely followed my nose. The smell was nauseating: a mixture of sweaty bodies, human excreta, curry, cooking, urine and fire smoke. The Tamil coolie, when wishing to relieve himself, merely squatted where he was, particularly in the dark at muster time.

All the manual workers on the estate were known by the Chinese word 'coolie'. Contrary to present-day ideas the word coolie was not considered in any way derogatory, and I shall be using this word until my narrative reaches the post-war period when it was replaced by the term 'estate worker'.

On arrival at muster I was met by R. P. 'Pete' Peters, the senior assistant – and at least 100 pairs of inquisitive eyes. He introduced me to the kranis (clerks) and conductors. The kranis were also Indians, but of a higher caste, well-educated, and they spoke fluent English. The conductors were responsible for the supervision of the labour force in the field, the direction of the various gangs to their allotted tasks and, above all, the standard of tapping. They had to ensure that there were enough tappers for the daily cropping. One could usually expect about 10 per cent of the labour force to be absent at any given time, because of illness, disinclination to work or, more often than not, a hangover from imbibing too much toddy, a powerful alcoholic beverage distilled from coconut milk.

The kranis called the roll and noted absentees. Later they completed the divisional muster reports which showed where the field gangs were working, the number of vacant tasks, and the number of sick reporting to the 'dresser'. This was a man with elementary training and much experience in basic medical matters – the day-to-day illnesses such as malaria, diarrhoea, minor injuries and also, of course, pregnancy. Their skills varied, but on the whole they were very competent. In fact, I had greater faith in the competence of the dresser than in several estate doctors I could mention.

When muster was over Peters told me to go back to the bungalow for tea and then to meet him at the estate office at 6.30 am.

I liked Pete immediately. He was about 28 and would have been planting for four or five years. He was married, and his wife Easter was with him. A very good rugger player, he had more than once represented the South vs the North, the ultimate accolade in Malayan rugby. This at a time when each side would have had a least one Blue, possibly an international trialist (usually a Scot), and most certainly several Services caps.

At 6.30 Pete began the job of teaching me to be a rubber planter. I was now a 'creeper' – the term used for very new junior assistants, who crept around the estate trying to look as inconspicuous as possible, not knowing their backsides from their elbows, and not being able to speak more than a word or two of either Malay or Tamil. After he introduced me to the senior office krani, a stout and very cheerful Southern Indian, we set out on foot to inspect one of the divisions. The estate was divided into three divisions, each with a senior conductor in charge, with a junior conductor, a krani, and two or three kanganis (foremen) under him.

Rubber trees are not indigenous to Malaya. They grew wild in Brazil, hence their botanical name *Hervea Braziliensis*, and the Brazilians, wishing to protect their world monopoly of this increasingly important raw material, prohibited the export of any plants, seedlings or seeds, under severe penalties. However, in 1876, the British botanist Henry Alexander Wickham, later Sir Henry, collected a quantity of seeds and smuggled them out to the Royal Botanical Gardens, Kew, where they germinated. A number of seedlings were sent out to Singapore, but none survived. Shortly afterwards more were despatched to Ceylon and there they did prosper. From these, 10 young plants were shipped on to Malaya and planted in Kuala Kangsar, Perak. As late as 1980 one of these original trees still stood in the grounds of the District Office.

In the late 1880s several hundred seedlings were planted as shade trees for the pepper on Kamuning Estate, Sungei Siput, Perak, and they were still there in all their splendour nearly 60 years later. I was most distressed when I returned to Kamuning in October 1945 to find that these historic trees had been felled for firewood during the Japanese occupation.

By 1897 there were some 34,000 acres of rubber planted in Malaya. Forty years later there were 3,250,000 acres, of which 45 per cent were owned by British, European and American companies and the rest by Asians.

Pete showed me how to tap a rubber tree. Thin slivers of bark are cut from the trunk, in a diagonally downwards direction, and the latex – as the sap of a rubber tree is known – flows from the incision into a small earthenware cup which is attached to the tree, usually by a length of wire. The tappers start work at 6 am and continue until about 11.30, when they would break for a meal, usually rice and curry, brought out to them by their wife or children. At noon they would begin to collect the latex from the cups, pouring it into buckets. If the trees on his task were of reasonable quality a good tapper would collect about six gallons of latex, although this yield was considerably improved when bud-grafted trees came into production in the mid-1930s.

When the latex had been collected, the tapper would sling the buckets over a kandar stick across his shoulders, and wend his way, often at a jog, to the collecting point where the contents of the bucket would be weighed, a sample taken for density, and the actual amount of rubber calculated. In those days a tapper was awarded a 'name' for one day's work, but later, in order to encourage higher production, he was paid on a yield basis, so much a pound weight tapped. This way the tapper earned more and the company achieved the higher production required, but the conductors had to be even more vigilant to ensure the trees were not damaged by over-enthusiastic tapping.

A 'kandar' was a tough piece of wood, about six feet in length, with wire hooks at each end on to which the buckets were hung by their handles. Again, I never ceased to be astonished at the way a frail-looking Tamil could carry 12 gallons of latex, weighing about 120 pounds, often for several miles without stopping, and rarely spilling a drop.

The Tamil, like most Indians but by no means all, is basically a gentle person, but when roused can become an absolute fiend, especially where women are concerned. One night, when I was back on Sungei Plentong in 1934, I was having supper when the dresser came in, placed a small bloodstained package of newspaper on the table, which he unwrapped to reveal a bloody piece of meat some two inches square. When I asked what it was he replied, 'Ramasamy's ear.' It seemed that Kupan, my cook, had returned from the toddy shop to find Ramasamy astride his (Kupan's) wife. With a roar he had leapt on them both, and in the ensuing fracas had bitten off the ear. I suggested that he was lucky it was only his ear that was amputated.

I later had all three in my office and successfully mediated between them, fining Ramasamy the cost of treating his wound at the JB hospital, docking a similar amount from Kupan's next pay, and lecturing his wife on the necessity for marital fidelity whilst being in the privileged position of living at the manager's bungalow and enjoying a higher standard of comfort and living than she would otherwise. Nowadays, of course, it would have been a matter for the police, probably a custodial sentence for Ramasamy, a divorce for the Kupans, and criticism of me for presuming to act as I did without the necessary qualification in counselling.

During our first walk around the division together, Peters explained that my duties entailed not only general supervisory work but also the compilation of the check rolls. Check rolls were the absolute curse of all junior assistants. Briefly, they were the official estate records of expenditure on labour. The names of all the labour force were written down in a column on the left of the double page in the roll book, and daily a tick or a cross was entered against each name to signify whether the individual had worked or not. If the coolie had committed a misdemeanour, such as faulty tapping or being late for work, he would be awarded only a half name. The number of names earned each month by the person concerned would be totted up in the right hand column. It follows, therefore, that the totals of the horizontal columns had to tally with those on the vertical. Invariably there would be a difference, usually an odd half name. Many were the times that I have sat up half the night trying to find the missing half name, to balance the books. In addition to these daily work records, details of cash advances, rice issues and any other relevant information were recorded on the right hand page. These check rolls were an absolute nightmare, but had to be kept accurately as they were part of the audit. Often I had to enlist the help of the office clerk to track down my mistake. The rolls had to be checked by the junior assistant in his own time, which I always considered unfair, and when I was in a position to alter this custom I did so without hesitation.

The first few months are gruelling and frustrating for a new junior assistant – as, I suppose, with most jobs. One would work nearly all hours that God gave, but without the experience to do anything much but to 'creep'. I would be up at 5 am, attend muster at 5.30, return to the bungalow for a shave and some tea and fruit, back to the office at 6.30, or straight out to walk around the tapping, taking in the weeding and drainage gangs. At about 11, I would return to the bungalow for a meal, midday rest (in Malaya this was known as a 'lie off') for an hour before going out to oversee the measuring of the latex, check up on the weeding gangs again, until about 2.30, when I returned to the office to listen to coolies' complaints and requests, mediate on quarrels and disputes, and generally act as the father and the mother to the estate workers. No one appeared to query the ability of a rather immature, unmarried 20-year-old to proffer sound advice on marital problems and life in general.

Should there be extra work laid on for the afternoon, for example extra weeding or tapping, or road or bridge repairs, the assistant would be required to supervise this too. There were many days when I worked from 5.30 am until nightfall at about 7 pm, with only a hour or so off in the day. And then there were the infernal check rolls.

Once a week the assistant supervised the distribution of rice to the labour force. The amount varied with the size of the family. Rice was purchased on the open market in bulk, and sold to the workers at cost.

It would take about three months for a new assistant to settle down and learn something of what it was all about, and about six before he began to earn his keep. Language was a difficulty. Not only did one have to learn Tamil, but also Malay. In India there was a system whereby junior officers, in both the civil and military services, were provided with 'munshis' (teachers), but not so in Malaya. Consequently one studied books, asked the conductors and clerks to translate, and generally picked up the languages as one went along. I think it was in the mid-1930s that most companies in Malaya introduced language exams for their European recruits, which, if passed, meant additional pay. In the event I soon became fluent in both Malay and Tamil, and was later to learn to speak passable Hakka (the Chinese dialect spoken around Taiping, in Perak), even though I did not have the help of a 'sleeping dictionary', as many young men did.

In a man's lifetime there are turning points or landmarks, often several, which have a definite bearing on one's future. One which affected me happened about four months after my arrival at Sungei Plentong Estate, probably in August 1930.

A wide stream ran through the middle of the estate and this often used to flood, and as the main estate road ran over this stream there were constant difficulties. It had been decided to change the course of the stream, and to sink three large pre-cast concrete culverts to replace the, by now, somewhat rickety bridge, and its quagmire approaches. As this was a comparatively major project it had to receive Board approval, and this was only forthcoming after Barton had left to go on leave. The work was carried out under my supervision, but in all honesty I did nothing except shout the occasional 'surrukka veile' ('work quickly' in Tamil), while trying to look managerial but, of course, fooling no one. I still lacked confidence and was hesitant to initiate anything, even when it was obvious what was required.

When the rains came the lack of an intelligent approach to the new road and bridge building very soon became obvious, the quagmire returned and the road became almost impassable. I was in the office one afternoon and happened to mention the problem to Peters. 'Yes,' he said, 'and what the fucking hell are you going to do about it?' I was so incensed that I stalked out of the office and strode up and down wondering how I should react. No one had ever spoken to me like this before. Should I complain? Luckily I was unable to decide what to say, so I went back to the bungalow, collected my motorbike, summoned the divisional clerk and, with him on the pillion, set off for the trouble spot. Together we observed the scene, and, not for the first or the last time, my surveyor's training stood me in good stead. We had not built up the approach roads sufficiently on either side of the culverts. We had not built up the crown of the road. We had not dug ditches either side of the road to take away the water. In fact, the whole thing was a perfect example of how not to remedy the problem.

I took the clerk back to the lines and ordered him to collect about 20 men to work until dark to drain the water away from the pot holes and ruts, and to make a start on digging the side drains, on overtime. The following morning he was to bring the same gang, continue with the drainage work and to start excavating laterite (red-coloured gravel). He was also to tow the heaviest roller he could find down to the site. In the afternoon, when the sun had had time to dry out the surface, the coolies were to build up the approach roads with a crown of at least six inches with the laterite, and then to roll and roll the surface until it was as hard as concrete. This was done, with the final touches completed the next day. The results were first class, and the culvert was still functioning satisfactorily when I visited the estate on government security business in 1951.

Peters never said a word. But I had done something off my own bat, used my initiative. From that moment on I walked around the estate with a degree of confidence, dealing with problems, such as cutting out a diseased tree or upbraiding a tapper for sloppy work, as I saw them. I was now earning my keep. In fact I was no longer a creeper. In retrospect, I owed Peters a great deal for his snarling remark.

The manufacturing process of rubber was primitive in those days compared to the present, laughably so. In the early Thirties, production was generally limited to ribbed smoke sheet and scrap. Only the largest estates had creping batteries.

The process was simplicity itself. After being weighed, the latex was tipped through a strainer into a large aluminium-lined coagulating tank, approximately fifteen feet by three by one foot deep. When the tank had been filled, the density would be measured and recorded, and either formic or sulphuric acid added. The frothy scum was then removed and aluminium slats slotted into the tank at one and a half inch intervals. The following morning the slats would be removed, the wet flabby sheets removed and passed through a series of rollers, rather like an old-fashioned mangle, which would squeeze out the water, flatten and impress a ribbed diamond-shaped pattern onto the sheets, which would then be hung in the smoke houses to dry, for about 10 days. After which one had what the rubber industry knew as RSS – ribbed smoked sheet.

Next the rubber was graded into categories. If the greater proportion of an estate's production was not graded No. 1, questions of the management would be asked not only by the local agents but also by the secretaries in London. Most rubber was sold by tender in London, much of it 'forward'. It was a very serious matter, again leading to a close investigation of the estate management concerned, if a consignment was subsequently rejected as not being of the specified standard.

Barton went on leave within a very few weeks of my arrival. After his departure I had the large bungalow to myself and felt very lonely. In the evenings, when not engrossed with my check rolls, I read a lot and studied my Malay and Tamil language books. The famous one was Wells' *Cooly Tamil*. I remember saying over and over again 'ompath airati tolairati tonnut ompathu', Tamil for nine thousand nine hundred and ninety-nine. Not desperately useful, but it allowed me to get my Rs rolling, as one must do in Tamil.

I was bothered by mosquitoes at first, and later by flying ants and stink bugs. After a dry spell the ants would fly out of the ground and make for the nearest light, so that the room would soon become ankle deep with their corpses. Stink bugs, the shape of ladybirds but larger, would drop into one's drink and would taste quite abominable, quite apart from the smell. Other than the mosquito nets around the beds, the Sungei Plentong bungalow was not mosquito-proofed.

In addition to all the flying bugs, the ceilings were the playground for little lizards called cicak (pronounced 'cheechah'). They are attractive little creatures whose favourite pastimes, when not devouring mosquitoes and other insects, are ensuring the survival of the species, and defecating. They also have the disturbing habit of shedding their tail when frightened.

My catering and housekeeping was done by my cook/boy, whom I placed on contract. For so much a month he would feed me and keep his wages from the balance. It was the common system for bachelors, and worked well. The tuan always bought his drinks and the ice. Refrigerators, even kerosene-powered ones, were unheard of. About once a week the estate lorry would go into JB and bring back a 50-pound block of ice in a tin-lined box, with the butter, soft drinks, beer, etc piled around the ice.

Only one estate bungalow in 50 had electricity, although it was usually available in the towns. We had oil lamps, or power lamps, fed from a cylinder. The snag with the latter was that the first flying ant to arrive usually broke the mantle. There were no radios either. These came on the scene in 1934 or 1935. I recall listening to the Queen launching the *Queen Mary* on Clydeside when I was back again on Sungei Plentong as acting manager.

Soon after Barton's departure the Peters invited me round to their bungalow for dinner and to meet Easter's mother, Lady Fraser, a most attractive and charming widow of a high court judge in India. Easter, too, was a very pretty girl. I looked forward to my invitations to spend time with them, as they were also very witty and good company.

It was the normal practice for an acting manager, even if he was the senior assistant from the same estate, rather than from another, to move into the manager's bungalow. Peters decided to remain in his own senior assistant's bungalow, rather than go through the upheaval of two moves in six months. This was understandable as Easter had made a very charming home and garden, whereas the manager's bungalow, although spacious, was modern and rather stark.

A week or so later Pete suggested that I should accompany them to Johore Bahru to visit the club, and to begin to meet some of the other Europeans of the district. One of the first I met was S. V. Jones, a senior civil servant. He was captain of the Johore Bahru Cricket Club, and was keen for me to play. As I had arranged to buy Pete's old AJS motorbike the travelling would present no problem. Jones eventually became colonial secretary to the Governor in Singapore, Sir Shenton Thomas, and was in this position at the outbreak of war with Japan. Unfortunately, Duff Cooper, who had been sent out by Churchill as co-ordinator of countries under the British flag, or some such extravagant title, took an instant dislike to Jones and he was forced to resign. Although extremely able, Jones was a very taciturn man, and his rather austere outlook on life would not have endeared him to such bon vivants as Duff and Lady Diana Cooper.

Churchill later compounded his error by promoting Duff Cooper to resident minister for Far Eastern Affairs, with cabinet rank. This appointment was a near disaster. He upset everyone, civil and services alike, even more than before, which would have been no bad thing if done several years earlier, but by then it was far too late, and only compounded their problems.

Through cricket especially I made several friends, one in particular named Fielding, a junior assistant manager with the Hong Kong & Shanghai Bank in JB. He had an MG sports car and we used to go into Singapore once a month for dinner, or to watch cricket on the Padang at the Singapore Cricket Club, and meet other young cricket enthusiasts. I went out to Malaya on a salary of $225 (Straits dollars) a month, plus $25 servant and $12 motorcycle allowances. Two hundred and sixty-two dollars a month, about £30 sterling, was good pay. A good meal in a first-class hotel, say the Raffles, would cost about $5, including a few drinks.

For young men of my age, after work was done, games loomed large in our lives. The most popular games amongst the Europeans were cricket, rugby, hockey, tennis and golf. With the Asians it was cricket, hockey, soccer and badminton.

All races played all games with and against each other. When I played rugger for Perak the most ferocious forward in the side was a Sikh solicitor from Ipoh. He removed his turban for the match and played with ribbons in his hair. Had he lived in England I am sure he would have won a cap. I understand that he died on the Burma Railway, one of very many thousands, including several of my friends and many of my acquaintances. And, of course, many Indians played cricket to a very high standard.

I am glad to say there was no colour bar as such in Malaya. The bar was not colour but financial. If one's water carrier could afford to he could sit next to you at the cinema or on the night mail train. Contrary to headlines I read many years later in the British gutter press, there were Asian members of many clubs throughout Malaya, although most preferred their own sports and social clubs. And, of course, the royal families in the states were ex-officio members of all the clubs. Jean and I were to become friends with several members of the Johore royal family when we were on Ulu Remis Estate in the 1950s.

At school I had concentrated on cricket and athletics, and did not take up rugger until I got to Malaya. It was Pete who introduced me to the game, and before long I was playing for Johore, the first season on the wing, thereafter at wing forward. Except for my sojourn in Sumatra I was to play rugger every season until the outbreak of war. I played for the state sides of Johore, Penang & Province Wellesley, Kedah and Perak against all the other states, with much enjoyment both on and off the pitch. Throughout my life I have always found that games players, particularly of team games, were more often than not reliable and dependable people. But the concept that team games build character is considered very doubtful nowadays, if not positively dangerous.

The captain of the Johore side during my first season was a police officer named John Dalley. He was to gain fame later by leading a force of irregulars, mainly released political detainees, known as Dalforce, during the defence of Singapore. These Chinese Communists were later to form the nucleus of the Malayan Peoples' Anti-Japanese Army (MPAJA) which operated throughout the War from their camps deep in the jungles of Malaya, supplied and trained by Force 136. Unfortunately, they would later be the enemy during the civil war known as the Malayan Emergency which began in 1948.

I learned a very salutary and painful lesson early on in my rugby career. When I was playing on the wing for Johore against the United Services and going hell bent for the line, ball in hand, I saw my opposite number coming for me with arms outstretched for a tackle. I jumped to clear his arms, but not high enough. I crashed to the ground, completely knocked out, and very lucky to have escaped a broken neck.

My tackler was a Lt G. J. Bryan, one of the large family of sporting Bryans, all of whom were of county or international calibre. I met him next when we were both feeling the effects of a most enjoyable New Year's party at the Hotel Europe in Singapore, he considerably the worse for wear and collapsed in the washroom. I joined him in one or two choruses of newly learned rugger songs, before calling a rickshaw for him. In 1945 I had to visit Army Headquarters in Singapore and was able to remind Brigadier Bryan of the previous occasions we had met.

There was, of course, no airmail to the East in the early 1930s. Mail took the best part of a month to reach us by sea. But letters arrived as regularly as clockwork. Jean wrote long and very dear letters, full of news of what she was doing, and getting these was really the highlight of my week. My father, too, although very busy as chairman of Alfa Laval, wrote every week until he was killed by a flying bomb in 1944.

Nineteen thirty was not only the start of a great adventure for me, but was also the year when the world depression really hit us in Malaya. In October our salaries were reduced. It was a case of take it or leave it. Most of us took it, and were grateful to have a job. My pay went down to $215 a month, about £25. But this was still sufficient to live comfortably, as I did not drink excessively, and as long as I had access to the JB Club library and could play cricket and rugger, and the letters from home arrived regularly, I was happy.

One night I went crocodile shooting with Pete and two Malays. We hired a sampan and, armed with rifles, paddled out into the Strait of Johore. The Malays had torches. These they shone along the mud flats and shallows, and very quickly reflected the yellow eyes of the crocodiles, which were either resting on the flats or gliding along just below the surface of the water. We aimed between the eyes, and shot four, three rather small and young ones, not more than four feet long, but the fourth was an eight footer. What particularly amazed me was the way that the Malays would jump out of the boat, grab the crocodile by its tail, and sling it over into the bottom of the boat before climbing back in again. I was very frightened for them, because every time we fired several crocodiles would take off from the banks, with a tremendous thwack of their tail, and come towards us. I half expected the sampan to be overturned at any moment.

After a couple of hours we returned to the jetty, and were starting to put our catch into the boot of the car when the large one suddenly came to life and knocked one of the Malays sideways with a swish of its tail. Pete put another shot into its head. Only the belly of a crocodile is used for shoes or handbags. No doubt Easter got a pair of shoes from our night's work, but I was disappointed that I was not offered even one of the smaller ones as I would have liked to have been able to send the skin home to Jean.

While on the subject of crocodiles, when I was back in Johore in 1934 a young planter from a neighbouring estate disappeared without a trace. About a month after his disappearance I was on my way to JB in my car when, passing over a bridge, I noticed some Malays excitedly pointing to something below them. I stopped to look, and saw that someone had killed quite the largest crocodile I had ever seen. He must have been a good 18 feet in length. When the Malays opened him up they found the missing planter's watch and wallet in his stomach. If this had occurred four years previously, I do not think I would have been quite so keen to go out on the crocodile shoot!

Having Pete's AJS motorbike I was able to get around several of the nearby estates and began to have quite a social life. I have to say now that my experience does not bear out Somerset Maugham's comments, in *A Writer's Notebook*, that all us planters were 'whisky-swilling, rough and common men' who spoke English 'with a vile accent or broad Scotch'. Although some undoubtedly did speak broad Glaswegian Scots, many more spoke the beautiful soft lilt of the Highlander or Aberdonian. And, of course, many of us had been educated at public school and university.

One of the planters I got to know was 'Fergie' Ferguson, later to be a divisional manager on Ulu Remis Estate when I arrived there in 1951. On Christmas Eve he had a party at his bungalow, during which he produced his Johore Volunteer Force rifle, and, even worse, some ammunition. It seems that the JVF kept their personal weapons at home rather than in the battalion armoury. Along one wall of the dining room was a row of rugby team photographs, with the team captain, as usual, sitting in the middle of the front row with the dated rugger ball clamped between his knees. Very tempting targets. Too tempting. Especially after quite a lot of drink had flowed. We took it in turns to take potshots at the rugger balls, although after a little while, when the shooting became wildly erratic, I joined Pete and Easter under the dining room table in fear for our lives. Mercifully the ammunition ran out fairly quickly.

A few days later everyone was phoned and invited around again to Fergie's bungalow, as he wished to show us something. He took us into his bedroom and opened the door of the cupboard that backed on to the wall with the now very tattered photographs. Not only was the cupboard ripped to pieces, but not a single piece of clothing had survived the fusillade. All his suits, trousers, jackets, shirts and ties were ruined. Worse still, having gone through his clothes, the bullets had ploughed on out through his bedroom wall, through the rubber, through the coolie lines and most were embedded in the wall of a conductor's house. We were all horrified at our stupidity and criminal folly. Perry, the manager, was quite rightly furious and threatened to report us to the police. Luckily for us he did not, as our companies could well have been looking for just such an excuse in the slump to send us home.

We all chipped in $20 to help Fergie buy new clothes.

The months passed very quickly after I had settled down, and with the friends I had made both on and off the games field, I began to feel less lonely. I was also gaining experience as a planter and earning my salary. Barton was due back from leave in January 1931, and I learned that I was to be transferred to Gajah Muntah Estate in Atjeh, Sumatra.

When the day came for me to leave Sungei Plentong, I said my goodbyes to Pete and Easter with real sorrow, for they had both been very kind to me. And it was entirely due to Peters that I was no longer a creeper but a fully fledged junior assistant and about to take over my own division aged 21 with only occasional supervisory visits from the manager.

Sojourn in Sumatra

January – December 1931

The company had reserved a cabin for me on the Dutch liner *Patria*. In a fit of generous mental aberration they had booked me first class. A far cry from the old *Achilles*.

My friend Fielding had driven me down to Singapore in his MG, and after a curry tiffin at the Raffles, had joined me on board for a farewell drink or two. We sailed in the late afternoon for Belawan Deli, the port for Medan which was the main town in Sumatra. The crossing was smooth. The tropical moon was full. I was travelling first class at the company's expense. This was the life!

For some reason I had always thought all Dutch women were stout mevrouws. I realised I was totally wrong because in the cabin next to mine was the loveliest creature I had ever seen. She dressed by day in what were, in the Thirties, called pyjama trousers, and by night in a long close-fitting shimmering gown. I could not keep my eyes off her. But, to my disgust, she seemed entirely satisfied with her small, fat, but obviously very rich, gentleman escort.

The country around Belawan is flat and uninteresting, almost a swamp, and, on that day in January 1931, particularly hot and sticky. On disembarking I took a taxi to Medan and reported to McAuliffe's agent. It was early afternoon when I arrived and Medan was enjoying the customary siesta. However, the chief clerk, a benevolent Chinese, was in the office and he told me that a room had been booked for me at the De Boer Hotel, and that I was to catch the Atjeh tram for Timbang Langsa, Atjeh, the next morning. He gave me my ticket and sufficient money to cover the hotel bill and other expenses, and sent me round to the hotel in the firm's car.

The De Boer Hotel was first class with large, airy bedrooms, kept moderately cool by the shades over the windows and the ever-revolving fans. That evening the local inhabitants were having a dinner dance, and I was interested to see how many Dutch men had native wives. The British seldom married local girls, sticking rigidly to protocol and marrying women of their own race and colour. There were, of course, exceptions. Jean and I were to know several mixed marriages, all of which were very successful, and accepted, at least by the European community. Such marriages were a lot less acceptable to the other races in Malaya, who considered it very infra dig to marry an orang puteh (white man). But I was always curious to understand why the Dutch, from the same social and religious background, who happened to settle in South Africa rather than to have continued on across the Indian Ocean to Sumatra and Java, should have had a totally different attitude towards the native populations of their adopted countries.

Despite its name, the Atjeh tram was in fact a proper train, but narrow gauged. The carriages were fairly primitive, and we stopped at every station on the 150-mile journey between Medan and Langsa. This took eight very tedious hours, as we rarely went faster than 15 mph. At Langsa I was met by my new manager, Rollo Gyllenskold, who was a Swede, and his German wife. It took about an hour and a half by car to reach the estate, firstly through padi fields and cultivated areas, but this gave way to secondary, and very soon to virgin jungle. The road was just loose shingle for most of the way. We seemed to be driving deeper and deeper into the jungle, and further and further away from civilisation. I had thought that Sungei Plentong was isolated! But eventually we got clear of the jungle and came to the plantation. I could see that the rubber trees were of very high quality and well husbanded.

Both Gyllenskold and his wife were very kind and I immediately got on well with them both. Our friendship deepened over the 12 months I was on Gajah Muntah, and continued after their retirement from the East in 1933 until I lost contact in the War. They settled in Zurich. Between them they spoke eight European languages and used to discuss which they should teach their children.

Gajah Muntah ('vomiting elephant' in Malay) was a first-class estate in every way. Gyllenskold told me about the division that I was to manage. It was even more isolated than the main division. He also told me that he had engaged a Chinese cook/boy named Ah Fong, who had already moved in.

The following day Gyllenskold drove me out to my bungalow. It was much smaller than the manager's bungalow on Sungei Plentong that had been my home for the last six months. Built in the usual style on wooden piers, it consisted of an open verandah with one end mosquito-proofed for use as the sitting room. There was a small dining room and a small bedroom, with a mosquito net around the bed. The bathroom had a large Shanghai jar and a lavatory on a dais, like a throne. There was no running water, so both flushing the lavatory and showering was carried out by scooping water out of the Shanghai jar. At least it was better than the thunderbox which was the most common form of sanitation in the Far East. There were seldom any long baths as we know them today. If a hot bath was required the tukang ayer (water carrier) heated up the water in four-gallon kerosene tins in the kitchen at the back of the bungalow, carried them upstairs to the bathroom, and poured it into a galvanised bath. But more often than not one required a cold shower, and the cool water from the Shanghai jar was breathtakingly refreshing after a hot sweaty day.

There was, however, one drawback to these old-fashioned bathrooms. They provided a cool haven for snakes, scorpions and centipedes, and although the tukang ayer was supposed to check before calling you, it was always best to double check for oneself.

I immediately took to Ah Fong, an elderly Chinese who had worked for some time at the Hotel Europe in Singapore. I never found out why he should wish to bury himself away so far from civilisation. When I was transferred to Kedah in December 1931 he came with me. He was probably the best cook I had throughout my time in the East.

There was no view from the front of the bungalow as the rubber trees came right up to the compound boundary. But from the back one could see over the rubber to the jungle-covered mountains beyond. Although much of the jungle in Malaya has since been felled, I understand that this part of northern Sumatra remains substantially the same to this day, and continues to be the habitat of all manner of wild animals, including tiger, elephant, orangutan (literally 'jungle man' in Malay), panther, bear, wild boar and many kinds of deer and monkey. The almost human shrieks of the monkeys provided a continuous background noise throughout the day, and half the night.

As we left the manager's bungalow I had noticed that the compound was enclosed within a high barbed wire fence. Gyllenskold explained that the Dutch were still considered enemies by the Atjehnese, so most bungalows required this protection. In addition, the Dutch army regularly patrolled the area.

Atjeh has a long and interesting history. During the 16th and 17th centuries it had been closely associated with Turkey, and was the centre of Islamic religion in Sumatra. The sultans had become extremely powerful, attacking the Portuguese colony of Malacca, and conquering as far as Pahang on the eastern side of the Malay peninsula.

When he was resident at Bengkoolen in Sumatra in 1819, Stamford Raffles, the founder of Singapore (and of the London Zoo), had signed a mutual defence pact with Atjeh and although this had not been subsequently renewed the Atjehnese had always considered themselves as allied to Great Britain. Holland had attacked Atjeh in the 1870s, so beginning a war that was still in progress, even if only in a desultory way, when I arrived in 1931. Atjehnese guerrillas were still active in the hills behind my bungalow, ambushing the odd military patrol, and attacking estates and other Dutch-owned property. But because of the pact signed by Stamford Raffles we British were safe, and it was unnecessary for us to live behind defences. As it was for Gyllenskold, who never closed his gates.

Gyllenskold warned me that it had been rumoured that a honey bear, taking advantage of the empty bungalow, was in the habit of entering the garden and robbing the oil palms which grew behind the house. The fruit is very juicy, and much favoured by many animals, particularly snakes and rats. The honey bear, in spite of its pleasant-sounding name, is far from sweet-tempered. In fact, it was a dangerous animal. As heavy as a tiger, one blow from its paw has been known to split a man almost in half.

I was not unduly worried, as I was not intending to dispute the ownership of the palm oil trees. Unfortunately, I had not been told the whole story. One night, shortly after having moved in, I had not been in bed for more than half an hour when I heard soft thudding up the back stairs, more thudding and a lot of disagreeable grunting outside my door, and this continued along the verandah and down the front stairs. The bear had obviously become accustomed to taking a short cut through the bungalow. I was a little worried in case it decided to explore the house further, as the only weapon I had was my hairbrush. The next day I had a bolt put on the bedroom door.

Having stuck this intrusion for about a week I decided on a cunning plan. On its next visit I waited until it was exactly outside my bedroom door then shouted at the top of my voice. The bear bolted. Ah Fong and the tukang ayer came running, thinking that I was being murdered. But I achieved the result I wanted. The bear still visited, but it never again took the direct route to its supper.

I quickly settled down to my new environment and, despite the loneliness, enjoyed life. Other than the divisional coolie lines about half a mile away, the next point of habitation was the manager's bungalow, the factory and main lines about three miles away. The nearest town, Medan, was 150 miles to the south. The nearest neighbour, other than Gyllenskold, was a German, some three hours walk away through the rubber and jungle. I had no transport. No telephone. No wireless. The only shop was the general kedai in the village, near the estate entrance, run by a Chinese.

I was sustained by the mail from home which arrived every week. The letters and newspapers were at least a month old when I received them, but as the flow was constant it did not seem to matter. Not being able to read Dutch there was no point in taking the local paper; even that took a week to reach us from Batavia (now Jakarta). So major events, like Britain going off the Gold Standard, and the formation of the National Government, had been faits accomplis for at least a month before I became aware of them.

I had a portable HMV wind-up gramophone, and Jean and my father kept me supplied with the latest Jack Smith, Layton and Johnstone, and Ronald Frankau records. I was not to know the classical repertoire until Jean arrived in Malaya in 1935, since when it has given us untold hours of joy. I also got my Father to send me a punch ball. With this, and a 16-pound weight I had found in the stores and used to put the weight, and some reasonably long distance runs through the rubber, I kept very 'fit. But I missed my games-playing very much.

Mental stimulus came from the library in Medan, where I could borrow up to 14 books at a time. These were sent up in a box by the railway and returned the same way. I read mostly biography and history, and the occasional thriller.

Once a month I bought a bottle of Veuve Clicquot from the local kedai. Quite why he should stock Champagne I never knew, unless one of my predecessors had a penchant for it and the Chinese shopkeeper, thinking it essential drinking for all Europeans, continued to get it in.

I still look back with nostalgia to those far off days in Sumatra. The utter peace. The only noise, nature. The only daily human contact, my labour force of charming Javanese or Atjehnese, who, incidentally, spoke what was known then as 'rajah' Malay, different to the language spoken generally in Malaya and less easily understood by most Europeans.

The estate was first class, unlike most of the other estates owned by Ridsdells in Malaya and Sumatra, and obviously owed a lot to Gyllenskold's management. In addition to the fine mature rubber, there were jungle clearings, all beautifully terraced, nurseries where the seedlings were propagated, and numerous other things of professional interest, all of which were lacking on Sungei Plentong.

My days were full of interest, but the nights were long and lonely. I wrote letters, read, played the gramophone, and went to bed soon after 9 pm.

Twice a month I went over to the main division to supervise the cash payments to the labour force. Having no transport, I would walk the three miles. On those days I invariably had tea, and quite often dinner, with Gyllenskold and his wife, after which the Bols gin would flow, often to such an extent I would have to stay the night before staggering back to my hilly division early the next morning in time for muster.

One Sunday I was surprised to see a European march smartly into my compound, followed by his bearer. He introduced himself as de Jong, the assistant on the next estate. He had very kindly walked through the five miles of rubber and jungle to see me. Like all Dutch whom I have ever met he spoke excellent English. He departed after tea, after much unaccustomed talking by both of us, with my promise to visit him a fortnight later. This I did, taking an Atjehnese from my labour force as a guide. The walk took about three hours each way, so it could only be done on a Sunday, which was an enforced day of rest by law.

I made quite a few visits to de Jong. There was, however, one thing about him that did not appeal to me. He kept two orangutan, and they used to ride around his verandah on tricycles. Although young, they were fully grown. They had a habit of making a beeline for me and climbing all over me, much to my disgust. Eventually I had to tell de Jong that unless they were made to stop this caper I would not be coming over to see him. Thereafter they were kept under restraint. My next visit was when de Jong gave a party in celebration of something or other, and he had invited his manager and his wife, both of whom were Germans, and some neighbouring planters. I had taken Ah Fong with me to carry my gramophone and records, so we were able to dance to Viennese waltzes and polkas, much to the enjoyment of the Germans present. Ah Fong and I staggered home through the jungle in the pitch darkness of the small hours, I leading the way with a torch which, as I swept the beam from side to side, lit up eyes everywhere. It was most eerie and I was very glad to get home.

I was having breakfast one morning when a coolie came rushing up to the bungalow shouting, 'Tuan, Tuan, mari lekas, ada ular banyak besar' – Tuan, Tuan, come quickly, there is a very large snake. I took my rifle – as a weapon, next to useless against a snake – and ran with him the quarter of a mile to where one of my weeding gangs was working. They had come across a giant python fast asleep, having just had a meal – we were to find out later that it was a young pig. The coolies had hit the snake on the head with their cangkul (hoes) and it seemed unconscious. I could scarcely believe my eyes. Its head was a good 12 inches across, and when we eventually straightened it out it measured 33 feet 6 inches.

I sent a messenger post haste with a chit to Gyllenskold telling him about this enormous reptile and asked him to come to the lines as we proposed to carry the still unconscious snake over there. It took 10 coolies all their strength to lift it. It was still unconscious when we got there but as Gyllenskold arrived and we were examining it gave a swish of its tail and started to wriggle. We gave it a couple of clouts to the head to put it to sleep again.

It really was a quite remarkable specimen, and, except for the abrasions to its head, quite undamaged. Gyllenskold was equally amazed. Luckily, on receiving my note, he had telephoned a German professional hunter who lived at Langsa who promised to leave straight away, bringing a drug (probably opium) to keep the snake alive but unconscious until he could get it back to Langsa to kill and skin it.

The hunter arrived in due course and was most impressed with the snake and confirmed that it was undoubtedly the largest snake ever caught in the Far East, if not the world. We took photographs of it, both on the ground and being carried by the coolies. I certainly appeared in at least one of these. But unfortunately they have all disappeared. Mine was, of course, left in Malaya when Jean left Kamuning in a hurry in December 1941. Copies which I sent home to my and Jean's parents have been lost over the years. I would be interested to find out whether 33 feet 6 inches is still a record for a snake.

I presented the python's skin to Gyllenskold's wife, and she hung it up on two sides of their bungalow dining room. I assume they took it home with them when they retired, so it could well still be in Zurich. Even if their descendants had disposed of it, it could be in a natural history museum. In retrospect, I am deeply sorry that this magnificent specimen of nature was slaughtered just for a keepsake, like so many elephant, tiger and countless other magnificent creatures.

I had been on the estate for about six months when the conductor informed me that a tiger spoor had been seen near the boundary with the jungle. Having confirmed this I sent a message to Gyllenskold who sent over a tiger trap. This was a most fearsome-looking apparatus, made of iron and shaped like a shark's jaws. It must have weighed two hundredweight. We bought an old goat and tethered it near the trap. The following morning a coolie came running to my bungalow to tell me that the goat was dead and that the tiger was caught in the trap.

Grabbing my rifle and collecting some tappers on the way, I arrived at the spot only to find that both the tiger and the trap had gone. The poor animal had pulled the trap clear of the ground, despite its weight and firm anchoring, not to mention the agony that he must have been in, and dragged it off into the jungle, where I could hear him grunting and snarling, about 20 yards in. I hesitated what to do. I had never seen a tiger before, certainly not a wounded one. And I was not a good shot. After a little while, whilst waiting for Gyllenskold to arrive, the noises stopped, so with some of the braver coolies, armed only with their tapping knives, we went into the undergrowth. There, amongst much gore and blood, we found the trap with the tiger's front paw in the jaws. The poor brute had either gnawed through its own leg, or had writhed sufficiently for the trap to have severed through the joint. There was nothing we could do. It would obviously soon die, and in great pain.

I have always made it a point when managing people, of whatever nationality, never to ask them to do something that I could not do myself. I was therefore determined to become a first-class tapper. So, much to the amusement of the coolies, I learnt the necessary skills and continued to keep my hand in until I took over Ulu Remis palm oil estate in 1951.

I used to study the daily tapping records and when I came across a task yielding less than the average for the area I would go out and see the tapper concerned at his work. If I thought he was not getting the best out of the trees I would instruct him to go ahead, clean the latex cups and remove the previous day's scrap. I would then follow behind and tap the trees. The tapper would then collect the latex and we would weigh the results of my efforts. More often than not I was able to improve on his yield, and so both increase the overall production, even if only marginally, and enhance my 'face' as a manager.

Should it not be convenient to accompany the tappers in the morning I would go out on my own in the afternoon. On one particular afternoon I was checking the bark consumption over the previous month when I heard from behind lots of female giggling. I turned and saw about half a dozen teenage Javanese girls cavorting about and generally playing the fool. They suddenly lifted their sarongs above their waist, danced a little jig, then turned and ran away still laughing, coffee-coloured bottoms swaying as they ran. It certainly was a merry sight, but not conducive to the peace of mind of a young bachelor trying to live a celibate life. It was fairly common for bachelors to take 'housekeepers' into their bungalows. On balance I think this was a good idea, because it not only ensured that random promiscuity was reduced, but also that the girl was well looked after. This was, of course, a lot more common in Sumatra, and I suppose the rest of the Dutch East Indies, than in Malaya.

I have often wondered whether the girls had the idea that it would be a good thing for the young tuan to adopt the ways of the East and were advertising their charms, or whether it was just girlish high spirits. Nowadays, I suppose, it would be called 'prick teasing'.

Sometime in November 1931 fresh tiger spoor was seen again within the estate boundary, close to the jungle. Gyllenskold was visiting my division on that day so we both went to inspect these new foot marks. Judging by their size the tiger was a large one. Coolies told us that they had heard a tiger near their lines and in the vicinity of the padang where their goats and cattle were tethered. If this were so, it would indicate that it was getting on in years and after easy prey. And that it could become dangerous, possibly man eating. We decided to tether an old cow nearby and build a platform in a tree overlooking it. Gyllenskold and I would then sit up there and wait for the tiger to return, as we were certain it would.

At about 6.30 pm, armed with rifles, torches and flasks of Bols gin, we climbed the ladder to our platform. It was uncanny being within 20 yards of the jungle, hardly daring to breath, and almost deafened by the cacophony of the tropical night orchestra, unmercifully attacked by mosquitoes. After a couple of hours, when we had almost given up, Gyllenskold suddenly gripped my arm and pointed to a spot by the jungle edge. Then I heard the muffled pad and heavy breathing. Then silence. Except that the poor cow had obviously sensed something and was trying desperately to escape, mooing in distress. Then it was all over. We heard a rush, a snarl, a brief cry of pain from the cow, and then the sound of ripping flesh.

At this point Gyllenskold told me to shine my torch. I focused it on the largest tiger I had ever seen, not that I had ever seen a wild one before. For a split second it stared back at us with large, unblinking yellow eyes and then leaped back into the jungle and vanished. The leap was astonishing, every bit of 30 yards.

The chances of the animal returning that night were minimal. However, discretion being the better part of valour, we waited another hour before risking climbing down from our platform and returning to my bungalow.

The next night we repeated the operation. Only this time we tied the torch to the tree, focusing its beam on the remains of the dead cow. We went through the same couple of hours of expectancy, mosquito attacks and, this time, the dreadful smell of the putrefying cattle carcass. Then we heard bones being scrunched. We had not hear the tiger's approach. Of course, we could not be certain that it was the tiger. Gyllenskold raised his rifle, as did I but leaving a hand free to turn on the torch. On Gyllenskold's order I pressed the switch. The beam settled on the tiger. He looked up at us again with those large yellow eyes. Gyllenskold and I fired together. The beast made no sound, but slowly collapsed on to its side, and after a moment or so stopped all movement. After ten minutes we judged that it was dead, so we warily got down and walked over to inspect our kill.

It was a beautiful beast, but, as we had suspected, old. Quite literally long in the tooth. About a dozen coolies, hearing the shooting, turned up, cut down some poles, and carried the tiger back to the lines where we could examine it more closely. It was then that I noticed that its right front paw was missing, severed at the joint. Against the usual laws of nature this tiger had survived its previous ordeal at the hands of man and, even more surprising, had returned to the same place where it had suffered so much torture before.

Having no camera, we were unable to record our kill for posterity. It was skinned and cleaned without delay, to adorn the manager's wall as another trophy. But I remained struck by the sheer beauty and the courage of this magnificent beast, and, thinking also back to the python, I shed a tear for these animals and resolved never to kill any of them again, except in self-defence or, if absolutely necessary, for the pot.

We were to smell tiger on several occasions both at Waterloo and Kamuning estates, and to see their pug marks, but I would not permit their shooting. Luckily none caused any problems.

During the seven months I was in Johore I was fortunate to avoid going down with malaria. My luck was not to continue. One day, in the middle of August 1931, I began to feel very queer. I had no thermometer but I knew I had a high temperature. I became increasingly ill, and towards evening I became aware that Gyllenskold was bending over me – I was to learn later that Ah Fong, recognising the symptoms, had sent for him. The next thing I remembered was waking up in hospital. Apparently I had been unconscious for 12 hours, including during the journey in to Langsa in Gyllenskold's car.

The doctor told me that I had been very ill with malaria but that I would now improve, the fever having broken. The Eurasian nurse instructed me to turn over on to my side, and I could not understand why even when she told me that she wanted to take my temperature. This was when I learned that in most European Continental countries temperatures were not taken with thermometers placed under the tongue as in Britain as, apparently, it was considered to be more accurate to take it from the rectum. I thought this most undignified, but was not up to arguing. I was in hospital for about 10 days before I was well enough to return to the Estate.

I left the estate only twice in the 12 months that I was there, my visit to hospital being one of them. The other time was when I accompanied Gyllenskold and his wife on a day trip to Medan. I forget the exact purpose of the 300-mile round trip, but I remember having a large rijsttafel – which became a firm favourite of mine – for lunch at the De Boer Hotel.

The day of 26 September 1931 was an occasion for double

celebration – my own 21st birthday, and my engagement to Jean Cuthbertson. The Gyllenskolds joined me for a special dinner prepared by Ah Fong, helped by a large hamper sent out from England by Jean's parents, I think from the Army & Navy Stores in Victoria Street. They specialised in such things, especially for the Services, at that time stationed throughout the Empire. We washed it all down with at least two bottles of Veuve Clicquot. Jean's father knew a diamond merchant in Hatton Garden, and I had sent money home to her to buy an engagement ring from him. Unfortunately it was stolen by the Chinese boy of a friend in KL in 1937 and not recovered, and although by then I could afford a very much more expensive replacement, Jean never considered it to be other than a nice diamond ring.

My time at Gajah Muntah was getting short. The Depression was really biting, and I was worried that I might be made redundant, even though I knew that Barton and Gyllenskold had sent in good reports of me. European staff were being axed and labour forces cut. Only high-yielding trees were tapped in order to lower the cost of production. Camps were established for planters who had been axed but unwilling to return to Europe, the main one being at Port Dickson, on the coast in Negri Sembilan. The unfortunate planter was provided with bed and board and a government handout of $10 a month. There were, of course, advantages in staying in Malaya. The climate, the friendly atmosphere, the avoidance of the drudgery and heartbreak of looking for a job in an England with unemployment of over 3,000,000 and, most important of all, the fact that one was on the spot if and when the world economy took a turn for the better and rubber was in demand again.

I was lucky. The London secretaries decided that I would be more useful to the Group on Sungei Gettah Estate, near Sungei Patani, in Kedah. I suspect both that Ernest Ridsdell had some influence on this decision and also that, because of my young age, the company could get a reasonably competent unmarried assistant more cheaply than a married one.

In addition to achieving some competence in my chosen profession, I had become fluent in both Malay and Tamil during my first 18 months out East, had adapted myself to the way of life, and had become quite a good games player. In short, I had gained confidence.

One day in December 1931 the Gyllenskolds drove me down to Langsa where I embarked on a small Straits Steamship Company vessel bound for Penang. These ships were only 800–1000 tonners, mainly cargo carrying, but they had a few first-class cabins which were very comfortable. I treated the Gyllenskolds to lunch and we said our fond farewells.

So ended my spell in Sumatra, a very lonely and isolated outpost of the Empire, albeit Dutch rather than British. After the initial loneliness I had become very attached to the beauty of my surroundings, the people, the utter peace, the wildlife and, above all, to the Gyllenskolds. All of which, on reflection, had enabled me to concentrate on learning my job, the languages, the modus vivendi of the peoples native to South East Asia, to an extent that I might not have been able to do in the less isolated estates on the Malayan mainland.

Kedah Days

January 1933 – April 1934

The sea voyage from Langsa to Penang took just under 18 hours, and we anchored in the roads shortly before breakfast. I went ashore and made my way to McAuliffe, Davis & Hope's office where I renewed my acquaintance with Jock Reid. After a chat about things in general, including the price of rubber, the Kedah rugger team, my time in Atjeh and, I was gratified to learn, the good reports he had received from Gyllenskold about me, I was told to report back at the office at noon when Cecil Tuke, the manager of Sungei Gettah Estate, would be calling to collect me and to take me back to the estate. In the interval I went around to the Hong Kong and Shanghai Bank and opened an account with about $300, my savings from my salary in Sumatra. This was considered quite a lot of money in those days, but high living was to reduce this little nest egg fairly rapidly.

As a rule my first impressions are fairly fallible, but in this case they proved to be correct. Tuke was thickset, very reserved and, to me, a dislikable man. As I got to know him better my liking for him did not improve. He had no charm. He was secretive, and ungenerous in money affairs – nowadays we would call it tight fisted. For instance, although he was getting at least double my salary, whenever he invited me to accompany him to the cinema I had to pay both for my ticket and my dinner. The dinners were invariably at the rather dreary Station Hotel rather than at the more glamorous Runnymede, or even at the Penang Club where he was a member. And I am sure that it was not done in the interests of my pocket. He was a non-smoker and teetotal. He did, however, like cricket, which was something in his favour.

Tuke suggested that we should take the funicular up to Penang Peak where we could have lunch. This must be one of the most spectacular views in the whole of Malaya. Especially for someone whose horizon is usually limited to rows of closely spaced rubber trees. Georgetown was spread out beneath us with all the landmarks that were to become so familiar. The roads and straits full of shipping, including on that day a large German two-funnelled liner, Bukit Mertajam, Kedah Peak and the mountains behind. Penang Peak was a holiday centre, a cool hill station to escape the heat of the mainland. Some tuans besar were lucky enough to live up there and commuted to their offices in Georgetown. Their syce would be waiting for them at the funicular station at the bottom with their car.

Francis Light, who was born and brought up in the tiny Suffolk village of Dallinghoo, founded Penang towards the end of the 18th century, when employed by the East India Company. Despite a marked expansion of trade with China there were as yet no port facilities under British control between India and China. Malacca, the only port on the west coast of the Malay Peninsula, was Dutch, they having captured it from the Portuguese. The East India Company decided, therefore, that Penang would be a convenient staging post. John Company had also decided to try to obtain a slice of the Atjeh spice trade; at that time Atjeh was the world's leading supplier of pepper.

In the meantime Light, who was based at Madras, had formed a friendship with the Sultan of Kedah. For some years Kedah had been at war with Selangor and the Sultan had appealed to the East India Company for military assistance, and, as part of the bargain, had offered to lease Penang to the East India Company. The treaty was concluded in 1786, and Francis Light became the first governor of Penang, and was to remain so until his death in 1794. He is buried in the churchyard in Georgetown. Incidentally, his son founded the city of Adelaide in Australia.

We crossed over to Butterworth on the mainland by ferry, a journey of about 20 minutes. These ferries were very old even in the 1930s, sideloading and coal fired. At Butterworth I was delighted to see a large Singapore Cold Storage depot, so let Ah Fong loose to buy the basic necessities for my new bungalow. There was also a small bar. Over the next 25 years I was to call in at Perry's Bar for 'satu empat jalan', one for the road, many, many times (see Glossary).

The road from Butterworth to Sungei Patani headed northwards, through some of the most attractive scenery in Malaya. As far as the eye could see there were padi fields, dotted with little islands of habitation, usually the traditional Malay wooden house on stilts, with an atap roof, surrounded by fruit trees such as durian, mangosteen, lime and coconut. There would be chickens scratching around in the earth underneath the house and a goat or two tethered nearby. I understand that one can see the same scene 50 years later, but each little house now has electricity, and a large television aerial on the roof. There is no closed season for padi planting, so one would always see the farmer, knee deep in the water, behind his buffalo and plough, with padi plants grasped in his hand which he would plant by plunging them into the mud. And the ever-present central Malayan mountain range in the background, covered with rain clouds.

The padi fields continued into Kedah when, somewhere near the village of Sungei Pasir, they gave way to the regimented rows of rubber trees of, mainly, European-owned plantations. The road ran through Sungei Patani, then a small town which housed the Kedah administration headquarters, the Sungei Patani Club, a golf course, law courts and dozens of small shops selling everything imaginable, owned usually by Chinese, although occasionally by Indians. Like all shops in the East, these would be open-fronted onto a covered pavement, separated from the road by a deep monsoon drain.

Sungei Gettah Estate lay a further 10 miles or so beyond Sungei Patani. One turned off the main highway on to a laterite road for about five miles. It was gloomy, with large, mature rubber trees spreading their branches right over the road, and in dry weather the red dust penetrated everywhere. There were three large European-owned estates along this road before it petered out into the jungle. The first was Sungei Gettah, then Bukit Lembu, and finally Sungkap Para.

I stayed the night with Tuke, after having had a quick look at the assistant's bungalow which was a couple of miles away from the main offices and factory. It stood in a clearing in the rubber, about 50 yards from the main estate road. Constructed of wood, it was unlike most estate bungalows in that it was not on wooden stilts or brick piers, but a two-storey house. The sitting and dining rooms and the pantry were on ground level, whilst upstairs there were two bedrooms and the bathroom. Each bedroom had a mosquito-proofed cubicle for the beds. The sanitation was the usual jamban (thunderbox), and the water, for all purposes, was stored in a Shanghai jar. On the whole the bungalow was very comfortable.

Tuke was a very taciturn man and seemed quite incapable of starting a conversation, whilst I was completely tongue-tied. After living for nearly a year without regular social intercourse I had nothing to say for myself. I was a month behind national and international news. As I began to go out and to meet other people, and neighbours began to call on me, I soon became very aware of my inadequacy. There was scarcely a topic on which I could talk, except rubber, and even then not too intelligently. I still had much to learn.

However, I soon settled down, as the routine was very similar to that I had been used to in Johore and Atjeh. And, of course, I had a Tamil labour force again, rather than Atjehnese. The latex from my division was transported daily by bullock cart to the factory on the main division. We did not get lorries until 1934.

The change between the complete isolation and loneliness of Gajah Muntah to the hurly-burly of Sungei Gettah was unbelievable at first. On most days at least two cars, several bullock carts and many pedestrians passed by my bungalow. After about a week I heard a motorcycle turn into my drive, much to my delight. It was Dan Wright, the assistant from Bukit Lembu Estate. This was our first meeting, and we were to remain the best of friends until his death nearly 50 years later. He was to take me to the Sungei Patani Club on the back of his motorbike, to introduce me to other young planters, and to help me to overcome my shyness and introspection.

The next visitor was Bob Chrystal, the manager of Bukit Lembu. He was married to Babs, an Australian whom he had met on holiday at Brastagi, the hill station in Sumatra. They married in 1928 and had Gerald and Helen by the time I first met them in December 1931. I fell under their spell immediately. Their bungalow was within half a mile of mine, and I passed it every time I went to the far end of my division, and usually got a cheery wave from Babs.

As the shyness wore off I began to enter into the social life of the district. I played golf on Saturday afternoons, usually followed by drinks with other young planters, civil servants and agency men. So that I should no longer be dependent on Dan's pillion, Tuke suggested that I buy his Big Six Norton motorcycle. I was now independent. I could go to Sungei Patani, some 15 miles away, Penang, about 40 miles further on, and, of course, visit my various neighbours. Compared to Atjeh, I felt that I was living in suburbia.

At the Sungei Patani Club I met another young planter who was to remain a close friend for the next 40 years, Walter Northcote-Green. Greeno introduced me to the Penang Cricket Club, and, although it was late in the season, I got in a few practice games. As so many planters had been laid off because of the slump, Kedah found it difficult to raise an eleven so had amalgamated with Penang. I forget how long this arrangement lasted. I was to become president of the Kedah Cricket Association in 1954, so I assume that the two states parted company again either just before the War, or immediately afterwards.

It may seem that life was one long round of gaiety. This was far from the case as, even with my own transport, it was rare for me to leave the estate on more than one evening a week, and then only to a neighbour. I did get to the club over the weekends for a round of golf or a game of cricket or rugger, followed by a few beers and supper, whilst a trip to Penang was rarely more often than once a month. Despite the cheapness of everything, salaries were not high, and I soon ate into the savings that I had accumulated in Atjeh. Also, to go anywhere I had to pass Tuke's bungalow, so that he could hear my motorbike and note the time of my return. Anyway, assistants were kept very busy from 5 am until teatime at about 4.30 pm – when, more often than not, there were the accursed check rolls to maintain. I have more than once arrived on the muster ground still in my white dinner jacket, much to the amusement of all concerned, to change immediately afterwards before going out around the rubber at about 6 o'clock. It was always a matter of principle for me to be on time for muster, however riotous the previous night's party had been, or however far I had had to travel to return to the estate, and it was something I always insisted, when I became a manager, that my assistants did, much to the annoyance of some of them.

After a few weeks I could see that Ah Fong was not happy, and I was not surprised when he came to see me one day to say that he had made a mistake and that he should have stayed in Atjeh. I was very sorry to see him go but could well understand the reasons. I paid his fare back to Langsa. Before he went he fixed me up with another Chinese cook/boy who had worked for the Chrystals.

All was well for a few weeks until Bob and Babs came round for drinks one evening. The first thing Babs spotted was her fruit bowl on my sideboard, the first of many such items we were to discover over the coming weeks. There was much embarrassment on my part, but none on the cook's. Babs gave me the bowl, but this was lost, together with everything else we owned, when the Japanese invaded.

Cookie did not last long for one day he was recognised by a dresser from the state leprosy hospital and carted off to complete his treatment. Whilst I am sure that the risks for me were practically non-existent, I did feel somewhat uneasy for several months afterwards.

My new cook/boy was Ah Kim, a young Chinese. He was always very cheerful, married, a good cook and honest. But he was an habitual gambler, and this eventually got him into very serious trouble. Ah Kim remained with me throughout my stay in Kedah, and later joined Jean and me on Kamuning. He left us only when his winnings could no longer sustain his opium addiction, in 1937. I paid Ah Kim $25 a month contract (about £3) and from this he fed me more than adequately, and kept the balance for his own wages.

Shortly after I arrived on Sungei Gettah one of the Indian clerks gave me an attractive little kitten, and I was to become very attached to it. In those days I had large white tablecloths which covered the round dining table, reaching almost to the floor. The floor was of cement, painted red and highly polished. One night I was sitting at the table, having supper and reading. The kitten was playing under the table, hissing and spitting. It became rather aggravating, so I gently tried to nudge it away with my foot, but without success. The hissing and spitting continued, only beginning to sound rather angry.

Tiring of its game I lifted the tablecloth – and had the fright of my life. Standing at least two feet high was a cobra, with inflated hood, hissing at the kitten. My bare ankle must have missed the snake by only a couple of inches each time I had tried to nudge the kitten. I leapt up, grabbed a golf club, yelled 'boy!', yanked the kitten away with the club head, and tried to hit the snake on the head – not easy in the confined space under the table. When the boy arrived we lifted the table clear so that I was able to have a good swing and soon despatched it. It was a good six feet long. Afterwards I realised that the cobra, which can usually move like greased lightning, was unable to get a grip on the polished floor. Otherwise my kitten would most certainly have been killed, and I would have been severely bitten on the leg, although I would probably have been able to reach the estate dresser in time to get the antivenom injection. Thereafter I always made a point of peering under the table before sitting down for a meal.

Another night I was asleep in my mosquito-proofed cubicle when I woke to see a man bending over the dressing table. He was standing with his back towards me going through the drawers. I watched him for a moment or two, but other than that he was Chinese I did not recognise him. Letting out a bellow, rather as I had done with the honey bear in Sumatra, I leapt out of bed but tripped on the mosquito netting, so he got away, running into the bathroom, down the back stairs and out of the back door. As the intruder seemed to know the house intimately I came to the conclusion that he might have been a servant for a previous occupier of the bungalow. Nothing appeared to have been taken, and I was not troubled again in such a way on Sungei Gettah.

Towards the end of 1932 my life changed again. It was now at the very worst time of the Depression. The price of rubber touched the all time low of 1½ pence per pound. It was decided that Tuke would take over Jabi Estate, near Alor Star, and I would assume the assistant managership of Sungei Gettah, under fortnightly supervision by Tuke. He would live on Jabi, and I would move into the manager's bungalow on Sungei Gettah.

The whole arrangement was, of course, a cost-cutting exercise by the Company, but it meant real promotion for a young planter of just 22, especially as Tuke's visits soon became only monthly. I was aware of some jealousies, particularly from some of the older assistants in the area, but I was lucky that, in the short time I had spent out East, I had worked on three contrasting estates, under three different managers, in rapidly deteriorating financial circumstances, and had started planting several years younger than the norm. I owed a lot to my previous managers, and especially, of course, to Peters on Sungei Plentong. To Tuke must go the credit of instilling in me the very valuable experience and lessons of producing rubber for next to nothing, paring production costs to the bone. My experience over the next two years, in the worst of the slump, stood me in excellent stead in the years to come.

I have always acknowledged that my subsequent success was in part due to the advantage I had over many planters, of the same vintage, whose careers were interrupted by the retrenchment during the years 1930 to 1935. I was genuinely fascinated with the whole process of producing rubber, from seedling to auction in London, whereas I felt that several of my contemporaries were more interested in the good life and took up planting merely to enable them to have it, and so, perhaps, were not so committed to assimilating experience, learning the languages, getting to know the peoples and the flora and fauna of Malaya. To me the social life was a bonus which I grabbed with both hands, but a bonus nevertheless.

Several of my friends and acquaintances have described the humiliation of not only searching for a job, but also in the work they were sometimes forced to do, and it is not surprising that most hurried back to Malaya as soon as the world economy improved. I am thankful that I was spared this.

There was no question of selling forward, but of realising the assets as soon as possible. I sold all the rubber I could sell to local Chinese rubber merchants, cash on delivery, buyer collect. I managed to get the cost of production down to the selling price of the rubber. And we always had the liquidity to pay the labour force and the suppliers. Only when these were paid could I draw my salary and expenses. Quite often I could not, and these would be credited to me.

The manager's bungalow was built on pillars, on a hill, which allowed me to look over the rubber trees to Kedah Peak, so I again had a view. I could tolerate any bungalow, no matter what its deficiencies, providing it had a view. The bungalow was large, with a verandah on three sides, and both bedrooms and the sitting room were mosquito-proofed. The bathrooms had the usual thunderboxes and Shanghai jars. The garden was wonderful, full of jacaranda, tulip, and flame-of-the-forest trees, and always a blaze of colour.

After several tumbles off my motorbike, usually due to a combination of the loose laterite gravel on estate roads and over-indulgence in alcohol, painful experiences but not seriously injurious, I began to contemplate buying a car. I felt secure in my job, there had been no adverse criticism from my manager or visiting agents. Furthermore, Tuke had a small 10 HP Fiat for sale, which had belonged to a former manager from a neighbouring estate who had been axed. I had made the decision to buy this car one night when I had landed in the ditch, with the Norton on top of me, and the red hot exhaust pipe resting on my thigh. The next day I sold the motorbike to a local Chinese garage for $75, and bought my very first car for $100 (then about £12).

It was a super little car and never let me down. In 1934 I drove it all the way down the Malay Peninsula to south Johore, and when I went home on leave in January 1935 I left it with the local Chinese shopkeeper in lieu of what I owed him. I must say, he was not too happy. Being Chinese he was really only interested in payment in currency. Or gold.

Sometime towards the end of 1932 Tuke invited me up to Jabi Estate one evening for dinner. The estate lay astride the Jitra road, east of Alor Star. In December 1941 the invading Japanese army were to use this road as one of their main lines of attack, and the area around Jabi was the scene of much bitter fighting.

After the usual abstemious evening I left at about 10 pm for the two-hour journey home. I had passed through Alor Star and was on the main north-south trunk road when I began to feel very sleepy and to keep my eyes open became a very great struggle. The realisation that I had left the road and was heading for the ditch certainly woke me up, but there was nothing that I could do before I was waist deep in water. Luckily the Fiat was an open two-seater so that there was no danger of drowning, but having scrambled out, I stood on the bank, wet and miserable, surveying my pride and joy. A passing lorry driven by a Chinese and carrying vegetables to the market in Penang stopped and gave me a lift to Bedong, where I was able to get a local taxi to take me back to Sungei Gettah. The following morning I went over to the Chrystals and used their phone to speak to my friend Eddy Gardener, the local PWD engineer. He agreed to recover the car and to tow it to Sungei Patani for draining out and repairing. He did this the next day for me, but I was quite rightly charged for the PWD services. He told me later that he had received a rocket from his superior, even though the PWD had made some money out of the episode, as apparently their accounts department was not geared up to sending out invoices for services rendered to private citizens.

The damage was quickly repaired and I had my car back within a couple of days. But never again did I drive when I was over-tired, except in wartime. I always pulled over for a quick forty winks.

I was now playing cricket regularly for the Penang Club, often on both Saturdays and Sundays. Also, we raised a Sungei Patani Club side which played other towns in northern Malaya. On one particular Sunday we had a game against Taiping, away, and Greeno, another young planter named Tyndale-Powell and myself drove down with Pat Daintry in his Ford. After the game, for some reason or other, we had to drive straight back, forgoing the usual after-game beers. Just outside Butterworth Pat said that he was suddenly feeling very tired. Mindful of my experience in the Fiat, I took over the wheel, and we proceeded on our journey home.

As we were passing through Sungei Pasir village a Tamil suddenly darted out into the middle of the road in front of us. I stood on the brakes but nothing happened. I grabbed the hand brake, still nothing happened. At the same time I swerved to the right, but the Tamil ran into the near side mudguard. I somehow eventually managed to stop further down the road and we ran back to find the old Tamil lying moaning and groaning, and obviously very drunk. He died before we could get him to hospital, it turned out of a ruptured spleen.

Paddy McNamara, the local OCPD, was soon on the scene and took statements from us all. He later tested the brakes only to find them almost non-existent. To add to my problems, not only did I not have a Kedah driving licence, but Pat had not even licensed the car.

I knew that I was in a lot of trouble. I had visions of being sent home fairly smartly by a company which could quickly fill the vacancy many times over. Fortunately we were able to prove, from the time we had taken to get from Taiping to Sungei Pasir, that we had not been speeding, and we could also produce corroborative evidence that we had each imbibed only one shandy after the match. However, the next day I was charged with (a) causing a death by a rash act; (b) driving a vehicle without efficient brakes; (c) driving a vehicle without a valid driving licence; and (d) driving an unregistered vehicle. The case would be heard in the Sungei Patani Court the following March – three months ahead. Pat Daintry was most apologetic, but there was nothing he could do except, perhaps, to appear on my behalf in mitigation.

I had many sleepless nights before the trial. I worked even harder than usual during the days, and spent most of my spare time with Dan Wright, playing cards and generally trying to keep my mind off the forthcoming trial. I did not tell either Tuke or the agents of the mishap – a great mistake, because, of course, word would soon have got around the expatriate community, but I was still young and immature. I forget whether I even informed Jean of my predicament.

At last the day of the trial arrived. To add to my anxiety, under Kedah law defendants were not permitted the services of defence counsel: one had to conduct one's own defence. The magistrate was a Malay, the prosecutor Paddy McNamara, and the witnesses the three other occupants of the car.

The postmortem report was read out in court by a hospital dresser. The Tamil had died of a ruptured spleen, and there was much toddy in his stomach. The evidence showed that the chap had been drinking heavily and the witnesses confirmed that he had suddenly darted out into the road and had run into me, rather than I into him. The magistrate enquired whether I had been drinking and the prosecutor could offer no evidence that I had. After a little deliberation the magistrate found me not guilty on the major charge and fined me $100 for the minor ones. My relief can be imagined.

As soon as the case was over, all concerned jumped into cars and headed off to Alor Star to watch an interstate soccer match. I went with Paddy McNamara, whilst the others were driven by the magistrate, at breakneck speed, in his open Alvis.

Despite the fact that I had not told Tuke about the incident, he knew all about it and was most sympathetic when he next visited the estate. During the time before the trial I also received great encouragement from Stewart Edgar King, the protector of Chinese, based at Sungei Patani. Known throughout Malaya as 'S.E.', he was some years older than we planters and was looked upon rather as a father figure. Dan, Greeno and I would often gather at his bungalow to chat half the night away. S.E. was a mine of information concerning all things Chinese. Shortly after coming down from Oxford and being accepted into the Colonial Service, he had been sent to China for three years to learn Cantonese, Mandarin and at least one other dialect, probably Hakka.

Because of the large number of Chinese and Indian immigrants in Malaya, the former attracted by the chance to display their native entrepreneurial skills in a prosperous country, the latter usually imported by the British to provide labour for the estates, and road- and rail-building, it was considered necessary to maintain government departments solely devoted to guarding the interests of these minority nationalities. The protectorate also controlled immigration, the application of banishment orders, provided defendants with interpreters and legal assistance in court cases, acted as arbitrators in marriage and marital disputes, monitored the Chinese secret societies, and refereed disputes between rubber estate and tin mine managers and their labour forces. In my experience no Chinese or Indian appealed to his protectorate in vain, and they were quite capable of taking on other government departments on behalf of their 'clients'.

During the wet season of 1932–3 we experienced in Kedah the heaviest rainfall ever recorded in a day in Malaya. The precipitation measured 17 inches. When this is compared to the average rainfall in England of 26 inches in a year one can get some idea of a tropical storm. It did not let up for 24 hours, and the flooding was immense. Luckily my bungalow was on a hill, but not so the staff quarters and coolie lines. All work on the estate was stopped until the floods subsided and we could restore the living accommodation to some degree of normality. It was worse still at Kuala Kangsar in Perak, where to this day a flood line of 17 feet above ground level is recorded on the post office wall.

At the beginning of 1933 Eddy Gardener, the Kedah PWD officer, moved on and his place was taken by Lal Laffan. Lal and his wife Midge were very good to the young bachelors of the district, and particularly myself. I suppose because I was younger than most. I was certainly a great deal less mature. Midge was a very beautiful young woman and most of us fell for her. She was certainly my favourite golf partner.

The Laffans took me on several excursions. We hired a launch and went out to the uninhabited island of Langkawi, little knowing at the time that I would be visiting it again in 1944. We also went picnicking to the Perlis Caves. These limestone caves are several hundred feet high in places and were the home of millions of flying foxes. A great Chinese culinary delicacy, they are really large bats, some with a wingspan of over six feet.

Looking back, I realise that the years 1932 to 1934 were my formative years. I grew up. I was building on the foundations laid by my mentors, namely my father, my school, Peters, Gyllenskold, even Tuke. I did not realise it at the time but another very important figure had entered my life. The longer I knew Bob Chrystal the more I liked and admired him. He was certainly the quickest witted man that I have ever met. He could be caustic and sometimes even cruel in his remarks, like many men with first-class brains. He was to teach me a great deal about life and I unknowingly absorbed the lessons. He was certainly a hero of mine. Looking back over a reasonably long life, during which I have been privileged to meet quite a few men of outstanding integrity, courage, humour and intellect, I would unhesitatingly place Bob at the top of the list.

I played a lot of cricket and rugger and I steadily improved at both games. I opened the batting and the bowling for the Penang

Cricket Club, and played wing forward for the Penang & Kedah Rugby Club. In 1934 Penang & Kedah reached the final of the Malaya Cup, against the United Services. The final was always played on the Padang in KL, in front of the Royal Selangor Club, known throughout the country as The Spotted Dog, or, more simply, the Dog. There used to be two large china Dalmatians, one each side of the main stairs, in memory of the dogs owned by a club secretary back in the Twenties.

I was very disappointed only to be a reserve, and was not alone in thinking that I had been underrated by the selectors. The selectors, coincidentally, were all Penangites and only chose three from Kedah, including me. This was the first time that Penang had reached the final, so I suppose they were loath to share their time of glory with Kedah. Like all reserves I secretly hoped that one of those chosen would fall sick, but no such luck. It must be remembered that there were always several army regiments and headquarters staffs stationed in Singapore and mainland Malaya, in addition to the Royal Air Force (RAF) and the Royal Navy (RN). Their Lordships at the Admiralty always seemed to ensure that a battleship or cruiser would just happen to be visiting the Singapore Naval Base at the opportune time, with officers on board who just happened to be full Services caps or internationals, so the Services sides were always very strong and, of course, fit. Penang lost.

We had travelled down by train, and had a very convivial weekend in KL, before embarking at Port Swettenham for the return journey by Straits Steamship to Penang. Pat Daintry was the Penang & Kedah fullback and had played a blinder. On reaching Penang, Pat and I spent the day in the cool of Penang Peak. A thoroughly enjoyable three days.

Pat was staying with me at the time, pending transfer to Tonghurst Estate, a small property east of Kulim and rather isolated. Later on, when he had moved, I spent the weekend with him. On our way home late at night, we were driving through some jungle near Tonghurst when a tiger jumped out across the road only a few yards in front of us. Pat slammed on the brakes (they worked this time!). The tiger stopped and stared back at us for several moments, fully illuminated by our headlights, before bounding off into the jungle. This was to be the last time that I was to see one of these magnificent creatures in the wild, although I was to smell them on several occasions in future and to see their pug marks.

Late in 1934 the Company granted me a week's local leave, and on Tuke's recommendation I booked a return passage on a Straits Steamship coaster to Victoria Point, in southern Burma. We sailed shortly after tiffin, and were in sight of land all the way, passing Langkawi Island again to port, and then Siam (Thailand) and the island of Phuket. The coastal scenery and the hilly hinterland were very beautiful.

Jean's long letters were a source of great joy to me. They arrived weekly as regular as clockwork, and were filled with all her news, descriptions of her various activities in her amateur dramatic and operatic societies, and her progress in singing and playing the cello, for both of which she was to gain gold medals from the Royal Academy of Music. She and her parents also used to send me out books and magazines, and overseas editions of several newspapers. I could also get The Straits Times each day so, unlike during my time in Sumatra, I was reasonably acquainted with what was happening around the world.

Whether the reports that began to appear in the newspapers concerning a man called Adolf Hitler in Germany, and the activities of his 'brown shirts', and news coming out of Manchuria about the Japanese, had anything to do with it I do not know, but the Kedah Volunteer Force was formed in 1934. I was number nine to sign on. Shortly after we had been kitted out and learned the rudiments of foot and rifle drill, we were inspected by General William Dobbie, the general officer commanding, Malaya, on the padang at Sungei Patani. Dobbie was later to become famous for leading the defence of Malta, for which the whole island was awarded the George Cross.

By 1934 the worst of the Depression was over and international trade was picking up. The price of rubber was improving. With more finance available estates could increase wages, plan replanting programmes and improve the living conditions of their labour forces.

Until the mid-30s most of the resident Tamil labour force lived in 'lines', buildings some 200 feet long, on stilts, about eight feet high, and divided into rooms of about 15 feet square. The whole family lived in this room, with the area beneath their space used for cooking and storage. Each line had its own wash house and latrines. Far from ideal but, strangely, well favoured by most of the Tamil coolies. In fact, when estates began to replace the old lines with the new cottage-type houses, many of the older Tamils were most reluctant to move. One of the drawbacks to the new type of line was that it was more difficult to pack the floor and walls with cow dung. This was used for many purposes, such as fuel for cooking and for smearing on wounds.

A few of us formed a weekly four at bridge and we met in each other's bungalows in rotation. The regulars were Dan Wright, Walter Northcote-Green, Ralph Inder and myself. One evening we foregathered at Ralph Inder's. Ralph was a tough little Cockney, just old enough to have fought in the Great War. I do not know whose idea it was to smuggle a Malay girl into his bedroom, although knowing my friends I can make a shrewd guess. Anyway, half way through the evening we persuaded Inder to go into his bedroom. He returned about half an hour later with a satisfied smirk on his face. No one said a word; he merely cut for the next hand and we went on playing.

After I left Kedah in April 1934 I saw little of Ralph Inder until he turned up at Sungei Siput in 1950. Shortly after breakfast one day in early July I was standing talking to Louis Denholm, who was to take over from me on Kamuning when I went on leave, when we heard a sudden burst of automatic gunfire intermingled with spasmodic rifle fire. This obviously came from Dovenby Estate which we were overlooking from our hillside. I remember saying to Louis: 'Here we are, going quietly about our business when over there one's best friend is being murdered.' Poor Ralph was not my best friend, but he was certainly an old friend. He died of multiple bullet wounds 24 hours later.

It would appear that early on that morning communist terrorists had slashed a lot of young rubber trees on Dovenby. Ralph had gone out to investigate and the bandits were waiting for him. Ralph and his escort of two special constables were outnumbered six to one, but they put up a good fight. One of the special constables was killed and the other badly wounded, and the bandits got away with their weapons.

It must have been early in March 1934 that I was told that Barton had asked for me to act for him on Sungei Plentong when he went on home leave. By this time Barton had been appointed visiting agent for the Ridsdell Group, so the confidence that he must have had in me was most encouraging.

The agents agreed that I could have 10 days leave, including the three days that it would take me to travel the length of Malaya, nearly 600 miles, to the south of Johore. S. E. King had been transferred to Ipoh, and Pat Daintry was acting on another Ridsdell estate near Batu Gajah, just south of Ipoh. So I arranged to have three days with each, before resuming my journey southwards.

After a number of farewell parties and the usual promises to keep in touch, I set out for Ipoh, some 140 miles away, getting there at about stengah time. S.E. broke the news that Pat was in Batu Gajah Hospital with a compound fracture of his leg, sustained whilst keeping goal in a soccer match. My plans, therefore, had to be altered. I accepted S.E.'s invitation to stay the whole six days leave with him.

I went to the hospital first thing in the morning. Pat was in good heart but very concerned about the estate. He persuaded me to go to Harewood Estate to look at the mail, deal with anything obviously urgent, and generally make myself useful. This latter would entail arranging to collect the payroll money from the bank and paying the labour force. I spent the best part of my six days holiday looking after Harewood Estate. On reflection, I was to do similar things over the years on many occasions, with scant recognition and even less financial reward. The modern word is sucker.

I took the north-south main road through Bidor, Tapah, Tanjong Malim, KL, Seremban, as far as Tampin where I turned off to Malacca and took the coast road to Muar where I stayed the night. The following day I pressed on via Batu Pahat, and Rengam, finally arriving at Sungei Plentong in the late afternoon. It would have been quicker to have stayed on the main road all the way, but I enjoyed the excursion and seeing the old town of Malacca, with its Portuguese and Dutch buildings, and the fort. At both Muar and Batu Pahat one had to cross the rivers by chain ferry, sharing the crossings with traditional roofed Malaccan bullock carts.

Johore Again

August 1934 – February 1935

Barton had not changed since I saw him last. As cheerful as ever. He must have seen a change in me, though. During the intervening period I had grown from callow youth to young manhood. We had about a week together before he left for home, and in that time he introduced me to the International Club in JB, with a membership open to all nationalities. It had its own nine-hole golf course. I met several members of the Johore royal family at the club and was invited to the Istana on several occasions. The Sultan had homes in England as well as in Malaya and was completely British in behaviour and attitude. This meant that he served alcohol to his guests, unlike the Sultan of Perak who served only orange juice when one was invited to the Istana in Kuala Kangsar.

In addition to Sungei Plentong Estate, Barton managed a small estate up the Johore river which was only accessible by boat. The company had a launch to ferry staff and supplies, which I used for my twice-weekly visits. I felt as if I were Sanders of the River. There was a telephone, too, so the head clerk used to report to me daily. Because I was also looking after this smaller property my salary was raised from $300 to $425 a month. That was about £600 per annum, a bank manager's salary in England at the time.

I suppose that I had been back on the estate for about two months when I received an invitation from the British Resident and his wife to a dinner party. Such an invitation was, of course, tantamount to a royal command. On the appointed evening I donned my dinner jacket and presented myself at the Residency. My fellow guests were Sir Andrew Caldecott, the acting governor of Singapore, and Lady Caldecott, the Senior Controller of Labour (Tamil) whose name I have forgotten, and the Dutchman Professor Van Steyn Callensfells, who was a world-famous palaeontologist. He was a giant of a man, at least six feet six inches tall, and weighing 25 stones. He had a huge black beard which reached almost to his waist. I learned later that Arthur Conan Doyle had based Professor Challenger, the hero of *The Lost World*, on him.

As the evening developed it became apparent why I had been invited. After all, I was still one of the more junior planters in the area, even though I was an acting manager. The professor was digging for Neolithic remains and had heard a rumour that there was a cave on the summit of a jungle-covered hill on Sungei Plentong Estate which might be interesting. I was asked whether I could guide the professor's assistant and two Dyaks to the hilltop to confirm or otherwise the cave's existence. I naturally agreed, but pointed out that there was no path so that we would have to blaze a trail, although I presumed that this would present no problem to the Dyaks.

The professor was a great character and told anecdote after anecdote, mostly to do with palaeontology. I cannot remember any except one about gin. In his deep guttural voice he related how 'one night I drank one hundred Gordon's gins. The next morning I had a headache. The next night I had one hundred Bols gins. The next morning I had no headache. I always drink Bols gin.'

We agreed on a day and Callensfells' assistant and the Dyaks arrived. Meanwhile, I had already found out that some of my labour force were in the habit of trapping wild boar in that part of the jungle, so I had arranged for them to clear a path for most of the way. We made it in a couple of hours and found the cave which was about 30 feet from the top. As it looked promising, the palaeontologist set up camp and started to scrape away, while I climbed the remaining short distance to the summit – a fortuitous decision that was to have momentous consequences some 11 years later.

There below me was the whole of the Strait of Johore, and immediately in front, seemingly at my feet, was the Royal Navy's Singapore Dockyard, with its dry dock capable of holding the largest battleships in the world, and several large warships at anchor nearby or berthed at the dockside. I gazed at this unique panorama for a long time and cursed myself for not having a camera. But the scene had evidently become indelibly etched in my mind.

I was delighted when the rugger season came round again and I managed to establish myself in the Johore state fifteen, at wing forward. It was generally acknowledged that the 1933–4 Johore pack was one of the best ever seen in Malaya. I remember most of the names to this day – Saunders, MacKenzie, Bailey, Duncan Campbell, Forbes Wallace, A. N. Other, Cameron and Hembry. Forbes Wallace, then the OCPD Johore District, became a particular friend. Duncan Campbell was a massive Scot, tremendous in body and voice. Good enough to have sung professionally before coming out to Malaya, his singing of 'The Road to the Isles' was particularly memorable, and no after-match beat-up was complete without it. Having survived over three years on the Railway, he was to be killed soon after his return to Scotland when the tractor he was driving overturned.

One day, towards the end of 1934, Forbes Wallace and I went down to the Seletar airfield on Singapore to see the arrival of the leaders of the London–Melbourne Air Race. We saw the eventual winners, Campbell Black and Scott. In 1934 such an event caused great excitement throughout the world.

One day I had a message from Bob Chrystal that he would be doing some VA-ing in the Rengam district and that his company, Guthrie's, were inviting local planters to see a demonstration of the Reginato Sheeting Battery, and that I should come along. There I met the inventor of this machinery, Batista Reginato. He was an Italian planter who owned several rubber estates in Malaya, and was later to be responsible for those owned by the Sultan of Johore. So began my long friendship with 'Uncle Regi'. When in 1952 I was transferred to Kedah, our neighbours were his nephew Bepi and his beautiful young wife Elena. Regi and his wife Otilia were interned as enemy aliens in 1940, when Italy entered the War, much to the disgust of his many British friends, as it would not have been possible to find anyone more pro-British than Regi. The authorities, as ever not prone to reasonable decision-making, shipped them off to an internment camp in Australia, where they were to remain until well after the end of the War, let alone until after Italy came over to the Allies' side in 1943, when they should have been released, having, quite literally, been forgotten.

My time on Sungei Plentong was now getting short and I was counting the days to Barton's return when I could go on my first home leave. Sandilands Buttery booked me on the Dutch liner *Marnix van St Alldegonder*, a far cry from the old *Achilles*, and I ticked off the days on my calendar.

During December I strove to harvest a record crop, and succeeded, a thoroughly tactless thing for an acting manager to do. Record crops were a manager's privilege. In the event Barton was able to comment adversely about the condition in one of the tapping areas. I had been extremely worried about the amount of bracken which had been allowed to grow in this particular division. Bracken is a sign of acidity, and rubber trees do not like acid soils. I had called in Bill Ackhurst, an expert from the Rubber Research Institution, whose opinion was that the bracken should be slashed to ground level, which we did. However, this let in the other enemy of rubber trees – lalang. This is a twitch, similar to that which grows in England, but with roots that penetrate many feet down into the earth, with needle-sharp points that bore into the rubber tree roots. Bill Ackhurst should have known better, and I should not have been so keen to show my efficiency. However, everything else met with Barton's approval, and I eventually received a £50 bonus from the London directors.

I had arranged with Bob Chrystal that he should join me for dinner at the Raffles, where I was staying the night before I sailed, and that we would have a night out on the tiles. The bedrooms, overlooking the famous lawn with its fan trees and canna beds, were off the wide verandah and were large, cool and airy. The bedroom was about 30 feet square, with a sitting area, a separate dressing room and a large bathroom, all marble floored, with punkah fans on the ceilings.

When at last the day of my departure arrived I drove to JB where I handed over my trusty Fiat to the somewhat reluctant Chinese merchant in lieu of the money I owed him, and hired a taxi to take me into Singapore. The initial thrill of the thought of leave had worn off. I now felt very tired. I had overworked my contract by over six months, and although comparatively fit because of the active open-air life I led, and the games-playing, the climate with its monotonously high humidity and heat, and, I suppose, the rubber plantation, obviously had a depressing effect on me. I badly needed a change of climate, scenery, and company. And to see Jean again.

So far I have hesitated to mention sexual matters. This because of both diffidence, and the firm belief that such matters should be of no concern except to the individuals concerned. However, having given my daughter-in-law Linda an undertaking that my memoirs would include 'warts and all' it is probably appropriate at this juncture to describe my experience to date.

In a word, nil. Because of my engagement to Jean I had been determined to impose discipline and celibacy, and, not without strain, I had succeeded. This was old-fashioned even for the 1930s, as well as appearing, no doubt, priggish. But there were very few single European women available and I remembered my father's short lecture on the dangers of promiscuity, and I think this fear was never far from my mind whenever the temptation became strong or the opportunity arose. Remember, penicillin and other modern drugs were not available at the time, although, I think, M&B was, just. (May & Baker sulphonamide tablets, used to treat gonorrhea.)

It is a popular misconception in Europe that Asian women are more promiscuous than European women. After more than 25 years in the East I can say, without hesitation or fear of contradiction, that the very opposite is true. Asian women have a far higher standard of sexual morality and marital loyalty than their Occidental counterparts.

When I was in Kedah I had met Sir John Campbell, first cousin to the Duke of Argyll. Sir John, by then well into his 60s, was a great character, lived in Perlis and owned a tin mine. Whenever he drove down to Penang he invariably stopped off at the Sungei Patani Club for a sharpener or three. He had formed his own company of yeomanry during the Boer War, and because of my father's service in the Imperial Yeomanry in South Africa at that time I was very interested in his reminiscences, and usually joined him. He looked very like C. Aubrey Smith, the Hollywood film star and one-time

England cricket captain.

Sir John was living with a well-known Chinese lady, Juliette Loke Yew, whilst Lady Campbell lived with an Australian ex-jockey, Dick Campbell, in Penang. A real Somerset Maugham set up. Sir John and Lady Campbell had three daughters, the eldest married to a doctor in Singapore, the second to a schoolmaster, and the youngest, Marjorie, still living with her mother. During my last days in Kedah, before moving down to Johore, I took Marjorie out to dinner several times, and I enjoyed her friendship and sense of fun. I was also aware that Lady Campbell sometimes looked at me with a rather calculating eye, but whether in fear that we might become attached or hope that we would do so, I do not know. Jean and I used to meet Marjorie occasionally in Penang over the years.

Juliette Loke Yew was the sister of a Chinese millionaire, of which there were many even in the 30s, who intensely disliked the idea of his sister demeaning the family by living with a European, so, the story goes, gave her £10,000 to leave Sir John, which she did – but immediately went to live with another Scotsman, a planter named Carmichael, in Sitiawan.

The Raffles holds many memories for me over the years. Towards the end of 1934 I had been on a shopping expedition to Singapore with a friend, I think for presents to take home on leave, and we had gone to the Raffles for tea and to watch the dancers at the usual thé dansant. We recognised the Rajah Brooke of Sarawak, the Ranee, and their three daughters sitting at a nearby table. No one seemed anxious to ask the princesses to dance, so I went over, bowed to the Rajah and Ranee, and asked if they would permit me the pleasure of dancing with their daughters. The Rajah nodded, and I spent the rest of the time dancing with all three. They were very attractive girls. One married Lord Inchcape, the middle one married Harry Roy, the dance band leader, whilst the youngest married an all-in wrestler. Years later the Rajah's nephew and heir, who was in military intelligence, stayed with me in my flat in Calcutta.

Bob Chrystal turned up and we immediately ordered several large stengahs, to get the evening off to a good start. We were chatting, deciding how we were to spend my last evening in Singapore, when we were approached by an elderly lady and a young man who asked if they could join us. About two weeks earlier I had been introduced to the couple, Lady Tichborne and her son Greville, who were travelling around the Far East, basing themselves in Singapore. The 'Tichborne Case' was a cause célèbre at the end of the previous century – I think involving a long lost cousin from Australia laying claim to the title.

The Tichbornes invited us to join them for dinner, which of course we did, and afterwards they asked if we would take them to the New World, an entertainment park full of dance halls, Chinese theatres, Malay wayang, shooting galleries, souvenir stalls, restaurants, satay stalls, pimps, prostitutes and perverts, ice cream stalls, anything and everything one could think of. And more besides. We walked around for some time before settling down in a dance hall to watch the taxi girls and their customers who were mostly British serviceman. The New World was almost the only place that ORs (Other Ranks, as non-officers were known in those days) could go for any entertainment. Officers would have the entrée into all the hotels, swimming clubs, restaurants and private houses, whilst ORs did not. A thoroughly bad system which was not to change until well after the Second World War.

We stayed at the New World until it closed in the early hours when Lady Tichborne said that she would like to go to a nightclub. I only knew of one, a sleazy dive run by a Tamil prostitute, where the Johore rugger team sometimes ended up after a match. I remember that the madame had a bottom waggle that was every bit as pronounced as Marilyn Monroe's some 25 years later. We stayed there, drinking and dancing until after 4 am, when we left to take the Tichbornes back to their hotel. Bob, who was staying at the Europe, then suggested that we had a nightcap there. It was after dawn that I finally went back to the Raffles by rickshaw. Rickshaws could be hired at any time of the day or night, the runners sleeping in them, springing instantly awake as soon as a potential customer came by.

As the boy was due to bring me tea and papaya at seven there was no point in going to bed, so I merely bathed and changed and did what little packing there was before having my breakfast and taking a taxi to the docks where the *Marnix* was alongside. I thus paid dearly for the privilege of staying at the Raffles on this occasion

Bob had promised to come aboard to see me off, but I was not a bit surprised that he failed to put in an appearance.

I find it difficult to adequately describe the unique feeling experienced by most people at the moment of departure for home leave, on a luxury liner, after long and arduous years spent many thousands of miles from home and family. In those days a contract for junior staff was for five years, and for senior three.

We sailed at noon. Most passengers stayed on deck, waving to the friends who had come to wish them Godspeed until they became a blur on the quayside, before drifting away to the bars or to their cabins to supervise the cabin stewards unpack. My cabin companion was an elderly sea captain going home on retirement from a lifetime spent in Far Eastern waters. He had first come out in a tea clipper in the 1880s, and was a fund of Conradesque reminiscences. My table companions were the Captain, a rather dull Dutch couple and two young French girls who were to disembark at Colombo. Conversation was rather stilted as the couple, most unusually for Dutch, spoke but little English, and the French girls none at all.

The first port of call was Belawan Deli, where I had disembarked almost exactly four years before. Seeing the dreary low-lying coastline again made me very thankful that I would still be on board when the ship sailed in a couple of hours. On leaving Belawan Deli I felt that the journey home had really begun. The passage to Columbo was quiet, calm and uneventful, and was always considered the 'settling down' part of the trip. Passengers sort themselves out, join the various on-board activities, and form friendships.

The Captain and I went ashore at Colombo to have lunch at the Galle Face Hotel, another famous hotel in the Raffles mould, which I was to get to know very well in the war years. Thereafter we called in at Port Said (the *Marnix* was oil-burning, so no Tamil coolies), Algiers, Genoa, and eventually Southampton. I had been away from England for more than five years.

Marriage & Managership

July 1935 – May 1936

No words I have can adequately describe my pleasure at being at home. So many friends and relations to see. So much to tell and to hear about. And, above all, the joy at seeing and being with Jean again, and at learning about the preparations in hand for our wedding.

The first impression on arriving home was the smallness of all the houses compared to those I had been used to in Malaya. Even the quite large houses, by English standards, of my parents and friends, appeared tiny, and, above all, airless.

We celebrated my sister Molly's 21st birthday at the old Holborn Restaurant, in London. It was good to be with my brothers Gordon and Bill and to learn about all they had done, at first hand, during my absence. Bill had joined Alfa Laval as a sales agent for their milking machines, covering Yorkshire and Lancashire, a position that he was to hold for the rest of his working life. He was by now a scratch golfer and playing regularly for the Yorkshire county team. Gordon had spent some time in Canada, where he had led a communist-inspired demonstration in Vancouver – not, I am sure, because of any political sympathy with the cause, but merely the love of a scrap, especially with the authorities. My father was managing director of Alfa Laval, and about to move to Walton-on-Thames, where he was building a house, to be nearer to the new factory and company headquarters he was developing at Brentford.

Jean's father, Bruce Cuthbertson, was London manager of the tube manufacturer Accles & Pollock, and was to make a name for himself as instigator of the company's sales slogan 'Give us a tube and we'll put another inside it'. An American company sent them a tube the size of a human hair. Accles & Pollock duly obliged. In the war to come he became the director in contact with the Ministry of Supply, and was responsible for the contracts for, amongst other things, millions of Sten gun barrels and many more millions of lengths of tubing for wireless aerials. From the latter he went on after the war to develop the world's first all-metal fishing rods.

Jean and I went to Twickenham and saw England play Ireland, and later in the summer, after our marriage, we were frequent visitors to Lords, where I was able to watch Wally Hammond bat again. I presume that this was Gloucestershire against Middlesex, as I did not see the Test match against the South Africans, which they won, in spite of a very strong England team.

We were married quietly in Upminster church, with just the immediate family and very few friends present, and left immediately on our honeymoon. This cost only slightly more than £50 for the fortnight, during which we toured England and Wales.

The time went all too quickly, and before long it was time to say our goodbyes. I had called in at the London office to see Halliday, the company secretary, and he told me that Tuke, whose leave had coincided with mine, had complained that my name had appeared in *The Straits Times* as having played cricket not only on a Saturday, but on the Sunday too, and what had I to say about it? I merely replied that it was a two-day State match, Penang against Perak, and that I thought it very poor form, but well in keeping with his character, for Tuke to have waited more than 12 months to complain to the secretaries personally, rather than to have confronted me with my heinous offence at the time. For a relatively junior planter to criticise a senior manager in this way was almost unheard of, but it was a sign of the confidence that I now possessed. I thought that poor old Halliday would have apoplexy. However, he told me that the directors had decided to offer me the managership of Waterloo Estate, Padang Rengas, in Perak – a small estate some six miles north of Kuala Kangsar.

This was very good news as, apart from a step up the ladder in my chosen profession, Kuala Kangsar was an attractive little town, with a club, a nine-hole golf course, and shops. It was also the capital of the state of Perak, the centre of government, and where the Sultan had his Istana (palace) and royal mosque.

At the beginning of July 1935 Jean and I waved our farewells to our families and friends at Southampton, little realising, in spite of the fact that it was obvious that the war clouds were gathering, that it would be nine years before I was to return to England. In Germany, Herr Hitler had attained power, it is sometimes forgotten by democratic means, and it was reported that Krupps had launched a vast expansion in their armaments production. Mussolini was preparing to invade Abyssinia, and Japan, which had already occupied Manchuria, was shortly to attack China.

We sailed on the brand new German liner *Potsdam*, the more knowledgeable amongst the passengers recognising that the ship had obviously been designed as an armed merchantman. The *Potsdam* was captured by the British during the War, and renamed the *Empire Fowey* and served as a troopship for many years. When we passed through the Suez Canal we saw several Italian troopships. The troops jeered at British ships and cheered the German ones, of which there were many (presumably involved in stockpiling war materials).

The journey down the Red Sea and across the Indian Ocean was uneventful, except for the odd tropical storm, but was obviously a great new experience for Jean. She became an expert exponent of liar dice and ship's champion at deck quoits. She was an excellent sailor, and we were to enjoy many happy sea trips together over the next 40-odd years, always preferring to take a ship rather than a plane.

On disembarkation at Penang, and after reporting to McAuliffe, Davis & Hope, I went to Borneo Motors and bought a brand new Morris Ten saloon, a first-class little car, into which we loaded our barang (luggage) and drove off to our first married home.

Waterloo was a small estate, very hilly, and fairly isolated (but not in comparison with Gajah Muntah). The rubber was in first-class condition, although the factory and machinery were antiquated – as one would expect with a Ridsdell estate.

We soon settled in to our new home, and Jean quickly made the bungalow attractive with curtains and cushions. We bought our own drawing room and dining room furniture, in place of the rather plain, poor quality chairs and tables supplied by the company. The wireless set given to us by Jean's father gave adequate reception to both the Singapore and Empire Service stations. And, of course, we had my wind-up gramophone. After a little while the packing cases containing all our wedding presents arrived and we had great pleasure in unpacking everything, and seeing, for the first time, the complete set of Harbridge cut glass most generously given to us by a cousin. Only one sherry glass was to survive the war, which I found in a local dispensary in early 1946 being used for urine testing.

I gained my place in the Perak state rugger team, and scarcely missed an interstate match in three years. I transferred to the Perak battalion of the Federated Malay States Volunteer Force (FMSVF) and trained as a Vickers machine gunner. We paraded on the padang at Taiping, usually under the command of Lt Frank Vanrenen, a proprietary planter (that is he owned and managed his own estate) on the Chenderoh Road, down which the Japanese would make one of their lightning flanking movements in 1941.

Waterloo did not extend me. It was under a thousand acres, all mature rubber, with no jungle reserve into which to expand. Ted Wilkie, the general manager, who made periodical visits, told me bluntly that I should look around for another, better job in one of the bigger companies, and that he would keep his ears open. The effects of the Depression were wearing off, the demand for rubber was growing, mainly because of re-armament, so the price of rubber was rising quite quickly, but working for a somewhat moribund company, with little or no assets set aside for development, offered no challenge for an ambitious young man.

Outwardly Jean appeared happy, but discussing our early days together, long after our retirement to England, she said that she was desperately homesick and lonely. I must have been very unperceptive and unfeeling not to have realised this, because I had gone through the same experience. I was extremely happy, with a new wife, doing work that I loved, in familiar conditions, able to speak the local languages, and newly promoted to managership (albeit, a small one) at the early age of 25. Jean, though, had to spend hours on her own, in a strange land, unable to talk even to the servants. Fortunately, there was soon to be a change for the better.

When the Chinese cook/boy left we engaged an Indian in his

place. All went well until one evening we returned from a rugger practice at Ipoh to find the mosquito windows wide open, and the cook/boy nowhere to be seen. I went around to the kitchen area and found him swaying like barley in the breeze, very obviously drunk. This he emphatically denied, which only increased my temper so that I hit him across the side of the head with my open hand. He collapsed and lay flat on his back on the floor. I threw a bucket of water over his head, dragged him to his feet, and ordered him to pack his belongings and leave. I sent for the office kebun (gardener) and instructed him to get the cook off the estate in fifteen minutes.

I went to the drinks cupboard and, like Mother Hubbard, found it bare. So here we were – at 7 pm, miles from anywhere, two people coming to dinner, no cook, and no drink. Except for a dozen or so bottles of beer. So all was not lost as Frank Vanrenen was a great beer drinker and so, we hoped, would be Bill Harvey, our other guest. Jean managed to produce some food whilst I poured out the beer, which appeared to be very frothy. Frank took a sip and immediately spat it out. We found that all the bottles had been broached and filled with soapy water. Luckily we all had a sense of humour.

The next evening we went to the Kuala Kangsar Club where we met Paddy McNamara, the same man who had prosecuted me in Sungei Patani in 1933, who was now the OSPC (Officer Supervising Police Circle) at Kuala Kangsar. Over drinks I described the events of the previous evening. Paddy asked his name and then disclosed that he too had employed the same man and had had exactly the same experience. He had locked him up in a cell overnight to sober up before dismissing him the next morning.

About a week later I received a letter from a solicitor in Taiping advising that he was acting for my ex-cook who claimed that I had thrashed him on the back with a bamboo lathi (stick), so injuring him that he had go to Taiping Hospital, where the doctor had issued a certificate to the effect that there were severe lacerations on his back that could have only been inflicted by a beating. Also, I had dismissed him without paying him his last five weeks salary. Either I paid him $200 or he would take out a summons against me.

I went straight into Ipoh the next day to consult my own

solicitor, George Tyrrill, the son of the famous Malayan judge Mr Justice A'Beckett Tyrrill, and told him everything, including Paddy McNamara's experience. George said that he would defend me and that it would be an open and shut case. The first snag arose when I asked Paddy to appear as a witness for me. He said that he could not do so for he had incarcerated the cook without entering a charge, which was illegal. The second was that Jean was expecting John within a matter of weeks and I did not want her to have to be cross examined by the solicitor representing the cook, a European named Gartside whom I disliked intensely.

On the day of the hearing Paddy relented and agreed to appear as a witness for me. I denied thrashing the plaintiff, but admitted to knocking him over with the flat of my hand. I said that he was so drunk that he would have probably fallen over anyway. Also, that I had not paid him his wages for the few days in April as the value of the drink he had consumed was far more than the few dollars I owed him. The cook, under oath, swore that he was teetotal.

Paddy then told of his experience, and how he had been forced to place the inebriated cook in a cell for the night for his own protection, in case he had injured himself!

The magistrate, a Malay who later became a distinguished High Court judge in KL, found that the cook was lying, that I had not beaten him, and that Jean had paid his salary for the previous month, March. But he awarded costs against me because I had not paid the cook's wages for the four days in April, notwithstanding the value of the stolen alcohol. I thought this rather unfair.

It later transpired that the solicitor's clerk had met my cook in a coffee shop, and, scenting a case to defend, had taken him home and beaten him, before taking him on to the hospital for the doctor's report. Gartside undoubtedly knew exactly what was going on. He was that sort of man.

There was to be a sequel nearly 30 years later in Suffolk. Our friend Dick Duckworth, a former British Resident of Selangor, who had retired nearby, invited us to his house to meet the current Malaysian High Commissioner, who was staying the weekend. I eyed him, I hope surreptitiously, for a few minutes and then asked him whether he had ever been a district officer and magistrate in KK. He had, in 1936. He remembered the case well, as the cook was to appear before him in similar circumstances again. We had a very cheery evening reminiscing.

There was a story going the rounds at that time about two bachelor planters who messed together and who became aware that the level of their sherry bottle was constantly going down, and they suspected the cook of taking a daily swig. To teach him a lesson they emptied out most of the remaining sherry and each peed into the bottle, before replacing the cork. After a few days, the contents of the bottle having diminished as before, they accused the cook of drinking their sherry, which charge he vehemently denied. However, he did explain that he always laced their soup with the sherry, just as he had been instructed to do by a mem he had previously worked for.

The weeks went by, and through rugger matches, Volunteer parades and evenings at the Kuala Kangsar and Ipoh clubs, we met fellow planters, government servants, tin miners, solicitors and agency men and their wives, and began to entertain at our bungalow and to be entertained at theirs. Most importantly, Jean was able to meet other women, to discuss the things that women do, especially, I would imagine, now that her baby was due within a matter of weeks. We still had no telephone, which was a disadvantage.

A very welcome visitor was Jean's uncle Ben Guy. Ben Guy was the Far Eastern representative for Buchanan's Scotch whisky, and both looked and acted the part. He was known from Bombay to Tokyo as 'Honest Ben Guy'. A great enthusiast for the turf, he always planned his itinerary around the various gold cup race meetings at Calcutta, Rangoon, KL, Singapore, Bangkok, Hong Kong, Shanghai and elsewhere. He appeared to know everyone and everything. It was through Ben Guy that we were to know Charles Martine, then manager of the Penang office of the Borneo Company, and his dear wife Pat, who were to remain such special friends for the rest of their lives.

Charles was about 10 years older than me, and had served during the last few months of the Great War. A man of great integrity, courage and stamina, he was captured at the fall of Singapore and carried the scars of many savage beatings from Jap guards for the rest of his life, never knowing a day without pain

During the war, when I was stationed at Barrackpore, I traded on my relationship with Uncle Ben when I called on Buchanan's agents in Calcutta. I managed to get a case of Scotch out of them for the officers' mess. It had completely run out of whisky and had been unable to replenish the stocks until my timely arrival.

Some weeks after the court case Jean and I were having tiffin with Ted and Lillian Wilkie on the nearby Eaglehurst Estate when the telephone rang and after a longish conversation I heard Ted say, 'Humphrey, I think I know the very chap, and what's more, he's sitting here now.' He put the phone down and said that the man on the line was Humphrey Butler, manager of Kamuning Estate, Sungei Siput, one of the very best estates in the Guthrie Group. Humphrey Butler was looking for an experienced planter to replace his senior assistant who was being transferred to another estate to act as manager, and did Ted know anyone?

Ted strongly advised me to apply, pointing out again the limitations of a company like Ridsdells. Guthrie's reputation was second to none and the chairman was John Hay (later to be knighted for his services to the rubber industry), the foremost name in the rubber world. I agreed to see Butler, so Ted phoned back and arranged a meeting for me that very evening.

I drove down to Sungei Siput as arranged. Kamuning Estate – Kamuning (Perak) Rubber & Tin Company Limited, to give its full, formal title – was situated astride the main north-south road, about 15 miles from Kuala Kangsar and 19 miles north of Ipoh – the 19th milestone was exactly opposite the estate entrance. I arrived at stengah time. Humphrey Butler and I took to each other immediately and it was agreed that he would telephone Guthrie's in KL first thing the next morning to arrange an interview for me with the managing agents. After this briefest of discussions Humphrey introduced me to his wife Sheila, thus establishing a firm friendship between the four of us that was to last until their deaths more than 30 years later.

I travelled down to KL on the night mail a few days later and duly presented myself at the Guthrie office where I was first interviewed by 'Long' John Anderson, son of Sir John, one of the founders of the Guthrie empire back in the late 19th century. After only a very few words I was taken in to see Roy Waugh, the senior visiting agent. Again, after only a very few words, Roy Waugh asked to be excused and returned in a short while and said, 'The job's yours, if you want it.' It was agreed that I would join Guthrie's as soon as I could obtain my release from Ridsdells.

A few days later I was due in Penang to play for Perak in an interstate rugger match, so I made an appointment to see Jock Reid at McAuliffes to arrange my release. Jock was very understanding and promised to cable Ridsdells in London first thing on the following Monday morning, with a recommendation that I should be released from my contract. As Guthrie needed an answer quickly I was to telephone Jock on the Tuesday afternoon to ascertain Ridsdells' reactions. This I did, to learn that London was prepared to accept two weeks' notice, but on condition that I repaid three quarters of the cost of my fare from England to Penang.

In those days, of course, companies only paid the fares of their employees. A wife's fare was the responsibility of her husband, so that Jean's fare was not involved in this calculation. I must say, I was somewhat aggrieved at Ridsdells' stipulation in view of the extra time that I had put in on my first agreement. However, I was not prepared to allow this to be an obstacle to my joining Guthrie's.

I moved to Kamuning in early May, little more than a week before John was due to be born. Jean had gone to stay with Pat Martine in Penang, to be near both her doctor and the hospital. The actual handover of Waterloo Estate to Ted Wilkie and the move took no more than a couple of days. The Kamuning lorry and my car were sufficient to transport all our chattels the 20-odd miles.

I was sad to leave Waterloo. It was, after all, our first married home, and my first managership. But, strangely, we never once returned. I know that Jean came to enjoy the peace and beauty of the place, once she had overcome the homesickness, the totally new and strange way of life, and after she had begun to learn the rudiments of the Malay language. She has often reminded young wives of Ruth's words to Naomi: 'whither thou goest, I will go; and where thou lodgest, I will lodge; thy people shall be my people' when they have complained about having to follow their husbands to out-of-the-way and uncongenial places.

Our wireless occasionally gave us trouble, but we heard the broadcast bulletins at the time of the death of King George V and the accession to the throne of Edward VIII. I invited the English-speaking Tamil clerk to listen to the new king's broadcast to the peoples of the Empire, after which he said, 'He is in all our hearts.' Before the end of the year, of course, he was out of many of our hearts, mine included. I am bound to say that he never struck me as being out of the right mould. And we knew nothing then of his shenanigans with Wallace Simpson.

So began our 14-year stay at Kamuning Estate. We were to regard them as quite the happiest and most productive and formative years of our lives.

Kamuning Estate

May 1936 – December 1941

After the small estate that I had left, Kamuning was a revelation; it seemed vast. It was more than 8,000 acres in area, of which over a thousand was jungle reserve. It had over 100 miles of roads, and a modern factory. It was very hilly, and was dominated by a large limestone outcrop, which rose up from just behind the senior assistant's bungalow and was visible for miles around. This, the Gunong Tunjuk (also known as Lion Hill), served as a landmark for aircraft navigation and was also used occasionally by an itinerant hermit. From time to time a light would appear on it, presumably when the hermit was in residence. On Coronation Day 1937 Paddy Jackson and I climbed to the summit and planted a Union Flag which could be seen fluttering for months until it was finally torn to shreds by tropical storms. In December 1941 it was reported that a red light could be seen on the top, placed there, it was suspected, by Japanese sympathisers or fifth columnists as a guide for their aircraft on their way to bomb the airfield at Ipoh.

The first rubber trees had been planted on Kamuning in the early 1880s as shade for the coffee and pepper, when the estate was owned by the Malay Peninsula Coffee Company, under the management of D'Estere Darby, who later went on to found the great trading company Sime, Darby & Co. In 1899, when the coffee market crashed, the estate was sold to John Anderson and Loke Yew, a Chinese millionaire, who appointed Guthrie's, of which Anderson was then chairman, as managing agents. Kamuning was floated on the London stock exchange in 1909.

Some of the best-known names in Malayan rubber industry history had, over the years, served on Kamuning – D'Estere Darby, Darcy Irving, Shelton Agar, George Henning, St Claire Morford, Roy

Waugh, Humphrey Butler and Robert Chrystal. I feel privileged to have followed them.

I have often examined my feelings towards Kamuning. If one can love one's country it cannot be impossible to love a rubber estate, surely? As an estate it had everything. It was large without being too large. It had magnificent views from its many hills. It was on the main road, within easy reach of both Ipoh and Kuala Kangsar. There were many shops in Sungei Siput village and an excellent market, only five minutes away. It had mains electricity, the telephone, a good, pure water supply piped in from the jungle, high-yielding rubber trees, sound finances with adequate capital reserves, and jungle reserves to permit expansion.

As senior assistant I was responsible for my own division as well as for the factory, which included manufacture of crepe rubber sheet, which was new to me, the grading, packing and despatch of the finished product. The factory was powered by two huge single-cylinder Ruston & Hornsby diesel engines. These were started each morning by heating the fuel with charcoal and a dozen coolies heaving on the giant pulley belt. They were museum pieces, but had served with the minimum of trouble for nearly 50 years, until I replaced them with electric motors after the war. The loud explosion and the puff of black smoke signifying the engines had started were the signals for me to go down to the office each morning.

At six in the morning on 23 May 1936 Humphrey Butler phoned with the news that Jean had given birth to our son in Georgetown Hospital, Penang, late the previous evening, and that all was well with both mother and baby. I left for Penang at once, breakfasted at Parry's Bar at Butterworth, and eventually reached the hospital to find Jean sitting up in bed nursing John, both looking very happy. I sat with them for some time before Pat Martine arrived to take me off for a celebratory tiffin at the E&O Hotel nearby, where we were joined by Charles, after which I took a rickshaw to the post office to cable the grandparents with the good news. I cabled 'Plain John arrived', which was not exactly what I had wanted to say, as Jean and I thought our son to be a very handsome baby, but that he was to have only the one Christian name.

I stayed that night with the Martines. The Borneo Company bungalow was one of the largest and most beautiful on the island, cool and airy, with a large, well-tended garden. After an early supper Charles took me off to the Penang Club, quite a privilege, as at that time only tuans besar could be members, and the new baby's head was well and truly wetted.

I had a very busy week back at Kamuning and phoned the hospital in Penang every evening to check on the progress of Jean and my new son. Both were in excellent health and spirits and looking forward to returning home. I set off to Penang again early the next Saturday and called in at Wearne Brothers, the leading car dealers in Malaya, and changed my car for a brand new Standard Twelve. So, in the course of about a fortnight, I had become a father, changed my job, and bought a new car, all on about £40 a month. Looking back, the change of car was a needless expense, but one that I have often repeated over the years. Apart from in the war years the only car that I have ever had provided for me was the armoured jeep on Kamuning Estate at the start of the Emergency, in 1948.

Kamuning presented every facet of planting practice, from seed collection, germination in the estate nursery, planting out and husbandry, tapping and rubber manufacture, estate and machinery maintenance, labour management, contracting, accountancy and budgeting, civil engineering (road making and bridge building), jungle clearing and terracing. Even tin mining. There was much to learn and much on which I could employ the skills and expertise that I had acquired over the previous six years. The days passed very quickly.

Humphrey Butler made a point of going around part of main division every Tuesday and Thursday. We would meet at the office at 6 am, walk around the division until nine, back to the bungalow for breakfast, meet again at 10 for another couple of hours of walking and inspecting until about 12.30. I would then usually go back to the manager's bungalow for a beer and a chat with Humphrey and Sheila, before returning to my own. After tiffin and a lie off we would meet again at the office at about three for a couple of hours of paperwork. The junior assistants would be working on the check rolls and discussing their problems, and receiving advice and orders. As senior assistant it was also my job to see that forward contracts were ready on the due dates and despatched by lorry to Sungei Siput railway station. In essence the duties of a senior assistant on a large estate were similar to those of a regimental adjutant or the first officer on a ship. The captain's right hand man. In fact, Humphrey, with his nautical background, came to refer to me as his 'flag lieutenant'.

Humphrey Butler was a great character, a planter of the old school. A strict disciplinarian, he could relax completely off the estate. He was well into his mid-50s when we first met. After leaving Bedford School he had joined P&O as an apprentice and was proud of the fact that he had sailed around Cape Horn in a windjammer. Having attained the rank of fourth officer he had left the merchant navy to become a tea planter in Ceylon, but thinking that the newly developing rubber industry in Malaya offered better prospects, had joined the Dunlop Rubber Group in 1910. He became general manager in the early 1920s, then probably the most coveted appointment in the Malayan rubber industry. He could rightly claim to be one of its pioneers. He resigned on a matter of principle, but often said to me that on reflection he was sure that he had been over-hasty. He was quickly taken on by John Hay of Guthrie's and, after a few years on an estate in Johore, was appointed to Kamuning in 1928.

Humphrey and Sheila were a formidable team. They also formed a comedy duet and performed in many amateur shows. He served on the Federal Legislative Council, and was formally to be addressed as 'The Honourable Mister'. This certainly appealed to Sheila, who was a very dear friend but something of a snob, and never failed to remind one that Humphrey was first cousin to the Earl of Hereford, and that she had been educated at Cheltenham Ladies' College. Humphrey had been married twice before, but the third marriage, to Sheila, was long and happy. They had three boys, aged 37, 17 and 7 at the time of our first meeting, the youngest, Tony, by Sheila.

The great day arrived when I fetched Jean and John home from Penang. Jean had now completely recovered her health and was able to cope with both the new baby and with settling in to her new home. With our new car she was able to visit friends on neighbouring estates, and to go shopping in Ipoh, where nearly everything that could possibly be needed could be bought. There was an excellent branch of Singapore Cold Storage for food, including, for example, pheasant and partridge from China. Cookie went every morning to the market in Sungei Siput for fresh fruit and vegetables, eggs and chickens, and household stores. A far cry from Atjeh.

I forget who recommended them, but Jean had not been back for many days when we engaged Alagamah as ayah for John and her husband Soopan as cook, thus establishing a happy relationship that was to survive the war. Unlike most house servants, who were either Malay or Chinese, they were Indians, although Jean spoke to them in Malay. As with many young European children, because of his ayah's influence, John was to become fluent in Malay almost before he was in English, even occasionally having to translate for Jean. Soopan was destined not to survive the Railway, but, as will be related, we were reunited with Alagamah after the War, and she stayed with us until we left Kamuning in 1951 when she returned to India.

In 1937 we felled and cleared 68 acres of jungle reserve to form the Sungei Buloh division, on the other side of the main north-south road and railway, and planted different clonal rubber plants in small blocks replicated eight times for experimental and comparison purposes. The plants were supplied by the Guthrie Central Experimental Estate at Chimera, where a lot of the research for the rubber industry was undertaken.

In the early years of the century, when most of Kamuning was under either pepper, coffee or jungle, illegal tin prospectors excavated many pits in search of the mineral. Some of this prospecting resulted in pits many feet deep, and while some had been filled in over the years, there remained many, covered by undergrowth, that had not been. These presented an ever-present danger to the unwary. Some such pits were discovered during the 1937 jungle clearing on Sungei Buloh. One day Donald Gray, who had stayed the previous night with us following a Negri Sembilan vs Perak rugger match, Humphrey and I were walking along a terrace when we suddenly came across one of these mining pits. When we looked down to the bottom, about 20 feet below us, we saw the floor to be a heaving mass of snakes, mostly kraits, probably the most venomous snakes in Malaya. Needless to say the pit was back filled that very day.

Another incident was even more alarming. Ford had left and Paddy Jackson was the Sungei Koh assistant. One morning a breathless coolie rushed into my office with a message that the Tuan Sungei Koh wanted a long rope most urgently. I asked why and was told that someone had fallen down a hitherto unknown mining hole. I sent the rope but to my astonishment the coolie returned an hour later with another message; the rope was not long enough. I found this difficult to believe, but sent out another one of similar length, with instructions that the two ropes should be knotted together. My curiosity aroused I accompanied the coolie back to the scene, to find Paddy and a gathering of distressed-looking Chinese coolies and Indian conductors. The pit was only about six feet across, but the depth must have been well over a hundred feet, as the two rope lengths only just touched the bottom. Quite how it was dug and the soil removed is a mystery. There was complete silence from the unfortunate man below. I considered that it was unfair to ask anyone else to volunteer to descend the depths and I had no intention to do so, so after a couple days vigilance with no sound from the bottom, we presumed that the coolie was dead. In all probability his death had been instantaneous.

A Coroner's Inquest was required, but there was no body, so it was held at the scene of the accident – one's nose provided all the necessary evidence that the man was dead. Immediately after the inquest Chinese death rites were performed and the hole filled in. This took over a week. The whole matter received some adverse comment from the Coroner and was extensively reported in the local press so a determined effort was made to find and backfill other pits.

The first five years of our married life were full ones. Quiet evenings alone together were welcomed for their rarity. Entertaining for the mem was simple, requiring only the planning of the menu and the seating of the guests. We held weekly bridge fours in each other's bungalows, and played the new game Monopoly whenever possible. Whilst I played rugger I was in strict training, so mid-week drinking was usually restricted to ayer limos (lime and water). But, of course, the post-match parties on Saturday evenings, and the curry tiffins on the Sunday, more than made up for my mid-week abstinence.

My old friend from Johore, Forbes Wallace, had now been posted to Kuala Kangsar as OCPD, and he strengthened the state pack. Our centre was T. M. Hart, an Oxford double Blue (rugger and cricket) and Scottish International. Together with our wives we made a lively sextet. John's christening was performed by Nigel Williams, who was also the state scrum half. I had first met him at rugger practice at Taiping and, packing in the back row, was on the receiving end of the scrum half's shouts of 'let it out, you buggers, let it out'. On enquiring who the scrum half was I was rather surprised to be told that it was the local padre.

On one of our earlier visits to the Ipoh Club we were joined by my old acquaintance from Johore, that giant of a man Professor Van Steyn Gallenfels. He was digging for Neolithic remains on Phin Soon Estate, near Sungei Siput, with Pat Noone, who was the Government ethnologist. I shouted 'boy!', ordered a beer for the professor, and was only a little surprised to see that it came in a chamber pot. He drank about half in one noisy gulp, and the rest in two. Remembering the story about the one hundred Bols gins, I ordered another 'mug' and beat a hasty retreat.

As Phin Soon was close to Kamuning, we visited the dig, and met Pat Noone for the first time. Pat was deeply interested in the aboriginals of Malaya, mainly the Semai and the Temiar tribes, who lived in the Perak jungle. Even 10 years later, during the Emergency, they still only very rarely ventured out of the deepest ulu. I was sitting in Pat's bungalow in Taiping one early evening when to my surprise several Sakai (as the aboriginals were generally known throughout Malaya) filed on to the verandah, squatted on the floor and just stared at us without saying a word. Of course I stopped talking and waited for one of them to speak, but they did not. The silence was uncanny. Eventually Pat explained that I was a stranger, so they would not speak until I had left, which I did immediately.

Pat married Anjang, a Temiar girl, the daughter of one of the headmen, and we used to meet them on Pulau Pangkor, the beautiful island off the coast of Perak. She used to swim in the nude, although very discreetly. She certainly had the most beautiful figure I have ever seen. Pat evaded capture in the war and lived in the ulu for many months with the aboriginals, before being murdered by, it was rumoured, a member of Anjang's family.

At that time Kamuning had three open cast tin mines, leased to a Chinese kongsi (company). Each month the recovered tin was weighed – another of the senior assistant's jobs – so that the estate's share could be calculated. The mines were overseen by a Sikh, Sohan Singh, a tall, fine man who was totally fluent in English, Malay, Tamil, several Chinese dialects and, of course, his own Punjabi, and was employed by Kamuning to look after its interests. Sadly, soon after the end of hostilities in 1945 the local Chinese resistance killed him on the suspicion, I am sure groundless, that he had been a collaborator with the Japanese. He was shot on the railway bridge leading to the Sungei Buloh division, and for a long time it was rumoured that Sohan Singh's restless spirit was still abroad. Certainly Jean used on several occasions to have a feeling that she had company when she crossed the bridge on her early morning walks.

In addition, we employed Harry Hannay as our mining consultant. 'Uncle' Hannay was a tall handsome Scot who had gone out to Malaya soon after the Boer War, so that when we first met him in 1936 he must have been in his 60s. I know that when he saw us off at Penang on our way home to retirement in 1955 he was 83, still ramrod straight and agile, despite having been imprisoned by the Japanese in the Sime Road Gaol, in Singapore, for three and a half years. On his release he had gone straight back to re-open his mining consultancy in Ipoh. When we said our last farewells he had not been 'home' for 40 years. Malaya was his home.

Hannay was a great character. As a young man he had been what was then called an adventurer. He was one of only a very few men to hold the Polar Star. He had served in both the Boer Wars, and the Great War. Charles Martine was his nephew – hence the 'Uncle' – and it was generally considered within their family that he was the original for Richard Hannay of John Buchan's novels. There were certainly coincidences. Uncle Hannay was a mining engineer, a Scot, had spent time in South Africa (where he had met Buchan), and had undertaken intelligence work for the Government – all of which also applied to Buchan's fictional Hannay.

When we were living in Kedah in 1954, Uncle Hannay and another old friend of his from the pioneering days of the early 1900s, Pop Cunningham, who was about the same age, and had raised the Sarawak Rangers, stayed with us for a night. I was, of course, fascinated by their tales, and only wish that I had been able to record them. The following day, after Hannay had left to go north, Pop whispered to me, so that Jean would not hear, 'If you ask me, Boris, I don't think Uncle is in the least bit interested in his Perlis tin mines – I think he has girl problems.' All I could think of saying was: 'Well, Pop, I hope I can be accused of having girl problems when I am 83.'

Jimmy Egan was another character. An Irishman, he was inclined to get rather pugnacious in his cups. He was responsible for the elephant patrol along the Lintang to Jalong road. Once a month he would mount an elephant and patrol the 20-foot-wide path cut between the jungle and the cultivated land to observe whether there were any traces of wild elephant having crossed the cleared strip. In which case Jimmy had to report the fact to the Perak state game warden, who would then track them down and try to turn them back into the jungle. I used to accompany Jimmy occasionally on these patrols and bivouacked for the night in the jungle – again, little realising that I would be doing the same thing, but in even less comfort, only five years later, behind enemy lines.

In 1938 I was selected with two other volunteers to represent the Perak Battalion in the Malayan Command Skill at Arms competition. I was never much use as a rifleman but did become more than competent with the Vickers machine gun, and although only a private I was appointed the company instructor. The gun had a crew of three: the Number One to aim and fire, the Number Two to feed in the ammunition belt, the Number Three as stand by. Each in turn served in the different positions. In the competition we had to fire at least 75 rounds in 30 seconds, 25 rounds a man. This had to be done four times and the results of the 300 rounds fired assessed. The four targets were about five yards apart, at a thousand yards. The beaten zone at this range was about five yards. All went well and the Perak Volunteers were as good as the regular army, until it came to the final shoot.

We wore the standard British Army issue 'Bombay bloomers', the wide-legged khaki shorts that came down to the regulation inch above the knee. The stockings came up to an inch below the knee. The Number One sat on the ground with his legs bent up astride the gun, so that he could aim by the sights on top of the barrel. Halfway through my final shoot I felt a searing pain at the top of my inner thigh. Letting out a yell I released the trigger and grabbed at the red-hot spent cartridge that had just been ejected from the machine gun and disappeared down my trouser leg. We were, of course, disqualified, but, in view of the fact that Jean had come within a cat's whisker of having grounds for divorce, my teammates were sympathetic. However, the colonel was unamused and I was carpeted for having let down the battalion, and denied promotion to lance corporal, I thought unfairly.

Late in 1937 we started to make plans to fell and clear 1,200 acres of reserve jungle, and to terrace the hillsides, and construct the roads for the new Sungei Buloh division, which was to be planted up the following year. This was exciting work. Not many of my contemporaries would have had the good fortune to be involved in such a project. Few estates had jungle reserves and fewer still the necessary financial resources to be able to undertake such major expenditure, on which there would be no returns for at least seven years. Not only would there be the initial investment, but also the mounting annual expenditure of husbandry, weeding, road maintenance, etc to bring the trees to maturity.

In 1938 Jean became pregnant again and we looked forward to a sister for John. But it was not to be. Following a course of quinine injections for a bout of malaria, she was admitted to Batu Gajah Hospital where she miscarried. At that time there was no alternative to quinine for treating malaria.

It took Jean some time to get over this disappointment and to regain her health. She had now been out in Malaya for three years and, in addition to the malaria, which at any time can be extremely debilitating, and the miscarriage, she was finding the monotony of the constant heat and humidity getting her down. We arranged for her to go home for a spell of leave, so she and John sailed on a new East Asiatic Line ship, which took 31 days to get to Tilbury. We chose this Danish line as the fare was cheaper than on the usual P&O or Blue Funnel ships, and because each cabin had its own bathroom.

She was away for nearly six months and greatly benefited from the change of climate and for seeing her parents and family and friends. I was very glad to have her back in Malaya as it was obvious to all that we would soon be at war with Germany – in spite of all the 'to-ing and fro-ing' of Chamberlain to see Herr Hitler – and Malaya, or so we thought at the time, would be far safer.

During Jean's absence I led the usual grass widower's existence. I played cricket most weekends. I had also taken up golf fairly seriously, although I was never to reach the same level of excellence as my brother Bill. Local club cricket was of the same high standard to be found in most of the main towns in Malaya, with the usual sprinkling of Blues and Services caps. At Ipoh we also had the famous fast bowler Lal Singh, who had played for India in five test matches against England. I once had the privilege of opening the bowling for Perak with him.

Training for the Volunteers became much more serious in 1938. The parades became more frequent and could no longer be looked upon as a pleasant couple of hours prior to a session in the bar. Our annual camp at Port Dickson was now run by the regular army, which introduced a sense of realism. At least realism for a war in Europe. There was no question of jungle training. I was commissioned just before the annual camp, after which, as a brand new second lieutenant, my Volunteer duties increased to the extent that I was involved in training in one form or another on most Sundays: not even the prospect of war was permitted to interfere with an Englishman's games-playing on Saturdays. I was given command of a rifle platoon, the platoon sergeant of which was a stalwart Malay called Eusuff, who also came from Sungei Siput, so I often used to give him a lift into Kuala Kangsar or Ipoh on drill days. The close relationship that I built up with this fine man was to stand me in very good stead some

10 years later, at the start of the Emergency. I attended many tactical exercises without troops (TEWTs) run by regular army officers, most of whom had only recently come out from England, or Egypt, or India. The problems set by these officers were still very definitely orientated to war in Europe, the desert, or the North West Frontier. I do not remember having even one discussion about jungle warfare; modern armies evidently would not be able to stray very far from the main roads. Even then I thought this a bold assumption.

Guthrie's encouraged their planters to take annual local leave, and from 1937 we started our yearly trips to Fraser's Hill, a hill station 6,000 feet above sea level, where the days were cool and the nights could be positively cold. Guthrie's owned the Whittington Bungalow which could accommodate about 20 people, so one was always assured of meeting kindred spirits amongst the other paying guests. The staff was well-trained, and the log fires in the evenings made for a relaxing break. There was a good nine-hole golf course, a small club with a well-stocked library, and many varied and interesting walks. The flora and fauna, particularly the birdlife, were so different to that which one normally saw on lowland estates, that there were always lots of interesting things to see. After the war I was to become a director of Whittington, but by then we tended to go up to Cameron Highlands, as it was nearer – one could go there for the day – and Fraser's tended to become over-full with the younger KL-ites and the military.

We were spending one Sunday at Cameron Highlands with Pat Martine and, amongst others, an acquaintance by name of Crowther-Smith. Pat had borrowed Rajah Brooke of Sarawak's bungalow. One night after dinner, when the girls had gone to the bedroom to powder their noses, the men, as was customary, went out to water the cannas, followed by the resident dog who, as it was obviously the custom, also raised his leg – but on this occasion squirted all down Crowther-Smith's beautifully creased white drill trousers. Ever afterwards he was known as 'Trouser-Smith'. He was to die most gallantly during the battle for Singapore.

During 1939 I was admitted to Batu Gajah Hospital to have my appendix removed. By way of convalescence, and in view of the fact that I had now been back in Malaya for four years, having had but one spell of home leave in eight and a half years, and was beginning to feel rather run down (I had also had a couple of bouts of malaria), Humphrey persuaded the agents in KL to agree to my taking a fortnight's sick leave, on full pay and at Guthrie's expense, which included Jean and John. This was most pleasant and unexpected as, prewar, companies did not pay their employees when they were on leave, nor, as I have mentioned, the fares of their employee's wife and children.

We decided to take the Straits Steamship *Kuala* for the round trip from Penang to Moulmein, the Burmese port south of Rangoon, further north than Mergui which I had visited in 1934. I thought that Jean would find the trip enchanting and the sea breezes most welcome. The *Kuala* would be sunk by Japanese shellfire while it was evacuating European women, mostly nurses, at the fall of Singapore, with great loss of life. We were to lose several friends on that ill-fated voyage, many of whom were 'rescued' from the sea, taken on board the Japanese cruiser, raped and then, it was rumoured, murdered by simply tossing them over the side. I have often wondered whether the Japanese captain was ever called to account for these hideous crimes. I hate to think that he 'honourably' went down with his ship. And we are supposed to let bygones be bygones, even after 40 years?

The whole trip was most enjoyable and, as expected, Jean was entranced with the scenery. In some places the deepwater channels were so close to the islands that it was possible to throw bottles on to dry land on either side of the ship. The jungle came right down to the water's edge and we once saw a panther slinking away from our unwarranted intrusion. I also remember a mass of sea snakes swimming alongside the ship. These snakes are very poisonous; they look just like land snakes, but with a flat vertical tail like a fish.

We spent an interesting couple of nights at Moulmein, and amongst the sights saw Kipling's 'old Moulmein Pagoda' and 'the flyin-fishes play', but not, alas, 'the dawn comes up like thunder outer China 'crost the Bay' – that was poetic licence. We had become friendly with a fellow passenger who was governor of Moulmein prison, and he loaned us his car and syce. We saw the elephants at work in the Steel Brothers' timber yards, moving great baulks of teak around, some of the older, more experienced ones without even the supervision of a mahout.

Our return journey followed exactly the same route as the outward trip, and again we were to marvel at the helmsman's skill in negotiating the narrow passages between the islands. On New Year's Eve 1938 a Straits Steamship Company vessel, on its way from Penang to Singapore, had run aground on the rocks off Pangkor Island, off the coast of Perak, and was a total wreck. As we sat at the captain's table one evening I asked him, by way of small talk, which silly ass had celebrated Hogmanay so much that he had wrecked his ship – a very foolish question, because not only could there have been very exceptional circumstances for this shipwreck (there were), but it might have been the very person to whom I was talking (it was).

The pleasant two weeks did us both the power of good. On our return to Penang we tiffined with the Martines, who were in the process of packing up to move to Kuching, in Sarawak, and promotion for Charles as it was the senior managerial job in the Borneo Company. We rescued a Chinese carpet that they had discarded and took it home rolled up on the top of our car. Shortly after I got back to Kamuning after the War to find our bungalow had been totally looted, I was browsing around a shop in Sungei Siput when I spotted a rolled-up carpet standing in a corner. I unrolled it and immediately recognised our Chinese carpet. The shopkeeper swore that he had bought it quite legitimately in Ipoh, and it could not have been looted from my bungalow. But I would brook no argument, gave the man $20 and marched out with the carpet under my arm. It looked good in its old place on the sitting room floor, and I wrote to Jean with the good news of its recovery. When Jean returned to Kamuning in July 1946 the first thing she said when she entered the sitting room was 'That's not our carpet!'. Nevertheless, it served us well, and was only discarded when we moved from Suffolk to Canterbury in 1972. A good $20 worth – about £2.50.

Whilst all this was going on the news from Europe, in the letters from home, in the newspapers and on the wireless, became increasingly ominous, and it did not take a genius to realise that we would soon be at war with Germany again. Many of us contemplated returning to England to join up, but it was pointed out, quite rightly, that we could contribute far more to a war effort by staying on in Malaya and producing those vital commodities, rubber and tin. In any case, some of us, but by no means all, considered that we could well be required to defend this part of the Empire against the Japanese in the not too distant future. Nevertheless, we worried for our families in Britain, most of whom had been involved in the Great War, so we were aware of the horrors to be expected, and the sacrifices that the nation would be required to make. But it simply did not enter anyone's head but that we would beat the Hun again.

We were having supper with a few friends, including the Butlers, and the Northcote-Greens who had come down for the weekend, on 3 September when we heard news of the Declaration of War from the Prime Minister's own lips. In spite of expecting it, all present were stunned, and the party broke up in a sombre mood. On reflection, though, it cannot be too usual for a dinner party to be broken up by the declaration of a world war.

For the first few days after the declaration we lived in fear and trepidation as to what we would hear on the news. But when it became apparent that there were to be no immediate and devastating air raids on London we relaxed and life returned to normal.

Training of the Volunteers increased and staff sergeant instructors were seconded from various regular battalions to assist. Attendance at annual camp, usually at Port Dickson, had always been encouraged but was not compulsory. In 1940 it was made so, and for all able-bodied Europeans under the age of 35, whether they had previously served or not. Thus hundreds of men who had hitherto avoided military training were called to the colours. In order to improve the standard of fitness and training it was decided that the Volunteers would be embodied for a minimum of a month. We old hands took great delight in seeing the 'box wallahs' doubling around the parade grounds and padangs, cursing and sweating profusely, often under the command of their office and estate juniors. I had two senior Guthrie managers from the KL office in my platoon and, whilst I did not pick on them, they certainly were made to perform as well as everyone else. One of them, Peter Taylor, became a good friend and eventually managing director of Guthrie's, Malaya.

Towards the end of September Humphrey Butler informed me that the company wished him to retire at the end of the year. He was 59, a good four years over the normal retirement age, but nevertheless very fit and at the top of his profession. Naturally we were all concerned as to who would take over, and you can imagine my delight when I learned that it was to be Bob Chrystal.

Doctor David Reid Tweedie had arrived in Sungei Siput by now, together with his Pathan bearer Thulasi. Reid, as he was to be known throughout Malaya and beyond, had spent several years in the Indian Medical Service in the North West Frontier province. I shall never forget his arrival; dressed in a plum-coloured suit, he looked like a caricature of an East End Jew – short, tubby, large bald head, prominent nose and heavy blue jowl. For a short time, I must admit, I viewed him with suspicion, but very soon fell under his spell. Reid and Jean and I were to remain close friends for the next 30 years. As I write he still lives in the 'White House', perched on a hill, on the Kamuning Estate, and still in practice in Sungei Siput, in spite of having a large house in Surrey where his wife Ruth lives. John and Linda stayed with him during one of their visits. Not so long ago he appeared on *Whicker's World*, on BBC Television, with his faithful Thulasi still in attendance. Reid boasted that he had not removed his shoes or boots himself since the mid-1930s. That was what a bearer was for.

Bob Chrystal arrived to take over Kamuning early in December 1940. The actual handover of the estate did not take very long, but the numerous farewell parties, given by everyone from the estate workers and office staff, to the British Adviser, spun out the Butlers' departure for several weeks, during which Bob and Babs stayed with us in the senior assistant's bungalow. One party was particularly memorable. It was given by the Chinese community and held in a Chinese restaurant in Ipoh. The alcohol flowed freely. There were many speeches, in English, Tamil, Malay, Punjabi and several dialects of Chinese, all of which were translated by Sohan Singh into the other languages of those present, each speech followed by the cry 'yam seng', after which the full glass is emptied in one. At a late stage in the proceedings I went for a pee, stepping over a large block of ice in the middle of the lavatory floor. Whilst I was in full flow one of the boys came in with a tray of glasses, said, 'Tabek, Tuan,' and, to my horror, proceeded to chip off lumps of ice and drop them into the glasses before returning to the party to serve another round of drinks. I could only conclude that the whisky and brandy were sufficiently strong to disguise any unusual flavours, and hoped that the large quantity of alcohol we had consumed, which for the Chinese would have been the very best five-star cognac, had killed off any germs.

After dinner some of us went on to the local dance hall and stayed until the early hours. It seems that when we came to leave I sailed down the steps, sat myself in a rickshaw and demanded to be taken to Sungei Siput, all of 19 miles away. We set off and I soon fell asleep. Luckily the rickshaw driver was recalled to the dance hall where Jean and the Butlers were waiting with the car. My syce was the only one with any money so he had to settle up for the rickshaw. Apparently I fell into the monsoon drain when we got home, stumbled up the stairs, woke up John, undressed by splitting my jacket in two, threw myself onto my bed, but missed it by a good few feet and crashed on to the floor. I was not at all popular with the mem.

Bob and Babs, together with their daughter Helen, settled in very quickly before departing to spend Christmas at Cameron Highlands. The war seemed a long way away, although the wireless became a much more important feature in our lives than hitherto. I had booked to telephone home but was told that the lines were now reserved for official communications only.

Bob returned shortly after Christmas, leaving Babs and Helen at Cameron Highlands. About a week later he was taken desperately ill with a perforated duodenal ulcer. It seemed that he collapsed during the night and the boy, hearing the groans of agony, ran to McNicholl, the new junior assistant, whose bungalow was nearby, who called Reid Tweedie. They rushed Bob to Batu Gajah Hospital where they contacted Mr Chitty, one of the best surgeons ever to go to Malaya. He was waiting for them when they arrived, confirmed Reid's diagnosis, and immediately operated. Another hour and it would have been too late.

I knew nothing of these goings on until McNicholl told me at muster in the morning. I telephoned the hospital and the sister advised that Babs should be told to get there as soon as possible. I telephoned Babs, told her the news, and arranged to meet her at Tapah, where the road up to Cameron Highlands turns off the main north-south road. We found Bob in a critical condition and barely conscious. Happily, after two days on the danger list, Bob began his remarkable recovery and we could all relax. It is still difficult to believe that, within 15 months, Bob was to take to the jungle and to stay there, living with the Sakai, for over three and a half years.

When Bob came out of hospital the company rightly insisted that, after regaining his strength, he should go on accelerated leave, and he and Babs and Helen left for Australia in June 1940. Bob had advocated my appointment as acting manager during his absence and the directors agreed, much to the annoyance of a number of other Guthrie staff who considered that they had prior claim to this senior position. This was made very plain to me when I went to a meeting that several senior Guthrie planters had to attend in KL a few months later, when it was obvious that 'young Hembry' was not very popular. In fact I rather enjoyed it, as I knew that I was there solely because of my ability rather than seniority of service. It still rankled some 14 years later when Jean was asked to act as Sir John Hay's hostess at a gathering at Port Dickson. One planter's wife made it very clear that she still thought her husband, both older and senior in service, had been slighted all those years before.

As was the custom, Jean and I moved over to the manager's bungalow where, after redecorating the verandah to Bab's wishes, we settled down to enjoy the added space and, above all, the large swimming pool and tennis court. We entertained a lot and Jean enjoyed the large mature garden, ably assisted by the two Tamil kebuns, one of whom even knew the Latin names of some of the plants.

Early in 1941 it was my turn for the compulsory two-month Volunteer embodiment at Port Dickson. Guthrie's sent Ian Murray, a cheerful and very efficient Scot, to take my place on Kamuning for this period. We were destined to be in tandem for most of the rest of our careers. He acted for me on Kamuning again when I went on leave in 1947, he took over from me on Bukit Asahan Estate, in Malacca, in 1952 and again as general manager of Ulu Remis Estate, Johore, in 1953.

We had not been in the manager's bungalow very long when both Jean and I heard running footsteps along the whole length of the verandah, across our bedroom and into the nursery. I flashed the torch but saw no one. Then, only a few weeks later, when Mary Rawson, who was staying with us whilst her husband John, the manager of Changkat Salak Estate nearby, was away for Volunteer embodiment, asked us one morning what I was doing running along the verandah in the middle of the night. Jean explained that it was not me but that we too had often heard the footsteps. We had heard servants' talk that the bungalow had a ghost but had taken no notice, especially as neither the Butlers nor the Chrystals had remarked about it. It was a wooden bungalow and the most likely explanation was that the timbers were contracting in the cool of the night after the heat of the day.

But footsteps are footsteps. And some 22 years later, when the Butlers stayed with us in Suffolk for a weekend, and naturally there was much reminiscing, Jean raised the matter of the haunting and asked whether they had ever heard the footsteps. They looked at each other and Sheila said to Humphrey: 'I think it's safe enough now to tell them the story, don't you?'

Back in 1929, when their son Tony was a small baby, his amah (nanny) was the cook's wife. They were an excellent couple in every respect. However, there came a day when Sheila became aware that all was not well in the servants' quarters. She had seen a strange Chinese woman hanging about and had asked who she was. It seems that she was the cook's number one wife who had suddenly turned up from China, and was most unwelcome. Matters soon deteriorated to the extent that there was continual and very loud quarrelling, often well into the night, until eventually the Butlers insisted that one of the women, preferably the latest arrival, must go. Very soon after this ultimatum the newcomer, obviously demented, seized baby Tony from his pram in the garden and ran with him up the bungalow steps, along the whole length of the verandah, through the main bedroom and into the nursery where she threatened the baby with a knife. She was overpowered and taken to Tanjung Rambutan mental hospital where she remained for some months. But when she was eventually released she returned to the estate, and very soon the trouble reoccurred.

The Butlers had arranged to take some local leave and before leaving had instructed the cook to get rid of his first wife before they returned. If not, all three would be dismissed.

When Humphrey and Sheila returned a fortnight later they were pleased to find that the woman had left and was presumably on her way back to China. Peace reigned and quietness returned to the servants' quarters. However, after a little while, Sheila noticed that Amah was frequently in tears and appeared very distrait. Sheila said nothing because there could be several explanations and anyway Tony was being looked after in the old excellent way. But eventually they could stand it no longer and Humphrey and Sheila summoned the couple and said that unless they told them exactly what the problem was they would have to go. After denials that anything was wrong they finally broke down and told the following story.

One night, when the Butlers were on leave, Cookie and Amah went down to the village, leaving number one wife in their quarters. When they returned, sometime after midnight, they found that the other woman had hanged herself from a beam in the servery, just behind the dining room. (Jean used to hang her jelly bags from the same beam.) They were at their wits' end. Everyone knew of the constant quarrelling, so it was most unlikely that the police would believe their story and they would be arrested for murder. So they decided to bury the body in the garden. They carefully removed the flowers from the bed, dug a deep hole in which the body was laid, backfilled, and with equal care replaced all the flowers.

The next day they told everyone that number one wife had left the previous evening to return to China, in compliance with the tuan besar's orders. The story was, of course, believed without question. But as the weeks went by they became increasingly worried about what would happen if ever the body were discovered. Who would possibly believe their story now? If it were true, why had they not reported it at the time?

The Butlers, too, were worried stiff. If the body was eventually discovered, could they be charged as accessories after the fact? If they informed the police, would a perfectly innocent couple be arrested for murder? They thought about it long and hard, and finally decided to say and do nothing, and the matter remained a secret until revealed to Jean and me in the quiet of a Suffolk garden.

I believe that the cook and amah were innocent. Be that as it may ... the flowerbed under the verandah, outside the bedroom, grew the finest cannas I have ever seen.

The Volunteers training was now taken very seriously. Several of the instructors had seen action in France the previous year and had escaped from Dunkirk. But the training continued to be concerned very much to open warfare, when most of us could see that it bore very little relevance to a campaign in the jungles of Malaya. I remember suggesting at the time that it would be more sensible to train us, at least the planters and miners, for intelligence and liaison work, for attachment to the regular army, where our knowledge of the local languages and the terrain would be of most use. But it was pointed out that it was doubted whether we would be required to fight in Malaya, and that the training would be of great benefit for the reconquest of Europe. The small arms training was, of course, not wasted.

It was sometime in 1940 that I had two adventures with snakes. Snakes were common on Kamuning, as they were throughout Malaya, and one met them daily around the estate. On the whole they were timorous creatures and did their best to get away, as will almost all wild animals.

It was about noon, I was walking along a path in the rubber with my mongrel dog Bill, when some 20 yards ahead he started barking furiously. I recognised the bark; it signified either a snake or a scorpion. He, like other dogs I have owned, seemed to have a sixth sense for danger. I walked forward on my guard when a few yards away I saw a large snake curled up on the path, rearing to a height of about two feet. It looked like a cobra to me – which was dangerous enough – so I picked up a length of fallen branch and shied at it. It hit the snake which immediately reared itself up to about five feet, and, spitting furiously, rapidly advanced towards us. I turned and fled, followed by Bill. The snake was gaining on us, when we came to a fork in the path. I took the right, Bill the left. Thank God the snake followed Bill. I ran on for another 50 yards or so and was joined by an equally frightened dog. The snake was a hamadryad or king cobra, one of the few that would attack without provocation and whose bite is positively deadly.

The second episode occurred one tiffin time. We were just sitting down when Ayah rushed in crying, 'Tuan, Tuan, there is a big snake at the back. As big as my arm.' As there was not a slimmer person alive than our ayah Alagamah, a snake the thickness of her arm could easily be despatched. So, grabbing a golf club and, still in my stockinged feet, I ran down the back stairs and caught a glimpse of the snake's tail disappearing into the long grass beside the hen run. I managed to hit it with my 7-iron. The next second, and given the space, I could have leapt backwards a full 20 yards. The thin little snake had turned and reared itself every bit of six feet high, spitting. Its body was thicker than my thigh let alone Ayah's arm. It was quite the largest hamadryad that I have ever seen. There were gasps of fright from the two kebuns who had gathered around to watch the fun. From the safety of the verandah, to where we had all retreated in double quick time, we saw the snake lower itself and slide under the chicken wire of the hen run.

Ayah said that she had first noticed the snake curled up under a lime tree in the garden near which John had been playing earlier in the morning. There was no doubt, therefore, that it had to be despatched as soon as possible. But how? I was not a shot in those days and did not possess a gun. My service revolver would be useless. But first of all I had to get into the hen run, through the loose piece of wire which was all of two feet high, on my hands and knees. I realised that this did not afford me the easiest means of escape, nevertheless, I crawled into the run, having armed myself and the kebuns with long poles, and surveyed the scene. No snake to be seen. So I crept up to the old tree stump in the middle of the run and saw a hole amongst the roots, peered down and was glared at by two of the most evil-looking eyes imaginable. The snake was curled up, about two feet down. I pondered the problem of how to kill it when I remembered my mother telling me that, when she was very young and living in Johannesburg, the family's Zulu garden boy had enticed a mamba out by puffing smoke from his pipe down the hole. I certainly had no intention of blowing cigarette smoke down this particular hole, so I called for an old piece of sacking which I wrapped around the end of a pole, doused it in kerosene, set light to it and rammed it down the hole and held it there. There was a furious response from the snake, in addition to much hissing and spitting, and just when I thought that it was gaining the upper hand, the struggles subsided and when they had stopped I withdrew the pole and after a little while the badly burned and stupefied snake slithered out and was quickly despatched. It was over 13 feet long. I felt no remorse, as I had done with the python in Sumatra, because I thought about John playing around the tree stump, within only a yard or so of the brute.

The Chrystals duly returned and it was my turn to make arrangements for our long leave, only the second I was to have in nearly 11 years. As the company had forbidden its European staff to return to Britain because of the war in Europe, we decided to go to Australia. I would go on ahead and look for a flat at Cottesloe, on the coast near Perth, whilst Jean and John would spend a month or so with Charles and Pat Martine in Kuching, Sarawak, before joining me. We took the night mail to Singapore and I put Jean and John aboard the *Vyner Brooke*, spent the night with John and Gwen Pickering, and early the next morning flew off in a DC3 for Darwin. It was the first time I had flown. Fifty years ago one seldom flew above 4,000 feet so were able to appreciate in the cool the indescribable beauty of the East Indies islands, the Flores Sea, the Celebes, and the wonderful colours of the coral reefs. We landed around midday for lunch, and for the night at Bali for dinner, a swim and a good night's sleep in a comfortable hotel. Except for the Himalayas I have never seen beauty anywhere in the world to exceed that of the East Indies Archipelago. I have only ever enjoyed one other flight so much as this one – the return journey from Darwin to Singapore, some four months later, in an Empire flying boat. I always regretted not having the chance to fly from England to Singapore by flying boat.

The next evening we reached Darwin. The contrast to the beauty of the Malaya and the Dutch East Indies was total. The airport hotel was modern and clean, but the town was deplorable. Darwin contained many poor whites whose houses were made from flattened kerosene tins and packing cases.

After another comfortable night I had an early start in a McRobertson Miller Airways Lockheed Hudson, piloted by two Australians with the broadest Aussie accents one could imagine. Flying over Carnarvon I overheard 'Rices 'ere terdye.' 'What's that yer sye?' 'Rices 'ere terdye.' After a little while I gathered that there was a race meeting at Carnarvon that day.

There was a story going around Calcutta in the war about an English ward sister who had stopped by the bed of a very sick Aussie pilot and said, 'Sergeant, you know you did not come in here to die.' 'No,' was the reply. 'I came in yesterdye.'

Two stopovers I remember vividly. The first was on a strip on a sheep station, quite literally 500 miles from anywhere. Just the station homestead, the dormitory shed for the aboriginal drovers, a half million acres of land, and half a million sheep. I have never seen so many flies. The butter was black with them. The twice-weekly arrival of the mail plane and its crew and passengers were the only contacts the sheep farmers had with the outside world.

We then flew on to Port Hedland, where the inhabitants were celebrating the hundredth consecutive day of temperatures above 125 degrees Fahrenheit. Port Hedland was famous in the gold rush days of the last century. I recall seeing Japanese 'pearl fisher' boats in the harbour when we departed the next morning. These were to be seen in every port between Singapore and Perth. The Japanese were busy charting every harbour in the region.

During the flight I teamed up with fellow passengers Jock and Isobel Campbell who were also going on leave from Malaya. Our families were to see a lot of each other during our three months' stay at Cottesloe. In March 1942 Jock and another 20-odd Malayans made an extraordinary escape from Padang, in Sumatra, to Ceylon in a prahu. He was later sent to Australia by SOE to organise and command the equivalent there of Force 136. At one time he shared ownership of a racehorse with Bob Chrystal and all us friends were pleased when the poor animal had to be put down. In loyalty to Bob and Jock we always backed their horse, but it never finished in the first three. Jock was eventually to become managing director of SOCFIN, but, alas, did not live long in retirement to enjoy his well-earned wealth.

We had three most enjoyable months in Cottesloe doing all the usual things of a seaside family holiday, but all the time conscious of the events taking place in Europe. Although the Battle of Britain had been won and the danger of invasion had been lifted for the immediate future, the news from the Middle East was depressing. We seemed to be on the retreat everywhere. Luckily we were ignorant that far worse was to come. Jock and I called in at the Royal Australian Air Force recruiting office to offer our services, but were turned down as soon as we said we came from Malaya. They did not recruit from the colonies. Our feeble joke concerning colonies and convicts was not well received.

We took a trip down to Albany, the southernmost tip of Western Australia, with nothing between us and the South Pole, and stood on the cliffs, several hundred high, and saw and heard the famous blowholes. On the way home in the dark, we were travelling along the main road, with forest on both sides, when suddenly a massive body descended from the sky to land on top of the bonnet. A kangaroo had decided to leap the road and had obviously misjudged the distance. He immediately leapt off and disappeared into the bush on the other side of the road, leaving a large dent.

One of the outstanding memories of our stay at Cottesloe must be the morning we looked out of the window and saw about a dozen of the largest liners afloat steaming into Fremantle harbour, amongst them was the *Queen Mary*, the *Queen Elizabeth*, the *Mauritania* and the *Ile de France*. They had been sent to Australia to be converted into troop ships, out of harm's way.

Our stay in Cottesloe came to an end and we flew to Melbourne, stopping en route at Adelaide after having flown over the Nullarbor Plain, once again miles and miles of nothingness, except the railway line which went, quite literally, dead straight for hundreds of miles. After a night at the Menzies Hotel in Melbourne we took the flight to Hobart.

Tasmania was a total delight. Years behind the rest of Australia and still very British, with many county, town and lake names the same as in England. We stayed the first week at the Wrest Point Hotel, one of the most luxurious hotels in one of the most beautiful sites I have ever seen. Unfortunately the cost was way beyond my means so, after a week, we moved into a comfortable pub in Browns River, about 20 miles outside Hobart.

It was winter in Tasmania and there was usually frost on the ground when I played golf in the mornings. By lunch the frost had thawed and we would play with John on the beach in the warmth of a good English summer day. We met and made friends with two Malayan couples and a couple from Burma, the Fairleighs. I met them again in Calcutta in 1943 after they had made the terrible trek out of Burma during which many hundreds died of starvation and disease. They had carried their little girl on their backs.

Whilst we were at Browns River I received from home a cutting from *The Times*, setting out the whole of Sir John Hay's chairman's report on Kamuning Estate for the year 1940/41. I was particularly pleased to read: 'Your manager, Mr Robert Chrystal, was unfortunately taken ill some months ago and was compelled to go to Australia for treatment. During his absence Mr Boris Hembry, the Senior Assistant, took over the management of the Estate, and I would like to say a special word of appreciation on the manner in which he has acquitted himself in this very important charge.' More important, the Board voted me a special bonus of £150. The report went on to say 'As to the condition of your estate, it is only necessary once more for me to assure you that it is upkept in first-class condition and that the yields we continue to obtain from them are on a generous scale.' As I had been both senior assistant and acting manager throughout the year under review I found it most gratifying that my efforts had been publicly acknowledged. My father pointed out that it was most unusual for individual staff names to be mentioned by chairmen in annual reports.

We then took a train to Sydney. The first part of the journey to Albury, on the border of Victoria and New South Wales, was aboard the luxury *Spirit of Progress*, but because the gauges of the rail tracks were different in the two states, we had to change trains and continue on the second stage of the journey in far less comfort. My brother Gordon, by now living in Sydney, had booked us into a hotel in the King's Cross district. To our dismay we discovered that it was a temperance hotel. However, it was very comfortable, the food was excellent, and we could drink in our bedroom.

Gordon had come out to Australia in 1937, and I had succeeded in tracking him down through Alfa Laval's Sydney office. He was in great form, and was living in a hostel. He was something of a Lothario and boasted that of the 15 girls at the hostel he had bedded 14. (The 15th, Mary, he had first to marry.) Gordon was shortly to join up and was to become the sergeant-at-arms on the *Queen Mary*, very definitely a case of poacher turned gamekeeper. We spent several enjoyable days in a hired launch exploring Sydney Harbour and all its beautiful inlets. We went aboard the *Queen Elizabeth*, at that time the biggest ship in the world, which had come round from Fremantle for its refit. The famous Bondi Beach we found disappointing, much preferring Manly.

The evening before our departure for Singapore, Gordon and Mary joined us for dinner, followed by a small party in our hotel room. We had smuggled bottles of beer into the hotel in suitcases, and when these ran out Gordon went out with the case for replenishments. Apart from the beer fumes, we all smoked, so that in no time at all the bedroom smelt like a public bar, despite the open window. Sometime after midnight Gordon and Mary decided it was time to go home. We staggered along the corridor. I was following Gordon and I knew instinctively what was going to happen. Sure enough, he lurched on to a bedroom door, which immediately flew open, and we were greeted with female screams and dire threats that the police would be called.

Having seen our guests off the premises I returned to our

bedroom where there were still a dozen or so empty bottles in evidence. It was far too late to do anything about these so I stuffed them into the wardrobe in the hope that we would be off the premises by the time the chambermaid got around to the room, and went to sleep. The chambermaid duly appeared with our tea in the morning, sniffed, slapped the tray down, said that she would report us to the manager, sniffed again and departed. I was not unduly worried, and when paying the bill I explained that I had found a long lost brother and that we had enjoyed a mild celebration. All the manager said was 'Good on yer, mate. Wish you'd asked me.'

I was not to meet Gordon for another 21 years.

We flew from Sydney in a flying boat, the *Canopus*, quite the most pleasant way of travelling by air. We sat in wicker armchairs, had plenty of room to stroll around, to look out of the windows or to go down to the bar on the lower deck. We flew at about 150 miles an hour at a height of only five or six thousand feet, so there was always much to see. We put down at Brisbane, Townsville and Cairns, having flown low over the Great Barrier Reef and seen quite the largest shark I have ever seen, swimming lazily among the coral reefs. Even from a 1,000 feet it seemed huge.

The next day we left soon after dawn, landed at Dili, on the Portuguese island of Timor, where we saw the usual Japanese 'fishing' boat, and then on over the breathtakingly beautiful islands south of Java, stopping the night at Surabaya. The following day we flew on over Java and, having some time to spare, the pilot took us over the Krakatoa volcano and the Sunda Strait which separates Java from Sumatra. Luckily I was blissfully unaware that I would be sailing through the Strait, in desperate circumstances, only a few months later.

Having reached Singapore in time to catch the mail train north, we stayed the night at the Station Hotel in KL. I called in at the Guthrie's office to catch up on all the news, before taking the train to Sungei Siput where we were met by Bob and Babs Chrystal and driven back to our bungalow and home.

So ended a most memorable leave. It had cost less than £250.

We soon settled back into life's usual routine, except for mounting anxiety about Japanese intentions. The news from the other side of the world was brightened somewhat by the reports of our victories in North Africa, and the realisation that Britain had apparently survived the worst of the Blitz. Changes had been made to the high command in Singapore, Air Chief Marshal Robert Brooke-Popham taking over as commander-in-chief Far East, with a command extending over Singapore, Malaya, Borneo and Hong Kong. Duff Cooper had arrived as cabinet minister in residence. The 'impregnable fortress' of Singapore was being reinforced by troops almost on a daily basis, and the Royal Navy, so we understood, had a formidable presence in the area. So the Government in England evidently took the defence of Malaya very seriously.

Not long ago I re-read the following from Winston Churchill's *The Second World War* – 'The defence of Singapore must be based on a strong local garrison and the general potentialities of sea power. The idea of trying to defend the Malay Peninsula, a large country four hundred by two hundred miles at its widest, cannot be entertained.'

Ignorance was bliss, so far as we were concerned.

We enjoyed peace for about three months.

On 1 December, having been around the estate as normal, I returned to the bungalow for breakfast and Jean told me that the Perak Volunteers adjutant had telephoned and that I must ring him back as soon as I got in. I told Jean that it could wait until after breakfast. In due course, having walked over to the office, I returned the call to the adjutant and received a somewhat peremptory instruction to mobilise at Taiping Racecourse forthwith. I argued that this was impossible at such short notice as I had an important job to do. The adjutant left me in no doubt that it was an order. I discussed the matter with Bob, who also took a pretty dim view of it, but we concluded that it was most probably only a mobilisation exercise so I had better go, but only after I had sorted out a few things with the other assistants and the office kranis. I then went back to the bungalow for tiffin and a lie off.

Jean drove me over to Taiping where I learned that the battalion had been formally embodied. This was somewhat worrying, but I kissed Jean and John goodbye and said that I would require collecting again in a couple of days.

I did not realise that we were not to meet again, and then only briefly, until April 1944, over two years later, and that I had seen the last of very nearly all our possessions.

Retreat

December 1941

I reported to B Company headquarters, where most people were still of the opinion that the embodiment was all only a 'dummy run', and that we would soon be home again. Some of the Europeans continued with their businesses from the Taiping Club, much to the annoyance of the colonel and adjutant. The company arrived in dribs and drabs and by noon on 2 December we were nearly at full strength. I was having tiffin in the Taiping Rest House, which we used as the officers' mess, when I was ordered to draw all my platoon stores and to proceed at once to Nibong Tebal to take over the guard on the bridges. Nibong Tebal, known locally as 'No Balls to Bang', is a small town on the Krian River, important because the main north-south road and railway line crossed the river at that point, only a few yards apart. We took over from a platoon of Gurkhas.

On being commissioned I had taken charge of a rifle platoon in B Company, under the command of a Captain Percival, a planter from the Taiping district, a Great War veteran, and a fine man. In addition to our old rifles, the platoon was also armed with four Lewis guns of 1918 vintage, for use against low-flying aircraft.

We spent five uneventful days guarding the bridge before being relieved by a platoon from E Company commanded by an old friend, H. J. Cockman. In civil life in the MCS in Ipoh, H.J. had won an MC in 1917, and was to be killed, as was Percival, in the final days of fighting for Singapore.

We got back to Taiping early on Sunday the 7th, and after a meal and only a couple of hours rest were ordered to move to Sitiawan, together with a mixed company of riflemen and Vickers machine gunners, with orders to guard the airfield there. At 0230 hours on 8 December we stood to and were told that the Japanese had landed on the coast near Kota Bahru, a small port on the North East coast, up near the Siam border, and that they had bombed Singapore. It was with a sense of relief that we also learned, shortly afterwards, that they had bombed Pearl Harbor as well, thus bringing the Americans into the war. So this was it. The balloon had well and truly gone up.

My first thought was to contact Jean. I managed to telephone her from the Sitiawan Rest House and told her to get to Singapore and out of the country as quickly as possible. If Jean and John were safely out of the country a great load would be lifted from my mind. Jean said that she would leave immediately, although doubted whether she would have the courage to shoot Gay, our lovely labrador, and would have to get Bob to do it. In the event, only some few minutes after having spoken to me, Ayah came to her with the news that Gay had been run over and killed by an army lorry at the entrance to our compound.

Jean's journey by car to Singapore, by ship to Java, another evacuation to Australia, and then across the Pacific and Atlantic oceans to England, is a saga in itself.

Shortly after hearing of the formal Declaration of War, Terry Dale, the detachment commander, addressed us saying, 'We shall defend this airfield to the last man and the last round. If we cannot defend it alive, we shall defend it dead.' Far from finding this inspiring I felt it most depressing. I could see no earthly reason why I should be expected to lay down my life for an outsize football pitch which was quite incapable of taking anything larger than a Tiger Moth, and which was obviously of no strategic importance whatsoever.

It was at Sitiawan that we heard of the sinking of the *Prince of Wales* and the *Repulse* by Japanese aircraft on 9 December, having been sent out with no air cover to destroy the invasion forces. Unfortunately, they were within range of the enemy air forces based in Indo-China, so stood no chance, and went to the bottom with much loss of life. The arrival of these two fine ships in Singapore, only a matter of days before, had convinced us all the Royal Navy meant business and that we would at least be protected from a sea-borne invasion. Looking back, our confidence was based on our long-held belief that Britannia ruled the waves and that the Royal Navy was invincible. The sinkings cast us all into the depths of despair, and we realised, for the first time, that the Japs would be a formidable opponent and that we would have the gravest difficulty in holding on to Malaya.

One afternoon we had a report from the local police that enemy parachutists had been spotted a few miles away and that they had sent an armed detachment to investigate. I was ordered to stand by with my platoon to act as reinforcement if necessary, but was stood down half an hour later when the police telephoned to say that the parachutes were Chinese womens' voluminous trousers hanging on a washing line.

On 12 December the battalion received orders to move to Ipoh to take up a defensive position around the aerodrome. I was in the leading lorry when, half way over the Blanja pontoon bridge across the Perak River, about 20 Jap planes swooped down on us. I felt a sitting duck and feared the worst, but the planes flew on, obviously with more important targets to attend to. We arrived in Ipoh during an air raid. It was most disheartening to see the enemy planes doing exactly as they pleased, with only spasmodic ack-ack fire in retaliation. There was no sign of our air force. We were not to know then, of course, that of the very few aircraft that we possessed most had been destroyed on the ground during the first few air raids on the airfields in Singapore and KL. We deployed around Ipoh airfield and dug in.

The news from the front was depressing in the extreme. The enemy had gained everywhere. On 12 December the Japanese attacked across the Siam border into Kedah. They used the tactics that they were to use in all their campaigns in South East Asia. They attacked our positions frontally in some strength, usually with armoured vehicles, whilst sending an equally large force in a flanking movement, often through the jungle where we had been told it was impossible for armies to operate, and attacked us in the rear, cutting off our line of retreat.

News came through that all European women and children and other non-combatants had been evacuated from Penang and Kedah, and were being so from Perak and the Northern states in the east of the country. But the Government's declared scorched-earth policy was only feebly carried out. Many Europeans failed to destroy the stores, equipment and factories in their charge because they were convinced that it would only be a matter of days, or weeks at the most, before British and Allied troops would recapture all the ground lost.

Ipoh airfield was comprehensively bombed on 20 December. Ipoh had been evacuated and the Japs were reported to be about 40 miles north, in the region of Kuala Kangsar, and not far from Kamuning. I had been allotted a defensive position around a Bofors gun which was manned by regular army gunners. We were digging trenches and gun pits for our Lewis guns when we heard the sound of approaching aircraft. By that stage we realised that they could only be the enemy. I spotted them quite high, I suppose at about 15,000 feet and well out of range. I was counting them and had reached 38 when I saw the bombs begin to fall. I shoved my platoon sergeant into a half-completed trench and fell in on top of him just as the first stick landed. I felt so helpless and exposed and thought that the end was nigh. But the noise of the explosions receded and when the raid was over I cleared the dust and gravel from my eyes and was horrified to find a crater about 20 yards from my trench and that the Bofors gun position had taken a direct hit and gun and gun crew had completely disappeared. We were bombed again a couple of hours later, by which time we had finished digging our trenches, and suffered no more casualties.

The following day we were very pleased with ourselves for having shot down with one of our platoon Lewis guns a strange-looking aeroplane which had flown low over the airfield. The pilot, who managed to crash-land nearby, was unhurt but not best pleased. He was Dutch, and had gallantly flown up on his own to provide us with air cover. My platoon had managed to shoot down the one friendly aircraft we were ever to see over Ipoh.

About two days before Christmas, with the Japs reported at Tanjung Rambutan, only a few miles from Ipoh, we were ordered to demolish nearby kampongs in order to clear fields of fire. Obviously we were to make a stand. At least Ipoh airfield, far larger than Sitiawan, might just be worth fighting for. But the battalion was suddenly ordered to withdraw to Kampar, some 15 miles further south. We were bombed continuously on the way down but suffered no casualties. When we arrived there we were immediately put to work again clearing fields of fire, and wiring. As we were near both the railway and the main road we were continually machine gunned and bombed. It was all very wearing.

We spent Christmas Day preparing our defensive positions. Stand to was at 0400 hours and, except for the interruptions because of the air raids, we worked solidly throughout the day until darkness, when the quartermaster produced a couple of turkeys and a quantity of whisky, no doubt looted, for the officers' mess. We finished up with a singsong.

The regular army fell back to the positions that we had prepared, and we withdrew to Bidor, some 20 miles further south, again being bombed and machine gunned every hour or so. For days we could hear the sound of battle at Kampar. Then, inevitably, the regular army's positions were outflanked and so had to withdraw, having to fight their way through an enemy road block behind them as usual, whilst attacked continually from the air. By this time, too, the Japanese had taken Penang and, having captured many small ships and, of course, the car ferries, ferried their troops down the coast to land behind us. These tactics caused much despondency and led invariably to precipitate withdrawal as soon as it was rumoured that the enemy had landed behind our lines. It was not until the savage battles in Arakan and the Imphal Plain later on that General Bill Slim persuaded the Army that when the enemy penetrated behind our defensive positions it was they who were cut off from their supplies and lines of communication.

It was disheartening to see the skies black with smoke from burning rubber stocks. We learned later that the Jap advance had been so rapid that they had overrun many estates before the scorched-earth policy could be put into effect. And it was very sad to see the European bungalows looted and wrecked, very often, obviously, by British troops, with torn photographs of children and family groups, some most likely never to be together again, scattered on the floor. The madness of looting in war-torn countries is something to which I can never become reconciled. No forces are immune to the chance to plunder, and the British Army is no exception – as I was to see again in Singapore soon after the Jap surrender. Only there it was even less excusable, as the looters were British generals and their senior staff officers.

It was at Bidor that we finally lost the last of our Malay troops. Except one. There had been a steady wastage every day as we moved southwards. The majority of other ranks were Malays whose families lived in the kampongs around Ipoh and Kuala Kangsar and it was totally natural that their first thoughts should be for the welfare and safety of their wives and children, and for their smallholdings. There was some criticism at first from several Europeans, but not from me. I was sure that, in similar circumstances, I would have done the same. My stalwart platoon sergeant Eussuf stayed on until we reached Port Dickson on New Year's Day 1942. After arranging for him to draw his full entitlement of pay I formally discharged him and told him to return to his kampong. I have always regretted that I did not press for him to receive an award for his loyalty and soldierly qualities. An outstanding man, who never once doubted that the British would return. I was to rely on him again in equally trying circumstances six years later.

The battalion had commandeered civilian lorries, and most were in very poor condition. That allocated to my platoon was the ropiest of all. It had no brakes and was all over the road, in spite of my efforts to keep it on an even course. I drove this lorry from Ipoh to Kampar, then to Bidor, and finally the 200 miles to Port Dickson, this last leg in one day. I insisted on leading the convoy so that I did not endanger the lorry in front and its stores in case the convoy had to halt suddenly. I was a nervous wreck when eventually we arrived at PD, having had to steer into the roadside bank in order to stop whenever we were strafed or bombed. We were not the only troops on the move, which only added to the difficulty. Luckily most, but not all, were going in the same direction as us. We still could not understand why there was not a single RAF aircraft to be seen.

It was a great relief to arrive at Port Dickson. Here we were able to bathe in the sea, to get our filthy uniforms dobhied, and to relax after more than three weeks of constant strain, hard work and occasional danger. The battalion had been reduced in size to little more than about company strength, so there was much re-organising to do. Unaccountably we were not bombed, even though PD was the headquarters and training depot of the Malay Regiment as well as, now, the various state Volunteer battalions. I suppose the Japs considered that they could cause more mayhem by concentrating on KL, Singapore and the retreating regular army on the main road.

It was on 2 January that a notice appeared calling for volunteers for the following special duties:

1. 'Tiger' patrols behind enemy lines.
2. Front-line transport drivers.
3. Vickers machine gunners, to be attached to the regular army.

After some deliberation I opted for the first job. I was too much of a loner to be a good infantry officer, and the thought of a small independent party roaming behind the enemy lines seemed more in my line than driving a lorry.

After volunteering I heard nothing for a few days, during which we were busy preparing beach defences. I saw quite a lot of Paddy Jackson as he was on the same detail. He did his best to dissuade me from pursuing the matter of the 'tiger' patrols, pointing out that I was a married man with a child and that I was unnecessarily putting myself at risk. I must say, his arguments nearly persuaded me to withdraw. In the event it was Paddy who did not survive; he died on the Burma Railway. He and several others had escaped to Sumatra where they had found a junk and managed to sail it to within a hundred miles of Ceylon before being picked up by a Jap destroyer and taken back to Singapore to join the other POWs. Then he was sent up to work on the Railway.

Of all our friends who died in the war years I think Jean and I miss Paddy as much as it is possible to miss anyone. He did not marry, so left no wife and family to mourn him. But there is a middle-aged woman, who, unless her mother discloses the secret to her, will never know that her true father died in Siam in 1944.

On about 4 January I was ordered to report to the Orderly Room where I found the colonel talking to Ronald Graham, a great friend who was a planter on a neighbouring estate in Sungei Siput. I had heard through the grapevine that Ronald, together with Frank Vanrenen, had been on a very successful tiger patrol behind enemy lines and had ambushed and killed a Japanese brigadier and two lorry loads of soldiers. As soon as I saw Ronald I knew something was in the wind and my heart sank when I remembered Paddy's exhortation.

It appeared that I had been selected to make up a party comprising three ex-Volunteers, three regulars and a wireless operator, to infiltrate behind Japanese lines, in order to interfere with their communications, and to gather intelligence. It was estimated that we would remain behind the lines for about three months, when it was expected that the Allies would advance north and recapture all the territory that had been lost. The CO made it clear that it was a voluntary assignment and that it was not too late to back out. I must admit that I did hesitate for a moment, but the idea of joining up with Frank and Ronald, whose wives were also close friends of Jean, quickly dispelled my doubts. Within five minutes I had packed what few belongings I had, bade farewell to Paddy and my company, and set off by road with Ronald to KL.

I cannot remember how I was able to establish contact with Mary Rawson in Singapore at her friends the Del Tufoes (after the War Tony Del Tufoe was to become the deputy high commissoner; Mary was at school with his wife), but I knew that she would know of Jean's and John's whereabouts if anyone did. Mary had left KL with several senior MCS staff and had reached Singapore where she had attached herself to the Colonial Secretariat. I was overjoyed to learn from her that Jean and John had got away from Singapore on 31 December, ostensibly bound for Australia. Mary was to be severely wounded when the ship she was on was bombed and machine gunned on its way out of Singapore only days before the surrender, and was to be in pain from the shrapnel she carried in her back for the rest of her life.

Except for a brief attachment to the 4/3 Madras Regiment, at Barrackpore, I was to serve in clandestine forces of one kind or another for the remainder of the war.

Stay Behind Party

January 1942 – February 1942

As it was late when we left the PD camp, Ronald and I decided to stay overnight in Seremban with our mutual friends Geoffrey and Eve Allan. Geoffrey was in the Posts & Telegraphs Department and was required to stay at his post until very nearly the bitter end to ensure that communications were maintained.

During the drive Ronald was only able to fill in the barest background of the unit which I was joining and I got to know more in due course from Freddy Spencer Chapman. Early in 1941 the Special Operations Executive (SOE) had set up a small organisation in Singapore to prepare for guerrilla warfare in Malaya. This was No. 101 Special Training School (101 STS), under the command of Lt Colonel Jim Gavin. Six weeks after its formation it was joined by Major Spencer Chapman, who eventually took over command from Gavin. The school was established at Tanjong Balai, about 10 miles west of the city of Singapore, with its object to recruit and train personnel, European and Asian, civilian and military, in guerrilla warfare, intelligence gathering, sabotage and other such activities, as required by GHQ Far East. A Royal Marine officer, Lt Colonel Alan Warren, acted as liaison officer with GHQ.

A plan to set up 'stay behind' parties had been proposed to the Governor Sir Shenton Thomas, early in 1941. Each party was to be commanded by either police officers or recruits from the Volunteers, who would know the languages and the countryside of the area in which they were to operate, and include Chinese, Malays and Indians. But after the inevitable delays the plans were vetoed because it was considered that any suggestion that the country might be overrun would have a disastrous psychological effect on the native population. Also it was thought that there would be an unacceptable drain on European manpower.

This decision was only reversed in November 1941, a week before the outbreak of hostilities, by which time it was, of course, far too late to stand any chance of success. The first intake of Chinese, and then only 15, did not start training until 20 December. Two days later Freddy handed over command of the school and headed north to report to Colonel Warren in KL.

Shortly afterwards Freddy, together with Major Angus Rose of the Argyll & Sutherland Highlanders, Frank Vanrenen and another planter friend, Bill Harvey, had made the hit-and-run raid behind the lines which I mentioned earlier. This was in fact Freddy's first experience of the Malayan jungle, and from about the second week in January 1942 until the end of April 1945, when we succeeded in rescuing him by submarine, it was to be his home.

Ronald had met both Warren and Spencer Chapman and was full of praise for both. When we arrived in KL he took me straight to Colonel Warren's office and introduced me to him and Freddy. I, too, took an immediate liking to both men. Freddy and I were to remain the greatest of friends until his tragic and unnecessary death in 1971.

After some questioning, Warren expressed approval of me, told me that he would arrange an immediate commission for me in the British Army with the rank of second lieutenant, and sent me off for a medical. Having been pronounced fit I was briefed about the forthcoming operation, and detailed to take a commandeered lorry to collect stores – food, water, ammunition, high explosives – in preparation to driving with Ronald to the rendezvous with Freddy and the rest of the party at Tanjong Malim.

Our party was to consist of Freddy, John Sartin (a regular army sapper and newly commissioned), Ronald Graham, Frank Vanrenen, Bill Harvey and myself (planters), E. O. Shebbeare (game warden), a forestry officer named Shepherd, Ah Lam (radio operator) and Joli, the last two being Chinese. To quote Freddy Spencer Chapman: 'Sartin was a regular sapper and though I should always be chary of taking a regular soldier on a job like this, he had become sufficiently irregular after instruction at 101 STS, while Vanrenen, Harvey, Graham and Hembry were rubber planters with commissions in the

Volunteers and absolutely ideal for such work; they had spent all their working lives in Malaya and spoke Malay and Tamil fluently.'

I spent a couple of days assembling the stores. I also insisted in having the lorry painted khaki, as I was not particularly keen to be seen driving around in a bright red and blue ammunition truck. Gavin was a great help, and without his ability to pull strings and rank to overcome various quartermasters' objections, I doubt whether I would have been able to get half what we needed. Even with the enemy only a matter of hours away the Army still insisted on all the appropriate requisition forms being signed before the issuing of stores and equipment. I signed – and was to lose them in their entirety within three days.

Ronald and I stayed at the KL Station Hotel. As the town was being evacuated and all the usual places of entertainment closed, we found the evenings rather boring, except for the excitement of the air raids. It was amusing to see the hotel servants disappear as soon as the sirens went, leaving us to get our own meals. The Station Hotel and offices was a large imposing building, whitewashed, built in a very distinctive Moorish style, and an obvious target for the enemy bombers. I suppose we took unnecessary risks in not seeking shelter with the hotel staff, but we felt a stiff upper lip had to be shown. Anyway, we helped ourselves to very adequate free meals.

On 5 January we set off for the RV at Tanjong Malim, Ronald in a car as escort, I driving the lorry that was overloaded with our stores. Vanrenen and Spencer Chapman had already reconnoitred the point of entry into the jungle and the best place to unload the stores. These consisted of canned foods and water, the wireless transmitter, explosives and other demolition devices, hand grenades, and many thousands of rounds of ammunition. Freddy, in his wonderful book *The Jungle is Neutral*, said that it was quite unsafe to drive by day since the Japanese had complete control of the air and used to fly up and down the road bombing and machine gunning any vehicle they saw. I can confirm this. We left KL shortly after tiffin, I sitting on top of several tons of high explosives and ammunition, and at times appearing to be the sole target for the whole Jap air force. We constantly had to stop and bale out to take refuge in a roadside ditch, but unaccountably were relatively unscathed.

Some miles out of KL one of the lorry tyres was hit by machine-gun fire and rather than stop and change the wheel I continued driving on the rim until we reached a roadside RASC depot established in some rubber. Here, to my utter amazement, I found Bob Chrystal and Robby Robinson (the latter also a planter from Sungei Siput). Someone produced a bottle of Scotch, so we had several stengahs and discussed what had happened to ourselves to date and the whereabouts of our respective wives (all safe, thank God), while the damaged wheel was being changed. I also told Bob and Robby of our present intentions. Little did I realise at the time that our apparent keenness for the task in hand had persuaded both of them to volunteer for similar work. I do not remember being particularly enthusiastic, but I may well have pretended a false optimism. But it was from this chance meeting on the roadside that the epic story stems of Bob's three and three-quarter years sojourn in the jungle. Poor Robby died of malaria, but Bob survived, in spite of a recurrence of his duodenal ulcers, several near-fatal accidents, starvation and lonely wanderings through the jungle, to live a happy and contented life with Babs in Australia for more than 32 years.

Ronald led the way after the wheel change, by which time it was dark. After a harrowing journey finding our way through a constant stream of blacked-out traffic coming in the opposite direction, and another puncture which I again chose to ignore, we limped our way into Tanjong Malim where we were met by Frank at the deserted police station as planned.

I was delighted to see Frank again, and felt that we were at least trying to keep our ends up and that the envisaged party could more than hold its own against the enemy. This confidence, of course, could not have been more misplaced. In the event the whole scheme was a total shambles and, in the final analysis, led to the beheading in Pudu Prison, KL, of my three very gallant friends Frank, Ronald and Bill.

Frank had arranged accommodation in the rest house. He told us that the Army had informed him that we had the best part of a week to get our stores off-loaded and into the jungle, so we felt able to relax and enjoy a bit of a party with a tin-miner friend, John Weekly, and others of the Perak ARP, who were also staying the night on their way south. So, reasonably contented with our lot, we bedded down for the night, and were able to remove most of our clothes – a relief we would not know again for almost four weeks.

Early the next morning Frank, Ronald, Ah Lam and I set off in car and lorry to a point north east of Tanjong Malim where a track led off to a Chinese-owned tin mine and kongsi. This track had already been reconnoitred by Freddy and Frank when they had also established contact with some Chinese who were expecting us. In exchange for money, rice and opium – the latter two commodities we had found abandoned at the police station – the Chinese, under their headman Leu Kim, had agreed to help us unload and stack our stores under cover in the kongsi before moving them deeper into the jungle.

The first mishap occurred near the kongsi. The lorry, the punctured tyre now down on its rim, became impossible to steer. Trying to negotiate a sharp bend in the track I lost control and ended up in a deep ditch. However, we were well off the main road and Leu Kim's coolies were able to unload and move the stores to the kongsi without too much trouble.

Leaving Ah Lim to keep an eye on the stores, Frank, Ronald and I recced a track leading off into the jungle. We followed this for a mile or so until it ran parallel to a large pipe which carried the water supply for Tanjong Malim down from the hills. We came across an atap hut, probably used by the Water Board labour, and decided that this should be our initial base and that we would arrange for the coolies to carry the stores up and hide them in the vicinity.

The four of us returned to Tanjong Malim in the car, satisfied that the stores were well hidden, that, given the week which the Army had promised us, we were well ahead of schedule, and expecting that Freddy and the rest of the party would be waiting for us at the police station. We were disappointed but not particularly disconcerted that they were not, as the night was young and we were confident that they would turn up before long. We began to worry when midnight had arrived but they had not. However, we turned in for the night on the floor in the cells, sure that Freddy would arrive in the morning, but unable to sleep because of the noise of the never-ceasing stream of traffic heading south; ominously like an army in headlong retreat. We had scarcely laid down our heads when we were roused by a British officer shouting to enquire who the hell we were and what the hell were we doing? We told him. He then confirmed what we had suspected. The Slim River line had broken and the only British forces between us and the Japanese were two Bofors anti-tank guns sited on the bend in the road about a mile to the north of us.

So, here we were. No leader, no plan, no maps, no codes, no radio crystals, no explosives expert. No nothing – or words to that effect.

Not quite the start to the operation that we had envisaged.

But we decided to carry on with establishing our supply dump in the jungle, all the time hoping that Freddy and the others would turn up. We quickly loaded the car with more rice and opium and with not a little fear and trepidation set off northwards again for our track, passing the anti-tank guns a mile up the road, much to the surprise of the gunners, who expressed their views concerning our sanity in typically British Army fashion. I am sure they did not realise it, but their nonchalant steadfastness in the face of the enemy did much for our morale. We unloaded as quickly as possible and headed back to Tanjong Malim for another load, fully expecting to be fired on by our own guns in mistake for the enemy as we rounded the bend. We stopped to warn the officer commanding the guns that we would be returning. He stressed the need for haste as the enemy's forward troops were within a couple of miles.

On our way back, having loaded the car with everything that we could, as we knew that this was to be the last such trip, we stopped and chatted to the British Army rearguard. The young officer and his Lancashire gunners seemed quite unperturbed. Very recently I saw a photograph of two Bofors guns, and the description beneath read: 'Anti-tank guns sited on the main road near Tanjong Malim, protecting the withdrawal of the British forces.' I am certain that these were our two guns, as the bend in the road in the picture seemed familiar. It made me wonder what happened to these very brave countrymen of mine.

We handed over the rice and opium to the Chinese and were

happy to see our stores safely under cover in the mine godown. Ah Lam gave the instructions for them to be moved the following day deeper into the jungle to a site which we would recce. Then, having immobilised the car, we four set off for the hills. We had not gone very far when we heard the explosions which signified that the road and rail bridges at Tanjong Malim had been blown – and with them any hope that Freddy and the rest of the party could join us.

That evening Frank and I went back down to the kongsi to collect stores for our immediate use and to arrange for the rest to be brought up the following morning to the dump site that we had selected. We broke open obvious food cases and loaded our haversacks with a good supply of tinned fruit, raisins, chocolate, tea and a couple of bottles of whisky. The tins were very heavy and with the grenades, ammunition belts and Tommy guns we carried, the journey back to camp was hard work, as the path was steep and made very slippery by recent heavy rain. The plimsolls we wore did not help. Frank, for all his toughness of spirit, was a small man and did not have my strength for portering, so found the going very wearing. Before we left Leu Kim gave us firm assurances that the stores would be brought up as instructed and that the whole job would be completed by nightfall.

We had a scrap meal and lay down to sleep on a raised platform that Ah Lam and Ronald had constructed with bamboo. Unfortunately the whole thing collapsed, probably due to Ronald's stentorian snores, landing us all with a painful crash on to the ground. Only Frank saw the funny side of it.

At daybreak Ronald, Frank and I made our way back down to the kongsi to supervise the loading of the stores, leaving Ah Lam with instructions as to what to do should he suspect there was anyone else in the vicinity. Knowing the Japanese habit of using jungle paths to outflank roadblocks we believed that it would not be too long before they could stumble on our hut. Leu Kim came out to meet us with tears in his eyes – I think genuine – and with the news that his porters had decamped in the middle of the night, taking with them absolutely every item of stores. The Chinese had panicked when they heard that the Japanese were in control of Tanjong Malim and had let it be known that anyone found harbouring or helping Allied soldiers would be summarily shot. Leu Kim denied all knowledge of the coolies' whereabouts.

So now we had no food reserves nor wireless set.

But we did have each other. We had common sense. We had advantages that were not possessed by British troops, or even the enemy for that matter, in that we had knowledge of the native population and their languages. We had a compass. We were not afraid of the jungle, or its inhabitants, animal or human. And in Frank we had a natural leader in whom we had great confidence.

Nevertheless, we were very disconsolate when we returned to the hut to break the news to Ah Lam, to hold a postmortem and to decide what we were to do next. The operation, the raison d'être for our present situation, was obviously now a non-starter. We knew that there were other 'stay behind' parties in the field but, for sound security reasons, we had no idea of their whereabouts, so it was out of the question to try to join up with them. (Incidentally, Freddy had preferred the term 'stay behind' to the original official 'left behind' party, as the latter sounded too much like abandonment, but we were beginning to think that the first idea was rather more appropriate to our present circumstances!)

After a meal of bully beef, biscuits and hot tea we all felt much better. The situation was serious but not without its humour. Anyway, nothing could be gained by sitting on our backsides feeling sorry for ourselves. We felt confident that we could extract ourselves from our present situation and catch up with the withdrawing army. (Our confidence was, of course, entirely misplaced, as we had omitted to allow for the fact that the Army travelled, for the most part, in lorries on metalled roads, and was in headlong retreat.)

Frank, quite rightly, decided that it would be unwise to delay our departure from the hut as not only was our presence there known to the Chinese mining coolies, who might betray us for a reward, but it was also possible Japanese would use the track. We gathered what few stores remained and went deeper into the jungle, the last man doing his best to disguise our tracks. We found a small clearing and, not having had much over the past 72 hours we decided to try to catch up on some sleep. This proved impossible because the mosquitoes were hellish. In any case we were soon disturbed by a lot of chattering of a sort that was not usually associated with disciplined troops on patrol so, feeling sure that they were not Japanese, I went to investigate and found a party of Chinese who were fleeing from Tanjong Malim, which was now under the control of the enemy in strength with tanks and heavy artillery, and intent of getting up to Fraser's Hill by jungle paths.

We discussed constantly the possible reason for Freddy's failure to join up with us, and came to the conclusion that the unexpected and precipitate retreat of the British Army, and the blowing of the bridges at Tanjong Malim could be the only explanation. This added to our disquiet about the planning. The more we talked about it the more certain we were that we had been the victims of slapdash planning, over-optimism regarding the ability of the British Army to hold up the Japs, and inappropriate or poor equipment.

Towards the end of May 1945, after his rescue and while we were chewing the fat at my ISLD training camp just outside Trincomalee, Ceylon, Freddy gave me the full explanation for his non-arrival at our rendezvous at Tanjong Malim. (See Appendix A)

On about 10 January we began our attempt to catch up with the British Army. We still thought that we could get back to our lines in a week or so. We each took sufficient tinned food, milk and dates from our stockpile to last for about seven days and set off up the track that we had been told by the Chinese would eventually lead to Fraser's Hill, intending to turn off after five miles or so and then, with the aid of our compass, to head in a southerly direction for Kuala Kubu Bahru.

We set off, full of optimism, with me in the lead, about 20 yards ahead. Very soon it began to rain, a real solid Malayan tropical downpour. But, unusually, it did not ease off after an hour or so. After three hours we turned off in what we hoped was the right direction. The going steadily deteriorated and movement became very difficult and progress slow. The incessant rain made the track very slippery. I still recall the utter misery and discomfort of that afternoon and evening. We waded across two rivers, more than waist deep, and, to make matters even worse for me, I was wearing slacks and there was no sun to help dry them out.

In the evening we started to climb again. We had now left the path and were in deep jungle. Soon we got into nipa palm where the thorns tore strips of flesh out of us. What with this and the leeches we were soon soaked in blood. It was impossible to progress for more than a yard or so without having to slash a path with the parang. And all the time it rained. In the 11 years that I had hitherto spent out East I had never known it rain so hard so incessantly.

The Tommy guns soon proved to be quite unsuitable for the jungle as they had far too many projections which caught in every branch and root and had to be constantly disentangled, which slowed us down even more. So we chucked them and our ammunition away as unnecessary encumbrances, realising that if ever we had to use them in defence the game would be up, and there was little chance that we would wish to go on the offensive as our aim was to get back to our lines unscathed, to live to fight another day.

The ascent was at times almost perpendicular and our progress at snail's pace. Our hands were ripped by clutching at the vicious palms for support. Visibility was almost nil and, despite every effort to maintain a southerly direction, sheer fatigue often made us take the easiest path which, sometimes, was northwards. The leeches fastened on to us in their dozens. The best way to get rid of them was to apply a cigarette end to its body when it will let go and fall off. But it was far too wet to be able to light a cigarette so we simply had to pull them off, which usually meant that the head was left still gripping and sucking away on one's flesh. They penetrated everywhere, including my balls and the crack of my bum. I developed a suppurating ulcer, some two inches long, on my backside, which was not cleared up until I reached civilisation again and it could be treated with sulphonamide. It was excruciatingly painful. When one is exhausted and run down the likelihood of leech bites becoming septic is even greater.

Towards dark the rain eased and then ceased altogether. But if anything the going got harder. Eventually we had to stop through total exhaustion. We cut a small square area out of the thorn bushes and laid out our soaked groundsheets to sleep on. Our search for dry wood was fruitless, but after about two hours of fanning and blowing on the few twigs we were able to collect we managed to get a fire going and boiled some tea in our mess tin lids. We then lay down to sleep. A forlorn hope. To the leeches were added the attentions of very hungry mosquitoes. At dawn, even though we were far from rested, very cold, wet and utterly miserable, and far too despondent even to attempt another brew up, we resumed our hacking through the jungle in the hope of getting past the palm thorns and into some clearing where the sun, which we could see palely shining through the fronds above us, could penetrate sufficiently to dry us off.

After wandering up hill and down dale for several hours in approximately the right direction according to the compass, the thorn forest began to thin out, the going got easier, and eventually we came out into a rubber estate. Here I had a nasty shock for, leading the column as usual, I spotted a man in uniform, only about 50 yards away, but too far to see what nationality. Taking no chances we beat a hurried retreat back into the undergrowth, hoping that we had not been seen. After a little while Frank set off to recce the area. He returned to report that no one was in sight.

We decided to go back deeper into the jungle and to work our way round the rubber estate as there could well be Japs there. We crossed a fairly deep stream, which again meant a soaking, and were soon covered with even more leeches. The irritation was almost unbearable. We were in the jungle for about two hours before coming out on a cleared hilltop, covered in tall lalang grass and planted somewhat sporadically with fruit trees. Frank sent me ahead to recce – and I received another shock when I suddenly stumbled across a group of British soldiers lounging around an atap hut. I hastily withdrew into the undergrowth, called up the others and finally, having first assured ourselves that there were no Japs in the immediate vicinity, with extreme caution made our presence known.

There were 20 of them, including two sergeants, Lancashire gunners who had been cut off from their unit by Japanese tanks during the Slim River battle, and had escaped into the jungle. They had been five days without food or compass, without any idea where they were going, without hope, and very frightened – of the endless impenetrable jungle, the Japanese, the natives whose language they could not understand and who might betray them, and the poisonous snakes and other dangerous beasts that they imagined were everywhere. We handed over all the rations that we had so painfully carried with us. So now, on top of all our other problems, we really were without any food at all. We stayed on the hill for the rest of the day, drying out in the sun and looking at Tanjong Malim in the distance. We were now very hungry as our total food intake for the whole day had been six dates.

The senior sergeant asked us to take charge and lead them, as they were quite incapable of looking after themselves. We were reluctant to have them with us, as a larger party would certainly hinder our progress, but as we could not leave them to fend for themselves, we agreed. But we made it quite clear that, as British officers, we expected our orders to be obeyed instantly.

We spent the night around the hut in the orchard, very cold from the night air and soaked through again from the heavy dew. To make matters worse for me, my chosen resting place was close to a gunner who had acute diarrhoea or, more probably, dysentery. I dared not move in the dark in case I encountered the contents of his bowels, so put up with the disgusting noise and stench until I could move away in the morning.

After breakfast of tea and one biscuit each, Frank, Ronald and I discussed what we would do next. We could see Tanjong Malim quite clearly, so it was obvious that after two days' march we had not made more than a couple of miles. It did not take a mathematician to work out how long it would take us to hack through the jungle to catch up with the British Army which we assumed would try to make a stand at Seremban, some 80 miles to the south. We therefore decided to go through no more jungle if we could possibly help it, to make for the railway line and simply to march down it at night, making for Rawang, a few miles north of KL. At Rawang we could decide whether to continue southwards or to head west for the coast.

The broad Lancashire accents of the gunners caused us much amusement. Every second word was 'fook'. Their favourite expression was 'by the fook', and they used it so much that before long we were using it too. The young men now in our care were pretty poor specimens of soldiery. Entirely unsophisticated, poorly educated, and totally ill-prepared for fighting the Jap. Many had never known a pay packet before being called up, victims of the Depression. Nevertheless, they were typical of the material that, when trained and battle-hardened, beat the Hun at El Alamein and in Normandy, and the Jap at Imphal and in Burma.

Frank and Ronald went off to recce a way down to the railway line, and returned after three hours to report that they had found a route to the boundary of Escot Estate, until recently managed by my friend John Kennaway. We decided to make for Escot that afternoon and hole up there for the night. On arriving at the jungle's edge Frank and I set off to find the best way to the railway line. We had only gone a hundred yards when we came across a Tamil coolie who gave us directions. As it was too late to have hidden from him we had decided the best thing to do was to walk up to him quite openly and ask the way. We felt that any lack of confidence on our part would have discouraged assistance. Surprisingly, we did not fear betrayal. I have subsequently heard of Malays acting as 'headhunters' for the Japanese, but only know for sure of one incident – when Frank, Ronald and Bill were betrayed and later beheaded, and even then there were extenuating circumstances. But I do know of many cases where Malay, Tamil, Sikh and Chinese men and women refused to co-operate with the enemy and paid for their bravery and loyalty with their lives. We returned to the others, rested and set off at dusk, I in the lead as Frank was hopeless in the dark, eventually reaching a position about 500 yards from the main north-south highway where we lay up.

While the troops again rested we three discussed the next move, and it was decided that I would go forward with Ah Lam to the nearby village, where we knew from our Tamil coolie that Japanese troops were billeted, endeavour to contact a friendly Chinese and get him to lead us safely past any danger spots, to the railway. We set off and had not gone very far when two men sprang out at us from the shadows. Thinking they were Japs I fled, leaving Ah Lam rooted to the spot. But not hearing any shouts or shooting I stopped and slid into a ditch and, in the darkness, watched the three of them in deep conversation. After a few minutes a lamp was lit and Ah Lam called out to me to come out of hiding. I was still not entirely convinced that the men were not Japanese so approached somewhat warily, holding at the ready a stout stick that I had picked up. The two were Chinese coolies, who agreed to fetch a friend from the village who would, they were sure, act as a guide.

They said we were in great danger as the village was full of Japs, and convoys were constantly on the main road across which we were going to have to dash to reach the railway line. I arranged that I would bring up our party whilst they went off for the guide. Again, unaccountably, and in spite of their obvious lack of money, I did not fear that we would be betrayed. I made my way back to the main party, and led them forward to where Ah Lam was waiting with the coolies and another Chinese whom I took to be the guide. They had brought three packets of biscuits and two tins of condensed milk which were handed over to us. They refused payment for the food, or reward, but we insisted and pressed a few dollars into their hands.

Then the 24 of us, each holding on to a stick held by the man in front, stumbled along through the outskirts of the village that we could see was full of Japs – as we had no aircraft the enemy quite obviously saw no need to observe a blackout – myself in the lead, quite certain that any moment we would be challenged and fired at. The gunners following seemed to make a terrific noise in their army boots.

Food in a starved stomach is replaced by wind. The pain from the build up of gas can only be relieved by farting. This from a score or so of men, added to the sound of hobnailed boots, and much muttering of 'by the fook', had to be heard to be believed. I was glad that I was in the lead. Luckily the Japs in the village were either rear-echelon troops or had been withdrawn from the front line for rest and, in the euphoria of victory, were in no mood to take elementary guard-keeping precautions.

The guide, sensibly, had chosen to cross the road in the middle of a bend, so in the dark we could spot the oncoming headlights from either direction. After several interruptions from the constant traffic, we got the troops across in groups of four or five, Frank despatching them at one side of the road, I receiving them at the other, hastening them away to lie down amongst the rubber trees. From time to time we could see unescorted staff cars going by, in both directions, containing senior officers, which were very tempting targets for the six hand grenades we carried between us. But this would have been suicidal so we decided against it.

Our guide took us to the railway, about 50 yards through the rubber and departed, wishing us well.

We decided that it would be unwise for the whole party to be together so we split up into groups, each in charge of one of the three of us and the two sergeants, and set off down the line at five minute intervals. The recognition signal was to be the first few bars of Lupino Lane's 'Lambeth Walk', whistled. Incidentally, I was to use this for the rest of the war, with V Force in Burma, and ISLD in Sumatra and Malaya.

Kalumpang, the first station south of Tanjong Malim, was reported by our guide to have Japs billeted there, so I decided to make a detour through the rubber, to the west. Unfortunately, when we had reached the point where we could see the station lights we had to cross a river that ran parallel to the line to get into the rubber. We got the gunners across safely, and I took off my trousers and hung them around my neck. I could not help wondering how I would feel if I were caught on the other side with my trousers down. But at least they remained dry. On the following day I somewhat stupidly gave them up to a gunner, after which I wore my shorts. We split off into our smaller parties again.

The night was now pitch black, with visibility no more than a yard. I was in the lead as usual. After creeping through the rubber for about 20 minutes we suddenly found ourselves in a mangrove swamp. Instead of firm ground we were in mud up to our ankles and getting deeper with each step, and the tree roots, instead of being below ground were now knee high, so the deeper we sank into the mud, the higher we had to climb over them.

The next three hours were quite the worst that I have ever

experienced. The thorn jungle was bad enough, but at least in that one could sit down to rest. Here one would very quickly be over one's knees in the vile smelling mud. Added to which we were clearly lost. The muttered curses and the 'by the fooks' could have been heard a mile away. I lit a match and from the compass realised that we were going in quite the wrong direction. I thought that we must have bypassed Kalumpang by then so decided to head east to pick up the railway again. Eventually the going got easier and we came out into secondary jungle and shortly afterwards hit the railway line.

I cannot describe the utter slough of despond which surrounds and encapsulates a mangrove swamp. The sheer exhaustion that is quickly reached is aggravated by the appalling stench, the leeches, the myriads of mosquitoes, the impalings by the roots – usually at lower midriff level – the heat, and the fear of crocodiles and snakes which abound in these swamps.

Unfortunately we found that we had not bypassed the station, having re-emerged on to the line only a hundred yards or so from where we had left it. But I was so fed up by this time that I decided to follow the line straight through the station, and trust to luck, wondering how the other parties had fared and hoping for their sakes that they had avoided the mangrove swamp.

Just before reaching the station we came across a group of men, huddled together on the embankment. The constant murmurs of 'by the fook' identified them – more easily than the 'Lambeth Walk' – as a party led by one of the sergeants. They had simply walked straight down the railway line, seen no enemy at the station and passed through. After waiting for a couple of hours they had decided that they would return to where they had started in the hope of meeting up again with the rest of us. I decided that I would follow their example and led the enlarged party back down the line, through the station. After only a few minutes I heard our recognition signal being whistled and Frank and Ronald and their groups emerged from the trackside undergrowth. I was the only one to have encountered the swamp – much to Frank's amusement, my chagrin, and my little group's annoyance. They most certainly did not appreciate my local knowledge!

No one had seen any sign of the Japs or railway staff, but we did see the sidings full of trucks, all of which should have been destroyed or immobilised. We decided that our few grenades would not be sufficient for the job so, again, discretion being the better part of valour, we passed on by down the main track.

A mile or two further on the railway and main road ran within only a few yards of each other, for a distance of some two miles. We were about halfway along this section when we heard the sound of approaching vehicles and the whole countryside was lit up. We just had time to throw ourselves into the ditch which ran between the railway and the road, and for Frank to shout for everyone to keep their head down and their face towards the ground – confident that he would not have been heard by the enemy above their engine noise. A long convoy of trucks, armoured cars and tanks passed, heading south. I could not resist raising my head from time to time to make mental notes of its strength and composition. I was astonished at the quantity of our own vehicles, which had obviously been abandoned, as well as the number of enemy tanks. I counted at least 350 trucks, staff cars, tanks and armoured cars and concluded that I was seeing at least a brigade on the move.

It seemed quite uncanny to be lying within only a few feet of so many of the enemy. My only real fear was that the convoy might come to a halt for some reason and the troops debus. Nothing could have saved us from detection, and we would most probably have been shot on sight as they would not have had the time or the inclination to take and interrogate prisoners of war. But our luck was in, the vehicles disappeared into the distance, and silence returned.

As we set off down the track again it began to rain. I, as usual, was in the lead. We had not gone far when I spotted some men approaching from the south. Again we tumbled into the track side ditch expecting to be fired at by Japs alerted by the sound of slithering and splashing. But all we heard was 'by the fook' and soon recognised the missing group led by the second sergeant. They had pressed on southwards until spying two Jap sentries at a level crossing gate a mile or so ahead. We all felt that we had had enough of cross-country marches in the dark and so decided to continue down the line keeping

an eye open for these Japs which, if seen, we would overpower –
in retrospect a naive hope because, of course, they were armed and
would probably have had reinforcements nearby.

As it was now about five in the morning and dawn fast
approaching, and we had been on the move for over eight hours,
Frank decided that we would withdraw into the adjacent rubber and
rest up. Sleep was impossible, even though we were all dead tired. We
were filthy dirty, hungry, and bitten to blazes by mosquitoes.

We could still see the road. Military traffic continued constantly,
but there were no convoys. We saw many more captured lorries
loaded with troops, the occasional tank and Bren carrier and, really
worrying so far as our own safety was concerned, hundreds of soldiers
mounted on bicycles. Frank sent the gunners deeper into the rubber
as one or two of them were quite likely to stand up, if only to pee,
and be spotted by some keen-eyed Jap on the look-out for stragglers.

We rested until about midday, when I realised that we must be
near Guthrie's Kerling Estate, so I suggested that we made our way to
the coolie lines where we might be able to get help and something to
eat. Frank agreed, and we soon reached what was obviously an estate
road, which we followed, keeping to the trees about 20 yards in, as
the Japs could well have been patrolling these roads, until we came
to a Chinese kongsi. Here we were hospitably but nervously received.
The Chinese boiled some water and we mixed this with the one tin of
condensed milk that remained and shared it between all of us – each
man received a cigarette tin of hot watery milk. Elixir. Our first 'meal'
for 48 hours. We were given directions and, after walking for another
couple of hours over some very steep hills, we came upon a stream
that led us directly to the Kerling Estate village.

Here we received a magnificent welcome from the Kerling
employees, coolies and office staff alike, and were showered with
all kinds of drink and food which we devoured ravenously. A young
Tamil woman rushed up to me and said that she worked on Kamuning.
She had burst into tears on recognising me, anxiously asked about
Jean and John, and cried again when I had to admit that I had no
idea of their whereabouts except that I had heard they had managed
to leave Singapore. By knowing most of the Europeans on Kerling I

was able to establish a close relationship with the senior Asian staff. Nothing was too much trouble, in spite of the fact that these were very dangerous times for anyone befriending the British. These loyal people risked certain death to protect us bedraggled, starving and desperate strangers. As soon as I could, after the Jap surrender, I made a point of going to Kerling in the hope of finding the people concerned, and particularly the young woman from Kamuning. She had left, and only the chief clerk remembered the incident.

Kerling was a very isolated estate and scarcely produced any rubber during the occupation, so most of the staff would have dispersed in search of work elsewhere. I did, however, advise Guthrie's of the help given by these kind people, and I am glad to say it was acknowledged in the first post-war annual report and a donation made to the staff fund.

They prepared a substantial curry and also provided the bootless amongst us with socks and rubber soled shoes. Unfortunately my feet were far too large, so I had to continue to make do with my own torn plimsolls. Squatting down to eat in the rubber store we were given news of the battles that had taken place at Rawang and Kuala Selangor, and that the British were fast withdrawing to the Seremban area. This was very depressing, for how on earth were we ever to catch up?

They told us that the Japanese had already been to the estate and checked the rubber, rice and other stocks, and had threatened death to all concerned should any be missing on their next inspection. The Japanese had arrived on motorbikes and had appeared to be cognisant of all the details of the estate, including the names of the European and senior Asian staffs, production, etc. Before the war the Japanese had inundated Malaya with countless dentists, photographers, barbers, pearl fishermen and tourists, and all, almost without exception, were spies. They recorded estate details, mapped jungle trails, the strength of road bridges, and other information which would be useful to an invading and occupying army. The resident photographer in Sungei Siput for several years, generally liked and well respected, and used by all of us both for personal portraits and estate functions, turned up in the wake of the Japanese army as commissar for the area. In retrospect it was significant that most of these Japanese residents in Malaya left the country a matter of months before the outbreak of hostilities, presumably ordered to leave to avoid internment.

Frank, Ronald and I discussed destroying the rubber stocks, smoke houses and the factory, as had been laid down by the Government's scorched-earth policy, but decided against the idea. We were sure that the Japs would take reprisals on the estate workers, and, in any case, so many rubber stocks had not been destroyed that Kerling's would have made no difference.

We were urged not to delay our departure as the Japanese were expected to return the next day. The head clerk advised us to cut through the jungle separating Kerling from a SOCFIN estate named Nigel Gardner, from where we could join the railway again to head south. He also promised a reliable guide to lead us through the jungle. We agreed, but were beginning to have grave doubts as to whether we would ever catch up our retreating troops.

So we lay down in the rubber store on the blankets which the staff loaned us, too tired to mount guard, and slept. At dawn the following morning we were woken with hot tea and were introduced to the Tamil guide. After thanking the estate staff most profusely we set off through the jungle, following Sakai paths and wild boar trails, and must have covered nearly 12 miles in about eight hours when we came out near the Nigel Gardner estate office and lines, completely exhausted. The guide went ahead to ask whether we would be welcome, and about the possible movement of Japanese in the area. We were again most hospitably received. Another large curry was prepared and hot water supplied to bathe our feet and to wash ourselves.

Our feet were now in a very poor condition. I had three large blisters which made every step hell, and the thorn and leech wounds were septic and suppurating badly. All our wounds were expertly treated and bandaged up by the estate dresser, so at least they would not be subject to any further contamination for a little while. After the sumptuous curry we bedded down in a packing shed for the night. However, few enjoyed much sleep. Two hot spicy curries in quick succession after several days of near starvation played havoc with our digestive systems, resulting in great discomfort and frequent visits to the nearby rubber trees.

We were warned that a gang of Malays had been armed by the Japs and had been promised $20 a head for every British soldier they shot. I have always doubted this, even after being told that there are records of British Army stragglers being handed over to the Japs, maybe sometimes for a reward. Luckily, I experienced nothing but sympathy, kindness and assistance from all that we met, irrespective of nationality.

This SOCFIN estate had over 100,000 pounds of rubber in stock, and all the buildings and manufacturing machinery were intact. The manager had refused to destroy anything, despite government orders. On the whole I believe he was right. After all, the 'invincible' British were leaving the native population in the lurch, in the hands of a bestial enemy, and it would have been quite wrong to have added to their misfortune by denying them the ability to earn a living and to feed their families.

Frank recorded in his diary everything of note that we saw, heard and did, to be able to make a full report when we eventually reached base. In it he had also made many amusing comments about Ronald, myself and our Lancashire lads. We three were very happy together, with complete confidence in each other. Frank was an inspiration to us all. His first thoughts were always for the unfortunate men whom we were trying to lead to safety. I often used to glimpse him at the tail of our party, helping a crippled soldier, or offering words of encouragement.

The next morning, after a breakfast of fruit and tea, we piled on to an estate lorry and were given a lift along the estate roads as far as the Batu Arang coal mine railway line where we debussed and followed the track for about five miles, until we arrived at another rubber estate. Our Tamil guide warned us that the labour force was treacherous, having run the Asian staff off the estate, looted all the bungalows and generally run amok. We approached the factory and office warily, and passed the vandalised manager's bungalow. The squatters in residence looked very surly, so we hurried on with merely a cursory acknowledgement. We learned from a Chinese coolie that an action of some sort had occurred in a neighbouring village only two or three days before, so I went ahead to recce the situation, in case there were still Japs around, maybe licking their wounds. I hid behind a banana tree for 10 minutes or so, saw no enemy, so walked along the main path into the village, full of trepidation, with the intention of finding the kedai (shop) and some food. The shopkeeper was most apologetic but looters had been there before. And from the way he spoke I understood that they were British rather than Japanese. But I did find a dozen or so perfectly serviceable abandoned British Army lorries and a staff car. They even had reasonably full petrol tanks.

When I got back to Frank we did discuss taking one of the trucks, but felt that that would really be asking for trouble. Ronald suggested that they could possibly have been booby-trapped, maybe even by our own side. So we decided to make for Batang Bajantai on foot. Just past the village we had to cross a river by a demolished bridge that the Japs had partially repaired, in full view of the astonished villagers who turned out to watch. The area around the other side was littered with field gun shell cases, abandoned rifles and other war impedimenta, but nothing that would be of any use to us. So we pressed on. We had not gone more than a couple of hundred yards when an elderly Chinese rushed up and warned us that a lot of Japanese were coming up the road towards us from Batang Bajuntai. Also that the town itself was full of the enemy and must be avoided at all costs.

We hurriedly withdrew into the roadside rubber trees, out of sight from the road, and sat down in a hollow to discuss the situation. The Chinese said that for $1,000 he would lead us through the jungle to Seremban, south of KL. While we were at Kerling I had torn a map of Malaya out of an exercise book I had found in the estate school. Seremban seemed a very long way away. Getting there by circuitous jungle paths would add considerably to the distance, quite apart from the time factor. By the time we reached Seremban we could be reasonably certain that our troops would be at least 100 miles further south. However, we accepted the Chinese's offer, gave him some money on account, and set off at a cracking pace, heading for Batu Arang coal mine.

We covered the seven miles in less than two hours and arrived at our guide's house utterly exhausted. En route we had passed several Sikhs who were obviously police deserters. Japanese aircraft flew low overhead almost continuously, so we were constantly having to dive for cover. All the colliery buildings were intact, although the machinery had been destroyed or immobilised, and the staff bungalows vandalised either by retreating British troops or the colliery's own labour force. I suspect the former. We had our first bath for many days in one of the mining pools, although the effect was somewhat spoilt by our having to don our filthy clothes again afterwards. The Chinese gave us a meal, for which he charged us outrageously, but we were not prepared to argue. He promptly disappeared on 'urgent business' and we feared the worse, so Ronald and I stood look out on the likely approach routes. However, he returned as promised and at about six in the evening we set out for Sungei Buloh, 17 miles to the south.

To begin with I was at the rear, so was on the receiving end of the usual cannonade, but at dusk I swapped places with Frank and joined the Chinese guide at the front. For the next 10 hours we wandered through tin mines, rubber plantations, mangrove swamps and kampongs. We must have covered over 20 miles, but as most seemed to be in ever-decreasing circles it is surprising that we did not all disappear. The tin tailings were particularly tiresome, as most had been flooded so, for hours at a time, we sloshed about in mud up to our knees, always mindful of the fact that we might encounter a deep mining hole and vanish completely. During a brief rest it was realised that two of the gunners were missing, so I retraced our path and luckily came across them two miles back, and absolutely at the end of their tethers. It took a lot of persuading to get them to summon up their strength to rejoin the party. It was obvious that the gunners, except perhaps one of the sergeants, were beginning to doubt the wisdom of having joined up with us.

The old Chinese led us straight through a village that was all too obviously occupied by Japanese. He shouted at the top of his voice for us to keep quiet and not to be bodohs (fools), sweeping the beam of the torch from side to side. I can only think that the Japs did not investigate because they thought he was merely a drunk on his way home from a toddy session. Or they were drunk themselves. At any rate, they saw no reason to mount guard or to investigate the disturbance.

It was here that Ah Lam decided to leave us. He went with our blessing, as we had no need for a radio operator, was another mouth to feed, and he would most certainly have been tortured and executed if we were captured, whereas there was a fifty-fifty chance that the rest of us would be treated as POWs.

At long last we reached the main Kuala Lumpur to Kuala Selangor road where we collapsed into the undergrowth through sheer fatigue. We were so tired that we had no energy even to bestir ourselves, but only to lie low, when about 30 enemy motor cyclists, light armoured cars and lorries came by, headlights blazing, heading for KL. When these had disappeared, and after a rest, we retreated further into the rubber trees and headed off in the direction of Sungei Buloh. The guide said that he knew of a hut nearby which he was sure we could reach in three hours, providing that we had to make no more excursions. As we soon came to the estate boundary and the rubber had petered out into secondary jungle we took to the road, hoping that we would have sufficient warning of oncoming traffic to be able to dive for cover. But we had a shock when, on rounding a bend, we came across three Jap armoured cars parked on the roadside. Too late to do anything we simply marched straight on by, expecting at any moment to be shot from behind, but nothing happened. Maybe all the Japs were asleep without posting sentries. When we had rounded the next bend and were out of sight we discussed whether one of us should go back to drop a few grenades down the hatches, but decided it was too risky to try to approach the vehicles for a second time without being seen, and anyway the explosions would most certainly have alerted every other Jap in the neighbourhood to come looking for us.

We reached the hut, which was about 50 yards off the road and without much cover, shortly after 3 am, having been on the go for 10 hours. I was reluctant to stay there and was all for moving deeper into the rubber – we were amongst rubber trees that had obviously not been husbanded for many years, so there was undergrowth – but the others were all in and had collapsed on to the floor and I saw little hope of stirring them. So I lay down, thinking to myself that there was a most unpleasant smell, as if from a dead body, but was by then too tired to investigate.

We had not been asleep for more than 15 minutes when I heard a motorbike drive up and switch off its engine on the road immediately opposite our hut. I realised that Frank had heard it too. Nothing happened, no one approached, so I crept out to investigate. I crawled up to the roadside, expecting any moment to be challenged, but could see nothing. Hiding behind a tree I heard another vehicle approaching, with headlights blazing. I watched as the armoured troop carrier got almost opposite me when it too switched off its engine and headlights and coasted down the hill, disappearing into the darkness. I realised then that they were preserving petrol by freewheeling down hills. Frank decided that we should move further from the road, and Ronald and I took turns to stand guard for the rest of the night.

At dawn I returned to the hut and found, to my horror, that my suspicions had been correct. Within a couple of feet of where I had spread myself to sleep was what remained of a human body, a heaving, seething mass of white maggots. The skull had been completely stripped of flesh, and they were busy on the torso. There was no way of telling the nationality or the cause of death. I heaved to be sick. Unfortunately there was nothing in my stomach to sick up, so it was agony

As there was much enemy activity on the road we decided to stay in this vicinity for a few days, both to allow those with very sore feet – most, if not all of us – to recuperate, and in the hope that Japanese would move on, presumably as the front line moved closer to KL. We soon realised that we were quite near a railway station and trains were arriving every half hour or so. Ronald, Frank and I took it in turns to creep as near as we could to see the Japs unloading men, weapons, ammunition and rice bags and loading them on to lorries which immediately drove off southwards, so that we could take notes which we, I must admit by then, somewhat forlornly hoped would be included in our report when we eventually got back to base. As the trains were obviously ours, and had equally obviously come some distance, through tunnels and over bridges, we were not over-impressed with the efficacy of the scorched-earth policy ordered by the Governor.

During the three days of our sojourn there we had no more than three bananas per man each day to eat, and the only water available was from a small and very muddy stream running near the road. Consequently we could only collect this at night. I recall waking up one morning with my tongue so swollen that I could not swallow or even close my mouth, and I imagined all the diseases that I may have picked up by drinking contaminated water. Fortunately, the swelling had mostly gone by the next day, so I decided that I must have been stung by an insect whilst sleeping with my mouth open. We had managed to retain a bottle of whisky, now less than half full, used solely for medical purposes. My swollen tongue was judged to qualify.

The Lancashire gunners were a severe handicap to the three of us, for they limited our progress. There was no question of moving quickly and stealthily with 20 cursing and farting Tommies. But common humanity dictated that we could not desert them. Whilst their discipline was good, we felt that they would rather give themselves up and take what was coming. They got into huddles whenever we halted and stopped talking when Frank, Ronald or I approached. I could not really blame them, for we were fighting for different things. Malaya was our country, the local inhabitants, of whatever race, were our people who, with only very few exceptions, displayed great loyalty to us. For the conscript British soldier, and in spite of the fact that it was part of their great British Empire, Malaya was thousands of miles away from home, hot, smelly, full of mosquitoes and leeches, snakes, malaria and natives whose languages they did not understand. We sympathised, but our patience at times was sorely tried.

We decided that we had remained there long enough, so persuaded the old Chinese that it was time to move. He complained of aches and pains in his legs and begged for a little whisky. Ronald handed him the bottle and, to our horror and before we could grab back the bottle, he emptied half what remained on to his hands and proceeded to rub it into his legs.

We set off as soon as it was dark, and immediately got lost. We had to cross a river and the old Chinese had forgotten the whereabouts of the bridge. We lay up in the undergrowth while he went off to look for it. After three hours he had failed to return so we settled down for the night and agreed that we would move off at dawn as it became obvious that the old man had deserted us, despite being owed $500. The three of us took turns to stand guard, just in case we had been betrayed, which we doubted.

At first light we were on the move, not at all certain which direction to take, but were soon very lucky to meet up with a friendly Malay who gave us much helpful information regarding our exact whereabouts, possible escape routes, distances and where the Japs were most active locally. He also told us that, after a fierce battle, our troops were withdrawing southwards from the Seremban area. We realised that this news had effectively dissipated any hopes we had of reaching our own lines, now over 100 miles away. So here we were, in the third week of January, having been on the run for nearly three weeks, severely handicapped by lack of maps, nearly 200 miles south of the part of Malaya that we knew, physically exhausted and starving, and responsible for the safety of 20 British soldiers. Incidentally, we did begin to wonder exactly how they had become separated from their unit and seriously considered accusing them of desertion, but did not, as our suspicions could well have been completely unjustified, and anyway there was nothing we could have done about it.

So we decided to make for the Klang area on the coast where we thought we could commandeer a boat or get a friendly fisherman to take us either down the coast towards Singapore or across the strait to Sumatra. At about midday we came to the hydroelectric power lines that the Malay had told us led to Klang. These went in a straight line for miles; the rentice, the cleared strip underneath, consisted mainly of secondary jungle, sheet lalang and the occasional padi field, with an inspection path running through the centre. To either side was jungle, with occasional clearings of orchards, but virtually no habitation. For some time we were close to a main road and saw several Jap patrols both on foot and in lorries. On one occasion we hid in a banana grove and saw a plane land on a straight stretch of road. The pilot did not get out, even to stretch his legs or to pee, and after an hour took off again and headed south. Perhaps he was lost and was trying to get his bearings. Or just tired.

It took four days to march down the hydro line. The going was very steep in parts and, because of our exhausted state, we were seldom able to make more than five or six miles a day. We had no food except a few wild bananas and sweet potatoes. All the orchards were either out of season or the fruit had already been gathered. Morale was surprisingly good, and Frank, as ever, was a tower of strength, often helping a straggler along by his pack straps. Our packs, of course, were practically empty. I carried a razor, toothbrush and paste, towel and soap, spare socks and one or two odds and ends. True to British Army tradition we scarcely went a day without shaving. We washed our socks and underpants whenever the opportunity rose, and tried to relax while they dried in the sun.

The nights were particularly unpleasant, with what seemed to be extra heavy dews, which made it almost impossible to sleep because of the extreme cold. The days were exhausting, too, although the drenching rain helped to offset the heat. I suppose that our very poor state of physical health made the hardships more difficult to bear. But, in spite of everything, we were usually in good spirits and very rarely was a cross word heard. By now we had sorted out the cheerful from the grumblers, and had brought the NCOs into our discussions. We had lost all idea of dates and time; all we thought about was where the next meal was coming from, and getting a good night's rest. Our bowels were in a very poor state. Ronald's had gone for over 10 days without working. Our ulcers, and especially the one on my bottom, were suppurating worse than ever, and the stench was sickening. But we just had to press on.

On the second or third day we reached a kongsi occupied by Chinese hydroelectric power line maintenance workers. Here we were kindly supplied with tins of milk, sweet potatoes and hard-baked biscuits, which we shared out equally amongst the whole party, and instructed the gunners to take themselves off into the cover of a nearby orchard to eat whilst we three remained drinking coffee with the kepala (headman), discussing our predicament and trying to find out the war situation, of which our host knew very little. Our discussions were suddenly interrupted by the arrival of three Japanese soldiers in a car. We beat a hasty retreat into the kitchen at the rear, and then, when the car stopped at the front, into the blukar (tall grass) at the back of the kongsi. The Japs left after about 10 minutes, and we returned to finish our coffee and conversation. They had been checking up on the hydro line and had instructed the labour force to continue working as usual.

We collected the rest of our party and pushed on down the power line path towards the village of Kapar where we met some friendly Tamil estate workers. One said that he had a friend who owned a boat and was sure that, for a reward, he would agree to take us down to Batu Pahat, in Johore. Between the three of us we had nearly $100, the last of our money, and Frank took it to pay the Tamil boatman to help us. The rest of us went to ground and Frank went off alone with the Tamils. It was by now about seven, and night had fallen. When, by midnight, Frank had not returned Ronald and I became very anxious and imagined the worst: that he had run into Japanese and had been captured. But we decided that nothing could be done before dawn, so tried to get some sleep where we were.

At about six the following morning, to our very great relief, we heard the 'Lambeth Walk' and, after I had replied in kind, Frank arrived, exhausted almost beyond belief, having had a most frightening experience. He had been walking into the village, talking to the Tamil, when a torch suddenly flashed on him and, before he knew what was happening, was overpowered by two Japanese soldiers and frog-marched to the police station. The Malay police had long since disappeared but there was another Jap in the office. Frank was searched and relieved of all our money. Fortunately, there were no cells so he was kept in the charge room. At about nine o'clock terrific explosions were heard from the direction of KL, with much tracer fire in the sky. (We also had heard the noise, and learned later that it was the RAF mounting their largest raid of the campaign.) The three guards became very excited and stood jabbering and gesticulating in the doorway, forgetting about their prisoner. This was unwise. Frank grabbed the table lamp, threw it at his captors, hitting one of them full in the face. He punched the two others, knocking them both out cold, and fled. He had then spent several hours trying to find us in the dark, all the while whistling our tune.

By the greatest of good fortune he had then fallen in with a Malay who recognised him as the tuan for whom he had caddied at the Malayan Golf Championship at KL the previous year. The Malay took him back to his house, fed him and gave him a blanket and a charpoy for what remained of the night. At first light he and the Malay set out to find us, succeeding without too much trouble. Frank apologised for having lost the last of our money. Ronald suggested that the real reason was that he had found an expensive woman for the night.

The Malay and his friends rallied around and produced fresh bread, fish and fruit and we all gorged ourselves, with the result that our mouth and lips became so raw with pineapple that many of us could scarcely speak. The fruit, however, was the best of aperients, even working on Ronald.

We had a long talk with the Malays, during which it became obvious that we should abandon all ideas of making it back to our front line. Quite apart from the fact that the only bridge over the River Klang, which was wide at that point and crocodile-infested, would be strongly guarded day and night, they told us of incidents where the Japs had rounded up British Army stragglers and had simply shot them out of hand. This also meant there was little point in sailing down the coast. We would have to aim for Sumatra. One Malay said he knew of a fishing village about 17 miles to the north where he felt sure we could get a boat, and that he would lead us there, even though we told him that we were now without funds to reward him.

We had a long march that night, although the going was considerably easier than of late, and decided to lay up for the day in the abandoned manager's bungalow of a rubber estate. Our Malay guide was disappointed that we were not able to reach our destination, said that he could only spare a day for us, and disappeared. Whilst we rested and tried to remember what our guide had told us about where we were going, before continuing at nightfall, we saw five British soldiers walking along an estate road, about a hundred yards away. They were most reluctant to stop when I called out, but had second thoughts and came over. They were Argyll and Sutherland Highlanders, an officer, a sergeant and three ORs. They had been cut off many miles to the north and had been on the move for three weeks. They had spent the last few days hidden in a Chinese temple beside the river and had several times tried to persuade fishermen to take them to Sumatra. As they did not speak Malay it was hardly surprising that they were unsuccessful. But it was a miracle that they had managed to get this far without capture.

The officer was full of useful information, but was most reluctant to throw in his lot with us. They had been part of a much larger contingent which had gradually split up and gone their separate ways. We agreed that large parties stood little chance of getting away, but persuaded him to stay with us, at least until we had been able to speak to the local fishermen and sampan owners. Leaving the Argyll officer in charge, Frank, Ronald and I went off on our recce.

We soon found a creek with several sea sampans tied to the bank. We spotted what looked like a couple of likely looking craft and decided that, if we could not find the owners to sail us across to Sumatra, we would commandeer them and make the attempt ourselves. Our difficulty was that none of we three were yachtsmen, and we doubted whether any of the soldiers were either, so knew nothing about winds and tides, or how to operate the sails and ropes. But we were willing to give it a go.

When we got back to the bungalow and explained the situation, we found that most of the gunners did not wish to risk the sea crossing but preferred to try their luck on dry land, keeping to the coast on the principle that they would eventually arrive at the southern tip of Johore, only a few hundred yards from Singapore, which the British were sure to be holding. We pointed out that, in our opinion, this would have even less of a chance of succeeding than what we proposed; how were they to cross the River Klang and at least four other major rivers, and how were they to get on without the knowledge of the Malay and Tamil languages? But, except for two of them who beseeched us to take them with us, they were adamant. We were secretly rather relieved that the Argyll officer was not prepared to order the rest of the gunners to accompany us, as we felt we had a far better chance of escape without them. I must say the Argylls were magnificent. They obviously took great pride in their regiment, and it came as no surprise to learn after the war of the good account they had given of themselves in many rearguard actions during the retreat.

We gave the gunners all the information that we could, our compass, the map of Malaya that I had picked up from the estate school, a list of a few Malay words that we felt may be of use, all our food (very little of this), and also the whereabouts of the boats, in case they changed their minds. We agreed to give them 24 hours start before we began our own attempt to get away. It was a sad parting, because we had become used to each other. Their gratitude was quite embarrassing, particularly as, in our hearts, we knew that their chance of survival was slim. At best they would end up as POWs – we were not to know of the Siam Railway then – or at worst they would be shot or bayoneted to death. We never saw nor heard of them again.

The next day we moved down to the temple where the Argylls had been before, covering the five miles by daylight. We marched through a village, much to the astonishment of the locals. I bought some tea and milk at the village kedai with, quite literally, the last few cents that the Argyll officer possessed, and Ronald cadged some fish from a passing fisherman, so we had a good meal when we reached the temple. This was on a narrow track which led down to the river, so a lookout could give us good warning of anyone hostile approaching from landwards, and the seaward approach was mostly mangrove, so safe.

But we did have several callers, more from inquisitiveness than a desire to help, from whom we learned that a Jap patrol came twice a day. This made us wonder how long it would be before we were betrayed, but we felt it important to maintain an air of confidence at all times, making it apparent that they were our friends, so that we knew we were perfectly safe.

The next day Frank, I and the Argyll officer decided to look over the available boats. We spotted one that seemed suitable, large enough to take the 10 of us, and with lots of sails folded up on board. We still preferred to be taken over the strait so went back into the village to try to find the owner of the sampan in question. We walked down the main street, much to the consternation of most of the villagers. The exceptions were one old Chinese and an even older Javanese who insisted on taking us to the coffee shop and standing us tea and biscuits. We were tucking into these and learning the local gossip when the Jap patrol arrived on motorcycles, so we were hustled into the rear whilst the Japs had some coffee too, sitting at the same table as we had been a minute before – the seats must have been still warm. After half an hour they left – without paying for their refreshments – and we resumed our places at the table.

The old Chinese said that he would be willing to help us get away and would make the necessary arrangements. We never saw him again, but that same evening two Chinese fisherman came up the creek and gave us some fish, pineapple, rice and milk, and said they would return the following day with a larger vessel, to sail us across to Sumatra, for $500. We readily agreed, although we had not one cent between us, confident that we could get the money from the Dutch authorities.

After a quiet night and rather an anxious day the fishermen arrived just before nightfall with a sailing sampan, and we all piled in even though it was only built to take six at the most, almost euphoric at the prospect of freedom and a hot bath. It was then that one of the fishermen told us that our old Chinese had been shot that afternoon for giving incorrect information about the number of powered sampans he owned.

It was a lovely tropical night. The crew paddled out into the channel and hoisted the sail, before preparing a meal of pork and vegetables. They even produced a bottle of samsu (rice wine). Early the following morning we had a mild panic when a Japanese aircraft appeared flying low over the sea. We scrambled under sails and old sacks whilst it circled overhead two or three times before disappearing southwards. Soon afterwards the wind dropped completely and we were becalmed. With no shade at all the heat was terrific and we were all prostrate from the sun, heat exhaustion and under-nourishment. To make matters worse, I went down with malaria. My temperature soared and I started rambling. I learned later that the others took turns to shade me and to splash water over me to try to cool me down. Apparently Ronald went over the side for a dip but very soon clambered back on board again when a shark was spotted. At nightfall a slight breeze got up and we were able to make way again. Around midnight a sumatra sprang up – a sudden squall of gale force wind, thunder and lightning, and sheets of solid rain, all combining to make the Strait of Malacca, because of its shallowness, an extremely dangerous place for small craft, especially when overloaded as we were. The seas were mountainous and we came near to capsizing several times. It must have been terrifying, even to the fishermen. I was only barely conscious, lying awash in the water that we had taken aboard, but just aware of the unpleasantness around. The following morning the sumatra disappeared as quickly as it had arrived and we were back to the broiling sun. It would appear that this state of affairs lasted for three days and nights, during which my temperature, measured by the thermometer that Ronald had somehow conjured from his haversack, approached 104 degrees Fahrenheit, as I lay in the scuppers, unable to move and wishing to die.

On the fourth day we arrived within sight of Bagan Siapiapi, a large fishing village on the Sumatra coast, but our agony was not to be assuaged, as the tide was ebbing at a faster rate than the light wind was taking us in and, before we could reach port, we were left high and dry on the mud flats close to a fishing blaht. The stench of dried fish, offal, bird excrement and rotting seaweed, in tropical heat, is to be avoided.

That evening, with a rising tide and an onshore breeze, we finally made it into Bagan Siapiapi harbour. I staggered out of the boat and immediately collapsed. The others were not in much better shape, except for Frank who was his usual indomitable self. We had each lost over two stones in weight over the month. Frank immediately arranged for the Dutch administrator to pay off the boatman who set sail back to Malaya the next day. The local Dutch took us up to the rest house where we were soon tucking in to the first real meal we had had for a month – porridge, eggs and bacon, bread and jam – with the disastrous results that can be imagined. We were relieved of all our filthy clothes, and those worth saving were sent to the dhobi whilst we were given sarongs to wear. Our wounds and bites were attended to by the local doctor. I was given a massive injection of quinine and my ulcerated posterior dosed liberally with sulphanide ointment, and dressed.

We stayed in Bagan Siapiapi for two days. On the third evening we were taken by motorboat southwards to Benkalis, arriving there at about midnight. By this time my fever had returned and I was immediately taken off to hospital. Frank and Ronald joined a group of Malayan Volunteer Air Force officers who had been evacuated from Singapore, while the soldiers were taken to a military camp. I never saw any of them again, but 20 years later, at a drinks party in Bishopsbourne, we met the sister of the Argyll officer. He had got away from Sumatra to India and survived the war.

I had recovered sufficiently after two days to be allowed to rejoin my friends. After a few days gathering strength and writing our report on the events of the last four weeks, we began to think about getting back to Singapore. It was now the first week of February and the latest news was that the British Army had withdrawn over the causeway, which was then blown – and with it any hope of saving Singapore. Together with the road and rail link, the island's water supply from Johore was carried in a large mains pipe on the causeway. The enemy was now only a matter of 1,200 yards from Singapore, and could be seen strutting about the streets and jetties of Johore Bahru.

Despite the depressing news we were determined to get back to Singapore as soon as possible in order, amongst other things, to submit our report on our operation to the intelligence officers. In retrospect our determination in this respect was the height of stupidity. Our report would be out of date, the failure of our operation quite academic, and our usefulness on the condemned island minimal. To be fair, I think that we all realised this at the time, but we felt that we had a duty to try to make the report, not only confirm the negative results of our operation, but to find out what had happened to Spencer Chapman and his party and, perhaps above all, to ensure that any future operations would be better planned and equipped.

A Dane named W.O. Grut, a planter from the Telok Anson area and a pilot with the Malaya Volunteer Air Force, had a Tiger Moth and flew every second day to Singapore, returning the following day, usually with a government official as passenger. Grut agreed to fly each of us back to Singapore, starting with Frank. I was to be the last, to give me another few days to recover.

We had gone over the report that Frank was to make. It was a surprisingly full one, as it was quite remarkable how much we had recorded – Japanese unit insignia, numbers of tanks and troop carriers, the morale of the civilian population, the (lack of) demolition of road and rail bridges, rolling stock, estate and tin mines – all of which might have been valuable if it had not been too late. We all agreed that 'Operation Balls-up' had achieved next to nothing in the five weeks that we had been on active service, except, perhaps, the rescue of seven British servicemen who would live to fight another day.

Frank duly departed, followed by Ronald two days later, and then it was my turn.

Before take-off Grut warned me that the Japs had greatly increased their air activity, now that Singapore was under siege. The Tiger Moth's maximum speed was under 100 mph and the flight took about two hours. We flew at a height of 500 feet, on a beautiful tropical morning, under a cloudless blue sky. The straits and islands around Singapore looked so peaceful. Suddenly there was a whistle on the voice tube and I looked behind me to see Grut pointing at a Zero fighter diving down on us. It over-shot us, banked round in a wide circle and flew straight back towards us. I braced myself for the bullets, when it suddenly turned away and disappeared. Grut tapped me on the shoulder and raised his thumb. When we landed on Singapore Race Course he explained that the Jap had been unable to throttle back sufficiently to be able to shoot at us. I was glad to be back on the ground. Grut had a parachute. I had not.

Having landed I had to decide where I was to report. It seemed strange not to have to take cover every time one heard a vehicle. Soldiers were everywhere. But it depressed me to see how far morale had dropped. Even that of the Lancashire lads whom we had shepherded for over a month in far more trying circumstances, and, it goes without saying, the Scots', had been much higher. But, of course, we had not been on the receiving end of a constant barrage of bombs and shells. I hitched a lift into Singapore, having decided that I should report to Headquarters Malaya Command at Fort Canning. I walked up the hill and was directed to Army Intelligence where the very first officer to whom I spoke knew all about me, having debriefed both Frank and Ronald. After questioning he took me to see the Corps Commander Lieutenant General Sir Lewis Heath, at corps headquarters somewhere behind the Raffles Hotel. 'Piggy' Heath, who had a withered hand from a First World War wound, had distinguished himself in East Africa, but had been handed a hopeless task in Malaya. He was most affable, said that he had studied Frank's report, asked a few questions, and congratulated me on a first-class effort, after which the intelligence officer put a car at my disposal with instructions to report for further orders to a Captain Morgan at the Cathay Building. He was known as 'Careful Morgan'. His initials were F.L.

Before seeing Morgan I ran in to Harry Foston and two other Guthrie planters in the foyer of the building. Harry had a bottle of gin on him so we had a couple of 'sharpeners' and swapped our stories. My first question of Morgan was as to the whereabouts of Frank and Ronald. He said that they had already been given their new task and that I had been detailed for something quite different. I was most incensed and demanded to be allowed to accompany them. Morgan pointed out that this was impossible as they were due to depart at dusk. He explained that they were to join up with Richard Broome and John Davis to try to rescue a lot of our troops who had been cut off in the Batu Pahat area and to organise their evacuation by sea to Sumatra. The whole scheme seemed pretty cock-eyed to me, but, nevertheless, I still wanted to join them. John Davis, who was to win the DSO for his exploits with Force 136, told me many years later what had happened on this operation. (See Appendix B)

Morgan told me to get down to a wharf near the Singapore Cricket Club where I would find Frank and Ronald loading stores on to their boat, and to use his car. I soon found my friends and after boisterous greetings we repaired to the SCC pavilion for several gins. Frank said that he had asked for me to be in his party but as it was considered doubtful that the Tiger Moth service from Sumatra could be sustained for another day someone else had been selected. He said that I had an equally important task, requiring someone with war experience and a knowledge of Malay. Something about organising another escape route, and that Morgan would give me my orders. So we said our farewells. Their fate could have been mine.

Escape

Mid-February 1942 – Mid-March 1942

On the way back to Morgan whom should I bump into but Reid Tweedie; we had both jumped into the same monsoon drain as shelter during an air raid. He was sharing a flat nearby with a couple of other doctors. We arranged to meet later that day. He had left Kamuning with two cases of whisky, a few clothes and a treasured Persian rug which he did not want to lose. Reid slept on this rug during the three and a half years he was in the Sime Road and Changi prisons and returned with it to Kamuning in March 1946. He sold the rug to me for $50. It is under my feet as I write.

Morgan told me to take the rest of the day off and to report back early the next day. I decided to go down to Raffles Place to see whom I could find at Guthrie's. The office had been hit, it is said, by the very first bomb to have dropped on Singapore. They were now in temporary premises in one of the banks' buildings. There I found Bertie Essen, an old friend from Penang, who told me how he had been able to book a passage for Jean and John on the *Kramer*, bound for Tanjong Priok, the port for Batavia, with the intention of travelling on to Australia. This was good news and the relief was tremendous, and called for a celebratory gin or two. We were interrupted by another air raid and took shelter in the bank's strong room, surrounded by stacks of dollar notes and security boxes. I wondered what would happen to the boxes' contents.

Bertie told me that all upcountry bank accounts had been transferred to Singapore, so I was able to arrange for all our money to be transferred to the Bank of New South Wales in Perth, Western Australia, as I was sure that Jean would try to reach there. Bertie also told me that as the estates fell into enemy hands all staff, European and Asian, had been automatically dismissed by Guthrie's. Thus my salary had stopped in the middle of January.

On my way to the bank I met another old friend, Len Ogier, who told me that he had seen John and Jean board the *Kramer*, and that she had given him our brand new Austin in which she had driven down from Kamuning. I went back to the Patterson & Symon's chummery, where he was staying, to collect it. Len also told me that Charles Martine was staying in the Borneo Company mess. I immediately drove there, ignoring the air raid as it appeared to be concentrated somewhere up Bukit Timah Road, and found Charles and several others of my acquaintance. It was agreed that I should join them for the duration, although it was obvious that this would not be long. Food was in short supply, but whisky was not, so the mess boys were kept busy supplying us with stengahs until the early hours.

The following morning, I reported again to Morgan. The battle for Singapore had begun. The Japanese had crossed over the strait from Johore and the city was now under continual bombardment from their guns. At night the sky was ablaze with exploding shells and the fires from burning buildings. The sound of machine-gun fire was constant. Now and again we heard the thunderous explosions from naval guns. The oil storage tanks were blazing and covering everywhere with oily soot. Despite everything, there was no sign of panic, even though in our hearts we knew that the end was near.

At my meeting with Morgan and another SOE officer, Basil Goodfellow, I was ordered to take a lorry out to the army central stores depot near the Ford factory on Bukit Timah Road and load it with tinned food, water cans and a quantity of plastic explosive (what this last was for I never found out), and then to drive it to the harbour opposite the Padang, where I would find a Sergeant Lamb on board a small coastal steamer. The stores were to be put on board and Morgan, Goodfellow and two naval reserve officers would join us and we were to set sail the next day for Sumatra. The plan was to plot and provision an escape route along the islands between Singapore and Sumatra.

I collected the lorry and drove out to the depot where, to my surprise, I found Walter Northcote-Green and another friend from Ipoh, Bunny Byers, secretary to the Perak Racing Association. The lorry was quickly loaded up, although the water cans were empty, the mains to that area of the island having been blown up. Walter was very interested in what I was doing. I hesitated before telling him, because it was meant to be secret, but decided that there was no point in my establishing an escape route if was so secret that no one would benefit. To anyone with a modicum of intelligence it was obvious that Singapore would fall in a matter of days and it was the duty of everyone to escape if at all possible. While chatting over a beer I noticed several Bren guns stacked in a corner. Walter let me take one and, together with several full magazines, I carried it all the way to Colombo. I said my farewell to Walter with a heavy heart, uncertain that I would ever see my old friend again.

I drove back to the Borneo Company mess and, finding the water there still flowing, filled all the water cans. I then parked the lorry under the verandah and joined Charles and the others for the first stengah of the evening. We had a very cheery evening, in spite of the air raids and the shelling. Although several shells landed in the compound, none hit the house. It was not until morning, when I saw the shell holes in the garden and the direct hit on a nearby house, that I remembered the high explosives in the lorry parked immediately below where we had been enjoying ourselves.

I told Charles what I was doing and did my best to persuade him to accompany me, but without success. There was no military reason for him to be in Singapore. Sarawak had been evacuated whilst Charles had been in Singapore on Borneo Company business and to collect his elder daughter Virginia from her school in Cameron Highlands. His wife Pat had trekked through the jungle from Kuching to Pontianak, on the south-west coast of Borneo, with their younger daughter Patty, aged three: an epic journey of courage and endurance. They had flown by seaplane to Batavia, to where Charles, unable to return to Sarawak, had managed to fly with Virginia. Satisfied that his family would get off to Australia he had then flown back to Singapore, driven by, in my view, a mistaken sense of duty, only to be 'put in the bag' with so many other of my friends.

Immediately after breakfast and farewells I drove down to the harbour in the lorry, followed by Charles' syce driving my Austin. I made contact with Sergeant Lamb who, it transpired, was the brother of a planter I had known in Kedah.

Lamb and I spent several hours transferring the stores from lorry to sampan to ship, which was anchored about 50 yards from the jetty. At about noon the air raid warning sirens sounded and we saw at least 50 enemy bombers immediately overhead. We took cover behind a wall and watched as they showered the harbour and anchorage with bombs, hitting many ships and lighters, setting fire and sinking most. Our little ship was totally unscathed.

Having loaded the stores I went off in my car to report to Morgan, who told me that he, Basil Goodfellow and the RMNR officers would be boarding later that afternoon. I was irritated to be instructed, rather than asked, to take both his and Goodfellow's personal kit back to the harbour, particularly as both had a lot more than me, including their two Dunlopillo mattresses, which I had to strap on to the roof. I saw no reason why I should be expected to provide a private taxi service, even as part of the war effort. I called in to the Singapore Cold Storage and bought some more tinned stores, I thought, in my naivety, for my own personal use. In the event they were shared with those who had had less foresight.

When I got back to the ship Lamb and I made ourselves tiffin, after which we assumed our duties as stokers and built up a head of steam. We were then joined by the naval officers, looking very pukka in their newly dhobied uniforms, in marked contrast to us. Then, with Lamb's help, and with great reluctance, I pushed my car off the jetty into deep water. Many of my friends, far brighter than I, obtained chits signed by officers stating that their cars had been commandeered by the military, and so in due course were compensated. I foolishly neglected to do this, so received no compensation. I could even have signed a chit myself.

It was now 13 February. Towards evening Morgan and Goodfellow came aboard and we weighed anchor and set a course for the first of the islands. Blakang Mati and Pulau Bukum were ablaze from burning oil tanks, whether bombed by the enemy or blown up by ourselves, I am unsure. The whole ship was quickly covered with oily soot, which penetrated even down to the engine room. Lamb and

I took turns to stoke the boiler. I was also the ship's gunner, as I had the Bren gun and defied anyone even to touch it. In addition to the Europeans on board we had two Chinese; one to act as pilot and the other to help in the engine room. The old ship must have been all of 40 years old, with a wooden hull lined with tin plate. The lavatory consisted of two short planks jutting out aft from the ship, over the propeller, and with a handrail. One held on to this and squatted, and should there be a slight swell running the result was a most efficient bidet.

When on deck I could see that we were only one of many ships and boats of all shapes and sizes heading away from Singapore. Avoiding other vessels became so difficult in the darkness that we came in close to an island and dropped anchor for the night. Looking back we could see the fires raging on Singapore. We got under way again as soon as it was sufficiently light to see and reached an island which was deemed suitable for the first dump. Lamb and I went ashore and I made contact with the headman who agreed to find a hiding place for the stores, to provide some villagers to help with the portering, and to offer assistance to future escapees. We then returned to the ship, loaded a sampan, rowed back to the beach, unloaded and carried the food and water into the nearby jungle, doing our best to hide the dump from immediate view. Then back to the ship and down into the engine room to raise a head of steam for the next move.

We repeated this operation on five or six islands in the archipelago between Singapore and Sumatra, anchoring each night near land. In all this we received no help at all from Goodfellow or Morgan, which made me very angry and I said as much, in spite of being junior in rank, suggesting they lend a hand. But with no success. They always appeared to be deep in conference with the naval officers, or helping themselves to the tinned stores I had bought for myself in Singapore.

The Japs continued to bomb and machine gun the escaping ships and many were sunk with terrible loss of life. The atrocities perpetrated on those unfortunate to have been on the *Kuala* and the *Vyner Brooke*, for instance, are sickening to read about even 45 years after the events. I have never been able to understand how the Japanese, by and large, have escaped the equally much-deserved opprobrium of the Germans. Perhaps it is ill-placed guilt for dropping the atom bombs. My own considered opinion is that it is a pity that only two were dropped on Japan.

We attracted the attention of Jap bombers during our voyage, and had several narrow escapes from near misses. The sound of bombs exploding in the water was particularly frightening in the engine room. It was like a gigantic hammer blow against the ship's hull. We stopped on numerous occasions to pick up survivors from less fortunate ships, whilst continuing with our job of dropping off stores on the various islands. We reached Djambi, on the east coast of Sumatra, on 17 February, to learn that Singapore had surrendered unconditionally at 1500 hours, on Sunday the 15th.

During the trip Lamb and I had discussed our plans for when we reached Djambi. So far as we were concerned we were due to make for the Indragiri River, where we would join Frank Vanrenen and Ronald Graham or to take part in the rescue operations from Johore. The others decided that they would make for Padang, the main port on the north west coast of Sumatra, on the Indian Ocean, from where they hoped to be picked up by the Royal Navy.

We had not been tied up for long and everyone disembarked when the siren sounded and at least 20 Jap bombers appeared overhead. Our little ship received several direct hits and disintegrated before our eyes. What was left burned furiously. Everything belonging to those who were headed for Padang had been unloaded, but the few possessions that Lamb and I had disappeared up in smoke. I now had nothing in the world except what I stood up in, but having been in a similar predicament before I was not unduly worried. Fate seemed determined that I should not join my planter friends.

Lamb and I then decided that we would also make for Padang, although I must admit to further doubts about Goodfellow and his sense of responsibility to those under his command when I saw him rushing around attempting to get a car for himself, leaving the rest of us to travel by commandeered lorry. In the event none was available so the poor fellow had to slum it with us.

By now it had become apparent that of the remnants of 101 STS gathered on the quayside at Djambi probably only Lamb and myself held genuine military ranks and that the others were civilians with army insignia and honorific (some would say bogus) ranks, a state of affairs I was to find throughout my time in clandestine forces.

I volunteered to drive, certain that I had more experience than anyone else, and not relishing being bumped about in the back. Goodfellow, of course, sat next to me. The drive across Sumatra was uneventful. The countryside was beautiful, less developed even than Malaya. We stayed the first night at a very pleasant little town in the foothills of the mountain range that runs down the western side of the island. It had a clean and comfortable government rest house, so we were able to enjoy hot baths and clean bed linen and good food. The town post office was still functioning so I sent a cable to Jean at the Bank of New South Wales in Perth. She eventually received it, forwarded to Melbourne, some two and a half months later, and was greatly relieved to hear from me for the first time since early December. But, of course, by that time Sumatra had also fallen, so she had to accept that by then I was most probably a POW. The mountains exceed 12,000 feet in places, covered in jungle, and the views were breathtaking. The utter peace, except for our own engine noise, made the war seem very far away. I do not remember seeing any other traffic on the road.

We reached Padang late the next afternoon and found a well-established transit camp, with a large contingent of Europeans from Malaya in occupation, mainly senior government people, police officers, PWD and other administrators, most a lot better fed, clothed and equipped than Lamb and me, and obviously having been in residence for quite some time. We reported to the camp commandant and were allotted accommodation.

On checking something in Spencer Chapman's *The Jungle is Neutral* I found the following passage: 'The last of the organisation to leave Malaya was Major Basil Goodfellow who got out of Singapore and made his way to Sumatra by the escape route.' No mention of Lamb and myself, yet we had done practically everything except steer the blasted ship! I am not blaming Freddy, because he could only have written of what he had been told by Goodfellow or someone else in SOE.

We spent the first two days at Padang relaxing as best we could, and I drew some pay. On the third day a notice appeared to the effect that a destroyer was expected shortly and all wishing to take their chances should be on the quayside ready for immediate embarkation and departure. All our party duly congregated, with the exception of Basil Goodfellow who, having evidently received prior information – which I do not remember him passing on – would remain until the morrow when there was a cruiser expected. I met him again briefly in Calcutta in late 1944. I was unaware at the time that he had been contacted prior to my recruitment into ISLD and had reported unfavourably on me, suggesting that I should be returned to regimental soldiering as being unsuitable for clandestine forces – this after I had twice been mentioned in despatches for my efforts with V Force in Burma.

The destroyer HMS *Encounter* came alongside that evening, embarked all wishing to be taken off, and sailed within the hour. The officers were invited into the wardroom for drinks and a meal, but as there was insufficient cabin space the rescued had to find odd corners on deck to sleep. I had grabbed Goodfellow's Dunlopillo mattress when he had discarded it on the quayside at Djambi so was quite comfortable on a quiet part of the upper deck, until we were struck by a tropical rain storm. Alongside me was a naval rating sheltering under a large groundsheet, so I suggested that he shared my mattress while I shared his groundsheet. We were comfortable and dry, but the thunder and lightning and the sound of the torrential rain on the deck made sleep impossible, so we talked. He was a 'writer' on the *Prince of Wales* and was one of the few who had been rescued when it was sunk. He had been landed in Singapore from where he had escaped to Sumatra, and now had been rescued again. He said that he had been sunk in the Mediterranean, in the Atlantic and now in the Pacific (actually, it was the South China Sea, but I did not wish to spoil his story) and promised that as long as I was with him I would be safe. Alas, he was to be sunk again when the *Encounter* went to the bottom less than a week later. I have often wondered whether he survived yet again.

After sailing we were informed that we were headed for Tanjong

Priok, the port for Batavia. On arrival, at about noon the next day, we were met by Colonel Killeray, the head of the SOE Oriental Mission, who had laid on a lorry to take us and our kit (in my case just my Bren gun, toothbrush, razor and Dunlopillo mattress) to the Des Indes Hotel in Batavia. This was luxury indeed. The Des Indes was on par with the Raffles in Singapore and the Runnymede in Penang. I was beginning to learn that those in SOE looked after themselves well. After three months of active service varying from the bearable to the indescribable, the few days I was to spend here, at His Majesty's expense, were to be enjoyed to the full.

One of the first people I met on arriving at the Des Indes was Billie Graham, Ronald's wife. I was able to bring her up to date about Ronald's activities since early January until I had parted company with him and Frank in Singapore a week or so earlier. I dined with Billie on most evenings, and before I left she gave me a letter addressed to Ronald as she felt that I could well meet up with him again before she did. I kept this in my wallet until I was able to return it to her in London in 1944, although unaware then of his fate.

I made enquiries about Jean and John, but learned very little other than that they had got off to Australia. I also heard that Pat Martine and her daughters had passed through.

I became quite friendly with Ian Morrison, *The Times*'s war correspondent who was to feature in Han Suyin's autobiographical novel *A Many Splendoured Thing*, and who was to be killed during the Korean War; also with Jim Gavin and quite a few of the 101 STS staff from Singapore, all fellow residents in the hotel. All the while the Japanese were constantly bombing Tanjong Priok and occasionally Batavia, but we were getting used to it by now, so life went on with daily conferences with Killeray and other senior SOE staff, at which nothing much seemed to be resolved, until one day we were offered the option of getting to Australia, presumably as part of an SOE organisation there, or making our way to Chungking to instruct the Kuomintang Chinese in guerrilla warfare. I thought when I heard this latter suggestion that it was strange that it had not occurred to the powers-that-be that the Chinese had been indulging in guerrilla warfare against the Japs for at least the previous five years, and *they* could teach us a great deal. My sojourn behind the enemy lines did not involve guerrilla warfare, but I could at least recognise a Jap if I saw one, which was more than could be said for the majority of the other SOE 'specialists'. Most, including Lamb, opted for Australia and left that night, leaving only three of us to attempt the trip to China – although how we were to get there was not disclosed. I must admit I was sorely tempted by Australia, knowing Jean and John would be there, but pride, in retrospect misplaced, prevailed. However, it must be said that many of those who did go subsequently distinguished themselves.

The war news was entirely depressing. The Battle of the Java Sea was fought in the final days of February and many fine British and Dutch ships were sunk. The enemy landed on Java at three main beachheads, the nearest to Batavia some 25 miles to the south. Our situation was now critical, and we had to get away immediately. We could no longer rely on the Royal Navy as their ships were mostly on the bottom. The *Encounter*, together with the cruiser *Exeter* of River Plate fame, had been discovered by a very much more powerful Japanese fleet in the Sunda Strait, and sunk by overwhelming gunfire.

Realising that we had been deserted by SOE, in the company of a few equally desperate men I wandered around the dockside at Tanjong Priok looking for a ship capable of making the journey to Ceylon or Australia. There were several steamers moored alongside, some obviously semi-derelict, others very damaged from bombing or shellfire, and yet others seemingly in sound condition but, on closer inspection, discovered to be out of coal or holed below the water line. Shortly after midday we met two Straits Steamship officers who said that they had found a ship, abandoned supposedly as unseaworthy but which, from their rapid survey, seemed capable of getting to Ceylon. Furthermore, it had sufficient coal, water and victuals aboard. They could raise a few more naval officers, but would we like to volunteer as stokers and deck hands? Would we! By now I considered myself a fully fledged member of the National Union of Stokers. It was agreed that we would assemble on board at six that evening, which would give us time to collect as many stragglers as we could find who were prepared to risk a night dash through the Sunda

Strait – it would be suicidal to attempt to sail out of Tanjong Priok in daylight. Meanwhile we would have to risk the ship being destroyed at the quayside.

We hurried back to the Des Indes, gathered about two dozen other escapees from Malaya, and with our few possessions returned to the docks and embarked. The officers were waiting and quickly allotted cabins and duties. The few women volunteered for the galley and the elderly men were appointed deck hands, leaving the young, more able-bodied as stokers and engine room crew. I was also master gunner, my Bren gun being the only weapon we possessed.

Under my direction we stokers soon got up a good head of steam, and at dusk we slipped out of the harbour to sea. The date was 1 March. The Captain informed us that the only route offering any chance of success was via the Sunda Strait which, with luck, we could be through and out into the Indian Ocean before daylight. We would then steam due west, as far from the normal sea lanes to Ceylon as possible and out of range of shore-based aircraft, before heading for Colombo. We were all well aware that the Japanese navy was in strength in the Sunda Strait. In fact it later transpired that a large contingent of their warships was actually steaming eastwards through the strait at the same time as we were heading westwards, but mercifully the weather was poor so we were not spotted.

We kept a steady westerly course for five days before turning towards Ceylon, all the time gaining confidence that we had avoided the enemy. We would not have been so complacent had we known that a substantial part of the Imperial Japanese Navy battle fleet was between us and our goal. Admiral Sir James Somerville had lost the cruisers *Dorsetshire* and *Cornwall* and the aircraft carrier *Hermes* to the enemy. At the same time Jap carrier-based aircraft had bombed Colombo and Trincomalee, and their submarines had taken an enormous toll of our merchant shipping. The Japanese then withdrew into the Bay of Bengal, leaving their submarines to continue with the destruction.

We zigzagged our way northwards, thankful at the dawn of each day that we had been undetected, carried out our normal watches, and, off-watch, did our best to sleep. I guarded my Dunlopillo mattress almost as fiercely as my Bren gun. The engine room was incredibly hot; I recalled the lascar stokers on the *Achilles* in the Red Sea, back in 1930. Coming up on deck after a four-hour shift was bliss. Rations were adequate and there was plenty of drinking water, but I do not remember any alcohol. Nor do I remember any unpleasantness between anyone on board. Everyone, including the galley staff and stokers, was required to do their turn at plane spotting duty. One day I spent some time watching four enormous sharks, swimming lazily in our wake, diving and surfacing like dolphins. I remembered being told many years previously that sharks always followed doomed ships, but kept that theory to myself.

At daybreak on 8 March the Captain told us that he expected to reach Colombo at sunset. We all gave a hooray at this good news. At about three in the afternoon the bow lookout reported sighting a periscope. Immediate alarm and despondency. We had visions of being so near yet so far. We knew that it could only be Japanese. The periscope circled us twice before submerging. Anxious minutes were spent waiting for the torpedo to strike. All eyes were glued to the ocean surface to spot its course so I could attempt to destroy it with my Bren gun. We zigzagged more frequently. After about 10 minutes it reappeared, circled us again, and disappeared. That was the last we saw of it. The most likely explanation, we decided when we had reached Colombo and had heard the latest war news, was that the submarine had used all its torpedoes to sink shipping in the area, had spotted our wireless aerials and, realising that we were only a short flying time from Ceylon, would have reckoned on us radioing for help. The Jap submarine commander was not to know that we did not possess a radio. For the same reason he probably decided against surfacing to shell us. We could think of no other explanation. That very afternoon several merchantmen had been sunk by enemy submarines in the approaches to Colombo.

Soon after this excitement we saw the outline of Ceylon and just before sunset we reached Colombo roads and dropped anchor. The whole motley crew then gave three cheers for the Captain. 'Don't thank me. Thank God,' was his somewhat over-dramatic reply. We were not permitted to go ashore until the following morning, which we all found particularly irksome, but at least someone sent several bottles of whisky aboard, so we had an enjoyable party and I lay down on my Dunlopillo not entirely sober.

The next morning, before being allowed ashore, we were interviewed by an officer in naval intelligence. The first thing I did on landing was to make for the post office to send a cable to Jean at the Bank of New South Wales in Perth. This said, 'Still in the running. Suggest you make for England. All my love.' I thought that, if she could get there, England would be safer than anywhere in the Pacific area, in spite of the bombing and the food shortages. The whole of South East Asia had fallen, including the Dutch East Indies and the Philippines; Australia looked ripe for the picking, as did India. And if Australia fell, as seemed a distinct possibility at the time, even New Zealand looked vulnerable. I do not know why I did not think of my birthplace South Africa, where I had many cousins. Or Canada. But I knew that if she could not be with me Jean would prefer to be with her own family, and, with typical British arrogance, I did not believe that England would be conquered.

From December 1941 to October 1942 must have been the bleakest months of the whole war. Singapore and Malaya had fallen, the enemy was sweeping through Burma to the very gates of India, Ceylon had been raided, the British Far Eastern fleet almost wiped out and the remnants withdrawn across the Indian Ocean to Mombasa, the Axis had driven the Eighth Army back to El Alamein in Egypt and now possessed the whole of North Africa, the Germans were pushing down through the Balkans to Greece to threaten our oil supplies in Persia and Iraq, and the Battle of the Atlantic against the U-boats seemed to be going Germany's way, too. The only bright spot was that the Americans were now in the war. And yet I saw no despondency or alarm in the faces of the British, civilians or military. It really never occurred to anyone that we would lose.

I reported to army GHQ in Colombo where I was interviewed at length about my Malayan activities, then issued with money and a rail pass to Calcutta, and instructed to leave Colombo that night. And, to my chagrin, I was relieved of my Bren gun. I spent the morning shopping for clothes and toiletries. In those days officers had to purchase every bit of military clothing and personal kit. A second lieutenant's pay was £274 per annum, and, at one time when she was an ambulance driver in London, Jean was earning more than me.

We said our farewells to the civilians and the naval officers, and the soldiers in our party caught the night mail to Talaimanar (the rail head at the north of Ceylon), from where we caught the ferry to Rameswaram on the Indian mainland. There we entrained again and slowly wended our way northwards via Madras to Calcutta. I was fascinated to see stations bearing names famous from the time of Clive such as Pondicherry, Madras, Cuttack and Nagapattam. After Malaya, the poverty of India was heartrending. In fact, in all my travels, I have never seen such human degradation as to be found around Howrah, in Calcutta. The journey took three days. The carriage was hot and dirty, meals were taken in station restaurants when the train stopped, usually for about half an hour, for water and coal. Each compartment had a shower and lavatory, and the seats folded down as bunks. Even in 1942 it was quite an adventure to go from Colombo to Calcutta by train.

When we finally arrived at Howrah Station, Calcutta, the RTO (railway transport officer) sent us to the Great Eastern Hotel on Chowringhee, now an officers' transit hotel. Not quite the Des Indes, but then, of course, I was no longer with SOE.

Marking Time

April 1942 – July 1942

Calcutta was a vast city, then the second largest in the Empire. There were the government, commercial and European residential quarters, but the rest was a vast sprawl of indescribably squalid, appallingly filthy, congested slum, where 8 million inhabitants eked out a meagre and degrading existence, so wretched that no words of mine can adequately convey my first impressions. But, as time went by, and like the majority of my fellow Europeans, I became inured to the sights and smells.

There seemed to be quite a few Special Forces officers billeted at the Great Eastern. One, Barney Le Seilleur, questioned me about my experiences in Malaya behind the lines and the subsequent events leading up to my escape, before taking me to Calcutta Fort where I went through the same rigmarole again, but this time for a colonel. After this interview I was passed on to a staff captain whom I realised I had met several years before in Singapore, Maurice Yates. He told me to take two weeks leave and suggested that he should telephone a Darjeeling tea planter, Colonel Treanor, retired from the Indian Army, who put up officers for short leaves. This arranged, it was agreed that I would take the train to Darjeeling a couple of days later. Meanwhile I would stay on at the Great Eastern while it was decided what to do with me.

My first night in the hotel, in a comfortable bed with clean sheets, was marred somewhat by my being woken at about midnight by something running across my face. Turning on the light I saw quite the largest cockroach I had ever seen – over two inches long. I despatched it with my plimsoll. I could not deal similarly with the rats that stood their ground when I returned to my room, looking at me, before scuttling off into the bathroom. This was definitely not the

Raffles or the Des Indes!

I caught the night mail to Jalpaigury, at the foothills of the Himalayas, where I breakfasted at the station hotel, before taking the train up to Darjeeling. This railway must be unique. First surveyed and laid in the 1880s it was still using the original engines and rolling stock, all in excellent condition. The track wound its way up the mountains, sometimes so circuitously that one could look out of the carriage window and see the engine above going in the opposite direction. The views were terrific, and all the time one could see the high peaks through gaps in the cloud. I travelled this route on three occasions and much preferred the train to a bus or taxi. The hill peoples, mainly Nepalese, are magnificent, as one would expect knowing the Gurkha.

Shortly before we arrived in Darjeeling the clouds clamped down, blotting out everything, rather like an old London pea souper, and it began to rain so that when I took a rickshaw from the station to the Planters' Club I saw very little of my surroundings. The street lights were barely visible through the mist, the passers-by were huddled in shawls. I had arranged with Colonel Treanor that I would spend the first night at the club, and he would collect me the next morning. The club was cheerful and the manager and his daughter gave me a warm welcome. After a few drinks, an excellent dinner and post-prandial conversations with one or two fellow guests, I went to bed, feeling very lonely and far from home.

Nothing could have prepared me for the next morning. The bearer brought the usual chota hazri (breakfast) and pulled back the curtains to let the sun stream in. I could only gasp and gape at the most fantastic scene imaginable. There spread out before me were mile upon mile of the snow-covered peaks of the high Himalayas, and framed in the window, towering over everything else, even though 40 miles away, was Kanchenjunga, all 28,000 feet of it. Even from that distance I had to look up at the summit. Living in Malaya and having visited so many far-off places, I suppose that I had become somewhat blasé of beautiful surroundings and vistas. But this was different; totally overpowering. I could not dress and get outside quickly enough. I wandered up to the maidan, from where I could get a better view of the nearby hills and valleys and, above all, the mountains. To this day I have never seen such overwhelming beauty.

Colonel and Mrs Treanor collected me as arranged from the club and, after tiffin at the Gymkana Club, we drove out to their tea garden. The Treanors were delightful. In his early 50s, he had fought in France during the Great War and had served on the Frontier on several occasions since then. The tea garden – they were not called estates, as in Malaya – was 25 miles out of Darjeeling, on a series of hills, with the awe-inspiring backdrop of Kanchenjunga. The bungalow was on a plateau, with tennis court and swimming pool and surrounded by every known Asian and European plant and flower in full bloom. It was school holidays so their 17-year-old daughter and 15-year-old son were there too, and made a delightful family. Mrs Treanor mothered and fussed over me, and soon had me back to the best of health. The excellent food, the quiet days going round the tea garden on a pony, quite the best way to see over the tea bushes, and the long evenings in front of a log fire made the war in general and the last hectic three months in particular seemed a very long way away. The fortnight went all too quickly.

Shortly after four thirty on the morning of the day before I was due to return to Calcutta, the Colonel and I mounted our ponies and rode steadily uphill for an hour, until we reached the peak of Tiger Hill, nearly 14,000 feet up. We dismounted and he pointed towards the northwest and told me to look. Shortly after dawn, as the sun rose behind us, we saw the twin peaks of Mount Everest bathed in sunlight and crystal clear, more than 140 miles away. A minute later they had disappeared from view behind clouds. Fifty years ago it was a sight to boast about; today the experience is commonplace.

When I got back to the Great Eastern Hotel I found that my posting still had not come through. So, having nothing better to do I spent most mornings lazing at the Calcutta Swimming Club, the afternoons, after a lie off, writing letters and reading the newspapers to catch up with the war situation around the world, and then dinner and a movie with a little gang of like-minded officers, similarly apparently unemployed, many of whom, no doubt myself included, would have been referred to by a few regular officers of my acquaintance as 'temporary gentlemen'. I never learned whether this was because some of us wartime officers were not considered really gentlemanly enough to hold the King's Commission, or whether they referred to the military ranks held by many in clandestine forces.

Nevertheless, even then I felt something of an outsider, for often when I returned to the hotel lounge I would find three or four of my companions deep in conversation which would be broken off when I approached. On one occasion I heard someone say 'Good God, you can't get rid of him. He is the only one of us who has seen action and can recognise a Jap,' obviously referring to me. Later I came to realise that the foundations of SOE's Force 136 were being laid (in a typically British way) over drinks, in the lounge of an hotel, and Le Seilleur and the others were discussing the administrative arrangements of the organisation. Eventually, when operations were being planned, when I would have been of use, I was away in Arakan with V Force. A lucky escape.

I met Maurice Yates quite often. One day he told me that he had advised those responsible that, because of my knowledge of the Tamil language, I should be posted to the 4/3 Madras Regiment, then stationed at Barrackpore, just outside Calcutta. Shortly afterwards my posting came through.

Barrackpore, on the Hooghly River, was where Eastern Army Headquarters was located. They had taken over the large Georgian mansion which had been the winter residence of the Governor of Bengal. The 4/3 Madras Regiment occupied the race course, and Regimental Headquarters and the officers' mess were in the grandstand. The Madras Regiment, not to be confused with the Madras Sappers & Miners, who remained loyal and earned undying fame in the Great War, had been disbanded after the Mutiny – it was one of the first to mutiny – and only reformed in 1939. It was now a training battalion.

The colonel, who was seldom sober after tea, was a frightful bore. The many stories of Flanders and the Frontier he had to tell were amusing and interesting on the first half dozen occasions they were heard. But I do remember a certain Captain Noronha, the very finest of Indian officers. His English was perfect, his accent impeccable, and he was a great one for the girls. It came as no surprise to learn that he rose to become a full general and commander-in-chief during India's war with China.

I was very definitely a supernumerary, a general dogsbody for everyone and everything. I stood behind the company commander on parade. And I very quickly discovered that my estate Tamil was not the native tongue of the Madrassi for when I was in the process of giving orders to a sepoy in fluent Tamil he interrupted: 'Sorry, Sahib, no speak English.'

It was here, in my tent and by the light of a hurricane lamp, that I wrote up the events of the previous four months. Unaccountably these notes have survived to this day

I was attached to a unit on Dum Dum airfield to interrogate army stragglers who had made their way out of Burma, by tracks and across rivers in the mountains that separated Burma from India. I must have been one of the very few interrogators who knew what this had involved. Poor chaps, thousands of them and all in pretty poor shape, their uniforms torn to shreds, very often without weapons or equipment, and with no idea of the whereabouts of their units, or whether their units even still existed. It was our task to sort them out and return them to their own units or into holding units. We were also instructed to sort out the genuine stragglers from deserters, but this was impossible. I reckoned that anyone who survived the hellish retreat out of Burma was a hero in his own way. It was not the soldier's fault that the army he belonged to was ill-prepared for the impossible task it was called on to do. I have found that officers sitting on courts martial or boards of enquiry often had little or no first hand experience or knowledge of the matter over which they are sitting in judgement or enquiring into.

Shortly after this I was put in command of a platoon and sent down to Diamond Harbour, a promontory on the Hooghly some 30 miles south of Calcutta, and a possible landing place for an enemy invasion. It was a strong defensive position, and we were backed up by field and ack-ack guns. We were required to stand to at dawn and at dusk, and to do some patrolling along the river bank, but otherwise I spent my time wildfowling with Captain Noronha, and reading.

Towards the end of April I was sent as second in command of a company to escort a thousand Italian POWs being transported from Calcutta to Bhopal. This entailed an eight-day slow, dirty and hot rail journey across the widest part of India. As ours was a special train it was shunted into sidings whenever regular mail trains were due, and this meant long waits in temperatures of over 100 degrees Fahrenheit. To our annoyance the prisoners were fed by contractors at pre-arranged stops with excellent and varied meals, whilst we British guarding them made do with standard issue bully beef and biscuits. We soon altered this and instructed the contractors to feed the escort before the prisoners and with the same food.

The Italians were a cheerful crowd and very obviously glad to be out of the North and East African battles. They also kept us entertained with operatic excerpts, almost all having, it appeared, excellent tenor voices. They sang Verdi and Puccini as British troops would sing the latest Vera Lynn song or 'Roll Out the Barrel'. However, after a while they became bored and started pulling the communication cord, bringing the train to a sudden grinding and shuddering halt, which often caused a hold-up for the express trains following. After several repetitions I lost patience. With the Maltese interpreter I went along each carriage and threatened that the next time the cord was pulled unnecessarily I would remove one man from each carriage and hang him by his thumbs in the guard's van. We had not gone more than a few miles when, sure enough, we came to another screeching halt. It was evident that the Italians did not believe that the British would carry out their threat. I had about a dozen purple-faced, sweating, pain-ridden prisoners hanging by chains from the beams in no time at all. We went on our way without further interruptions. In fact I had released them after only about 20 minutes, but kept them in the guard's van for another couple of hours.

I was at Eastern Army Headquarters one morning when, to my surprise, I bumped into Angus Rose, whom, it will be remembered, had been on Freddy Spencer Chapman's first operation behind the Jap lines in Malaya. He was now with the 2nd Battalion Argyll & Sutherland Highlanders, also stationed at Barrackpore. We had a brief chat and agreed to meet up again at the cinema the following evening. After the performance Angus invited me back to his mess and over a few pegs he described a Divisional exercise that was to take place shortly, and asked whether I would like to be an umpire. I readily agreed, as it seemed interesting and would get me away from Barrackpore.

The Divisional scheme was to involve the Air Force and Navy as well as the Army and would be held in the Sundabans, a vast area of creeks and islands in the Ganges delta, and home to the Bengal tiger. I was ordered to take command of a ferryboat and to cover a certain area. The idea was for Red Force to simulate a Japanese sea- and airborne invasion, whilst Blue Force, the Division, was to repel it. I spent a marvellous week cruising around the rivers and creeks. I was able to instruct the ferryboat captain to take me wherever I wished within my allocated area. I felt as if I had my own private yacht. I noted all Red and Blue forces' movements, which were radioed back to Exercise Headquarters. Occasionally I would be instructed to inform a formation that they were hors de combat.

At sunset we would tie up at a riverside village, and after an excellent dinner I would stroll ashore and in broken Bengali talk to the villagers about what we were doing and why. They were obviously totally unaffected by the war and continued with their lives as they had done so for the last thousand years and more. Sometimes I would be invited by the village headman to his house to meet his family.

The sunsets were particularly beautiful, and I can still recall the hundred and one smells of a Bengali village – wood fires, cow dung, human ordure and cooking curry.

On completion of the exercise the umpires gathered back at Barrackpore to report and to discuss the lessons learnt. I was interested to see that amongst the 20 or so umpires I was the most junior by far, still the lowest of the low, a second lieutenant. The rest were majors or colonels who looked at me with some disdain until Angus introduced me as one of the very few present who like himself had seen a Jap at close quarters. This 'wash up' by the umpires brought home to me forcibly that I held very junior rank for my age. Most men of 32 were captains or majors, some even half colonels.

This was the first time that I had given any serious consideration to my lowly rank as hitherto, with 101 STS and during my escape, it had not seemed important. But I did realise that I had only held the King's Commission for five months, so even I could see it was a bit optimistic to expect early promotion. (The commission that I had held in the FMSVF was a Governor's Commission, similar to the Viceroy's Commission in the Indian Army.)

During that April and May, however, I also had another worry. For me they were probably the most anxious weeks in the whole war. Jean and John had sailed on the P&O liner *Strathallan* from Sydney bound for England and, as the ship had a good turn of speed, she was to sail alone, unescorted, across the Pacific, through the Panama Canal, and then across the Atlantic, at a time when the Japanese, known to have a good many submarines, were in the ascendancy in the Pacific, and when the U-boat was winning the Battle of the Atlantic. Of course, I had many second thoughts as to the wisdom of my suggestion that they return home, but by then it was too late. They were on their way. The battalion officers became almost as anxious as I was, and asked for news almost daily. All I knew was that they had sailed. Then one day a cable arrived reporting their safe landfall in Glasgow. I immediately passed on the good news to the colonel and we held a special dinner night in the mess in celebration.

At the end of May I was allowed another leave as, ironically, my previous visit had been considered as sick leave, so I contacted the Treanors and arranged to spend a couple of weeks with them. I repeated my journey up to Darjeeling, only this time it was more enjoyable, as the weather was fine and the views of the Himalayas more constant and breathtaking than ever. I was met at the station and taken straight back to the tea garden. By now I had formed a close friendship with the Treanors and it was like coming home. Sometime during the lazy and happy first week, when we were sitting chatting over a peg and I had voiced my impatience with my present posting, the Colonel said that only the previous week he had met a Brigadier Felix-Williams at the Gymkana Club who had told him that he was responsible for some sort of intelligence-gathering organisation operating behind the enemy lines in Burma. He had been most impressed with the Brigadier's enthusiasm, and suggested that I endeavour to contact him with a view to joining the organisation. I thanked him, said I would, and promptly forgot about it.

Midway through my second week there I began to feel ill and run a high temperature and fever, so the Treanors drove me to the British Military Hospital outside Darjeeling. The doctor took one look at me and ordered me to bed, for not only was I suffering from malaria but also, he thought, acute infectious jaundice (hepatitis), which diagnosis quickly confirmed.

The first night was hellish. The ward had previously been for Indian sepoys and the beds were still charpoys. Apart from the Scots ward sister, the nursing orderlies were convalescing British other ranks. I did not sleep for a moment. The next day I staggered away from my bed. It was alive with bed bugs. I shook the charpoy repeatedly until the floor was littered with the foul creatures. The charpoy was taken away and fumigated, but for the four weeks that I occupied it I itched.

My diet was fat free and desperately uninteresting, consisting mainly of porridge with treacle, and boiled chicken or boiled fish, twice a day, every day. Certainly no alcohol. There were six officers in the ward, one of whom was named Hornsby, whose family company manufactured the world-famous Ruston & Hornsby diesel engines that we had on most estates in Malaya. Jaundice is a very lowering disease, and after four weeks I was so depressed that I said to the doctor that I thought that if I did not get out of hospital soon I would surely die there. To my astonishment he agreed, and asked was there anywhere I could go to convalesce. I rang the Treanors, and within three hours I was asleep in the now familiar bedroom in their bungalow.

I did have several visitors while in hospital, including the Treanors, Joan Yates and a Mr Falkener. He was a retired tea planter who did his bit by visiting the hospital and chatting to the patients. He was most interested to learn that I came from Malaya, and revealed that he too had been a rubber planter there. He started naming planters he had known and became rather angry when I had to say that I had not heard of any of the first six he had named. It was obvious that he was beginning to doubt that I had been anywhere near Malaya, at least as a planter. Finally, in exasperation, he said, 'But you must know Tommy Menzies.' With much relief I could say, yes, I did indeed know of Tommy Menzies. He was an old planter of many years standing, married to Marie Ney, a famous stage actress in her time. I then asked Falkner when he had last been in Malaya. He thought for a bit and said, 'Let me see. I think I left there in 1910.' I had to explain that 1910 was the year in which I was born.

I made a rapid recovery at the Treanors. The complete change of surroundings, good nursing and improved diet did the trick. I was even permitted a few weak whiskies. After a week or so Colonel Treanor had a committee meeting at the Gymkana Club in Darjeeling and I went along with him. Having read the newspapers in the library I wandered into the bar and was quietly contemplating a chota peg when a distinguished looking man came in, wished me a good evening, and asked me if I would care to join him in a drink. I explained that I had to be careful and why, and limited myself to another small whisky with lots of water. We chatted for some time and he began to question me about my more recent past and the Malayan campaign. After a while he said, 'How would you like to go to Arakan?' I said, 'Very much.' Anything was better than Barrackpore. 'Where is it?' He replied, 'Burma. When you get back to Barrackpore go and see my military secretary and he will fix it up.' Military secretary? Alarm bells rang. I asked, 'Excuse me, Sir, but who are you?' 'Irwin. General.' My bar companion was Lieutenant General Noel Irwin, Eastern Army commander. We chatted for a few minutes more, when he excused himself and left. He explained that there was a clandestine unit called 'V Force' operating behind the enemy lines in Burma, under the command of a Brigadier Felix-Williams, and that he thought I would be suitable for it. Then I remembered Treanor's suggestion of a month before.

When I got back to Barrackpore I was summoned to see the colonel who questioned me about my meeting with the Army commander; the military secretary had already told him that he was to lose me. My commanding officer told me in no uncertain terms what he thought of me. 'Hembry, you bloody fool. Why do you want to volunteer for such a dangerous job? You are a married man with a family and this is a training battalion and you could stay with it for the rest of the war.'

A week later I was on a train bound for Chittagong and Arakan.

V Force

August 1942 – February 1943

Chittagong was a day and a night's rail and ferry journey from Calcutta. At that time it was the only railhead and port through which XV Corps, on the southern Burma front, could be supplied. XV Corps consisted of the 14th Indian Division, much enlarged with several additional brigades, commanded by Major General Lloyd. It was mobile on a mixed mule and mechanical basis, but was generally not battle-hardened nor, as yet, jungle trained. It was concentrated around Comilla and Chittagong, inside Bengal, with forward elements further southwards into Arakan. Further south still and eastwards was the operational area of V Force, whose task it was to provide warning of enemy activity and intentions. V Force was already operating around Imphal, to the north.

The RTO at Chittagaong directed me to the rear headquarters of V Force. This was in a large bungalow and was manned by one elderly officer who was expecting me, and a small signals section. I was ordered to proceed at once to Cox's Bazaar, a fishing village further down the coast and another short voyage from Chittagaong. The officer was also the unit's quartermaster so was able to issue me with a revolver and Thompson submachine gun. Now I felt more like a soldier. He also handed me the unit's mail to deliver. He told me that the unit's forward base was at Bawli Bazaar, in Burma, about 30 miles south-east of Cox's Bazaar, and only reachable on foot as the road-making had been delayed for weeks because of the monsoon. Not that that mattered as V Force had not been issued with transport of any kind. Later it was to get a jeep and a motorbike.

I duly embarked on a small coaster, not much larger than a tugboat. I had by this time accumulated several essential items of kit all of which were packed into a bedroll which went under the name of an officer's valise. This was a wonderful article of inestimable usefulness. The outside covering was of canvas and leather. Inside were a mattress, a pillow, and several large pockets for clothing and other articles, and it rolled up into one neat bundle. An officer in the Indian Army was never without one; next to his weapon it was the one essential piece of kit. Later on I made it even more comfortable by acquiring an inflatable li-lo. On the trip to Cox's Bazaar I spread my valise out on the deck and slept under the stars.

At Cox's Bazaar I was met by a Lt Colonel Calvert – not 'Mad' Mike Calvert of Chindit fame – who was also in V Force but was stationed in Calcutta where he was lucky enough to live with his wife in a flat on Chowringhee. Calvert informed me that Brigadier Felix-Williams was expected in a day or so and would be going forward to Bawli Bazaar and I was to act as escort. The Brigadier would ride a horse. I would walk. That suited me because I would rather be footsore than bumsore. It had taken me some time to recover from my rides in Darjeeling.

It was arranged that I would mess with a battery of Mountain Artillery. It was equipped with guns that could be dismantled and carried on Missouri mules. Most of the gunners seemed to be huge Sikhs. A young gunner officer showed me where to dump my kit and then took me along to the mess to introduce me to the battery commander and the rest of the officers. They were all regular soldiers with long service in various North West Frontier wars and skirmishes and they kept me enthralled over dinner with their reminiscences. I had two very pleasant days with them before the Brigadier arrived.

I took an instant liking to Brigadier Felix-Williams – 'Felix-Bill'. Pukka Indian Army, his regiment was the elite Tochi Scouts with whom he had served in the wilder sections of the Frontier, and with distinction in France in the Great War. He spent the night with friends in a neighbouring Punjabi mess, and the next morning we set out for Bawli Bazaar, Felix-Bill astride his horse and I trailing along some 10 yards behind. Marauding Japanese occasionally mounted ambushes along the track to Bawli, so I took my escort duty seriously. Progress was good, until late afternoon when it started to rain. Coming from Malaya I thought that I knew all about rain, but rain in Arakan is something altogether different, where 150 inches in three months in the wet season is common.

Felix-Bill, who had made this journey on several occasions, said that there was a dak bungalow (government rest house) some few miles further on where we would dry out and rest up for the night. What he did not mention was that it was on the other side of a chaung (river). When we reached the chaung we found the ferry on our side – the ferry was a punt, not much larger than those used by Cambridge undergraduates on the Cam. The Brigadier tethered his horse to a tree and we were poled across by the Burmese ferryman. Getting in and out of the ferry was almost impossible because the rain had made the chaung banks very muddy and slippery. We struggled up the opposite bank and made it to the dak bungalow. The wooden bungalow was built on stilts, as in Malaya, with a corrugated iron roof. The incessant rain beating down on it sounded like machine-gun fire. The dak wallah was a Maug (people who lived astride the borders of Bengal and Burma) who said that he would prepare hot baths and a meal straight away. The Brigadier sat down and I thankfully dropped my kit and valise on to the floor when, to my utter astonishment, he said, 'Now go back and get my horse.' I could not believe my ears and when I did I thought he was joking. He was not. I considered mutiny, as the punt could barely carry three people, let alone a horse. And it was not me who had been riding it. And, if anything, the rain had worsened.

In great disgruntlement I made my way back to the chaung, rousted out an equally disgruntled ferryman from his basha, and slid down the bank on my backside into the punt, and was poled across to the other side, where the horse was patiently waiting. I wondered whether he knew what was in store. Then the fun began. I untethered the creature and began to lead it down towards the water when we both slipped and landed on our respective posteriors. I thought for one moment that it would roll on top of me. Struggling to our feet we reached the water only to find that the boat had drifted off down stream. So we made our way to it, up to our hocks in slimy mud, and brought it back. How to get the horse on to the punt? I thought that, as Felix-Bill had made the journey before, perhaps I should go back across the chaung to ask him. But it occurred to me that this might be some form of initiative test, which, if failed, would mean my being RTUed (returned to unit), and I did not relish the idea of serving with the 4/3 Madras Regiment at Barrackpore for the duration.

We tried keeping the ferry broadside to the bank, but the horse could not or would not mount the craft and turn 90 degrees at the same time. Every time we got its forelegs on to the craft it drifted away from the bank and we would all end up in the chaung, and neither the ferryman nor I was strong enough to hold the punt steady. So I got the boatman to wade into the water and ram the punt end-on into the muddy bank. That way we got some stability whilst I coaxed the horse to embark. He gave every impression of having done it before, because, in spite of the boat rocking during the crossing, he remained calm. And all the time it continued to bucket down. The whole operation took well over two hours. When I reached the dak bungalow I thankfully handed the horse over to the dak wallah to dry off and feed and climbed the stairs soaked through, covered in mud from head to toe, and in a vile temper which I made no effort to disguise. But I swear I saw a glint of amusement in Felix-Bill's eye when he thanked me and passed over the bottle of Scotch.

The rain had stopped during the night and the weather was hot and steamy. We made an early start and arrived at Bawli Bazaar at midday. Felix-Bill introduced me to my commanding officer and those officers in camp. The CO was Lieutenant Colonel Archie Donald, well over six feet in height, as hard as nails and utterly fearless – the winner of two King's Police Medals for gallantry. Frank Bullen was a Malayan policeman, a Scot of frightening aspect with a red beard, who wore crossed cartridge belts like a Mexican bandit, hard drinking and hard swearing. He was seldom in camp and so I saw very little of him. Then there was Lieutenant Gretton Foster, a farmer's son from Coggeshall, in Essex. As I knew the area well, we had much in common and became firm friends. We spent many an evening talking about home, mutual acquaintances and, above all, the birds. The group was completed by a former Burma Forestry Service officer, and a doctor.

Donald had been in the Burma Police for many years, most of

the time in Arakan, so knew the whole area and its various tribes and languages intimately. He wore a bush shirt, always outside his shorts, socks and chaplis (Pathan sandals), 1914–18 ribbons, was armed with revolver and kukri, always carried a broken polo stick, and topped it all with an old-fashioned khaki pith helmet. He had a hooked nose, a fierce moustache and a bark much worse than his bite.

The first afternoon was spent listening to the Brigadier questioning Donald, and I was amazed at the colossal amount of information V Force had collected about Japanese movements, positions, units and their spy networks. I was to learn later that sometimes these were the same as ours. But we paid better. Donald's agents were everywhere and his sources of intelligence were legion. To my amusement the agents were all referred to as 'CFs' – Chittagonian Fuckers – even in official reports to Corps Headquarters.

The camp consisted of several large and well-made bashas with atap thatching. Each officer had his own bearer and the mess employed a good Maug cook. Rations were extremely generous; V Force was obviously considered a special unit judging by the 'officers' comforts' issue, for in every five gallon stores container was a bottle of Scotch. This in addition to rice, dried fruit, packets of potatoes and onions, tinned stores, tinned milk, tea and coffee and packets of cigarettes. The latest batch of containers had been badly packed, for the pungent smell of onions penetrated everything, especially the cigarettes, and one would have to be very hard up for a smoke to try one. But the CFs loved them. Compared to ordinary infantry soldiers we lived like fighting cocks.

That evening we had a sort of mess night, a little indulgence in alcohol loosened tongues, and I got to know my new companions a little better. The Brigadier told us some of his plans to extend V Force operations, and then dropped – so far as I was concerned – his bombshell. Having just completed a march of over 30 miles, in appalling conditions, I was to accompany him back to Chittagong, starting the next morning, using the same method of transport. I was very far from amused, started to remonstrate but thought better of it, so merely asked what the form was.

Having escorted the Brigadier on his return journey to Cox's Bazaar, I was to collect a party of six Pathans who had recently been recruited into V Force but found to be totally unsuitable, and escort them back to Chittagong. It would appear that, when they were not actually working, they were seducing the local village maidens which infuriated their menfolk. There were no complaints from the women, but some of our agents would not leave their villages for fear that the Pathans would get up to mischief in their absence. Having handed over these brigands I was to collect stores and large amounts of cash to pay our agents. I would then be allotted a reliable Pathan to help guard the treasure on the return journey, and porters.

The trek to Cox's was uneventful, and we made it by nightfall. This time it did not rain and Felix-Bill handled his horse crossing the river. We messed that night with the Punjabis and the following morning I bade goodbye to the Brigadier, who was heading north to another V Force unit, and went in search of my recalcitrant Pathans. I found them under military detention but still heavily armed, which struck me as strange. Apparently those in charge had tried to take away their rifles and knives but had thought better of it when the Pathans got angry. They then had given their word not to escape and honour on both sides was satisfied. I led the way down to the jetty and we sailed at nightfall. The peaceful, beautiful starry tropical night, the quiet lapping of the waves on the bow, and frequent recourse to the whisky bottle – happily shared and enjoyed by my Muslim brigands – made for a long and refreshing night's sleep.

I was woken the next morning with a cheerful 'chota hazri, sahib?', a mug of scalding tea put on the deck beside me, and a brown hand on which were several freshly made chappatis was held out towards me. Having breakfasted I rolled up my bedroll, and, hearing a lot of laughter, mug in hand I wandered aft to find my Pathan friends playing marbles on the deck – with live hand grenades. I beat a hasty retreat as far forward as I could get, expecting an explosion at any moment. But the pins stayed in place.

They were a great bunch of rogues and would have been wonderful in combat, but were totally unsuited to the work required by V Force, and I am surprised that they were ever recruited. It was probably the hare-brained idea of some box wallah at Barrackpore. But I was sorry to say goodbye to them when they were collected by the RTO at Chittagong.

I reported to V Force Headquarters and had made the arrangements to collect the stores and money and my Pathan personal escort, in time to begin the return journey the following evening, when I went down with a savage attack of malaria. I awoke the next day in a comfortable bed in the spare bedroom of the bungalow of the Chittagong Hospital doctor. With his help, and that of a particularly attractive Eurasian nurse, I fully recovered in 10 days. Meanwhile Donald had been informed of the delay.

I made the return journey to Chittagong, landed the stores, and spent the night with my friends the Mountain Gunners, whilst my escort set about recruiting porters. Once more we set off to walk to Bawli. I was becoming used to this 30-mile hike, but was still weak from the malaria and had to rest fairly frequently, which pleased the Chittagonians, but not the Pathan who made it pretty plain that he thought we were all sissies. He was tall and stout, with a truly wicked countenance and a large moustache. He dressed as if on the Frontier, with large baggy white (grey!) trousers, pullover and long top coat, woollen cap, and carried an old Lee Enfield, kukri, stabbing dagger, two Mills bombs and the usual crossed bandoleers. Our conversation was limited, but we got on well. I shared my whisky with him and ate with him, and he managed the porters. One of us always stood guard on the money.

We were given a boisterous welcome by Donald and the others, and my return with the money, official mail and stores for the next three months was celebrated by quite a party.

So far Donald had given me very little information about my job, so the next morning he called me into his office basha and took several hours briefing me about the Force, its current activities, its methods, its shortcomings, his future plans and my part in them. Our job was to be the eyes and ears of the 14th Indian Division. The division was spread out over tens of scores of miles, much of which was jungle. The RAF was unable to provide the necessary intelligence by reconnaissance as, in those early days, they did not enjoy air supremacy, and anyway the Japanese usually moved at night and, where possible, kept to the jungle.

I went on my first patrol two or three days later, with three CFs. My experience of the past months in Malaya stood me in good stead. The terrain over which we operated was similar, but the jungle was less dense. From Bawli down to the Teknaf Peninsula there was a coastal plain which was heavily planted with padi, and innumerable habitations – in Malaya we have would called them kampongs – scattered around on islands. I could have been back in Kedah. One had to be extremely circumspect in one's movements as the Jap was known to be in large numbers in the Arakan Yoma, a range of jungle-covered hills running north-south along the length of Arakan, and could spot us crossing the open padi fields. Also, they patrolled constantly and often in force.

My CF guide and interpreter, who knew as much English as I knew Arakanese, was a wily old bird, a local man who knew the area from childhood, so we were able to move under cover of high bunds (banked-up earth to control water courses) and the occasional clump of forest. Our entry into the little islands of habitation in the padi fields was always carried out with extreme caution as any one of them could have been harbouring a Jap patrol and we would have been sitting ducks. One or two CFs would discard their weapons – usually a Boer War rifle – and walk openly into a village and, over a cup of tea in the shop, would question the onlookers who always gathered around a stranger, concerning the whereabouts of any Japanese. When they were satisfied that the coast was clear the rest of us would move in. The village elders would usually provide us with the information we required to build up a picture of the enemy's movements and routine. If we thought there to be an opportunity of employing casual agents we would give the headman money with instructions to send a man into known Japanese-held villages to scout around and to return with all the information he could glean. Payment terms were strictly cash on delivery, as we were well aware that the enemy were playing the same game and that several Arakanese were double agents, so we became adept very quickly in discerning which information was genuine and which was planted or merely fabricated. On the whole the system worked well.

When we arrived at a village, whether during the day or night, we always forbade anyone to leave without our express permission, on pain of death. I only know of one instance when a villager disobeyed our orders and was subsequently executed, as he had been observed by a CF talking to a Jap patrol commander. On the whole the Arakanese much preferred the British to the Japanese although there was always the risk of someone falling to their blandishments, usually anti-colonial in nature, and giving us away. But most realised that British rule was more benign than Japanese and any who did work for the enemy would have done so for the money or for fear of retribution on their families. My first patrol was uneventful. We saw no Japs face to face but heard them moving around from time to time and laid up under cover until their patrols had passed by, sometimes very closely. I had several meetings with agents, received their reports, and paid out monies owed. I thoroughly enjoyed the experience. Memories of nights in the open under the stars, with the now familiar smell of cow dung, wood smoke, curries and spices, remain with me still. On the quiet nights out on patrol the war seemed miles away. After four days we returned to base and I made my report. I had a feeling, although this was never confirmed by Donald, that he had sent me off on my first patrol to a relatively quiet area – if anywhere in Arakan could have been considered quiet in those early days. The Jap, with their command of the air, continually strafed and bombed the 14th Indian Division's forward positions and their patrols if caught in the open. It was not until towards the end of the year, when we had built a few forward air strips, that we saw our own Hurricanes and Spitfires overhead. It was quite extraordinary the difference to morale that a few of one's own planes overhead made to those of us on the ground.

Because of my posting to Burma the steady flow of mail from home had dried up and months went by without my receiving a single letter, which was very disappointing. Strangely enough no one else was receiving letters either, and an air of gloom set in. Soon after my arrival Donald appointed me adjutant, despite my frequent absences on patrol. There were very few duties other than preparing the wage packets for the CFs and agents, sending and receiving the occasional signals, and dealing with queries from HQ. One day shortly after my appointment a large bulky envelope arrived from Cox's Bazaar. Donald threw it over to me, unopened, with the words, 'Put it in the trunk and if anything requires an answer it will answer itself in due course.' I did this for at least two months without any recriminations from HQ. Then one day, having nothing better to do, I decided to go through the tin trunk just to see what it was we had failed to deal with. I slit open one of the large envelopes and out fell at least a dozen letters from home. It was the same with all the other envelopes; each member of our unit having at least six. There were one or two official-looking missives, and these were returned to the trunk unopened. Not much was said by anyone for the next few hours as we read and re-read our letters and assimilated all the latest news from home. Thenceforth all such envelopes were opened as soon as received.

Towards the end of July 1942 Colonel Donald received word that it was intended to clear the enemy out of the Mayu Peninsula and to capture Akyab Island. V Force was ordered to step up its intelligence-gathering activities, to garner as much information as possible regarding Jap dispositions, numbers, units, supply lines and even the names of their senior officers. We doubled our patrols and were away for at least a week at a time, penetrating deeper into enemy-held territory. One morning I led my patrol out of the bush on to the bank of a deep chaung, looking for somewhere to cross, when we came under machine-gun fire from the other bank. We took cover, returned fire, and for about five minutes there was a real old-fashioned Guy Fawkes Night between us and the Jap section which we could see in the undergrowth opposite. We suffered no casualties and I doubt very much whether they did either for, apart from my submachine gun, we only had my CFs' old rifles which would have been hard put to reach the other side of the river, let alone to hurt anyone. I called cease-fire and waited to see what happened. As nothing did, after 10 minutes or so we withdrew and enjoyed a breakfast of chappatis and cold tea. I decided to abort that particular part of our recce as I was certain that the Japs we had engaged would have been greatly reinforced and on the look out for us.

It was on returning from one such patrol that Donald called me to his basha and, after discussing my report, said it was imperative that we got information about the defences of Maungdaw and that one of his old agents had found his way to us from that very village. I have the advantage of having in my possession a report marked 'TOP SECRET' – so secret that I see it was circulated to twenty-nine different recipients, including GHQ Eastern Army, IV and XV Corps, and numerous divisions and brigades – and I quote from it:

> The Brigadier [Felix-Bill] has just returned from Arakan with much information concerning the defences of the Maungdaw area. The GOC wished to thank personally the officers of V Force for the work done and excellent intelligence produced. This was mainly due to the excellent and often dangerous exploits of Lieutenants Hembry and Foster. In spite of extreme fatigue, fever and other ailments these officers were constantly going into Maungdaw and other defended places under the nose of the enemy and returning with the desired results. The information given by their agents always proved to be correct.
>
> An example is given below in an extract from a report by Lt Col Donald, commanding V Force in this area.
>
> It was 'Dick Turpin', a V Force agent who kept us informed by letter and hand drawn maps of the gun positions of the enemy. Such was the importance of this information that quite a number of these were immediately checked by Lt Hembry and found to be correct.

Donald was adept at choosing code names for our agents – one was called 'General Barebum' – and these were used – like CF – in all our reports. Dick Turpin was the son of a schoolmaster and so spoke limited English, and had been known to Donald for several years.

In view of the attack being planned Donald thought it absolutely essential that I personally checked the information provided by Dick Turpin, as it was doubted whether the sketches that he had made of the Jap strong points and positions were accurate enough for the

RAF bombers and the Army's 25 pounders to pinpoint. Thus it was that about 10 o'clock on a most beautiful full moonlit night a small native canoe, paddled by an Arakanese, could have been seen gliding silently down a chaung towards Maungdaw. Closer inspection would have revealed a large English subaltern stretched out full length in the bottom of the canoe, admiring the sheer beauty of the sky above and remembering the lines learnt at school:

> The moon shines bright – in such a night as this,
> When the sweet wind did gently kiss the trees,
> And they did make no noise; in such a night,
> Troilus, methinks, mounted the Trojan walls,

My plan was to make for Dick Turpin's house, which he shared with his wife and parents. This was on the outskirts of Maungdaw and close to the river. From there we would sally forth, under cover of darkness, to pinpoint the critical defences. The chaung was only about 50 yards wide so we were close to the enemy and I expected a challenge any moment. But the Japs did not seem to be keeping a very good lookout, perhaps because they did not believe a lone British officer would have the impudence to penetrate so deep inside their territory. We drew into the bank when we came within sight of the village and tied up. Dick Turpin went ashore and, when he was satisfied that we had been unobserved, beckoned me and together we walked along the path that led from the river to the village. When we reached a small plantation of fruit trees I stayed behind in cover whilst he went forward and knocked on the door of a small bungalow. After a moment or two the door was opened a few inches and a face peered out. A moment later Dick Turpin returned to collect me and we were inside the house. By the light of the oil lamps I could see there were four others in the room and I was introduced to Turpin's mother, father and another relative. They chatted for a few minutes in Arakanese, looking in my direction. Then the father turned to me and in very good English said I was most welcome and that I must join them in a meal. As it was now well after midnight I said that I did not wish to cause them any trouble and anyway would not the fact that the lights were burning, even behind shuttered windows, arouse Jap suspicions? The father said no; most householders kept their lamps burning, and that the opposite would be true.

It turned out that it was Dick Turpin's father who had drawn the maps, so I cross-examined him closely and got him to draw in more features, such as large trees, prominent buildings and other outstanding landmarks by which the RAF could the more easily identify their targets. Having come so far I thought that I might as well check one or two sites on the ground myself. As there was a curfew our movements had to be very discreet. Turpin went outside to scout around and returned a few minutes later to say the coast was clear. I followed him up the road, keeping to the shadows. Having gone only about 50 yards we spotted a group of Japanese sitting around a table under a tree, playing a dice game in the light of a hurricane lamp. Turpin whispered that they were the night watch. We skirted them and had covered another 100 yards when he pointed to a clump of trees out of which a gun barrel protruded. Further on was another gun pit with what looked like a Lewis gun, and a nearby building which was obviously a unit headquarters. I noted the unit sign by the door and decided that I had seen enough. When we got back to Dick Turpin's father's house I examined the map again and saw that the three positions which I had seen were correctly plotted on the map.

We said farewell to this gallant little family, made our way back to where we had hidden the canoe, and paddled away. As it was now nearly daybreak we drew into the bank once we well clear of the village, hid the canoe and ourselves in nearby undergrowth, enjoyed a breakfast of chappatis and cold tea, and settled down to rest up for the day. I was to take the first watch, but before Turpin had closed his eyes we heard chatter and laughter coming towards us, on the opposite bank. We watched as half a dozen Japanese soldiers, all armed but obviously off-duty, with a couple of Burmans, squatted by the chaung and started to fish. They stayed for an hour or so before deciding that they had caught enough and returned whence they came. We moved deeper into the undergrowth, took it in turns to sleep and keep watch, and set out at dusk for home.

The next morning, having reported my findings to Donald, he told me that he had an unpleasant task for me. In the course of the previous few weeks we had been joined by two Burma Government officials, Colonel Phelips and Sheik Mohammed, the latter a charming Indian who had been educated in England. They were preparing to take over the civil administration of Arakan as officers administrating recaptured territories, or some such title, after our attacks on Maungdaw and Buthidaung had succeeded. It seemed that our forces had captured three Arakanese who had been tried in a court set up by Phelips and found guilty not only of spying but also of terrorism. The three had led the Japs to a village where they knew two agents of ours were hiding, and they, all their relations, and the village elders had been shot. After which the three had threatened to accuse the remaining villagers of spying for the British unless they complied with their demands for money. They had been sentenced to death, and the executions set for that very day.

As I listened I realised what my unpleasant task was to be. Donald confirmed that, as adjutant, I was to take a dozen CFs to form the firing squad. I asked him whether he was going to witness the executions. He said no, he had important reports to complete. I said, 'Colonel, I remember you saying not all that long ago that you would never ask your officers to do anything you wouldn't do.' Donald looked at me fiercely and said, 'Hembry, you bastard. Okay. I will witness the executions.'

I formed up the firing squad and we had a few practice shots at paper targets pinned on to trees. I was very worried about their poor aim and the efficiency of their very old rifles. Promptly at six that evening the condemned men were marched out on to a patch of grass behind the camp, with their hands tied behind them. A Burmese priest asked each of them whether they had anything to say. They had not. I blindfolded each of them, pinned a piece of paper over where I thought the heart was, withdrew and ordered the firing squad, drawn up about 20 yards away, to take aim – four to each condemned man – and gave the order to fire. As I had feared, the executioners' aim was poor and the condemned fell to the ground, groaning. I asked the dresser, who was standing by, exactly where the heart was. 'Half an inch below the left nipple, Sahib.' With my Tommy gun I put three rounds into each man on the ground, and that was that. The bodies were taken away for burial with full religious rites, and Colonel Donald and I repaired to the mess in a sombre mood for several burra pegs.

Shortly after this I collapsed with another bout of malaria. The MO injected me with a large shot of quinine and I was taken back by motor launch to Bawli Bazaar, where I recovered in about a week, just in time to hear the big attack go in. The battle lasted only for a couple of days, but we were close enough to the front line to be deafened by the shelling and the sounds of the RAF dropping bombs on Maungdaw. A day or so later I accompanied the colonel to a Divisional conference. General Lloyd, a fine soldier who was to be killed later in North Africa, reported that the advance had gone well and that his objectives had been taken. The attacks had been made both sides of the Mayu range, along the coast and further east down the Kaladan valley. Maungdaw had been occupied without a shot being fired. The Jap intelligence had been good, for they were aware that we had superior forces, and had withdrawn. They re-took Maungdaw a couple of months later, by which time I had left V Force. By the end of the year the British forces were spread out along the coastal plain just north of Donbaik and still about 10 miles short of the end of the Naf Peninsula and Akyab Island, the prime objectives of the attack.

Few officers at the conference knew about V Force, and some of those present, extremely smartly turned out, viewed Donald and me with a mixture of amazement and contempt. I was not surprised. Donald was dressed as usual and I in the same way but in old plimsolls and with no headgear at all. After a little while, a young immaculately dressed staff captain from a British regiment turned to me and whispered, 'Who is that old bugger in the Kitchener helmet?' I drew myself up to my full height and whispered back, trying to appear shocked at the impertinence, 'That old bugger is my colonel!'

Christmas 1942 saw V Force comfortably housed in a large bungalow in Maungdaw, overlooking the maidan. We celebrated with the usual dinner and lots of liquid refreshment before tidying up the office and quarters in preparation for a visit by General Wavell, the commander-in-chief, Lt General Irwin, Eastern Army commander, Major General Lloyd, Fourteenth Indian Division commander, and various other senior officers, scheduled for Boxing Day or soon after. General Wavell had expressed a wish to inspect V Force officers and to thank them for their efforts. The assembled unit consisted of just Brigadier Felix-Bill, Colonel Donald, Gretton Foster and myself: the others were away on patrol. I briefed the mess orderly, whom I had christened Archibald because his real name was totally unpronounceable, to be prepared to produce tea if required, and to serve the top brass in order of seniority, which I would indicate. At that time I was wholly ignorant of the badges of rank of anyone above brigadier, so would have to try to recognise the faces.

Shortly after tiffin on the appointed day the three generals flew in to the little airstrip and were met by Felix-Bill in our new jeep, and driven back to our bungalow. Donald and his two subalterns were lined up and introduced to the generals. I was particularly pleased to be able to talk to Wavell whom I greatly admired. It was apparent that General Irwin or the Brigadier had briefed him about my experiences in Malaya, for he asked me some very pertinent questions and we talked for a good five minutes. The C-in-C then made a short speech, congratulating the V Force officers and agents, and confirmed that I had been mentioned in despatches and in due course could wear the appropriate insignia. Colonel Donald then told me, again in front of everyone, that I could put up my second pip as a first lieutenant. I must say, I went to sleep that night feeling rather proud.

The party then stood around looking slightly self-conscious when one of Wavell's aides whispered in my ear that the generals would appreciate a cup of tea. I sprang instantly into action, turned smartly and got as far as yelling 'Arch– !', coughed uncontrollably, and walked through to the mess room to issue the necessary instructions to Archibald, our mess orderly. Just in time, I hoped, I had remembered the C-in-C's Christian name.

It was while we were taking it easy over the Christmas period that Gretton Foster and I talked for hours, sitting out under the stars, usually with whisky in hand, about our youth and early days in our respective peacetime careers, and what we would do after the War. Both were confident that we would survive, and on the winning side. I knew that Gretton was not married, but asked whether he was engaged. He explained that he once had been, but his fiancée had broken it off. He had been a keen poacher and one evening, still wearing his poacher's jacket, he had taken her to the local cinema where during the film his fiancée had endearingly slipped her hand into his pocket – only to be bitten severely by his ferret. End of engagement.

The day after the generals' visit, Maungdaw was bombed, and our sleeping quarters received a direct hit and were totally destroyed. We lost one CF, and all our personal kit. We took shelter in a slit trench, conveniently dug by the Japanese during their occupation. Some of the bombs fell unpleasantly close. So once again my personal possessions had been reduced to what I stood up in. Fortunately, one of our officers was on leave in Calcutta at the time and we were able to get a signal through to him, and in only a week or so he was back in Maungdaw with new equipment and clothing for us all. But, there were no free replacements from the army. Every item of kit had to be bought by myself, charged to my account at the Army & Navy store in Calcutta.

At the end of December Donald and I went on an operation which involved a visit to Foul Point, the tip of the Mayu Peninsula, just opposite Akyab, then the Jap's area headquarters. I quote from the 14th Indian Division Intelligence Summary No. 26 dated 13 January 1943, which I retain:

Subsequent to the advance of our forces Lt Col Donald and Lt Hembry have organised a system of intelligence, with a few V Force agents and a number of locals, to get information about Jap movements from Foul Point to Lambagona. Both these officers have been to within a few miles of Foul Point, their agents going still further. On the 28th December Lt Col Donald reported that on the west of the Mayu Peninsula there were very few Japs in the hills. On the east, however, there were Japs in most of the villages, totalling from 300 to 400.

As regards Akyab, he estimated 3,000 Japs in and around the town, with another 300 on the north end of the island opposite Foul Point.

Reports like this, of course, give only the bare bones. No mention is made of the hours of planning, the risks involved or the dangers actually encountered. Donald and I had to walk through miles of open country well into Japanese-occupied territory to a secret rendezvous with a Mr Maracan, a well-known merchant and businessman who lived in a small village just north of Foul Point. Donald, in his own inimitable way, had nicknamed him 'Maracan of Arakan'. Maracan was very loyal and his efforts on our behalf were invaluable. We needed to brief him very carefully before he sent an agent into Akyab. We wanted to know all about the sea and land defences, the disposition and numbers of troops. The planners were contemplating an attack on Akyab simultaneously from landwards and seawards by the very much enlarged 14th Indian Division. If we could capture Akyab we would have a substantial port for landing tanks and other heavy equipment for the build-up of sufficient forces to advance south. In the event it was all pie in the sky, for the delay in following up our capture of Maungdaw and Buthidaung enabled the Japs to regroup, recapture their lost territory, and force us to retire. Akyab was eventually taken by XV corps nearly 18 months later.

I shall always remember our trip to Foul Point and back. Striding along with my colonel, he wielding his polo stick and all the time singing, 'Home, home on the range, where the deer and the antelopes play.' I did my best to keep him between me and the hills from where any shooting would most likely come.

The first Battle of Donbaik took place during the third week of January 1943. We had recently been joined by a new subaltern, Second Lieutenant Davies (I regret I do not remember his Christian name), and I thought that it would be ideal for his baptism of fire to take part in the battle. Before the start of the attack the enemy was to be subjected to a heavy barrage of 25 pounders, .37 mountain guns (howitzers) and a battalion of heavy machine guns, which would then creep forward as our troops advanced. I had decided to take young Davies to an artillery OP (observation post) to view the battle. Having been given the okay by the gunner battery commander I was told to follow the field telephone lines which would lead us to the OP. We soon picked up the cables and followed them. We seemed to be following them for miles. Disquiet set in after half an hour when we should have reached the OP within 10 minutes. I saw from my watch that it was 10.45. The barrage was due to begin at 11.00. The high ground on which the OP was located should have been in front of us, but there seemed to be no rising ground in front. I looked at my watch again. It was still 10.45. It had stopped. Davies' watch said 1100 hours. Panic stations. I looked around and spotted a hole in the ground made by a tree that had been uprooted by shellfire – probably our own artillery's ranging rounds. We fell into the hole at the very moment the bombardment began. It quite literally rained high explosives. I do not know exactly how long it was before the barrage lifted and moved on another 100 yards or so, but it seemed a lifetime. It was most probably only five minutes. Then the machine guns opened up. This was even more terrifying than the heavy guns, and lasted longer. Then these, too, moved on. We gave it another five minutes before we left the comparative safety of our hole. No sooner were we out in the open when bullets began whistling past our ears like angry wasps. We hurled ourselves back into our hole. Every time we lifted our heads ping went another bullet, sometimes so close that I could feel the hot air – or so I imagined – as it just missed. Obviously a sniper had survived the barrage. I suggested to Davies that he put his hat – as usual, I had no headgear, he had an Aussie army slouch hat – on to a nearby bush, with the idea of trying to spot the sniper as soon as a bullet hole appeared in it, whilst he was re-loading for the next shot. The crown was completely riddled before I saw a man halfway up a tree, and some 50 yards away. I told Davies to move his hat slightly and as soon as we heard the crack of the sniper's rifle we would both stand up and let fly with our Tommy guns. We did just that. After a few minutes we both raised our heads again and saw the very bloodstained body dangling from the tree.

The telephone line that we had followed was, of course, Japanese. They must have watched us following it into their positions. We shall never know why they did not kill us, unless they had wanted to take us prisoner to interrogate us.

We picked ourselves up and scurried off in the direction of our own forward troops, halting only to allow Davies to go back and get his hat. This was silly because we were immediately fired upon from another direction. It was then that we saw the mules.

To quote from V Force progress report to Eastern Army HQ dated 31 January 1943:

> During the Battle of Donbaik on 21.1.43 Lieutenants Hembry and Davies went into the fight to try their luck against Jap snipers. They had not been long thus engaged when they noticed some mules loaded with a mortar and some bombs wandering away without their darabis (drivers), so under enemy fire they caught the mules and brought them back to our lines. True enough they only saved the lives of a couple of mules, but against this it must be remembered that the Japs would have had a nice present of our mortar and several cases of bombs. All the more credit is due to young Davies as this was his first time under fire.

I was glad that no mention was made of my mistake over the Jap telephone wire.

We had led the mules a few hundred yards when a grenade went off very near us. We dropped to the ground, letting go one of the mules which wandered off to nibble at the undergrowth. I remember saying to Davies, 'Bugger me, where did that come from?' Just then we heard a groan from behind a bank. We let go of the other mule and each threw a hand grenade towards the noise and, after a few minutes of silence, crept up and peered over the bank to find not a Jap but a sepoy, badly wounded, wheezing and twitching horribly. I gave the poor man some water and saw that he had been shot several times in the chest but did not, I was thankful to note, appear to have received grenade shrapnel wounds. We pondered what to do whilst the battle went on merrily all around and over us. Then I told Davies to catch the mules again whilst I picked up the sepoy and slung him over my shoulder and we made our way back to our lines.

We had not gone more than a couple of hundred yards when we were surrounded by Sikhs. The Sikh officer viewed us with the gravest of suspicion. He could see that we were not Japs, but we could have been Germans. From time to time we had heard rumours that Germans were fighting with the Japs on several fronts, and we in V Force had tried on several occasions to verify this. We persuaded the Sikh officer that we were British, he relieved us of the mules and directed me to the casualty clearing station where I thankfully laid the poor sepoy down on to a stretcher. We then made our way back to V Force Advance HQ, made our report and treated ourselves to several large pegs of whisky.

It was at about this time that I was notified that I had been mentioned in despatches for the second time.

It was during the Battle of Donbaik that I witnessed a Sikh win the Victoria Cross. Some Bren carriers were badly shot up on the beach, put out of action and their occupants killed or wounded. Sergeant Packrat Singh of the 5/8 Punjabis drove his Bren carrier down the beach, under very heavy fire, calmly got out, hooked a chain on to one of the disabled carriers and towed it back to our lines. He then repeated the operation with the second carrier. I was about a quarter of a mile away in an OP and saw everything. I believe the award was immediate.

Sometime not long after Donbaik, Donald and I had returned from a rather special patrol and were sleeping, wrapped up in our groundsheets, not far from Divisional Forward HQ, when we were suddenly woken by cannon and machine-gun fire. We were partially undressed; that is to say we had removed our shoes and socks. I found and donned mine quickly, but my colonel was cursing and groping around for his, muttering, 'Where are my fucking socks, where the hell are my fucking socks?' I could not help bursting out laughing, which promptly produced a whole lot more curses. We grabbed our weapons and made our way to HQ, where there was not a little panic. There was more shelling and machine-gun fire coming from seawards and we assumed that the Japs were making a landing behind us, in their traditional way. We stood to all night to find, in the dawn, that we had been shelled by the Royal Navy who had got their co-ordinates wrong. Then, to cap that, the very same morning we were bombed by the RAF. They inflicted only minor casualties, but we did begin to wonder who our enemies were.

It was on my way back to our main V Force Headquarters, having hitched a ride with a gunner colonel, that we came across one of his unit's three tonners broken down by the side of the road. We stopped, having seen a Tommy's boots sticking out from underneath the engine. 'What's up?' asked the Colonel. Back came the answer from underneath the lorry, 'What's oop? I'll tell thee what's oop. The fooking fooker's fooked, fook it!' I had never before heard a word conjugated as adjective, noun, verb and expletive all in one sentence.

After First Donbaik (there were two such battles) Colonel Donald, Gretton Foster and I went on a fortnight's leave, leaving Davies in charge of our CFs. The road through to Cox's Bazaar having now been completed we took the unit's jeep, which I drove. There was still the odd Jap patrol infiltrating even this far so our weapons were always at the ready and loaded, but we were unmolested. Then from Cox's to Chittagong by steamer, and on to Calcutta by rail as usual, before checking in at the Great Eastern Hotel, which appeared to have been much improved since my last stay. The rats and most of the cockroaches had been banished.

I immediately telephoned the Treanors, hoping to be able to spend my leave in Darjeeling, only to learn that they were going down to Gopalpur, a seaside resort in Orissa, for two weeks, but would I join them there? After a couple of days in Calcutta spent replenishing my meagre wardrobe and visiting the 4/3 Madras out at Barrackpore, I caught the train for the night's rail journey to Gopalpur and a wonderful welcome from the Treanor family.

The days passed with nothing to do but relax, eat, sleep, bathe and talk. The only snag was the break in letters from Jean and the family, as they were still being forwarded to V Force in Arakan. This was unavoidable as, apart from the Treanors, I had not told anyone of my holiday plans, not even my colonel.

Imagine my surprise, therefore, when, on the Saturday afternoon at the end of only the first week, the dak wallah handed me a telegram instructing me to report immediately to a Colonel Heath at an address in Ballygunge, Calcutta. At first I simply could not understand how anyone could have known my whereabouts – the answer, of course, was that I had been traced through the RTO at Howrah Station who had dealt with the furlough warrant – and then I was angry because I had only had one week of my fortnight. I talked the matter over with Colonel Treanor who, as an old army man, advised compliance with the order. Thus I arrived back at the Great Eastern Hotel early on the Sunday morning in time for breakfast and a spruce up, before taking a taxi out to the address in Ballygunge. Ballygunge was the suburb where most of the burra sahibs of the great Calcutta trading and tea companies lived in considerable splendour. Many of the large bungalows had been commandeered by the various headquarters for their staff officers, quite a few of whom had the good fortune to have their wife and family with them. I duly found the house and knocked on the door. It was answered by a man dressed in grey flannels and open-necked shirt who introduced himself as Colonel Heath. I told him who I was and showed him the telegram. To my utter astonishment he looked at it, said it was Sunday, and told me to return at 'a reasonable hour' on Monday.

I had quite forgotten that wars stopped on weekends for box wallahs. It was shortly before tiffin time and the man did not even ask me in for a drink or offer to call a taxi to take me back to Calcutta. I waved down a passing army lorry and was given a lift back into town. The incident certainly put me off Colonel Heath, who was to be my commanding officer for the next two years. Henceforth I never liked or trusted him, nor, incidentally, ceased to be amazed at the speed with which he had achieved such exalted rank, fast even by the nebulous standards of clandestine forces, and particularly so considering his comparative lack of seniority in his prewar job.

I returned to the hotel, mystified as to what it was all about, and seething with rage. I was used to being buggered about, having orders countermanded and changed in the field where everyone is confronting the enemy and sharing the dangers, and the situation changing by the minute. I had not yet learned that the further away from any action the more likely it was to experience pettiness, the lack of any sense of duty or urgency of many staff officers, who often worked the traditional peacetime hours, even with the Japanese pressing against the very borders of India. I cheered up considerably when, much to my surprise and delight, whom should I meet in the bar but Freddy and Bill Ferguson, two planting friends from Sungei Siput. Both had been pilots in the FMS Auxiliary Air Force and were now in the RAF, having had further training in Canada. We had a very good party

I did not realise it at the time but I had seen the last of Arakan. Looking back over those years I can say with all sincerity that the time spent with V Force was for me quite the most rewarding and interesting of the whole war. Despite the dangers and discomforts I would far sooner have stayed with V Force, with its completely unselfish and dedicated officers, than be with ISLD, where I found – as so accurately described by Brigadier Bowden-Smith in a letter to me on the cessation of hostilities – 'a maelstrom of difficulties and opposition both from above and below'. And that was not including the Jap!

I would like to quote from the final paragraph of Colonel Donald's report to Eastern Army Headquarters dated 31 January 1943:

> Before closing this, my final report on Arakan V Force, I must record my deep appreciation for the services rendered by all my officers. They have all at various times been in very tight corners which they have taken in their strides, without thought of praise and rewards. I have indeed been fortunate to have these officers, and my final remarks on them are AS FIGHTING MEN THEY ARE SECOND TO NONE.

The capitals are Colonel Donald's.

ISLD

MARCH 1943 – APRIL 1944

The following day I took a taxi out to Ballygunge again, my anger only slightly abated but nevertheless interested to learn why my well-earned leave had been curtailed. After a brief discussion about my activities with V Force, Heath disclosed that he, too, was an ex-Malayan, with Nestlé, and asked whether I knew a Laurie Brittain. I said of course I knew Laurie, who was also with Nestlé, and his charming American wife Verna. She it was who told me the limerick that I have remembered to this day:

> There was a young lady of Madras
> Who had the most beautiful ass,
> Not round and pink,
> As you might think,
> But the sort with long ears and eats grass.

Verna, as an American, of course pronounced Madras, ass and grass to rhyme.

Heath then said that Laurie was in the building and would like to talk to me. I was delighted to see Laurie again, looking spruce in his pilot officer's uniform. Heath interrupted our enquiries about our respective wives and the quick résumés of our recent activities by saying that he had been given an important task by General Wavell, and that I had been recommended for the enterprise, which would not be without danger. I was curious. What could be possibly more dangerous than V Force? But before they could say more would I sign the Official Secrets Act? Curiouser and curiouser! I agreed, and the document was produced and signed.

Heath then explained that he was in charge of the Calcutta end of an organisation code-named Inter Services Liaison Department (ISLD), part of the Secret Intelligence Service (SIS), which had its headquarters in New Delhi. ISLD was charged with obtaining military and civil intelligence out of Burma, Indo-China, Siam, Malaya and the Dutch East Indies. He was building up the Calcutta office to manage the various country sections but had not, so far, got anyone except Laurie for a Malayan section. Would I go to Sumatra? I pointed out that Sumatra was not Malaya. He said that he was well aware of that, but I had worked in Sumatra, and the immediate priority was Sumatra. So, on the basis of the year I had spent planting in Atjeh, 12 years before, I joined the Secret Intelligence Service.

Heath went on to say that Winston Churchill was strongly in favour of invading Sumatra in order to set up the necessary bases from which to recapture Malaya, Singapore and the Dutch East Indies. The chiefs of staff were not in favour of such an enterprise, and certainly not until they had knowledge of the strength and disposition of Japanese forces in Sumatra. But no intelligence of any description had been forthcoming from Sumatra since its capitulation a year earlier.

As Heath and Laurie unfolded their plans and ideas I realised that I was now launched on something completely different, on an enterprise that would involve travelling by submarine, landing on enemy occupied shores a thousand miles from base and, if captured, being guaranteed a painful death. Whilst I did not reconsider my decision for one moment, my mind did go back to the comments of the colonel of the 4/3 Madras Regiment the previous year.

The first result of my new venture was promotion to captain, with a monthly salary of 1,000 rupees, which was now to be paid by the Foreign Office rather than the army. I was thus able to send more money home to Jean. However, I soon found that living in Calcutta and spending more time in an office meant smarter clothing and extra expenditure on messing and renting a private billet. I even had to buy a service hat. I sent for my large suitcase that contained all the civilian clothes I had bought when first reaching India and which I had left with the Madrasis when I went to Arakan. When it eventually arrived I saw that the locks had been broken. Except for two pairs of socks it was empty. So I had to go out and buy, for the second time in a year, a complete set of clothes. It was indeed expensive fighting for King and Country.

I was ordered to go to Darjeeling to attend a specialist signals course to learn Morse code. Naturally I was not averse to spending time in the mountains and duly presented myself to the course instructor at the Planters Club where I was to stay. The first persons I met in the bar were my friends from V Force, Frank Bullen and Gretton Foster. Not much Morse code was learnt that night. Nor by the end of the week, because all I had learned was SOS (which seemed appropriate) and V for Victory (which did not). I was hopeless. There was no question of my becoming a radio communications officer.

After a week I received a signal from Laurie Brittain to report back to Calcutta as soon as possible. For 'security reasons' I was not allowed anywhere near the ISLD office or mess, but was confined to the flat we shared off Chowringhee. Here we were visited daily by various intelligence officers who endeavoured to teach us enemy ship and aircraft identification – I already knew what a Zero looked like! – and to recognise Jap insignia of all services, many of which I already knew from my time with V Force. I was soon to become proficient enough to act as an instructor for trainee agents of many nationalities; British, Dutch, Siamese, Malay, Indian and Chinese trainee agents all passed through my hands.

The instruction lasted for about a fortnight, after which Laurie and I took the train down to Colombo. On arrival we booked into the Grand Oriental Hotel, comfortable enough but not up to the standard of the Galle Face. Laurie decided against the latter because he considered it far too conspicuous; we were on a 'top secret mission' and had perforce to remain out of sight as much as possible. Dear old Laurie revelled in the secrecy of it all, causing the less serious-minded members of the organisation much amusement. He was right, of course, because not only were our own lives at stake, but also the safety of submarines and their crews.

After the usual nightcaps in the bar – no amount of security considerations would cause Laurie to miss those – Captain Hembry and Pilot Officer Brittain went to their beds. The following morning

Squadron Leader Brittain appeared for breakfast. I asked whether I could put up a major's crowns to match his new stripes. Laurie was not amused when in jest I pointed out that he had leapfrogged me in rank. He said that I must get away from the hidebound attitudes to rank of the regular forces. We were now in something altogether different, where rank did not matter. Laurie always was a little pompous. But he remained one of my dearest friends.

That morning we had our introduction to Korps Insulinde. This was a Dutch commando-type unit formed mainly by escapees from Holland. Over the next few weeks we were to hear many stories of their daring escapades getting away from the Germans, through France, over the Pyrenees to Spain and Portugal or Gibraltar. As Sumatra was, of course, a Dutch possession it was considered only sensible to use Dutch forces for any operations there. Anyway, the only submarines then available to the Allies in the Indian Ocean and Bay of Bengal were three Dutch O-class boats. These were smaller than the Royal Navy's T-class submarines that were to arrive from the Mediterranean in a matter of months, but were more comfortable and had the benefit of rudimentary air conditioning.

Laurie then unfolded the plan for the forthcoming operation. In about three weeks' time a party of eight – six Dutchmen and us two Britons – would embark on a Dutch submarine, sail to the west coast of Sumatra and make landings in the Trumon area of western Atjeh. We were to contact villagers to obtain as much information regarding the enemy's troop strengths and dispositions as possible, and also to bring back to Colombo two intelligent and well-travelled native Atjehnese for prolonged interrogation. These unfortunates were to accompany us willingly or unwillingly, it mattered not which.

It was then that I pointed out to Laurie that I had more actual experience of this sort of clandestine operation than all the other officers in the unit put together, and so it was imperative that I should take part in all the planning. With some reluctance Laurie agreed to see what he could do, which in the event was nothing. The senior Dutch officer at the Korps Insulinde camp was a Major Pel, an officer of the old school, thoroughly dislikable, and distrustful of everything British. Luckily the commander of the forthcoming operation,

Captain Jan Scheepens, was altogether different. A really outstanding leader of men, he came from several generations of Dutch military stock. His father had won the Dutch equivalent of the VC in the Atjehnese wars, and Scheepens himself had long military experience throughout the Dutch East Indies. We all had complete confidence in him from the start. I formed a close friendship with him that lasted until he was killed by pro-Soekarno terrorists towards the end of December 1945.

The Dutch had a very great advantage over Laurie and me as they had been undergoing full commando training for nearly six months and were at the peak of fitness. Although my war to date had been fairly strenuous, my strength had been undermined by several bouts of malaria and the jaundice. Laurie's war thus far had been fought from behind a desk. I was 32, whereas Laurie was 41 and not much of a games player prewar, so I thought it particularly courageous of him to launch himself so wholeheartedly into the three weeks intensive training. Also, we were damned if we were going to give Major Pel anything to complain about. Scheepens was my age, the others in their mid-20s. I became fitter than I have ever been during the whole of my life, before or since.

The day started at sunrise with PT, followed by instruction in unarmed combat and silent killing, then a swimming race over a mile. After breakfast we took to the rubber dinghies. The camp was about a mile from the open sea on the banks of a tidal river. The boat training took the form of paddling downstream when the tide was flowing and returning when it was ebbing. To paddle a rubber dinghy against a fast-running current, fully clothed and armed, takes every bit of strength and skill a man possesses and I shall never forget the utter exhaustion after the first three hours. As with a chain, a four-man rubber dinghy crew is only as good as its weakest member. With two men paddling each side in unison, the craft can be held to a more or less straight course. Slackening by one man will throw it off course, or even into circles. The Dutch naturally set out to show up the effete British; but Laurie and I hung on and refused to display weakness despite being many weeks' training behind them.

We spent the afternoons jungle trekking, and the nights once again in the rubber dinghies, paddling several miles out to sea and then paddling inshore and landing on the beach. This was particularly tricky as the breakers would tip us over unless we kept straight and end-on to them. We had to keep our weapons slung across our shoulders otherwise they would be lost when we were somersaulted overboard when the dinghy turned upside down. When we landed we would pull the dinghies up the beach and hide them, before setting off on a compass course to find a village or some other feature or RV. The object of these exercises, in addition to toughening us up, was to teach us stealth, speed, accurate landfalls, cross-country marching and teamwork.

The three weeks passed in a flash and, although we did not achieve the standard of fitness of the Dutch, Laurie and I were more than capable of holding our own. The intensity and thoroughness of the training were to save our lives.

The final exercises took place on a submarine. The rubber dinghies would be stored on board deflated. To launch them they would be passed through the very confined space of the forward torpedo bay and up through the forward hatch when the boat had surfaced sufficiently to allow it to be opened safely. The dinghy would then be inflated by the submarine's crew on the forward deck, after which the shore party would clamber over the side of the conning tower and make its way forward to the inflated dinghies and lower them over the side by rope. This part of the operation was extremely hazardous as the submarine's ballast tanks bulged out about 10 feet from the side and then curved downwards. After 10 days at sea the boat's casing would be covered in slimy weed and be as slippery as an ice rink. To contend with these obstacles in a heavy swell required training, courage and a lot of luck.

On the day of our departure we went on board the submarine depot ship HMS *Plancius* which was anchored in Colombo Harbour and were introduced to the Captain S (for submarine) who discussed the operation in some detail, reminded us that the safety of the submarine was of paramount importance and took precedence over all else – including the success or failure of our operation – stressed its importance to the Allied cause, and wished us luck. We were then introduced to the commander of our submarine, the O24, which was tied alongside the depot ship, Lieutenant Commander W. J. De Vries DSC, RNethN.

Our party consisted of Scheepens, Van Tuyl (a future Dutch foreign minister), De Jonge (the living image of the actor Jack Hulbert), Bernard Hanauer (who had escaped from Dachau, and whom I was to meet regularly in the Special Forces Club in London over the next 30 years. He taught modern languages at Charterhouse School), two other Dutch officers whose names I forget, Laurie Brittain and myself – in my opinion the best-trained and fittest expedition ever to set out from Colombo.

So began Operation MATRIARCH. We sailed at sundown, and within sight of the harbour and accompanied by a surface ship, we made our practice dive. Even to an experienced submariner this was an anxious time. It only required a small mistake by one of the depot ship's crew, such as the failure to secure a torpedo tube hatch, to send us to the bottom. If the submariners were anxious, just imagine what went through a passenger's mind on his very first dive. All went well, and after about half an hour we surfaced, signalled goodbye to the tender and set sail.

For the first few days out of Ceylon we sailed on the surface night and day, as far as the Nicobar Islands, as we were out of range of land-based enemy aircraft. Thereafter the submarine would dive at dawn and surface at nightfall, and the whole routine would change. Night became day. Supper would be taken at 0700 hours, one slept between 1000 and 1800, breakfasted at 1900 and lunched at 0100 hours. It took me some time for my body clock to adjust to this, although Bob De Vries told me that for submariners it was usually the opposite; they tended to eat meals at very strange times when in port. The O24 had limited officer accommodation. The wardroom had six bunks only which the army party was only allowed to use when the owner was on watch (a system the Royal Navy called 'hot bedding'), so it was unusual for one to finish the 'night' in the same bunk as one started it. I spread my Dunlopillo under the wardroom table which gave me some degree of comfort, but I found it very difficult to sleep. Although total heaven compared to the British T-class boats in which I later sailed, which had none, the air conditioning was not very effective. The body odours and the smell from the galley were obnoxious and accounted, I am sure, for my subsequent detestation of onions. The food was good.

I enjoyed the utter peace when surfaced at night under the tropical moon and stars. Over the next 12 months I was to make another four such trips and by the time of the last I had become very proficient at identifying the stars and constellations, having spent many happy hours on the conning tower with the officers-of-the-watch tutoring me in astronomy and astral navigation.

Then one day we were called to the periscope and shown the stretch of shore on which we were proposing to land. We were off the coast of Atjeh, between the Simeulue Islands and the mainland. It seemed beautiful and peaceful. We cruised up and down all day at periscope depth so that each member of the army party could survey the scene in detail and take notes. We spotted a sizeable village near the shore and Scheepens decided that this would be our target. We would land about a mile north of the village, aiming to reach the beach at about nine that night.

The submarine surfaced at sundown as usual and steamed very slowly, using the batteries because sounds carry far at night and the diesel engines would have been far too noisy. Sometime after eight Bob De Vries took his boat in to the 10-fathom line, and stopped engines. By the time the shore party had assembled on deck the two dinghies had been inflated and launched over the side. In spite of a fairly heavy swell we all managed to get into them without accident and then, with whispered good lucks from the crew members on deck, we pushed off and started paddling towards the shore.

We had about a mile to go to the beach and good progress was made. The breakers gave us some trouble and I nearly lost my paddle, but we touched down on the beach on time and after careful scrutiny dragged the dinghies up into the undergrowth by some coconut palms. All was quiet. We walked along the beach to the outskirts of the village, spread out and lay down and observed the scene for some minutes. Seeing nothing untoward we made our way to the centre of the village where we came across a number of the villagers squatting around a fire. They were amazed to see us and could not understand how we had got there. We told them by seaplane. We explained what we wanted and asked for the headman, only to be told that he was away but would be returning shortly. Meanwhile, we must stay for a makan besar (feast) and they would tell us all they knew about the Japanese in the district. But, they said, the headman would be in a much better position to answer all our questions when he returned, as he was constantly travelling around the area and in periodical touch with the Japanese administrator.

The crowd of villagers had by now swollen to about 50 and each of us had our own group surrounding us, telling us all that they knew or, more likely, what they thought we wanted to know. Time dragged on and we had enjoyed their hospitality – I ate some chicken and vegetables and had a mouthful of toddy – but there was still no sign of the headman. I now realised that the villagers were behaving in their normal treacherous way towards the Dutch, and warned the others. I had seen the signs. Scheepens agreed and decided that we would return to the beach, re-embark on O24 and try another village further along the coast. We walked back along the beach, aware that we were being followed by a large crowd of villagers. Suddenly, about 100 yards short of where we had hidden the dinghies, they all disappeared into the shadows; there was not a villager to be seen nor heard. We cocked our guns, realising that we had been betrayed and were probably walking into a trap. When only 50 yards from the hiding place we came under fire from rifle and automatic weapons. Without waiting for any command we all rushed into the sea, plunged into the breakers and began swimming in the direction we thought that the O24 would be.

The firing increased and something heavier joined in; I think a two-inch mortar. Scheepens called our names and all eight of us answered. How anyone had escaped the first outburst of machine gun and rifle fire remains a mystery. I am certain that none would have survived if the Japs had held their fire for another few seconds. We swam for all we were worth away from the beach. I remembered what the Captain S had said and was certain that De Vries would follow regulations and leave us to our fate. The bullets zipped around us like hailstones, and when the mortar bombs burst in the water our stomachs contracted and expanded in excruciating agony. I thought I would burst and my guts spill out. Gradually we pulled away from the shore but I was getting very tired. Laurie said afterwards that from time to time all he could see was my army cap floating in the water beside him and he would say to himself, 'Poor old Boris, the poor sod has bought it,' only to see my head bob up again underneath it, look around, take a breath, and go under again. We swam for about an hour as the shooting died away, and just as I was thinking that we would have to turn round and swim back to shore we saw the outline of the submarine. Utterly exhausted we were pulled aboard, and I saw that I was the only one who had retained his trousers and headgear. The others were stark naked. However, we had all still got our Sten guns.

We owed our lives to the intensive fitness training we had undergone, to Bob De Vries, whom none would have blamed if he had left us to our fate, who disregarded Admiralty regulations by bringing his boat closer inshore than the 10-fathom mark (the depth a submarine must have to submerge), and to Jap impetuosity.

The submarine gathered speed and headed out into deep waters, diesel engines roaring.

After a meal we had a brief discussion about the events of the evening and then all collapsed into the empty bunks and slept soundly for a solid six hours. I suggested that, in view of the obvious continuing animosity of the Atjehnese towards the Dutch, we should all say that we were British. I knew from my days on Gajah Muntah 12 years previously that the locals held the British in high regard. But the Dutch would have none of it.

The next day we cruised along the coast at periscope depth looking for likely landing places, all the time keeping a look out for enemy aircraft. Our story of using seaplanes might have fooled the natives but would not fool the Japanese. Their air patrols would certainly have spotted any Allied vessel getting close enough to Sumatra to launch and retrieve a seaplane. We eventually identified a beach that looked suitable and a nearby village, and that evening launched another two rubber dinghies, and paddled ashore. This time, though, Scheepens very sensibly decided that, once we had landed, one of the Dutchmen would rope the dinghies together and paddle out to sea and remain a few hundred yards off shore until given the signal to return to pick us up.

The village was smaller than that of the previous evening. When we were satisfied that it was free of Japanese we entered and found the village headman and villagers extremely friendly – but then so were those the previous night. We told them that no one was to leave the village under fear of death, and this time the interrogations were carried out by Scheepens and Laurie whilst the rest of us patrolled the village and surrounding areas. At about 11 we heard the sound of a motor vehicle. The headman got very agitated and said it was the Jap patrol that had arrived during the day to warn that Dutch troops were likely to visit them, in which case the villagers had to tell them, the Japanese, immediately. It seemed that the Japs were going to all the villages along that stretch of coast, following the previous night's episode, warning about the retribution the villagers could expect if the presence of these Dutchmen was not reported at once.

We beat a hasty retreat, but not before telling the headman of the dire consequences that would befall his village if anyone should betray us. I do not suppose it would have taken him long to realise that we could only be bluffing whereas the Japs were most certainly not. We had landed about a mile from the village and had kept to the plantations instead of the beach, so the going was slower and more tiring. All the time the sound of the lorry was getting closer and we could see the lights through the palm trees, mercifully going in the opposite direction to ourselves. By this time Laurie was beginning to feel his age and was some 20 yards behind. Leaving the others to go ahead I waited until he caught up. He was staggering and groaning and gasped that he had 'had it'. I said, 'Balls! Give me your Sten,' slung it over my shoulder, and dragged him along. The others were now out of sight, so I decided that we would make much quicker progress by taking to the beach. I soon spotted them ahead clambering into the dinghies, Scheepens calling for us to hurry. I got very angry and said, 'You might have waited, you bastards!' Laurie by this time was almost out on his feet and I had difficulty in holding him up let alone dragging him to the boats some 10 yards out. To make things easier for me I unslung my Sten and flung it into the nearest dinghy. Unfortunately it missed, and disappeared under the waves. I was past caring. Scheepens waded over and helped lift Laurie into the dinghy and we were soon on board the submarine again.

We had gathered much useful information from our second sortie about where the larger Japanese forces were concentrated throughout western Atjeh, how many vehicles were to be seen along the roads, the presence of armoured equipment and, as important, we were able to make sketches from the descriptions supplied to us of Japanese unit insignia. We then made our plans for the third and final sortie. Going through all the notes that Laurie and Scheepens had compiled we were able to decide what needed explanation or further enquiries or confirmation.

Again, as soon as it was light the next day we reconnoitred more beaches at periscope depth and chose one with a substantial village nearby. I thought that it might be large enough to hold a permanent Jap garrison and therefore to be avoided, but as we saw no signs of their presence it was decided that this was to be where we would abduct the Atjehnese: the larger the village the greater the choice. It was also decided that Laurie would not take part in this third landing. The landing and meeting with village headman and villagers went according to plan. We lay up outside the village to observe the situation and, judging the coast to be clear, went straight to the coffee shop and ordered drinks. We were told that the Jap patrol visited twice a day, as regularly as clockwork, at 10 in the morning and five in the evening. But, just in case, I was posted as lookout at the southern entrance and two Dutch guarded the northern. I spent much of the time chatting to a young girl and her younger brother. Apart from more useful information they told me that their older brother had been taken away by the Japanese the previous day for questioning as someone in the village had told them that he could speak another language that was not Dutch. The Kempeitai (Japanese secret police) thought that it could be English and that the unfortunate youth might therefore have something to do with the foreign spies who were in the area. It was English, but after a beating, they let him go.

After talking for about an hour, during which Scheepens had decided which men he would take back with us, I was whistled in from my outpost. The men appeared just what we were looking for but both were extremely reluctant to accompany us. However, the muzzle of a Sten pressed hard in the back was sufficiently persuasive. In any case we would have made a show of kidnapping them, to protect their families, even if they had been keen to go with us.

We called in the dinghies, climbed aboard, made the prisoners paddle to keep them out of mischief and got back to the O24 without further incidence. The Atjehnese quickly settled down to the strange life on board a submarine, and soon became willing collaborators and imparted much more useful information. After further questioning by intelligence officers when we got back to Colombo, they were given new identities (quite why this was necessary I cannot imagine), and were settled in a village near the Korps Insulinde camp. I saw them again a year later; they were barely recognisable. Very fat, complacent, and living with Sinhalese women at His Britannic Majesty's expense.

As soon as we were safely back on board and the dinghies deflated and stowed away, De Vries headed northwards in the hope of finding enemy shipping in the vicinity of Kotaraja, Sabang Island and the north end of the Strait of Malacca. I was pleased that the search yielded nothing worth expending torpedoes on, so after four days patrolling we headed for home. Once past the Nicobars we stayed on the surface and I enjoyed again the peace and quietness and coolness of the utterly beautiful tropical nights. We reverted to normal surface routine and everyone's spirits brightened progressively the nearer we got to Colombo.

Before being allowed into harbour the submarine had to be degaussed. The hour or two spent on this most essential operation was most irritating to those of us whose only idea was to get ashore, bathe, change and enjoy dinner at the Galle Face Hotel, if possible with female company. Scheepens always appeared with an endless supply of Service girls. I danced the night away on several occasions with Maria Goldman, the wife of my FMSVF colonel at the time of the Embodiment at Port Dickson, back in December 1941. A FANY (a member of the First Aid Nursing Yeomanry, the Princess

Royal's Volunteer Corps), she was now secretary to Lt Colonel Christopher Hudson, who commanded the combined Anglo-Dutch Force 136-Korps Insulinde wing of SOE, and told me it that it was not a happy partnership. I could understand why.

After a few days recovering from our recent exertions and debriefings by several intelligence officers, Laurie and I departed by rail for Calcutta. Lt Cmdr De Vries was awarded a very well-deserved DSO, Scheepens and the other Dutch officers received Dutch awards. Laurie and I were given a bottle of Bols gin to consume on the rail journey.

We were glad to get back to Calcutta and our comfortable flat, but had to produce more reports and to undergo yet more debriefings. I was amazed at the number of military intelligence officers who seemed to have little else to do except to compile reports. All this took a week, towards the end of which we were told that Colonel Leo Steveni, the ISLD Director, and a lieutenant colonel whose name I forget, were due in from Delhi to meet us. The meeting duly took place in Heath's office – the same office from which we had previously been banned for security reasons – when the formation of the Malayan Country Section, ISLD was confirmed. Much to Laurie's disappointment we were told that the head of Section would be an ex-Malayan police officer, whom I shall call Smith for convenience, with Laurie as his second-in-command. The unnamed lieutenant colonel and the ex-Malayan shared the same homosexual proclivities. It was neither the first nor the last time that I saw membership of the queers' fraternity assist the second-rate up the promotion ladder. Incidentally, Heath, who was Laurie's junior in Nestlé, very obviously derived great pleasure from having their positions reversed.

I was to be the number three in the organisation and general dogsbody. Again, I made it clear that I expected to have a say in the organisation of the Section, its staffing, training and planning, as I had more operational experience than the three others put together, in spite of being the most junior in rank. My life, and that of any agents that I commanded, must not be placed at risk by amateurs; by this time, rightly or wrongly, I was beginning to think of myself as reasonably professional. This attitude of mine did not go down well with my seniors, although the Director did somewhat half-heartedly agree with me and suggested to the others that my views should be sought.

But I did wonder why the SIS would wish to get involved with such an organisation as ISLD, other than simple empire building. I was meeting Force 136 people on almost a daily basis and it occurred to me that there was little that ISLD could do that Force 136 could not or did not. ISLD's remit was to be solely involved in gathering intelligence. Although Force 136's was to cause general mayhem and to prepare guerrillas to assist our eventual invasion and recapture of Malaya and the other countries in which they operated, in so doing they could not help but gather much useful intelligence, so in my view there was unnecessary duplication. But mine not to reason why ...

My first job was to recruit European officers, not only for active service in Malaya, but also for training, briefing and debriefing, and as conducting officers. The Asian agents were to be recruited from Chungking, Madras Province and other southern Indian states. By devious means many Chinese Malayans had found their way to Chungking and several score proved willing to return to Malaya. These were invariably supporters of Chiang Kai-Shek, as the Communists had taken to the jungle. Of all the men recruited for service in Malaya there was only one who gave us trouble. I tried my best to have him shot, but the powers-that-be would only sanction imprisonment for the duration.

The recruiting of the European element was easy – here the 'old boy net' worked to our advantage. Most of the ex-Malayans arriving in Calcutta had passed through Maurice Yates's hands so we could trace those who were not already in Force 136 and take our pick. My job was then to find suitable training areas, far from the madding crowd, and with separate accommodation for each party. They had to be kept apart for security reasons. Here once more Maurice was useful. Through him I met a partner of McLeods, the large Calcutta trading house that also owned several tea gardens in the Dooars. Most of the younger European tea planters had joined the Forces, leaving many bungalows empty. Smith and I went on a tour of inspection and judged them to be ideal for our purposes. There were sufficient available to permit the training of four parties, and accommodation and office space for the instructors.

Training consisted of lectures on security, how to set up meetings with other agents, how to recruit agents, so-called invisible writing, communications, briefings as to the kind of information we were looking for, the establishment of safe houses, recognition signals, making contact with known sympathisers, even how to resist torture from the Kempeitai in the event of capture – a forlorn hope, so I immediately deleted it from the curriculum as a waste of time.

Poison capsules were issued to all our agents and conducting officers, but I am unaware of anyone actually taking them on an operation. I flushed mine down the lavatory.

Potential agents were soon forthcoming. The first batch consisted of two Tamils and three Siamese. I messed with the Siamese, two of whom were members of the Royal Family and all three were charming and sophisticated men with English public school and university education. The Indians were of the babu (clerks) class, so there was no doubt why I chose to live with the Siamese. This was a mistake, only rectified when I took the Indians to Ceylon for their training in sea craft. Left alone at night they caused trouble with the females on the tea garden. I did not blame them, but it led to numerous complaints from the managers, not to mention the estate menfolk. As they were not members of the armed forces I could not confine them to barracks. There was little I could do but to ask them to be discreet. One of them also developed an excessive liking for the demon drink. I began to wonder just how successful the proposed operation was likely to be, especially as, contrary to my stipulation, I had no part in its planning. That had been done by Heath, Smith and Laurie Brittain whilst I had been involved upcountry. I had further misgivings when I learned that I was to be the conducting officer, to get them to a beach on Penang Island and to endeavour to retrieve them from a Chinese junk near Langkawi Island, off the coast of Kedah, four weeks later. I voiced my opinion that these two men were not suitable, but was overruled.

In due course I handed over the running of the training school to my second-in-command and returned to Calcutta with the Siamese and my Tamils. The Siamese went off with their own Siam Country Section officers, leaving me to concentrate on my troublesome pair. They were in lodgings not far from our flat and, together with an expert in matters Japanese, we met every day in our garden to continue the training. This was mainly how to recognise Jap military badges and insignia, and documentation. One of their briefs was to return with Japanese-issued identity documents and movement passes. I thought the whole operation far too ambitious, considering our lack of experience in mounting such an operation and the poor quality of our agents. Whilst one had been to Malaya, the other had not and, as I knew from personal experience with the Madras Regiment, their Tamil bore little relationship to that language as spoken in Malaya. Again, my objections were overruled.

Late in November 1943 the three of us flew down to Colombo in a Dakota, the first of many such flights I was to make over the next 18 months. ISLD had sent someone to Ceylon to look for a suitable training area and he had found an ideal place – an island with a lighthouse, about halfway between Colombo and Galle, uninhabited but for the two lighthouse keepers. No women and no alcohol – except my own closely guarded supply of whisky. The ferryman was employed continuously for the first two days shifting stores, rubber dinghies, equipment, food and a hundred and one other things that we needed to set up a base. We lived in the lighthouse storeroom. I arranged a daily delivery from the mainland of fresh vegetables, fish and fruit, and a newspaper.

We spent a very happy and strenuous two weeks on our island. The training was almost entirely physical: swimming, cliff climbing, round-island runs, dinghy paddling and night beach landings. My aim was to make the agents so tired that their only thought would be to 'bash the charpoy'. I also had the dinghies deflated every night and kept the pump by my side – I was taking no chances.

One morning, when we were going for the first of our daily swims, we noticed a large black heap on the beach on the mainland just opposite us. On closer inspection I saw it was a dead whale. It was very badly gashed so I surmised that it had probably been struck by a ship's propeller or wounded by a depth charge. By midday the smell was bad enough; after two days it was indescribably awful, so much so that I began to think that we should find another camp. The stench permeated everywhere – our food, our clothes, and even my whisky. But after four days the kites and gulls had cleared the flesh and all that remained was the skeleton, and by the time we left the tide had washed away everything.

Then one morning an officer from ISLD Headquarters in Calcutta arrived with our orders. We were to return to Colombo and embark on the T-class submarine HMS *Tactician*, under the command of Lt Cmdr Anthony Collett DSC, RN. The old submarine depot ship *Plancius* had been replaced by the *Adamant*, recently arrived from the Mediterranean. With it had come a squadron of T boats, commanded by men who had distinguished themselves in the North Atlantic and the Med, of which Tony Collett was one. The Captain S was Captain H. Ionides RN, a massive man, well over six feet tall, and broad in proportion. The wardroom was bright and cheerful and ISLD and Force 136 officers were always made welcome. Pink gins at tuppence a tot enabled one to enjoy many a half hour without breaking the bank. I renewed my friendship with Bob De Vries, whose boat came in off patrol as I arrived. We were to remain close until he left for the United States late in 1944.

I was summoned to Captain Ionides's cabin and introduced to Tony Collett. We went over the operational plan and I was advised, again, that at all times the safety of the submarine and crew, and the exigencies of the service – by which he meant that if a suitable target presented itself, they would not hesitate to attack it – took precedence over my operation. I did not think this fair, but kept my counsel. Captains on the army general list do not argue with captains RN. I then supervised the loading of our stores and went below and settled my two agents into their temporary quarters in the forward mess deck. I stood on the conning tower as we left harbour, observing the naval drills which had changed little since Nelson's time.

After the trial dive, we resurfaced and resumed the routine life on board a submarine in these waters. Nights on the conning tower observing the stars were interspersed with at least two hours a day of further instruction for my agents, going through the dos and don'ts, trying to get into their skulls that if they gave themselves away they would most certainly be tortured and executed. I had no conviction that the operation would succeed for, quite apart from anything else, and as I had considered from the start, the two men were not what I would call agent material. This did not diminish their personal courage in any way, but was hardly fair on them if they were not the kind of people to keep, in modern parlance, a low profile. I issued them with both British Straits dollars and forged Japanese occupation currencies, and identity papers, also forged, and went through the plans to establish cells in Penang, Province Wellesley and northern Perak for the umpteenth time.

We had one brief panic. We were on the surface when the ASDIC picked up an object travelling towards us at great speed. It was too late to take avoiding action so we braced ourselves for the torpedo to strike. In the minute or so wait Collett swept the area with the ASDIC but could find no trace of another submarine or ship. Then suddenly the object veered away and disappeared. The only explanation was that we had picked up a shark or whale. The heads were in constant use during the next quarter of an hour.

To the uninitiated, use of the heads in a submarine is complicated, and fraught with danger to the user. Whereas a surface ship has no difficulties in disposing of sewage, it is an entirely different matter for a submarine. The heads are adjacent to the control room and when submerged permission must be obtained from the officer-of-the-watch before they are 'blown'. The officer will raise the periscope and have a quick look round to make sure that there are no enemy ships or aircraft in sight and then, in answer to the request 'Permission to blow the heads, Sir?' will reply, 'Permission granted.' The process is complicated and involves operating several knobs in the correct sequence. Failure to do this results in the entire contents of the system being blown back in the face of the unfortunate operator, whose job it is then to clear up the foul mess. When enemy ships or aircraft are about the heads cannot be blown in any circumstance as the contents, when reaching the surface, would be an instant giveaway of the submarine's position. Of course, Nature being what she is, it is when the submarine is in danger that one is in most need of the heads, so the situation within the submarine can be better imagined than described.

We arrived off Penang at about midday. Collett and I spent the rest of the daylight hours with our eyes glued to the periscope surveying likely beaches for a landing, and eventually settled for one that looked suitable. We surfaced as soon as it was dark and, while I gave the agents their final briefing and the dinghies were brought out on deck and inflated, Collett took the *Tactician* in as close as he dared. At about 10 we launched the dinghies and the two Tamils pushed off towards the coast. We waited for a couple of hours, saw no SOS signals, so withdrew into deeper water and started our routine patrol.

Just before dawn we dived and slowly entered the northern approaches to Penang Roads. Through the periscope I could see the ferries plying between the island and Butterworth, just as they had done in peacetime, although the majority of the passengers were in khaki, as were most of the vehicles. We spotted the masts of quite a few warships which were tied up to the wharves. The sight of the Runnymede, the E&O and the Cricket Club brought back many memories of happier times. We lay off Penang for a day or so, after which, seeing no worthwhile target, left to patrol the channel around Langkawi Island, to the north. Again we saw nothing worth expending torpedoes on, so after about a week we returned to Colombo and eventually drew up alongside *Adamant*.

Early in December 1943 I set off again in *Tactician* in the hope of finding my two agents as arranged, sitting on a junk off Langkawi Island. I was not optimistic. In addition, *Tactician* had two other tasks: to land three of SOE's Siamese agents on a beach south of Victoria Point, and to carry out a normal submarine patrol in the area. The SOE conducting officer was Captain Simon Reid. A man straight out of a Boy's Own adventure story, he was tall, very thin, bearded and, when on operations, armed with every kind of side arm and knife imaginable. He was also great fun, a fund of stories, but did not believe in wasting water on washing. Even when we met for dinner at the Galle Face on the first night of our return from an 'op', he had neither washed nor changed. I think he brushed his long hair, occasionally. He was a brilliant linguist, and although he had no experience of Siam and the Siamese, applied himself to learning the language and was fluent in a matter of weeks.

Before we sailed Simon and I were summoned to meet Admiral Sir James Somerville, the naval commander-in-chief. He questioned us closely about the forthcoming operations and expressed himself most forcibly about his dislike of clandestine organisations and the risks that they put on his ships and crews. Shades of Captain Ionides. I was beginning to wonder whose side some people in the Royal Navy were on. It was obvious that quite a few of them would have preferred to be allowed to get on and fight their own war, with their own priorities and in their own time, without 'interference' from anyone else, particularly 'brown jobs'. When I later reported this interview to Heath he went to some length to criticise me for even discussing the op with the Admiral, as we were SIS and not part of the military establishment, and the Admiral had no 'right to know'. I found Heath's comments irksome in the extreme, and totally unrealistic, and told him so. I asked why, then, did I go around with three pips on my shoulder if I were not to all intents and purposes in the military. And was he suggesting that junior army captains take issue with full admirals – especially if we wanted to use their submarines? I was later to learn that many senior officers of all three Services questioned whether the results achieved by clandestine operations justified the extra risks to ships and submarines and, later, aircraft, and the removal of personnel, from their mainstream forces. I must admit that the longer I was involved in clandestine operations the greater the sympathy I had with this view.

We underwent the usual routine, keeping to the surface until the Nicobars and then diving by day and surfacing at night. As was now my habit, I spent as much time as I could on the conning tower, taking in the wondrous sights of the stars, feeling the cool breezes and thinking of more peaceful times with Jean and John. After a week we reached the coast of Siam and, following the usual reconnaissance, Simon Reid off-loaded his agents and we watched them paddle away towards the shore. Collett then moved down to the area of Langkawi and we commenced our patrolling, inspecting all likely looking junks through the periscope, hoping to see the pre-arranged signal from my Tamils. We did this for three days without seeing their sign, so Collett and I agreed that they would not be coming. On the fourth day we surfaced and I had a dinghy inflated so that I and a member of the crew who had volunteered to come with me paddled across to a very surprised and somewhat frightened Chinese crew aboard a junk. Meanwhile the submarine submerged, to cruise around waiting for my signal to surface again to pick us up. Having hitherto always been inside one at the time, or not nearly so near, I was unaware of the tremendous noise, all the hissing and blowing, that went on when a submarine submerged and surfaced.

The Chinese junk skipper was very forthcoming with information about the Japanese in Penang. He also told me that the Germans were using very large submarines to transport rubber, that there was one such U-boat loading in Penang harbour at that very moment, and that they had a naval contingent billeted at the Runnymede Hotel. I gained important information regarding the permitted movements of civilians, and I relieved two of the crew of their identity cards. They were, of course, most concerned, but I told them that they should report the cards lost overboard. I spent well over two hours talking to the skipper and added a great deal to our meagre knowledge of the Japanese occupation. It was he who gave me the idea for my next major submarine operation when he told me the way the Jap shipping, bound from Singapore to Rangoon, would sail in convoy between Langkawi and the mainland.

Having gained all the information that I thought I could, I signalled to Collett and within minutes the *Tactician* surfaced about 50 yards away and we were hurriedly dragged aboard. We dived immediately and took one last look at the junks in the vicinity to see whether my two Tamils were about, but seeing no recognition signal we circled Langkawi Island, surveying the coastline for likely landing places and hideouts. I was beginning to formulate a plan to establish some form of presence on the island.

In spite of the present setback, I could see that Langkawi was ideally situated for at least two of our purposes: a naval observation post, to monitor the enemy shipping en route between Singapore or Penang and Rangoon, and an assembly point for agents going in and out of the mainland. I felt sure that we could recruit sufficient Chinese junk crews willing to co-operate to provide the ferrying to and from various points up and down the coast, especially as we would be paying very well for their services. I was aware that Force 136 had made several unsuccessful attempts to pick up agents sent in earlier. Too much had been left to chance and to the skills of the agents which, at that stage, were not great. This reflected on us, the clandestine organisations, as we were to a great extent still feeling our way. Although both ISLD and Force 136 were extensions of well-established organisations in Europe and the Middle East, the conditions in which we operated were entirely different. For example, no European could pass himself off as a native of the area in the way that one could in Europe and the Mediterranean countries. So we were forced to operate through third parties.

I discussed my ideas with Tony Collett on the return trip to Trincomalee, to where the submarine depot ship had now moved, and he could see no problems from the naval point of view. In fact he became quite enthusiastic and promised to use what influence he had with Captain S.

Heath had flown down from Calcutta and was on *Adamant* to meet me when we berthed, hoping that I would be able to report a successful operation. In those early days, although I was unaware of it at the time, there was considerable and, at times, most acrimonious rivalry between ISLD and Force 136. Heath was most anxious to succeed where Force 136 had failed. But I had long before realised that those early operations had little chance of success, because of bad planning, poor agent material, and an almost complete ignorance of the current situation in Malaya under the Japanese. In retrospect I can see that both these main clandestine units had about a year of endeavour with little or no success, followed by a year of almost complete success.

Heath and I spent Christmas Eve 1943 at the Galle Face Hotel, and flew back to Calcutta on Christmas Day. A postmortem on the entire operation was held at which it was concluded that our two Tamil agents had fallen into enemy hands. I felt that there was an equal chance that they had merely gone to ground for the duration, opting for quietness and safety, but did not say so. In fact I was maligning them.

When I returned to Malaya in September 1945, I made a point of meeting all the agents that ISLD had put into place, including my two Indian friends. It seems that the first few days on Penang Island had gone smoothly, but they had come under suspicion during the ferry crossing to the mainland. At Butterworth they had separated, having arranged to meet up again somewhere in Kedah, en route for our RV off Langkawi Island. However, one, the alcoholic inclined, was picked up soon afterwards and, after a fairly savage questioning and beating by the Kempeitai, was incarcerated in Taiping Gaol. The other, the womaniser, evaded capture and penetrated as far south as Sungei Siput where he made himself known to Fernandez, the Kamuning Estate dresser. He was able to tell Fernandez that I was still alive and would expect him to give all reasonable assistance to any of my agents that came his way. In the event Fernandez proved most reliable and, although he was not formally an ISLD agent, I was able to reward him for services rendered when I got back to Kamuning. Needless to say, I was very glad that my two Tamils survived the war, paid them their arrears in pay and flew them back to Madras.

Shortly after my return to Calcutta Laurie Brittain assumed command of the Malayan Country Section, ISLD, and I was appointed second-in-command. I had spent very little time in Calcutta during the previous six months so I was surprised at the growth in the number of personnel employed by ISLD, both administrative and field staff. Laurie had several ideas as to how they could be employed and, usually over lunch in the New Club, would expound his theories and wax enthusiastic about his plans. These, mercifully, never saw the light of day. But over one of these lunches I unfolded my scheme involving Langkawi. Straight away Laurie put it up to Delhi, who approved it in principle, so we got down to detailed planning. I chose as my number two – it never occurred to anyone that I would not be in command – Captain John Llewellyn, a fluent Malay- and Dutch-speaking Welshman. The operation was given the code name MULLET.

In describing MULLET I have the advantage of having a copy

of both the operational order and the submarine commander's subsequent report before me.

The intention of MULLET was threefold:

1. To establish an ISLD transit camp on the north-west corner of the island of Langkawi.

2. To engage a junk or junks to carry agents between the island, where they would be dropped or picked up by submarine, and various destinations on the mainland of Malaya.

3. To establish a naval observation post on the island, in order to monitor Japanese shipping movements.

The party was to consist of myself, John Llewellyn, three Straits-born Chinese (one of whom was a radio operator), Able Seaman Denning RN, Corporal Johnson RM, and Corporal Flynn RM. With the exception of myself, whom I felt still retained a degree of fitness since training for the earlier Sumatra operation, and was in any case required in Calcutta for further planning meetings, the main party gathered at a specially established camp near Trincomalee and underwent intensive fitness training under the supervision of the Royal Marines. The lighthouse island camp was for agents only.

The departure date was set for 10 February 1944.

All personnel and stores were loaded on to the *Tactician* on the 9th, and we set sail late on the next day. We arrived in the vicinity of Langkawi on the 19th and just before dusk sighted a large junk becalmed west of the island. Llewellyn and I boarded it and, much to our disappointment, it soon became obvious that it would not suit us. It plied between Kantan, to the north, and Lumut, on the coast of Perak, to the south, with no intermediate stops; and the skipper and crew were so terrified of the Japs that no amount of bribe could get them to co-operate. Our orders stated that, in such eventuality, 'the junk must be sunk and the crew removed in a manner to be decided upon by the submarine commander and the party leader'. When we returned to the submarine Collett and I agreed that any such action could sour our future relations with other junk skippers, alert the Japs, and bring additional hazards to our agents, so that, on the whole, it would be better to let them go. I did not think that our future plans would be compromised. Anyway, I had not been happy with that part of our orders and thought the matter should have been left entirely to my discretion. We decided to land the party on Langkawi on the following day, but as the landing party were preparing Collett received a signal from Trinco to patrol elsewhere immediately; the 'exigencies of the Service'. The *Tactician* headed out into the Indian Ocean in search of prey, but after two days of seeing nothing we were ordered to resume our interrupted activities around Langkawi. It was now the evening of the 22nd; we were three days behind schedule. We launched our two folboats (folding boats) and inflatable recce boats over the side, loaded stores for the whole six days and, in the small hours of the morning, paddled away towards the island. Collett agreed to remain in the vicinity, but warned that he fully expected to be diverted away on another patrol. The lives of agents always seemed less important the higher the rank in the Royal Navy; whereas the ship and boat commanders were prepared to work wonders for us, bent the rules, and often turned a Nelsonian blind eye.

The landing was compromised from the start. There was no moon and the paddle-in took at least an hour longer than anticipated, with the result that it was dawn before we reached the selected beach. But misfortune had already struck, for we ran into a fishing fleet of a least 10 large sampans. They were all manned by Malays – who took not the slightest notice of us. It appeared as if they were accustomed to seeing strange-looking boats at 5.30 in the morning being paddled furiously by Chinese and Europeans. There was nothing that we could do except continue on our journey. It was past six when we landed and hauled up our boats across some 20 yards of white sandy beach to the cover of an overhanging rock. We all felt terribly compromised and very despondent. But as it would be several hours before the Malay fisherman could have got back to their village to discuss our presence with their headman, and probably an hour or so after that before they decided to report our presence to the Japanese, if in fact they had decided to, I decided to unload our stores and to move them some 50 yards further in from the beach where Llewellyn had found a cave in a cliff, screened from the sea by dense undergrowth. We then sat down under cover and ate breakfast.

I was faced with a grave decision. On the one hand my party was at stake; on the other the safety of the *Tactician* and its highly trained crew of 60 was of paramount importance. The Japs would realise that such a landing party could only have come from a submarine, and ships and aircraft would scour the area until it was sunk. I had no doubt in my mind that the whole operation had to be abandoned and that we should recall the *Tactician* and leave the vicinity as quickly as possible.

Shortly after nine o'clock smoke was seen coming up from the south, and very soon we identified six destroyers of the Asashio class which proceeded to patrol up and down, six or seven miles off the island. We naturally feared the worst; that our presence was already known and they were searching for the submarine. However, we were heartened to notice that the fishermen made no attempt to attract their attention. After an hour the destroyers suddenly turned away and headed north as quickly as they had come. I immediately gave instructions for the red recognition panel to be placed out on the rock for 10 minutes each hour on the hour, as arranged with Collett.

In the afternoon we had to stop this as we sighted two large merchant ships sailing in the direction of Langkawi Sound, between the island and the mainland, but these became temporarily obscured in a rain squall. We also saw several aircraft and were convinced that there was a concerted effort to find us. However, after a little while, when the ships had passed out of sight and the planes had left the scene, I began to think that, perhaps, the destroyers were not searching for *Tactician* specifically, but rather keeping the sea lane under surveillance to protect their merchant ships, and that my idea of an OP on the island was not such a bad one after all. But there was obviously too much enemy activity to permit us a staging post there for agents.

As soon as it was dusk we loaded our boats and paddled seawards. I had taken the precaution of roping the boats together. In the event this was wise as there was a very strong tide running around the island, and it appeared to be changing direction constantly. Once again it was very dark and squally. From time to time I flashed out our pre-arranged recognition signal, but with still no contact with

Tactician after several hours, our spirits began to flag and imaginations to run riot. Had the submarine been sunk, or sent away on patrol far away? Had it failed to spot our signals? How long would it be before we were picked up by the Japs if we returned to the island? How long should we go on paddling before I decided to return to Langkawi? All these things were going through my mind when suddenly the ear-splitting trumpeting of a dozen bull elephants rent the air, closely followed by a stentorian shout of, 'Hembry, where the bloody hell are you?' across only a couple of hundred yards of water. I recognised Collett's voice immediately, but it was coming from behind us, to landward. Eight very tired but very relieved men were dragged on board after having been paddling for over five hours. (The elephants were, of course, the boat's siren.)

Tony Collett's first words to me were that he had received a signal from Trinco to abandon MULLET forthwith and to patrol the Malacca Strait with the intention of intercepting the Japanese main battle fleet which was thought to be heading north from Singapore. My immediate reaction was to ask fo return to Langkawi Island. Collett went on to say that he had signalled us at nightfall to re-embark as quickly as possible and had kept on doing so for some time. He denied seeing our recognition signals. He had also failed to spot the destroyers, the aircraft or the merchant ships.

I realised that we had left the island before he had started signalling. And when we had flashed our torches we were already to seaward of him, so he had been flashing his away from us, landwards. Only Tony Collett's sense of duty and comradeship towards us, and willingness to disobey an order, had allowed us to be rescued.

I quote verbatim extracts from the Submarine Commander's report dated 9 March 1944:

8. It is felt that MULLET had to contend with bad luck from the start. Alteration of plans, alteration of patrol for priority Naval operation, lack of moonlight etc.

9. The operation has, however, conclusively proved that Langkawi and adjacent island are indeed ideal as an observation and W/T station for reports on enemy shipping.

I confirmed similar findings in my report and that 'many large vessels were sailing between the island and the mainland, giving good protection from British submarines'. My idea to establish a 'safe house' and route in and out of Malaya for our agents would not be feasible, at least on Langkawi Island, although I did wonder whether there would be more suitable islands further south, around Pangkor Island for example. In fact, this did not matter, as help was shortly to hand in the form of the Liberator bomber, which could fly the return journey to southern Malaya from outside Calcutta in a matter of hours rather than days, and parachute our agents and their supplies directly into their target area.

The submarine stayed on the surface for the remainder of the night, and dived at dawn. We had not been submerged for more than an hour when the Officer-of-the-Watch spotted through the periscope a very large German submarine on the surface gliding slowly towards Penang. Tony Collett allowed me a quick look. It looked huge. Although it was almost out of range Tony decided to fire off a couple of torpedoes. He followed the tracks until they disappeared, whilst we held our breath and counted up to 60 when we hoped to hear the thud of the 'fishes' striking home, but we heard nothing. Most of us passengers were happy enough that they missed their target because, if they had hit, every Japanese ship and aircraft would have been out looking for us. Tony lowered the periscope and dived deeper, altering course to avoid the island by as great as distance as possible just in case the torpedo tracks had been picked up by the German's ASDIC. All was peaceful again, and we relaxed in the overcrowded and extremely smelly wardroom.

We spent the whole of the next day submerged, running south until nightfall when we surfaced to cruise slowly to the northern end of the Malacca Strait. When we dived at daybreak we must have been level with the Selangor coast on the one side and Bagan Siapiapi on the other. I did not know it at the time but there were another three T-class submarines with us, strung out across the strait, waiting for the Japanese battle fleet to sail through. Had they done so it would have been impossible for them to have avoided serious losses, but I doubt very much whether our four submarines would have escaped.

The sea depth in these narrows scarcely exceeds 10 fathoms, the absolute minimum that a submarine needs to submerge. From keel to the top of the conning tower is 40 feet, so even when lying on the seabed there could be only 20 feet or so of water cover. All this was common knowledge to us passengers, so we viewed the forthcoming naval engagement with grave misgivings.

Tactician patrolled backwards and forwards at periscope depth until about midday when smoke was seen. This turned out to be a tanker travelling east to west, probably from Port Swettenham to Bagan Siapiapi or Belawan Deli. Collett closed with the vessel and, after making sure that there were no naval escorts or aircraft in the vicinity, surfaced, and scrambled the gun crew and opened fire – he wished to save his torpedoes for the battle fleet. I was allowed on to the conning tower to watch the fun, but to our consternation the Japs retaliated with two medium-calibre machine guns that Collett had failed to spot on the tanker's deck, which splattered the conning tower around us. I beat a hasty retreat down the ladder, but when I was only half way down Collett sounded the klaxon for an emergency dive, whereupon the other ship's officers who were on the bridge tumbled down on top of me and we collapsed in a cursing sprawl of legs and arms at the bottom. Within a minute or two we had submerged and began to circle the tanker whilst Collett chose the best angle from which to sink it with torpedoes – all the time conscious of the fact that it would have signalled our presence and ships or planes would have been on their way to deal with us.

Collett gave the orders to fire two torpedoes and after the hiss of their release we counted to 30 when there was an almighty explosion. He called me to the periscope; all there was to be seen was some debris, a mule, and several human figures in khaki falling from a great height. If I had not witnessed it I would not have believed that a ship of that size could have completely vanished in a matter of seconds. Collett then lowered the periscope and we got away from the scene as quickly as possible – all of 10 mph on our batteries.

The next 10 hours were quite the most terrifying in my whole life. We were bombed and depth charged almost continuously. We could hear the enemy ships criss-crossing the sea only a few fathoms above us, and just when I thought they had given up and gone away, over would come the bombers to drop their loads, and then the ships again with their depth charges. We stopped engines and just sat on the bottom. Not a word was spoken except in the quietest of whispers and then only by the First Officer reporting the damage. A dropped spanner on the steel deck could have been heard on the surface hundreds of yards away. There seemed to be a leak somewhere because I could hear the sound of rushing water. And, of course, just when one most wanted to use the heads one could not, under any circumstances. The stench of sweat, fart and fear was indescribable. It was particularly difficult for us passengers, as we were not trained submariners, had no duties to perform or stations to man, and could only sit tight and fear the worst.

At last the Japanese departed, whether because they had used up all their depth charges or had concluded that we had got away, we could never be sure. Collett told me later that it was touch and go whether the oxygen would hold out. We were lucky, too, that the waters in the Strait of Malacca were very muddy or we could well have been spotted, and that the Jap ASDIC was not up to the German or our own standard.

After all that, the Japanese fleet failed to put in an appearance.

We sat tight for another hour, just to be certain that we were on our own, before starting the port engine – the starboard engine had been damaged and was beyond repair by our ERAs (engine room artificers) – and limping away at snail's pace. As soon as it was dark we surfaced, and opened all the hatches to let the fetid air out and the sweet smelling sea air in. And everyone used the heads. We dared not break radio silence until we were within a short distance of Trinco harbour, to report our presence so that we were not depth charged by our own forces. We were seven days overdue and had been written off, so received a great welcome from other ships, with much hooting of sirens and cheers when our Skull and Crossbones was hoisted. When we secured alongside *Adamant* the Captain S came aboard and ordered Tony Collett to 'splice the main brace'.

As soon as I was on board *Adamant* I sent a signal to Laurie Brittain at ISLD Headquarters in Calcutta confirming our return.

They had, of course, also given us up for lost so it was a great relief when they learnt of our safe return. Laurie replied with the news that I had been promoted to major, and that I would be taking over from him as head of Malayan Country Section as soon as I returned from leave in England. This last bit of news was most welcome, as it was now nine years since I had been back to England, and I had had only one home leave in 14 years. And, of course, I was overjoyed at the prospect of seeing Jean and John again. It appeared that ISLD Delhi had arranged for me to attend a special course.

When I got back to Calcutta there were all the usual debriefings and postmortems. During the long, slow journey home Tony Collett and I had long talks about the op and agreed that we should recommend to our respective senior officers that we should try again as soon as possible. Now, as it was to be my responsibility to organise such an operation, I could put in hand the planning and recruiting of suitable agents and personnel, so that they would be ready for my return.

At last the great day came. Laurie cabled Jean, 'Get rid of lodger, Boris on his way!' The flight from Calcutta to Karachi was in a Liberator bomber that had been converted to take passengers. On arrival at Karachi, Frank Smitherman, who was with the Burma Country Section of ISLD and on the same course as me, and I were informed that a dozen or so brigadiers, all recently sacked by Lord Louis Mountbatten, recently appointed as supreme commander, were being sent home and had higher travel priority than us, so we would have to wait. We hung around Karachi for over a week getting very bored and frustrated until we palled up with a squadron leader who was flying back to England in another Liberator (unconverted), and if we did not mind sitting on a whole lot of parachutes in the bomb bay, we would be welcome to hitch a ride with him and his crew. We lay back like Eastern potentates and, having stopped off at Habbaniya for fuel, limped into Cairo on three engines. It required two days to do the necessary repairs, as aircraft in transit had a low degree of priority with the maintenance units. More frustration for Frank and I, relieved only by the opportunity to stay at Shepheards Hotel, and to hear at first hand the experiences of those who had fought in the desert – and those who had spent three years living it up in Cairo at His Majesty's expense.

We obviously had gremlins aboard our Liberator because on landing at Gibraltar we bounced a good 20 feet in the air, crashed back on to the runway, and broke one of the our tail fins. I was beginning to think that in future I must keep my feet firmly on terra firma. Life in the air and under the sea was beginning to be dangerous.

We were put up at the Bristol Hotel, then an officers' transit camp, where to my amazement who should come into the bar but Colonel Steveni, my ISLD director, who, to my horror and great disgust, introduced me to his drinking companions with the words, 'Here is Boris Hembry, one of our officers who has just been to Malaya'.

We hung around Gib for a week, going down to the aerodrome each day to try our luck for a lift. On the eighth day our squadron leader pilot of the Liberator met a friend who was flying a Wellington back to England and he got us a ride, again sitting in the bomb bay, this time on mail bags. We flew as far out into the Atlantic as we could to avoid the Luftwaffe – Frank and I had not been issued with parachutes – and eventually landed at Lyneham, in Wiltshire, this time with no mishap. It was raining.

Home

April 1944 – July 1944

My first thoughts on landing on that Sunday morning were of Jean and John. I wondered how much they had changed since we had last been together on Taiping Racecourse, on 1 December 1941. A lot of things had happened to all of us since we had said our goodbyes. John, I was sure, would have grown a lot. And I had not seen my parents and family for nine years. I felt a thrill at being at home in England – many of us then really did believe it to be the 'sceptred isle' – even though it was raining, and there was a war on.

Smitherman and I made our way to London by train and went straight to the Royal Empire Society, in Northumberland Avenue, where I was a member. My other club, the Sports Club, had recently amalgamated with the old East India Club and was camped out somewhere because their clubhouse in St James's Square had been taken over by the American military. I immediately telephoned Granny Cuthbertson to tell her of my arrival, so that she could inform Jean who was not on the telephone at the little house she rented, when she came off duty – she drove an ambulance. She was on the phone within the hour, and at the sound of her voice the years seemed to slip away as if we had never parted. It was agreed that she and John would come up to Liverpool Street station where Dad would also meet us, and drive us all over to Walton-on-Thames.

That afternoon Smitherman and I made our way to SIS Headquarters in Broadway, off Victoria Street. Contrary to all expectations the office was open, although, of course, the director was away for the weekend. His secretary, an elderly FANY, was most courteous and said how disappointed 'Master' would be to have missed us, and would we please come back the next day. She then took us in to see the paymaster, a bad-tempered captain who suggested that I was 'another bogus major'. I put him wise none too politely.

The reunions at Liverpool Street station were utterly joyful. I saw no change in Jean. John, of course, had grown. And my parents looked much the same, too. They had been living for several years in the house they had built for themselves in Walton-on-Thames, and were now well established in the area.

My recollections of my first reactions to England in general and London in particular remain vivid. The countryside viewed from the train from Lyneham to Waterloo was simply beautiful – England in the spring takes a lot of beating. Everywhere was so lush and green and fresh. The India that I was used to was arid, dirty, stale and suffocatingly hot. I was prepared for scenes of devastation in London, but not for the scale of such devastation. The pictures I had seen and the descriptions I had heard had grossly understated the real situation. I was horrified to find so many old familiar landmarks razed to the ground or gutted by fire. I compared it to Calcutta which had experienced some bombing, but nothing like London. I understand that 2,000,000 Indians fled the city after one small air raid, which had left a few craters along Chowringhee and on the Maidan.

After a week at Walton-on-Thames we moved to the little house that Jean had rented near her parents in Hornchurch. The Cuthbertsons had altered even less than my parents. Grandpa was a stalwart of the ARP, which meant being on duty for most nights, in addition to his vital war work supplying tubes of all sorts for the armaments industry. My parents-in-law usually had RCAF (Royal Canadian Air Force) fighter pilots from Hornchurch aerodrome billeted on them. Just before I arrived they had had the sad task of parcelling up the belongings of one young pilot who would not be returning. He had always given his egg ration to John.

The course started on the third week of my homecoming and meant commuting to London on most days. But, to be honest, there was not much that could be of any use to me. Neither I nor my agents were likely to be able to penetrate the Japanese High Command to photograph important documents, or to sit in the middle of Tokyo murdering top brass. But I did go to several most interesting lectures at the Code & Cipher School at Bletchley Park, where we were taught methods of encryption which were simple and unbreakable, and 'invisible' writing. But, of course, I had no idea of the real contribution that Bletchley was making to the war effort. I am fairly certain that one of my fellow students was Kim Philby, but for security purposes we did not bandy our names around.

To my surprise Reg Heath turned up one day. He did not tell all and sundry that I had been to Malaya recently, but he did quietly tell me that I had been recommended for the DSO, and that it would be gazetted sometime soon. I felt very honoured, but did not honestly feel that I had done enough to merit it, certainly not compared to the many heroes of all three Services that one continually read about who had been admitted to the Order. I told no one but Jean – which was just as well, because, a few weeks later, Heath invited me to meet him for a drink at the Café Royal where he informed me that my DSO had been turned down, on the grounds that I had risked capture in Sumatra (which was rich, as I had no part in planning the operation and had only followed orders) whilst knowing too much about the Secret Intelligence Service (I knew next to nothing – even about my own section) which I could (almost certainly would!) have given away under interrogation by the Kempeitai. And anyway service in SIS/ISLD was 'unheralded and unsung' as I had known from the beginning. On reflection, I wondered whether Heath had in fact recommended me for the decoration, as he must have been equally aware that such awards were not given to field personnel of SIS, even those in uniformed quasi-military sections such as ISLD, so I doubt whether he would have even wasted his time. But I was rather disappointed all the same.

In May I was involved in a tragedy. Laurie Brittain's wife Verna – she of the ass limerick – was working for the American forces in Australia and Laurie had been trying to pull strings to get her transferred to India. Out of the blue her transfer came through and she set sail from Perth in a merchant ship. Somewhere off Ceylon the ship was torpedoed and sunk by a Jap submarine. The few survivors picked up by the Royal Navy included the captain who reported seeing Verna, with several other survivors, mostly women, being taken on board the Jap submarine before it submerged. This was the last anyone saw of Verna, her fellow prisoners, and the submarine. It is assumed that it was sunk by the Allies soon afterwards. Laurie sent me a signal describing the event so far as it was known and asking me to go down to Henley-on-Thames to break the news to her parents. This I did. But within a matter of weeks Laurie had been posted to Australia. Another unnecessary waste of a life.

My course was not very strenuous and I was able to spend a lot of time with Jean and John. We went to several shows in London, and even saw a cricket match at Lords between two Services sides each containing several well-known cricketers. But naturally we talked a lot about what had happened to us since our parting on Taiping Racecourse. Jean told me of the hectic drive down to Singapore, of the dive bombings on the road, of her impatience with some of the Singapore Europeans' attitude to the war, of her brush with Dawson, the managing director of Guthrie's, over payment of her fare to Australia, of the stay in Sumatra, of her trip to Australia and the filthy state of the ship, of her stay on the sheep station outside Melbourne, of the very great kindness of all the Australians that she met, of the desperate unescorted dash across the Pacific and Atlantic oceans in the *Strathallan*, and, latterly, of her work as an ambulance driver in and around the East End of London in the air raids. Some of the details were so lurid that I began to think that I had been having the soft life. I had never had to pick up incinerated remains of airmen, or to take corpses to the mortuary, or to drive in the black-out during an air raid, with buildings crashing around. And all the time bringing up a vigorous little boy. In India we had no real shortage except, on occasions, of whisky. I had my moments of danger and discomfort, but at least I was able to escape to the peace and beauty of the Himalayas, be waited on, entertained, and have days of idleness. Not for me the prolonged strain of the flying bomb and the rocket, the food rationing and clothing shortages. I came to realise that, on balance, many thousands of women had a harder war than their menfolk, something that I believe has never been sufficiently acknowledged.

It was whilst we were at my parents that the Second Front opened on 6 June. It was apparent during the preceding days that something momentous was afoot because of the never-ending sound of aircraft overhead. For those of us who scarcely saw an aircraft that was not enemy, the vast air fleets of the Allies were something to behold. There was an air of fulfilment about; Rome had fallen, bloody battles were taking place around Kohima and Imphal in which the Jap seemed to be taking tremendous punishment and were being beaten back, and the Americans were making good progress in the Pacific. It would all be over by Christmas – so it was said.

The first V1 flying bomb, the 'doodlebug', arrived during the night of 12 June, a week after D-Day. More than 200 fell on London and the Home Counties within a couple of days, followed by another 3,000 during the next few months. Jean, John and I were back in the little house in Hornchurch when the first V1s came over. Our first reaction was that the ack-ack guns were having a turkey shoot, but we soon realised that this was not so and that Hitler's terror campaign had started. I was really rather frightened, but the British civilian population seemed to take it very much in their stoic stride. To them it was only one more bit of beastliness from old Adolf which would be seen off like all the others.

On Saturday 17 June we all went over to Walton-on-Thames for the weekend. They were the last two days that my father and I were to spend together. That evening the doodlebugs came over in droves and we could hear the explosions all around. There was an ack-ack unit in the waste ground behind the estate and they were in action constantly. At about midnight we heard a great cheer go up from the gun position as they had brought down a flying bomb – right in the middle of Walton-on-Thames, causing an enormous amount of destruction. It also brought down a lot of soot from the chimney, all over the drawing room carpet, much to the annoyance of my mother but laughter from the rest of us, because she complained bitterly that the charlady had only just hoovered and it was most inconsiderate of the Boche. It was the last laugh that we would have for some time.

On the Sunday the Guards Chapel at Wellington Barracks received a direct hit during matins, killing the entire congregation of hundreds. On Monday my father left as usual to go to his office at Brentford. We never saw him again.

We expected him home shortly after six. When he had not returned by nine we became very anxious and I telephoned round the local police stations to find out whether any incidents had been reported that might have involved him. The answer was no. At about midnight my uncle Fraser Thompson, who happened to be staying with us, accompanied me to Walton-on-Thames police station and we got the sergeant to phone all the other police stations in the district, but again they drew a blank. None of us slept that night.

Shortly after nine the next morning a Mr Lomax, a complete stranger, phoned to enquire whether Claude Hembry had got home safely the night before. He was most distressed when I replied no. He said, 'Oh, my God,' and went on to explain that, as usual, he had met my father in the 'Groto' public house at Isleworth, on the way back to their respective homes, for a drink. After only one the air raid warning had sounded and Dad, refusing a second drink, said that he would get on home as he so hated the doodlebugs, and anyway his son was home on leave. As he approached his car a flying bomb landed, quite literally, on top of it. The pub, although badly damaged, still stood and all the people inside had escaped with a few minor injuries. Most of the blast had gone over the pub; apparently a well-known phenomenon. I rang Alfa Laval and arranged for Dad's old friend Nobby Clarke, the works manager, to meet us at the Twickenham mortuary to help with the identification. My father was buried the following day in Teddington cemetery in the presence of my brother Bill, the board of directors of Alfa Laval and myself.

Mr Rutherford, the chairman, told us that after a board meeting the directors usually went to a local hotel for a meal and drinks, but on this occasion Dad had refused, giving the same reasons as he had later to Mr Lomax, but had popped in for a quick drink at the Groto nearer home. I resolved never to refuse an invitation for a drink.

I was due to fly back to India at the end of the month, but was granted a further month's compassionate leave. Mother did not want to stay in the house on her own and decided to sell up immediately, lock, stock, and barrel, in my view a very great mistake. She kept a few heirlooms, but many were sold, to my everlasting regret. My mother moved in with Bill and Winnie in Yorkshire for a few months, before setting up home with her cousin in a flat in St John's Wood.

One day in July I was summoned to an admiralty research establishment in Teddington to look at a two-man midget submarine. For most of the day I listened to an enthusiastic young naval officer trying to persuade me that it would be ideal for operations off the Malayan coast. The idea was that it would be towed by a T-class boat to within a few miles of the coast, the two crew would then transfer to it and submerge, get to within a short distance of the beach, surface, and launch themselves off in an inflatable dinghy, having set machinery to sink the midget sub to the seabed, and a timing mechanism that would automatically bring it back to the surface at the appointed time. I was sceptical in the extreme. Supposing the alarm clock failed and we were left paddling around looking for the sunken boat? Or supposing it went off by mistake and it surfaced in broad daylight? Or perhaps we wanted to beat a hasty retreat earlier than planned? I said no thank you very much.

Towards the end of July I received a signal from Laurie Brittain that he was coming to England for a conference before going back out to Australia, so would carry out the handover of the Malayan Country Section at Broadway. This did not take long, although the section appeared to have expanded even more during my absence in preparation for our 'moment of history' – the invasion of Malaya.

My time in England was now getting short. Broadway had reserved a seat for me on a flying boat leaving Tenby in South Wales during the last few days of July, and I was to hold myself in readiness to leave at a moment's notice. I spent as much time as possible with Jean and John, although I had to go up to Broadway on most days for discussions concerning intelligence requirements for the forthcoming invasion. These were memorable mostly for the excellent lunches that senior SIS officers seem to be able to order for themselves at fashionable restaurants and their clubs, in spite of rationing.

I did experience one amusing incident whilst waiting at Gidea Park Station to take the train to London. A middle-aged lady came up to me and enquired why a fit young man like me was not in uniform. I was stumped for an answer so I merely said, 'Far too dangerous, Madam, far too dangerous.' She snorted, told me that I was lucky she had not a white feather to give me, and stomped off.

The Cuthbertsons received the dreaded telephone call. I was to report to the RTO at Paddington Station where I would entrain for Tenby the following morning. Like thousands of other servicemen I said my sad farewells to my wife and son, not knowing when we would all meet again. In the event we would be apart for more than two years. Grandpa Cuthbertson drove me to the station, we said our goodbyes, and I was on my own again.

The journey to Tenby was dreary and the train crowded. Even though I had a warrant for first class, the compartments were full of senior officers so I stood in the corridor all the way to Swansea, and it was well past dinnertime before I reached my hotel in Tenby. The elderly barman was ex-Royal Navy and had spent some time in Singapore. We reminisced over a shared jar of pickles and a few beers before I turned in. The next day the whole of South Wales was fog-bound so we could not take off until late the following night. My fellow passengers were two brigadiers. They occupied two temporary bucket seats, whilst I lay down, as usual, on mailbags, and travelled yet again in comparative comfort, all the way to Calcutta. We refuelled in Gibraltar sometime in the middle of the day, and landed at Benghazi for the night, before going on to Cairo, landing on the Nile.

Here I was afforded VIP treatment. There was a car to meet me from the embassy – presumably laid on by the 'firm' – with a young man who suggested that I might like to spend the day at the Gezirah Club, then one of the world's great social and sporting clubs. Quite apart from the magnificently appointed club house, it had every conceivable type of playing field and games court, a swimming pool and a golf course. I understand that both Wally Hammond and Denis Compton had played cricket there. I noticed the two brigadiers looking a bit forlorn, so I asked them to join me. We had a most pleasant afternoon and evening, before taking off on the next leg of the flight early the next morning. Having flown down to Australia by flying boat over the colourful islands of the Dutch East Indies and the Celebes Sea, it did seem strange to be flying in one over the desert. We refuelled at Bahrain, Karachi and Delhi, before finally landing back on the Hooghly at Calcutta.

Command

August 1944 – December 1945

The first week of my return I was involved in taking stock and reviewing the section's activities, plans, and the organisation. I had had little to do with the Calcutta office for nearly six months, during which time the Malayan section had grown beyond all recognition. A branch office had been opened in Colombo, with the task of managing the training camps at Trincomalee and on Lighthouse Island, as well as the equipment, provisions, and transport. We now had a British warrant officer small arms instructor, with John Sketchley in overall charge, having moved down there shortly before my return. The Calcutta office consisted of myself, Harry Hays as 2IC, a number of conducting officers, training officers up in the Dooars, and Japanese specialists based in Calcutta, the latter shared by all the country sections. I had a most efficient secretary.

However, I was disappointed to find, in spite of the orders I had given before leaving for England, that we did not appear to have any more agents in training, or any operations actually scheduled. A few outline plans did exist but they all struck me as pretty foolhardy, and doomed to failure before they started. Frankly, I wondered what Heath and my old friend Laurie had been up to, other than engaging in empire building on a grand scale, knowing that they would get approval for most increases of staff and equipment simply because we were the Malayan Country Section, and the next big British-led Allied invasion planned was on Malaya. The bigger their staffs the more important their jobs and, it was hoped, the more senior their ranks. I fear it was ever thus.

ISLD Headquarters seemed to have trebled in size, mostly with lieutenant colonels and wing commanders. Brigadier Bowden-Smith had now succeeded as our director; a charming man, but in the early days he was greatly hampered by the lack of co-operation between the two principal British clandestine forces, ISLD and Force 136, and also, I thought, by a lack of the support he had the right to expect from some of his own more senior officers. It was to be one of my achievements that, before too much time had elapsed, I and my opposite number in Force 136 had managed to overcome most of the difficulties brought about by the previous inter-unit rivalries.

With the transfer of Mountbatten and his vast Supreme Allied Command South East Asia (SACSEA) organisation to Kandy, in the central hills of Ceylon, the ISLD Delhi Headquarters had followed. The mess, run by a lieutenant commander RN, who seemed able to lay his hands on anything, was in a large comfortable bungalow. The Supremo (as Mountbatten liked to be referred to) often used to drop in and I chatted to him on several occasions over a drink.

The first thing I had to do was to instigate some operations. Nothing is worse for morale than to be sitting around with nothing to do. Officers and agents quickly lose their enthusiasm for dangerous work. Besides which, of course, SACSEA would be requiring information about Jap troop dispositions, their intentions and likely responses to an invasion of Malaya. What information we did have indicated that they were switching troops away from the Dutch East Indies to the South Pacific area to try to counter the Americans and Australians. But they still had formidable forces in Malaya, and must have been aware that an invasion was being planned so would be preparing their defences.

I was surprised to learn that so much planning for the invasion of Malaya was being carried out in London rather than locally, and that they were being advised, to a large extent, by ex-Malayans who had not been near the place for several years. This was most evident by the choice of landing place, near Port Dickson, which I knew to be unsuitable.

Fortunately I had a first-class leader around whom to build my first operation. Charles Knaggs had been recruited shortly before my return from England. He was a Chinese protection officer from Malaya, highly intelligent, and with a real aptitude for radio work. I immediately sent him to England, together with two or three others, to attend an advanced radio course, where the instructors reported that he was outstanding in all aspects of the work.

Whilst he was away I began planning my first operation, to be code-named EVIDENCE. I liaised with Force 136 to ascertain their areas of activity, both current and planned. I was told that in the middle of 1943 they had managed to land two Malayans, Richard Broome and John Davis, both of whom I knew from prewar, together with some first-class Chinese agents, by submarine on the mainland under the code name GUSTAVUS. They had established contact with elements of the MPAJA, (Malayan Peoples' Anti-Japanese Army, communist Chinese-led) and had sent back much useful information, including the good news that Freddy Spencer Chapman was alive and living in the jungle. Unfortunately, they had then gone off the air and there had been no contact for many months.

I therefore suggested to Heath and Colonel Innes Tremlett, head of the Malayan Section of Force 136, that, if nothing had been heard from GUSTAVUS by the time that Knaggs's party was ready, we would drop it as near as possible to the last known position of Broome and Davis, taking with them spare radios and batteries. I suggested that the reason for their being off the air was technical rather than anything more sinister because I felt sure that, if they had been captured, the Japs would have kept the radio on air, feeding us with false information and hoping that in return we would give away details of our other operations. Having made contact with Davis and Broome, the ISLD party would then continue with its own mission of establishing intelligence networks in that part of the country.

I was taking the first steps to improve the relationship between ISLD and Force 136. There had been much jealousy and rivalry previously, much of it inspired, I am sorry to say, by ISLD, which helped no one and had allowed, I felt, the Navy and the RAF, on whose services we both relied, to play one of us off against the other on several occasions. By the end of the war the co-operation between our two clandestine organisations could not have been closer. This was undoubtedly helped by the close friendships I formed with Innes and Claude Fenner his deputy, two more people I had known in Malaya before the war.

At first I felt that the two organisations would be better amalgamated under SOE, as there was much overlapping of responsibilities, and consequently duplication of effort. But from the beginning of 1945, when Force 136 concentrated almost exclusively on preparing the resistance movements for their part in the forthcoming invasion, and channelled all their intelligence through ISLD so that I could present a comprehensive review in my daily intelligence reports, having the two organisations made sense. Anyway, there was no chance that the Foreign Office would have agreed to lose ISLD.

During these early weeks I was planning that ISLD would have units in the field along the whole length of Malaya, covering the main lines of communication that the Japs would have to use to counter our invasion. I was also giving much thought to establishing intelligence cells in all the main towns – KL, Ipoh, Seremban, Malacca, Penang, JB and, of course, Singapore. This we eventually did all too successfully, as some of our cells were to form the basis of the Min Yuen, of which more later. There seemed no shortage of young men willing to risk their lives on these somewhat nebulous projects, to travel thousands of miles and then to parachute into an inhospitable country, with a fairly good chance that the Kempeitai would be waiting for them. Although almost all my volunteers were in the Army and, to all intents and purposes, would continue to serve as uniformed soldiers, they would receive no recognition whatsoever for their services and bravery, unlike those in SOE with whom, very often, they shared the very same aircraft or submarine, and the subsequent dangers and hardships. And ISLD, more often than not, had to drop blind, with no DZ (dropping zone) party waiting for them, to wave them away if the Japs were too close. There was to be only one exception to the awarding of decorations, as I will relate later, and I had to go to the very top to obtain that.

I decided that EVIDENCE would be in two parts. EVIDENCE 1 was to consist of Charles Knaggs, Donald Gray, a planter, George Brownie, a businessman formerly based, I think, in KL, and three Straits Chinese, Ban Ho, Ah Lieu, and the second radio operator Wong Weng Fong. Nothing having been heard from GUSTAVUS, I decided to drop them south of Sungei Siput, near Dovenby Estate, on an open area east of the main road. From there I felt it would not be too difficult for the party to make their way into the jungle around Gunong Korbu, where I was sure they would be contacted by the MPAJA who would take them to John Davis, assuming they were still alive and free. The second party would follow into the same general area at the next full moon.

Donald Gray was an old friend and very hard-playing rugger forward. I had heard that he was somewhere in India with the Indian Army, so I sent word that I wished to see him in Calcutta as I might be able to offer him more interesting employment. Poor Donald confessed, well after the end of the war, that he was not a bit keen on the job I had offered him, but it was difficult for him to refuse without loss of face – Asians are not the only ones to dislike losing face. Whatever his initial doubts, Donald was soon hooked and became a first-class member of the team.

The follow-up party, EVIDENCE 2, would consist of Douglas Lee-Hunter, Nigel Crompton and two Chinese, one of whom was the radio operator. Lee-Hunter had distinguished himself in Burma and had won the MC and Bar. Outwardly he was a cheerful, happy-go-lucky chap, but in fact was ruthless, cold and calculating, and completely selfish. Nigel was a regular gunner officer who had escaped from France at Dunkirk and, after service in Burma, had volunteered for an Indian Army parachute brigade and so was one of very few members of ISLD who came to us as an experienced parachutist. Neither had been to Malaya.

EVIDENCE 1 got away on 25 January in one of the newly arrived Liberator Mark IV bombers, fitted with extra fuel tanks in the bomb bay. I must admit to certain qualms as I saw the aircraft disappearing with six young men that I was sending away to drop blind into an area that I had not seen for over three years. But at least I was sure that the whole operation had been carefully planned, the personnel well trained, and as little as possible left to chance.

The drop was scheduled for just after midnight. Should the pilot fail to locate the DZ he was to return to try again the next night. There were three main possible hazards: enemy action, low cloud or storms over the DZ, and navigational error. There could be three attempts over the full-moon period. I knew of one Force 136 mission having to make the three attempts. As the round trip took over 20 hours one can imagine the feelings of frustration and discomfort for the aircrew and agents alike. In the event of an abortive drop the heavy supplies would have to be jettisoned as the weight would be too much for the aircraft, even with additional fuel tanks, to make it home. This, in turn, meant that we always had to have our stores triplicated. Aircrews were instructed that the one container that should never be jettisoned was the one with the radio set. But they were not told that this also invariably contained large amounts of currency, opium and, sometimes, gold.

The first news came in a signal from the aircraft: 'Operation successful'. Everyone breathed a sigh of relief. We were to learn later from experience that this signal only meant that the 'bods' and stores had been dropped, whether on to the correct DZ, or into the enemy's lap, was an entirely different matter.

Each ground party had certain scheduled times and radio frequencies for sending and receiving. We had hoped that EVIDENCE 1 would come up on the air within 24 hours of landing, so I naturally remained close to our radios throughout the time. But no signal came. I was not unduly worried; I thought that they might have landed close to the enemy where it would be unsafe to start fiddling with their wireless sets. But after four sleepless days and nights I did become very worried, and began to harbour doubts as to the wisdom of despatching EVIDENCE 2 in just over three weeks, even though I knew from reports of similar operations into Burma and Siam that had gone wrong that the Japs would invariably try to get the captured radio set on air. Hence each radio operator had a code, usually a few innocent words, which would be included in each transmission to confirm its authenticity. I did not completely despair.

On the sixth day, I was in my office with Harry Hays and our RAF liaison officer discussing details of an operation I was planning to put a team into northern Malaya, to cover Penang and the railway route down from Siam, when the radio operator rushed in shouting, 'They've done it, they've done it!' I read the actual signal which said,

'You might as well have dropped us into Sungei Siput police station stop all well stop exhausted stop in contact with MPAJA stop full report later stop.' The radio operator confirmed the signal genuine; the code words had been included. My first reaction, of course, was total relief. Reg Heath and other senior officers then burst in, having heard the news, grabbed my hand and congratulated me on our first successful op. I had to remind them that this was the easy part. They had yet to set up their spy networks, the whole object of the exercise.

Subsequent signals filled in the details. The six parachutists had been scattered over a fairly wide area, far nearer to Sungei Siput than planned, and in the middle of extensive working tin tailings. How they missed the high-tension electricity power lines or landing in some very deep mining pools is a mystery. Luckily some MPAJA informers had spotted the drop, as had the Japs who came quickly on to the scene, but not before our six had been collected and spirited away to the jungle edge, minus much of their supplies but with the precious wireless sets and spare batteries, and the cash and the gold and some food. The MPAJA took them over and led them deeper into the safety of the jungle and, after about a fortnight, they met up with John Davis and were able to deliver the spare wireless set and batteries.

EVIDENCE 2 was despatched as planned the following month and rendezvoused with Knaggs's team.

According to Donald, ISLD was not welcome by SOE, who appeared suspicious of our intentions and seemed to be under the impression that we were out to steal their thunder. Nothing could have been further from the truth – in fact the very opposite was true, as I had chosen the area of operation of my ISLD team to help Force 136 – but it was a good indication of the ill-feeling and lack of co-operation that existed between our two organisations, and this had even filtered down into the jungles of Malaya. But there was also ill-feeling and lack of co-operation within ISLD, between EVIDENCE 1 and 2. After the close-knit party consisting of Frank Vanrenen, Ronald Graham and myself in Malaya back in 1942, and my later experience in V Force in Burma, I just could not understand it, and turned a deaf ear to many of the complaints that came back. After all, they were having a cushy time compared to Frank, Ronald and me. We were not weeks in the same camp, receiving a major's pay and allowances which could not be spent, supplied with mail and other comforts by parachute. And, anyway, I had other far more important matters to worry about than agents' petty complaints.

Incidentally, my teams had gold wire sewn into the waistbands of their trousers. This could be cut up and used in emergencies for bribery or reward. There must have been many emergencies and much bribery, as not one inch was ever returned. My enquiries were always met by smirks and evasions.

The EVIDENCE teams split and went their separate ways and were soon sending back valuable intelligence. In addition to information regarding Jap dispositions, troop movements, units etc., there was also much information of a political and economic nature. Some of this set out in great detail the post-war plans of the MPAJA. When I got the first inklings of these I managed to have infiltrated two of my own agents, avowed supporters of Chiang Kai-Shek, into the MPAJA, so I could get it straight from the horse's mouth, so to speak. This was probably the most dangerous job given to any of my ISLD agents during the whole of the war – and it was not even against our enemy, the Japanese. It was plain that, as soon as possible after the surrender of the Japanese, the Communists intended to oust the British and to seize control of Malaya. I included all this in my daily intelligence reports and discussed the matter with Innes Tremlett and Claude Fenner, as I realised that the high volume of arms and ammunition that Force 136 were parachuting into Malaya was not all going to be used as intended, against the Japanese. They confirmed that they too were worried at the number of arms containers that were not being recovered from DZs. I raised the matter with Brigadier Bowden-Smith and he promised to discuss it personally with Mountbatten at the very first opportunity. Mountbatten's response was that it was our job to win the war and someone else's to keep the peace.

At the time I had to admit that seemed sensible. In June 1948 I was not so sure.

By August 1945 ISLD had six separate main parties in the field, usually based in the vicinity of a Force 136 unit, spread throughout the country, and each with their paid informers operating out in the towns, railway stations and workshops, coffee shops and estates. The full-moon periods from early 1945 until the end of the war were increasingly busy, with often five or six Liberators flying sorties, dropping personnel and supplies, on behalf of ISLD and Force 136, along the whole length of Malaya, during the three or four nights available. We also had to recruit many more radio operators to man our receivers in Ceylon, as they were open 24 hours a day, to maintain communications.

Before we moved from Calcutta I had recruited Colin Park, the son of Air Chief Marshal Sir Keith Park, commander of 11 Group RAF during the Battle of Britain, and recently arrived out in India as Mountbatten's chief of air staff. Colin was a fine young man, rather wild, and had been wounded in North Africa. I did not know, until shortly before he was to drop into Malaya, that he had a metal plate in his head, and suffered from the occasional blackout, otherwise I doubt whether I would have taken him on. Sir Keith and Lady Park were a delightful couple and I often used to dine with them in their spacious flat in Government House. They never once asked about the whereabouts of Colin, and I never felt obliged to offer them any information, although often Lady Park would hand me a letter addressed to him for inclusion in the next supply drop. I kept in touch with them until after poor Colin was killed by terrorists near Kamuning Estate, during the Malayan Emergency, whilst serving with Ferret Force. When I made him a major in January 1945 he must have been one of the youngest in the British Army: he was just 21. I dropped Colin into Johore with Harry 'Piper' Gray, another Malayan planter, a Scot who was never without his bagpipes and who I was to get to know on Ulu Remis Estate in 1951.

Towards the end of 1944 I had been called in to see Naval Intelligence who complained that they knew next to nothing about the movement of Japanese shipping around Singapore and the use they were making of the old Singapore Royal Navy Base, and could I help? I studied the maps long and hard when suddenly, lying in my bath one evening, I remembered the jungle-covered bukit on Sungei Plentong Estate, in Johore, overlooking the naval base, that I had climbed with Professor Van Steyn Callenfells looking for Neolithic remains, back in 1934. If I could get someone on that, or one of the adjacent hills, they would have a magnificent and uninterrupted view of the naval base, the docks and every ship that went in and out. So was born Operation MINT.

That night I pondered the problem and discussed it with Harry Hays well into the early hours. Then, as soon as I had my ideas down on paper, I went to see Heath who, impressed, sent the embryo scheme straight away to the P Division Committee, whose chairman, Captain Garnon-Williams RN approved of the idea in principle. My plan was to get a party down to Australia, whence they would go by submarine to land on the east coast of Johore, near Mersing, and thence by foot to the hill.

I had also decided on a leader for MINT. It would be John Hart, an officer with experience of landing agents into Siam by submarine, of mixed Dutch and British parentage, and tri-lingual in English, Dutch and Malay. I cannot remember the names of the others in the ISLD party.

A T-class submarine was diverted to Australia on completion of its patrol and Hart and his party were flown down to Fremantle by Liberator, an uncomfortable non-stop 16-hour trip, where Laurie Brittain and John Sketchley gave them their final briefings and saw them off. But there was much Japanese naval activity in the South China Sea, to the north-east of Singapore island, which had to be avoided – the naval operations staff considered, for once, the placing of this particular team to be more important than torpedoing enemy shipping – and very bad weather, which would have made a beach landing impossible. So the landing was called off and the submarine made its way back to Trinco through the Sunda Strait, the narrow waters between Java and Sumatra through which I had made my escape in March 1942.

I was extremely disappointed, but determined to try again at the first opportunity. Shortly afterwards Hart and his party embarked in another submarine, this time on a joint Force 136/ISLD operation code name CARPENTER/MINT, on 6 January 1945. The Force 136 contingent was under the command of Captain David Trevaldwyn, whom I was to meet again many years later when we moved to Canterbury to find he and his wife, an artist of great ability, living nearby in Whitstable. They went by way of the Sunda Strait and threaded their way through the islands around Singapore before successfully landing the SOE party and John Hart and his two Chinese agents on 6 February. CARPENTER was a very successful three-stage Force 136 operation. On the third stage they landed 20 Royal Marine Commandos who secured a strip of beach whilst they took off the crew of an American B29 Superfortress bomber that had been shot down during a raid on Singapore, and Sergeant John Cross and others of a party left behind in Johore in February 1942, and long since written off until news of their survival had filtered through to John Davis up in Perak. Cross and his companions were eventually guided to John Hart's camp, where they also found the American airmen, from where they were rescued.

John Cross was a remarkable man and he described his adventures most graphically in his fine book *Red Jungle*. He mentions me briefly:

> In Colombo we were met by Boris Hembry. He had been a planter in prewar Malaya, and had been one of Major Spencer Chapman's behind-the-lines parties in January 1942 ... I had been longing to get out of Malaya and back to civilisation, but now, curiously, it was a pleasure to join up with this man with a Malayan background. He was in radio touch with Hart and knew all about us. I could speak freely to him and he understood everything at once. Our interrogation at Kandy followed. It took the form of daily examinations by specialist officers in a hut at Supreme Headquarters. I did not feel it was a success. Perhaps I had developed some raw edges, but the political affairs officer seemed to be haranguing me rather than interrogating ... but the understanding Hembry gave me my head by suggesting that I should sit quietly in his quarters for two or three days while I made a written report, which was a much more successful procedure.

John Cross's reference to the interrogation sums up the behaviour and attitude of some officers who never got nearer the war than a headquarters office chair and the mess bar.

MINT was my most successful ISLD operation and the only clandestine operation using a submarine that I know of that gained the Naval Commander-in-Chief's full approval. So much so that, after John Hart's reports had resulted in the sinking of a Japanese cruiser and several other ships, together with much useful intelligence concerning shipping movements, he thanked me personally as we stood side-by-side in the headquarters lavatories. Many years later, while Jean and I were staying at his lovely house at Kyleakin on the Isle of Skye, Colin MacKenzie, the late head of SOE in South East Asia, told me that MINT had been considered in senior intelligence circles to have been the most productive intelligence operation in the whole of the Malayan war.

John Hart and his Chinese radio operators had narrowly escaped capture on several occasions. The Japanese had quickly realised that someone with a wireless set was operating across the strait and did their best to catch him. It was certainly nerve-racking for me waiting for him to come up on air. As soon as peace came in August 1945 I pressed for a DSO for John and received the usual response. But, as Winston Churchill once said, 'Up with this I will not put.' I wrote a formal recommendation to Brigadier Bowden-Smith, who agreed to pass it on to the Supremo personally, and lobbied every senior naval officer I met, including Mountbatten's ADC, advising them of John's contribution to the naval war effort. Eventually, to my very great satisfaction, I was able to signal to John that his richly deserved DSO had been gazetted. I remember his reply with pleasure: 'Thank you, but you deserve it more than I do.' Not so, but it was gratifying that he should say so.

My friend's story is nearly finished. When I flew to Singapore shortly after the surrender, John Hart and all the officers, other ranks and civilian agents, whom I had ordered to make for Singapore immediately on the cessation of hostilities, met me off the plane and escorted me to the building they had taken over as temporary headquarters. In only a matter of hours John began pressing me to send him on an operation to Java. His parents had been interned somewhere on the island and he was anxious to trace them. There was no way he could go unless it was on an operation. Against my better judgement I formulated a plan and forwarded it to my superiors who approved it. In October 1945 John flew to Surabaya where, almost immediately, he was ambushed and shot dead by Soekarno terrorists. I can only conclude that they thought he was a hated Dutchman. His totally unnecessary death has remained on my conscience ever since. There was no real military reason for him to be in Java. I should not have yielded to his entreaties. I made sure that the DSO was handed to his mother.

My days were very full. In addition to the six major parties, MINT, and a further two similar smaller operations in the field, more were being planned. Each morning I held a conference in my office at which all the incoming signals were discussed, intelligence dissected and analysed. I would be required to fly down to Ceylon at least once a week for meetings with senior SACSEA intelligence officers, Force 136, and to visit the ISLD training centres on Lighthouse Island and near Trincomalee. Whilst there I would often go aboard *Adamant* to discuss MINT, and enjoy a few pink gins with the Staff Officer S Lieutenant Commander Sheridan Patterson. While in Ceylon I had the use of my own Beechcraft, usually flown by a very able Sikh flight lieutenant. On my return to Colombo I would take the night mail train to Kandy to attend conferences chaired by Brigadier Bowden-Smith. Then back to Colombo to catch a Hudson or Dakota for the uncomfortable and often very bumpy flight back to Calcutta. It was on one of these flights, during a refuelling stop at Bangalore, that I saw three Mosquito aircraft crash within a few minutes of each other. They simply fell out of the sky, without warning, and for no apparent reason. The RAF put it down to lightning strikes in the clouds. Our departure was delayed for a couple of hours to allow the electrical storm to move on, but the event hardly boosted our confidence as passengers.

Soon after my return from England in July 1944 I had moved into the large flat vacated by Laurie Brittain, just off Chowringhee, and I invited Harry Hays and his wife Deb to join me. Deb soon created a real home from home, but after a few months she went off to join her sister in Bangalore, so we had the flat to ourselves and it soon became a temporary mess for officers in transit who were usually associated with intelligence work. One such was the Honourable Harold Tennyson, later Lord Tennyson. Harry told many amusing stories about his father, England's cricket captain in the 1920s, who was a great character. One I particularly remember also involved Harry whilst he was up at Oxford. He had picked up a girl in the bar of the Berkeley Hotel and after a night's dining and dancing, had taken her back to her flat. The next morning when he slipped her a five pound note for services rendered she said, 'You mean bugger – your father always leaves me a tenner.' Harry later became the representative in England for Veuve Clicquot.

Even after moving the Malayan Country Section Headquarters to Ceylon we kept on the flat as a base in Calcutta. Other visitors I remember were Peter Brooke, nephew and heir to the Rajah of Sarawak, and Leonard Cheshire VC, who stayed for a fortnight. A very quiet and unassuming man, he was on his way, as Churchill's representative, to witness the dropping of the atomic bomb on Hiroshima, although, of course, I did not know this at the time.

I moved my headquarters down to Ceylon early in March 1945, to be nearer the centre of things. SACSEA and ISLD Headquarters were up at Kandy, SOE Operational Headquarters were in the Mount Lavinia Hotel, and the Navy was at Trincomalee. MINT was now my only operation requiring a submarine; all others were positioned and supplied by Liberators now also based in Ceylon. I should have moved earlier, but we were all so busy with operational matters that I did not give it high priority.

There was already a complete signals unit there, with three or four codists, and I took with me Harry Hays, my RAF liaison officer, my FANY secretary, and my quartermaster, leaving only a skeleton staff in Calcutta to oversee the agent training establishment and recruiting.

I was so pleased to get away from the Calcutta box wallahs, many of whom appeared to spend more time out at the Tollygunge Club than at their desks. The office worked like clockwork under

Harry, leaving me to attend to the operational side of things. These were undoubtedly the hardest and most interesting months of the war for me. With the anxieties for other men's lives, there were times when I longed for the peace and quiet of the Arakan. During the early stages of an operation, when we were waiting for the first signal that they were safely arrived, and then settling down to jungle routine, there were many nights when I took Benzedrine to keep awake in case of an emergency and panic signals.

My relationship with Force 136 became even closer. I attended their weekly conferences when every operation was discussed in great detail, news of movements, resupply problems, troubles with the MPAJA and intelligence. I reciprocated as much as I was able – more, no doubt, than I should have done, because ISLD simply did not disclose its field operations and sources of information to anyone. I took a very liberal view of the 'need to know' principle. My friends Innes Tremlett and Claude Fenner well understood that I was unable to be as totally open with them as they were with me. By now Force 136 was a vast organisation, concerned mainly with organising, arming and training the forces that would rise up and attack the Japs when we invaded, like the Resistance in France in 1944. The collection and correlation of intelligence material was of secondary importance to them, but was our raison d'être, so they passed everything that came their way to ISLD for evaluation and dissemination as appropriate.

I was able to bring caution to bear on a matter dear to my heart. In January 1945 I had received evidence that Bob Chrystal was alive and living deep in the jungle somewhere in Pahang with Kuomintang guerrillas. Force 136 had a party not too far away and suggested they contact Bob, get him to the Perhentian Islands, off the Trengganu coast, with a view to lifting him off by submarine or flying boat. I thought this a daft idea. Bob had survived since January 1942 and it seemed crazy to me to risk getting him across to the islands now, with the end of the war now probably only a matter of months away. Fortunately Innes Tremlett agreed and the matter was dropped. In due course Bob and his friend Creer fell in with Dobree of Force 136 and Desmond Wilson, the leader of my ISLD team in Kedah.

To quote from Denis Holman's book on Bob's epic feat of endurance, *The Green Torture*: 'Chrystal was thrilled to hear from Desmond Wilson, a cheery Irishman with a heavy black beard, a member of ISLD, that his chief in India was none other than Boris Hembry who, the reader will remember, had been his assistant on his Sungei Siput estate ... Chrystal had always thought that Hembry had been captured by the Japs ... Chrystal was overjoyed that he would be able to send him a radio signal that very night. He drafted a signal, asking Hembry to inform his wife in Western Australia that he was alive and well.'

I received this and wrote a very guarded letter to Babs Chrystal, with no more than a hint that Bob was alive. I did not want to buoy up her hopes only for Bob to die before we could get him out. I posted it in a town pillarbox, rather than sending it with official mail, a mistake as it had obviously attracted the attention of a censor. I was invited to meet a senior security officer two days later, and was surprised to see my letter open on his desk. I was required to destroy it, having first received what I thought, in view of the letter's carefully worded contents and my own job, an unnecessary lecture on security.

I then had a better idea, one which I should have had in the first place. I signalled Laurie Brittain in Brisbane asking him to instruct John Sketchley to call on Babs in Perth and personally impart the news, but not before stipulating that she must not divulge it to a soul, not even to her own children.

When the time came for MINT and CARPENTER to be resupplied we organised a joint ISLD/Force 136 drop. The round trip of 3,500 miles took the Liberator nearly 22 hours, at that time the longest flight, in terms of mileage and duration, in support of a clandestine operation on record, for which the pilot, Squadron Leader Lewis Hodge (later Air Chief Marshall Sir Lewis Hodge, KCB, CBE, DSO, DFC) was awarded the DSO.

Sometime in April 1945 I was invited to dinner by Innes Tremlett. We often dined together at his small seaside bungalow, usually alone as we could discuss a lot of things more openly, away from the more formal large weekly conferences. On my arrival I was a little surprised to see Claude Fenner too, because not only did he spend most of his working days with Innes and would have been entirely au fait with all aspects of Force 136 operations, but also he had his wife and small daughter living nearby and naturally wished to spend as little time away from them as possible. However, over a stengah it quickly became apparent why he was there. They had decided to attempt to bring Richard Broome and Freddy Spencer Chapman home by submarine, and were interested to hear my comments and suggestions. I was all in favour. The distance that the two escapees would have to travel to the coast was not much more than 60 miles, and most of the route was under the control of the MPAJA. With adequate guides they should be able to reach the coast, possibly in the Pulau Pangkor/Lumut area, in roughly a fortnight from the word go, time to arrange for a submarine to be on hand. In the event the T-class boat originally intended for the rescue broke down and another, smaller, submarine had to be diverted. The pick-up was a success and Freddy and Richard arrived back at Trinco on 19 May – Freddy having been out of circulation for three years and five months.

Freddy and I had much to talk about, and we spent three whole days almost alone together. Our tongues never stopped wagging and our gullets never ceased swallowing. It was the longest and most enjoyable debriefing that I ever did. Along with all the joviality and enjoyment of his homecoming I extracted much useful intelligence information, particularly about the post-war intentions of our communist allies. Freddy's book, the story of his sojourn in the jungle, and what led up to it, *The Jungle is Neutral*, rightly became a bestseller. The Force 136 Air Liaison Officer responsible for arranging the RAF air drops was a very attractive WAAF, Flight Officer Faith Townson. Faith was billeted at the Galle Face Hotel and now and again we dined together. She became Mrs Spencer Chapman. After the war, Freddy and I met from time to time at the Special Forces Club in London, and corresponded regularly. He became headmaster of the British school at Plön, in Germany, and then of St Andrew's College, Grahamstown in South Africa. Disapproving of apartheid, in 1962 he returned to become warden of the Pestalozzi Children's Village at Seddlescombe in Sussex, from where he moved to Reading

University as one of the college wardens. We met at the SFC one night towards the end of July 1971 and I found him very distrait. On 7 August my dear friend and comrade-in-arms took his own life. I, like all those who had the privilege to know him, was devastated.

At about this time I was promoted lieutenant colonel – temporary and unpaid.

The war in Europe had ended, and the Japs were retreating everywhere but still putting up stubborn resistance. Life became even more hectic as we asked our agents in the field to acquire yet more information about the enemy's activities and dispositions. My intelligence reports became increasingly important as D-Day for Operation ZIPPER got nearer, and I was required to present the latest situation reports once a day. By now Force 136 had many teams in the field, so there was a lot of their intelligence to sift through and evaluate in addition to my own ISLD's.

I had received orders to sail with the Commander-in-Chief on his battleship, together with my signals unit, so that we could maintain constant contact with the ISLD teams on the ground. I did voice my continued doubts to Innes Tremlett as to the suitability of the proposed invasion beachhead and he agreed with me. But neither of us thought that the opinions of junior officers such as ourselves would be greeted with anything other than derision and annoyance, certainly not at this late stage, and anyway we both had our minds full with our own jobs.

All was set for a bloody battle when the first atom bomb fell on Hiroshima on 6 August, followed by a second on Nagasaki three days later. On 15 August the Japanese capitulated.

I must admit that my first reaction was one of disappointment. Quite apart from the enormous amount of work we had all put in to ensure a successful recapture of Malaya, we were looking forward to knocking hell out of the Jap and returning as a conquering army, thus in some way reinstating the British in the eyes and minds of the Asian population whom we had so badly let down in February 1942. And, I thought, the more Japs we killed in the process the better.

The disappointment quickly evaporated and gave way to a feeling of very great relief. Thousands of Allied soldiers' lives would be saved, including and particularly the POWs', as I had received evidence that, had we invaded, the Japs would have massacred every POW and civilian internee they held, male and female. Their safety quickly came uppermost in our minds and I signalled every one of my ISLD teams to report the whereabouts and numbers of any POWs or internees in their areas. The vast majority, of course, were in Siam, having worked on the Railway, and Singapore, although we were aware of numerous internment camps spread around the Dutch East Indies.

The Allied prisoners of all races had been subject to over three and a half years of the most savage and barbaric treatment by the Japanese, and were continuing to die in large numbers of disease and starvation, and the highest priority should have been given to getting help to them as quickly as possible. This was prevented by the combined chiefs of staff agreeing to General Douglas MacArthur accepting the overall surrender of the Japanese in Tokyo Bay with all the pomp and ceremony that he could devise. America was now the dominant partner and Britain had better accept it. We in SEAC were very bitter. The consequent delay could have had most serious consequences for our men still in enemy hands. The ceremony on board the battleship USS *Missouri* on 2 September was no doubt a magnificent and historic spectacle, but not worth the life of one Allied POW.

To quote from General Slim's definitive book *Defeat into Victory*: 'Our men and those of our Allies were daily dying in their foul camps. Thousands were at the limit of weakness and exhaustion. Had we delayed even a few days more in sending in supplies and relief personnel, many more would have died pathetically at the moment of rescue ... The evacuation of our prisoners had to wait the arrival of our troops.'

The mind boggles sometimes at the mentality of generals determined, I suspect for their own egos, to 'put on a show'.

Mountbatten and Slim, therefore, 'jumped the gun' and began flying in help before the formal surrender. They had already seen the first batch of POWs repatriated from Rangoon and knew what to expect. Some had passed through Colombo before I had left for

Singapore. To say that I was appalled by their appearance would be an understatement. Most of us seeing them felt ashamed to think that we had lived more or less comfortably whilst our fellow Britishers had been so foully degraded. The amazing thing is that, amongst my friends who had suffered at the hands of the little bastards, scarcely one showed any bitterness in later life. I could not have been so forgiving.

On the Saturday immediately after the surrender I was invited to a party given by Sir Keith and Lady Park. I drove up to Kandy by jeep as I intended to travel back to Colombo via Nuwara Eliya, in the mountainous tea-growing district of Ceylon. It was quite a long journey, much of it through jungle. Coming around a bend in the road I saw a large mound ahead in the middle of the road, at the same time aware of a most unpleasant smell. As I got nearer I saw it was a dead elephant. I managed to get around the carcass but the smell had penetrated everywhere and clung to my clothes so that, as soon as I arrived at the Parks' house I had to creep in through a side door and straight upstairs to my room to shower and change, thankful that I had been invited to stay the night. I found the party a little daunting. I was the only officer there under the rank of admiral, general or air marshal, except for a number of junior WAAFs, WRNSs and FANYs. I spoke to Generals Slim, Carton de Wiat VC, Browning, Oliver Leese and several others. I seemed to be the only member of the clandestine community invited.

Admiral Mountbatten sat down beside me as I was chatting to Lady Park and said, 'Thank you, Hembry. Thank you for all your hard work,' and asked whether I would be taking part in the Victory Parade that was being planned for Singapore. I said not. He got up and excused himself. But I was rather flattered. I was able to give the Parks a message from Colin and to show them on a map his whereabouts in Johore. Before I left the following morning Sir Keith gave me a letter for Colin and I was able to hand it to him when we met in Singapore 10 days later.

After a week or so, when I was sure of the cessation of hostilities, I instructed my teams to make their separate ways to Singapore, to commandeer suitable houses, and to prepare to receive me and the advanced party on about 2 September. I had arranged for two Catalina flying boats to carry Harry Hays, a driver, some secretaries, codists and signallers and myself. After a 17-hour flight – made more uncomfortable for me because, as the commanding officer, it was my 'privilege' to sit in the canvas rumble seat in the cockpit rather than to spread myself out to sleep as usual in the belly of the fuselage – we touched down on the old flying boat base at Seletar. With the exception of Charles Knaggs and Douglas Lee-Hunter, every man jack of my teams were there to greet me, including the two Chinese who had penetrated into Singapore itself, setting up a coffee stall opposite the main entrance to the Japanese GHQ, to report the comings and goings.

Charles Knaggs had died a month earlier from river fever, a form of typhus. He was buried by Donald Gray in secondary jungle about 40 miles north of KL. When I went north to find out what was keeping Douglas Lee-Hunter so busy that he was unable to obey my orders to come to Singapore, I found the grave, marked it prominently, and was able to advise the war graves people of its whereabouts. Charles now lies at Kranji, in Singapore, along with several others mentioned in this book. He, John Hart, and the two young British officers who disappeared near Trinco while out training in a folboat early in 1945, were the only casualties that we had during my time in the Malayan Country Section of ISLD.

The first two weeks were very hectic. I personally debriefed all my teams, compiled lengthy reports on their activities and the intelligence they had gathered, and began making arrangements for them to fly back to Calcutta prior to leave and demob. The Asians were paid off and travel arrangements were made for them to return to their homes, either in Malaya or, in the case of my two Tamil friends, to Madras.

As soon as I could get away I took the best of the 'liberated' cars and drove up to KL where I was reunited with Bob Chrystal. He was very thin, but otherwise appeared to be reasonably fit. We had a marvellous evening together with so much to talk about. But I was astonished to learn that Force 136 was not going to fly him to Australia. I telephoned Harry Hays and instructed him to arrange a flight without delay. Bob was off within 48 hours. I was delighted to accomplish something which Force 136 was either unable or unwilling to do.

Having got Bob transport down to Singapore I drove north to Ipoh, booked myself in at the Station Hotel and walked across to the Ipoh Club where I met Bill Ferguson, whom I had last seen with his brother Freddy in the Great Eastern Hotel, Calcutta, immediately before I joined ISLD. He was with the Rubber Unit of the British Military Administration, in my view one of their very few sensible appointments. The club steward had somehow conjured up several bottles of Scotch, which were consumed in fairly short time. The following morning I drove out to Kamuning Estate where I received a wonderful reception from those who remained of my prewar staff. I saw our bungalow. It was in a sorry state. I found a torn snapshot of Jean and Ronald Graham in our swimming pool, which I remembered having taken in 1941. The old manager's bungalow was not much better. I told Kandasamy, the office head clerk, that I intended to move in there but he advised against it as the Kempeitai had used it for their interrogation and execution centre for the district, and he doubted whether we could get any servants to work there. In fact, when I returned to Kamuning I had it pulled down and used a lot of the materials to rebuild my old senior assistant's bungalow, which then became the manager's. Kandasamy told me that he had kept a trunk containing some of our belongings which had been packed by our Tamil boy when Jean had left in haste in December 1941. I told him to retain the trunk until I returned, which I thought would be early in 1946. As luck would have it, Kandasamy's house was completely destroyed by fire soon after I left, so I never found out what was in the trunk. So Jean and I had lost absolutely everything. Everything except our opium stool which I found in a coolie's house. It remains a most treasured possession.

My car broke down, so I abandoned it and got a lift back to Ipoh on a passing army lorry. I telephoned Douglas Lee-Hunter in KL to send up one of the many cars that he seemed to have at his disposal. Meanwhile I stayed at the Station Hotel until it arrived the next day, and was driven down to KL. I never found out exactly what Lee-

Hunter was really up to. He pretended that he had a ring of agents working in the political and economic field, but it was obvious to me that he was involved in some lucrative racket – more like a Mafia boss than a major in British Intelligence. I got him back to India as soon as I could, but, because of his outstanding war record in Burma, with some reluctance I decided against further investigations into his recent activities.

From KL I flew back to Singapore in an RAF plane. Harry Hays was busy winding up our affairs. All the time I was being cabled by Guthrie's requesting that I should arrange to be demobilised in Singapore, and as soon as possible. They had offered me a senior position, which I had accepted. They were also pulling strings to get my release. The majority of Guthrie estate managers had either been 'put in the bag', or killed, or were in the forces elsewhere in the world. The fact that I had had only a three and a half month break in nearly four years did not seem to occur to them. Unfortunately, at the time, it did not occur to me either what I was missing. For instance, 90 days home leave on full pay. A demob outfit. And, above all, reunion with my family. These received no consideration at all from Guthrie's. I wondered at times, in the years to come, why I should have felt so much loyalty to that firm.

The death of John Hart was still weighing heavily on my mind when we nearly had another unnecessary tragedy on our hands. Colin Park had somehow got hold of some locally brewed 'hooch', a particularly poisonous form of toddy. Many British ORs were in hospital having drunk it, some had gone blind, others had actually died. Colin had disappeared, but I tracked him down to the BMH (British Military Hospital). He was in a sorry state, but recovered sufficiently in a fortnight to be packed off back to India.

By the end of November most of the winding up had been completed and I had filed the last of my reports. The penultimate paragraph warned that the Communists intended to take over Malaya at the first opportunity. My officers and agents were all off my hands, paid off or at home enjoying well-earned leave. Only Harry Hays, a couple of clerks and my FANY secretary remained. As we did not have a great deal of work, Harry and I took one of the several cars at our disposal and drove up to Kuala Lumpur. It was a large Humber Snipe, which did not run very well because the Japs had used a mixture of spirit and oil made from rubber instead of petrol. However, it got us there. Just. We left it at a Chinese garage, no doubt to be used as spares. We stayed at the SOCFIN mess with John Sketchley and Jock Campbell, who had been demobbed in Australia, and caught up with each other's news. Peter Taylor and several other Guthrie directors had arrived and were living in the Station Hotel. Peter was anxious that I joined them, but I declined. But I promised to go down to Port Dickson to open up the Guthrie estates in the area in December, whether or not my release had come through.

Harry and I then flew back to Singapore. For the past year I had been able to order, almost at will, if not my own aircraft, at least priority air passages. Henceforth I had to join the queue and take my turn after the top brass, civil servants of quite lowly rank, and absolutely everyone in the British Military Administration (BMA). The last-named, even in the short time they had been in Malaya, was already gaining a reputation for maladministration, extreme arrogance and high-handedness, and corruption.

Whilst finally packing up the office I saw Harry repeatedly eyeing a tin box which I always kept firmly locked under my desk, whether in Calcutta, Colombo or Singapore. Eventually he had been unable to resist asking what was in it. I, too, had been giving much thought to its contents for a month or more. We had had two abortive drops when, as the normal practice, all the aircrafts' cargoes had been jettisoned, except the case containing the radio. My tin box contained $52,000 in brand new notes, together with several yards of gold wire. The equivalent of £10,000 – a great deal of money in 1945 – was mine for the taking, with no questions asked. Harry's face, when I finally opened the box, was a picture of disbelief. I explained where it had come from and the dilemma I was in. Should we keep half each or hand it in? We were sorely tempted, but agreed that we would not wish to have it on our consciences. I took it around to the Treasury Department where the official I saw was most annoyed. It appeared that the money and gold would have been written off months ago, and it would be a difficult accounting exercise, and there would probably have to be an official enquiry, if it had to be reinstated. Did I really wish to return it? With reluctance, I said yes. It was a decision that I have regretted ever since – the more so as I am certain that the official, a member of the BMA, kept it himself.

I must not omit to mention the chow dog I took over from a surrendered Japanese army officer. Kim was to remain my faithful companion and shadow until his death in 1950. I had to learn some Japanese in order to talk to him. He had sabre slashes on his side where the Japs used to 'play' with him with their swords.

My release came through with effect from 12 December 1945. I said my farewells to my staff, loaded my belongings into my commandeered car, and set off for Port Dickson, Kim on the front seat beside me, after what I like to think was honest (too honest!) endeavour, and with a letter in Brigadier Bowden-Smith's own hand in my pocket.

He wrote:

Dear Boris,

Thank you very much for your letter of the 29th. It is very gratifying to know that you can look back on your days with ISLD with no regrets, for never would I have believed that any man could have been flung unseen and unknown into such a maelstrom of difficulties and oppositions both from above and below. If it hadn't been so absorbingly interesting and of such vital importance I could never have stood it. I can also say, quite truthfully, that I have had more drive, determination and support from you than from any other Head of Section.

I have always tried to improve our relations with 136 and Malaya was one of the hardest areas to get co-operation, but your arrival as Head of the Section immediately eased that task and between us in the end we had won through.

Whether you will be granted any visible proof of gratitude for your services I do not know, but you have definitely got mine.

A happy 1946 and all good luck. Hope to see you at

Ascot next summer, whether I get the job or not.

Yours sincerely,
J. L. Bowden-Smith

Kamuning Again

December 1945 – September 1947

My worldly possessions consisted of a suitcase of clothes, my officer's valise, a wind-up gramophone and some records, an American .30 carbine, a .22 rifle with silencer, a German Luger automatic pistol, a few boxes of ammunition and a Japanese officer's sword. The carbine was supplied by the OSS (Office of Strategic Services, the forerunner of the CIA), the rifle by ISLD, and the Luger and sword by His Imperial Japanese Majesty. The OSS did excellent service in many theatres of war, but what it was doing in our theatre puzzled me at first. However, I became friendly with several of their officers and very frequently went to beg some piece of equipment or other as they had large quantities of everything imaginable. The reason for their presence in India, Ceylon and eventually Malaya became obvious the nearer we got to VJ Day. Their ranks multiplied threefold, with men carrying briefcases rather than weapons. They were the spearhead of American big business, salesmen determined to get in on the ground floor of the vast South East Asian markets that had been starved of both everyday essentials and luxuries for so long. European factories were non-existent or, as in the case of Britain, fully geared to producing for the war effort. The Americans, of course, had spare capacity which they were eager to use. It did not endear them to us.

I had already made a recce of the Port Dickson area and arranged to move into the old APC (Asiatic Petroleum Company) mess – one of the very few bungalows that had not been vandalised, and right on the coast. The other occupants were the local British Military Administration officer who was acting as the district officer, a Royal Engineers officer who was assisting the Public Works Department, and Freddy Cunnyngham, an elderly proprietary planter of many years standing and something of an institution. I was made most welcome.

After four years of army life it seemed strange to be a civilian again, but a very great relief. Responsibility for the lives of others may sharpen the wits but it plays havoc with the nerves. I now looked forward to finding out how much of my old skills I had retained. My first task was to visit each estate in turn, and then to compose long reports describing their state and immediate requirements. These would be cabled to London as the KL offices were not yet functioning.

One day on Linggi Estate, as I was driving up to the office, I was smartly saluted by two very unkempt and obviously half-starved men. I stopped because of the salute, and even in their present state their bearing seemed soldierly. Astonishingly, they were two Gurkha riflemen left behind, badly wounded, in 1942! They had been taken in by Rajahdorai, the Linggi office clerk, nursed back to health, hidden and succoured for the duration of the war. I gave them some money, arranged for them to have a square meal in our mess, and then to be driven over to the nearest British Army camp, where the FMS Volunteers had been camped when I joined Freddy Spencer Chapman almost exactly four years previously. Rajahdorai was rewarded, but I have no doubt inadequately, as is the British custom. We still correspond at Christmas. He is now a millionaire, having invested in property, and lives in Seremban.

The estates in the Port Dickson area had suffered little damage other than by neglect. During the interval between the surrender and the actual landing of British troops the Chinese had removed many of the aluminium slats from the latex settling tanks, and until these were recovered – either by threats or payment – or replaced, factories could not resume production. Also, there were scarcely any latex buckets left. I got over this by approaching APC who sold me hundreds of empty four-gallon kerosene tins which I had cut in two.

I spent Christmas 1945 quietly in Port Dickson and New Year's Eve at the Station Hotel, KL, with Peter Taylor, now managing director designate of Guthrie's, Malaya, and a few other Guthrie box wallahs. They had all recently arrived back from England, so henceforth I was to deal with the KL office rather than directly with London. Everyone seemed to have had leave except myself.

I was dumbfounded when I learnt that Bob Chrystal had returned to Malaya, not even waiting to have Christmas with his family. He had returned at the Government's request to help round up the Kuomintang guerrillas still roaming around Pahang and the other eastern states and falling prey to MPAJA, who were murdering them for having been traitors to the communist cause. The supporters of Chiang Kai-Shek had helped him survive so, naturally, he wished to assist them now. The next thing I heard was that Bob had reached Fraser's Hill where he had collapsed and had been admitted to KL Hospital. As soon as he was fit enough to leave he came to stay with me at Port Dickson. It was wonderful to be reunited and we had a most rewarding month together, talking about the old happy days, his life in the jungle, and the enmity between the MPAJA and his Kuomintang friends. He then went back into the jungle, despite my repeated requests that he call it a day. He collapsed again soon afterwards and Peter Taylor asked me to accompany him down to Singapore to put him on a flight to Australia. Unfortunately there was a mix up over timings and I missed him. We were not to meet again until he and Babs came to stay with us in Suffolk in 1959.

The early days after the war were intensely interesting and very challenging. Everything was in short supply: food, clothing, medical services, common sense and integrity. This last was particularly lacking in the British Military Administration, who quickly became known far and wide as the British Mal Administration. Many of its members openly boasted that they were in it for 'a quick buck', to set themselves up for retirement at home. It was my misfortune to meet some of these types, members seconded to the Rubber Section of the BMA, one in particular on Kamuning, as I shall relate later. Only a few planters had managed to escape from Malaya in February 1942. Of those who did, those of military age who were not already in the Forces immediately joined up; those of middle age were usually posted to appointments in the civil service, and were spread far and wide. It is estimated that nearly 300 planters were killed, or died as POWs or internees – over a quarter of the entire prewar total. Thus, until the survivors started to drift back after home leave and recuperation, planters were thin on the ground. The numbers were made up by the BMA.

Such was the reputation for dishonesty and corruption surrounding the BMA name that, for example, many former employees of the Tanglin Club, in Singapore, which in those early post-war days was being managed by the NAAFI, part of the BMA, did not apply for their old jobs again until it was returned to civilian management at the end of March 1946. They thought that even to be associated with the BMA would damage their chances of re-employment.

Reid Tweedie told me that, when the prison gates were opened, his cellmate in Changi Gaol immediately went to his bungalow on Claymore Hill, where many tuans besar had lived, and was both amazed and overjoyed to find it exactly as he had left it three and a half years previously, even to the extent that his gramophone records and copies of *The Field* were in the same order as when he had departed. The house and contents had been well looked after by his servants and the occupiers, senior officers of the Imperial Japanese Navy (many of whom would most probably have trained at Dartmouth). Reid's friend returned to Changi for the night, to collect his few possessions and to say goodbye to his fellow inmates. When he got back to his bungalow the following morning his servants greeted him in tears. His house was empty, ransacked by the British Army. One of the uniformed vandals was even wearing a major's crowns on his shoulders! When it comes to looting, the British Army has few peers.

The main estate work consisted of obtaining supplies of rice and other necessities, and setting gangs to work to clear four years' growth of weeds. I got local Chinese tinsmiths to make tapping knives, and potters to produce cups for collecting the latex, and it was with great satisfaction that we started tapping on Port Dickson Lukut Estate in February 1946, the first estate in the Guthrie Group, if not in the whole of Malaya, to go into commercial production.

By February the bureaucrats had begun to return in large numbers to fill the civil service posts. One of their first acts made me extremely angry. They called in all the cars that we early birds had commandeered from the Japs. It did not matter whether the vehicles happened to be essential to the owner's occupation, or that that occupation was to do with the economic recovery of the country. I appealed to the highest authority in the BMA, but to no avail. I was told that if I did not hand in my car I would be arrested and held in custody, as martial law was still officially in being! I must admit I was sorely tempted to call their bluff, especially as I knew that the man I was dealing with had spent his entire war in the Navy, stationed in New Delhi, hundreds of miles from the nearest sea! My car was confiscated, no doubt to be driven by some junior civil servant seconded from the Colonial Office. I could never understand why Guthrie's did not put up more of a fight against this iniquitous ruling. I was required to drive my Studebaker into Seremban to hand it over; the civil servants were not even prepared to come out to collect it; I suppose it would have meant missing a few stengahs at the Sungei Ujong Club. I bought a clapped-out Austin Seven from a Chinese towkay, the only car I could find. On the way back to Port Dickson the rear end suddenly collapsed; the offside wheel had come off. Luckily I was near a Malay kampong and some of the menfolk lifted up the car while I refitted the wheel. I could not find the wheel nuts so removed one nut from each of the other three wheels, and drove the rest of the way at 20 mph. The estate engineer managed to keep the little car going until the following month when I went down to Singapore to pick up a brand new lorry for the estate, one of a batch recently shipped out from England.

It was good to see Singapore getting back to normal. I was delighted to see my old friend Dan Wright in the Guthrie Singapore office, and very pleased to learn that he had been appointed as one of the three visiting agents. Outwardly he had survived his three years as a POW on the Railway remarkably well, but it was not something that he ever cared to discuss, even with his oldest friends. He had got off the ship from England that very morning. I delayed my return to Port Dickson so that we could enjoy quite a few stengahs together before he caught the night mail train to KL.

My time in Port Dickson was getting short. Planters, old and new, were beginning to arrive in large numbers and I was able to hand over the estates one by one. I was anxious to get to Kamuning where I had officially been appointed manager. I knew from my brief inspection that it was in a far worse state than any of the Negri estates, and news I had received in letters from old members of staff who knew that I was returning to Sungei Siput was disquieting, especially about the temporary manager.

So, early in March 1946, I sat down behind the steering wheel of another new lorry that I had collected from the docks in Singapore the previous week, and set off for Kamuning Estate. Four years and three months earlier I had driven a lorry in the opposite direction. After a break in KL to talk to Peter Taylor I drove northwards to Tanjong Malim. Royal Engineers had put up a Bailey bridge to replace that which their predecessors had blown up in January 1942. I passed the police station where Frank, Ronald and I had spent that last night before taking to the jungle, and stayed overnight with Harry Hays on the SOCFIN estate Lima Blas, talking well into the night, in spite of the early start that I had planned for the next morning.

On my way again I rounded the bend north of Tanjong Malim where I had seen the Bofors gun, and passed the track which had led to the Chinese kongsi where all our stores had been stolen. I was to pass this way many times again and always had the desire to drive down the track to see whether our abandoned car and lorry were still there. But I never did.

I lunched in the Ipoh Club but saw no one I recognised, and arrived at Kamuning in the middle of the afternoon. I stopped off at the office where all the old office staff and a number of the labour force were waiting to greet me. Although I had made a very brief visit back in October, this time I was expected, and it was a tearful reunion all round. We all realised that I had come home. The temporary manager (TM) from the BMA stayed in his office. I took an instant dislike to him.

After the welcome, with speeches in English, Malay and Tamil, I took my leave and drove the short distance to my old assistant's bungalow, as I had seen on my previous visit that the manager's was uninhabitable. I had not been there for five minutes when I heard the patter of feet on the stairs and Alagamah, John's ayah, burst in and flung herself into my arms, weeping. We both wept, she with joy and I with both joy and dismay at her wasted appearance and lack of clothing. Her sari was an old mosquito net. After a few minutes exchanging news of her husband and Jean and John, I gave her $20 to go straight down to the village to buy at least one outfit of clothes. I told her that she was once again my cook/ayah and that she must sleep at the bungalow until I had ascertained the current servant arrangements. We were both happy to be together again, and I knew Jean would be equally happy to hear of Alagamah's return.

Having driven the best part of 200 miles by lorry, followed by an emotional reunion, I decided to call it a day. My bed had been made up in the same room occupied by the TM, so I unpacked the few things I had brought with me and had forty winks before showering and changing for supper. At supper the TM told me, rather diffidently, that he had adopted a Malay boy and would I mind if he shared our bedroom. I told him in no uncertain terms that I minded very much, and that if he wanted to share his bed with his boyfriend he should move out and live with him in his kampong.

The following morning I made my first sortie around the estate. My first impression left me intensely disappointed. I had expected to see it unhusbanded, but not to be in quite the derelict state it was. Two or three hundred acres around the central labour quarters, factory and bungalows had been felled for firewood. Only the main estate road to the Banda Bahru division was easily passable. The whole estate was under thick secondary jungle. But the rubber trees themselves, the revenue-producing capital asset of the estate, appeared in good condition. The TM had been on the property for nearly four months and it was impossible to see what he had accomplished during that time. When I returned to the office I made my thoughts abundantly clear. I spent that first afternoon in the office going through the accounts and was astonished to see that over $50,000 had allegedly been spent on clearing undergrowth and reinstating the roads. It was apparent that a monumental fiddle had been perpetrated.

I told the TM to remove himself forthwith from the manager's desk which I then promptly occupied, and told him that I expected him to leave the estate first thing the following morning, taking his 'adopted son' with him. He said that Mr Taylor would hear about this, to which I replied that he most certainly would and picked up the phone there and then and, in front of the TM, told Peter exactly what I had found, and that I was putting the matter in the hands of the police as a very obvious fraud had been perpetrated. Peter calmed me down and said, 'Let's have no recriminations,' which I found surprising at the time, but not so when later I learned that he had appointed several similar misfits and charlatans to other estates.

I was glad to find that practically all the old staff were available, including the Tamil headmen. I recognised so many of the old familiar faces and the genuineness of their welcome was most touching. I was back amongst friends. The old Chinese contractors appeared and we soon got down to agreeing contracts for clearing the undergrowth and eradicating the lalang from the areas that had been felled. Lalang did not normally thrive under the shade of mature rubber trees but ran amok when they were felled. It was eradicated either by forking or poisoning with sodium arsenite. We used to carry stocks of this sufficient to poison the entire population of Malaya.

I was anxious to see the 1938 clearings which I had planted up under Humphrey Butler. From the roads I could see fine thick foliage, allaying my fears that the trees had suffered to any great extent, but I took the very first opportunity to visit the clearings, with the very same Main division conductor who had supervised the planting out eight years previously. The undergrowth was out of control but, as I had thought, the rubber trees were in good order. We were walking along a path under electricity power lines when I saw a loose wire draped across the path. I grabbed it to clear it away and turned to the conductor to ask what he thought it was doing there. 'Tuan, drop it!' he shouted. I did. 'Tuan, you will live for a thousand years.' He told me that only the previous week a young Gurkha officer, Lt Murray-Duncan, had seen a similar wire across his path, and had been instantly electrocuted when he had touched it. I felt sick and had to sit down. The conductor explained: with the reversion to secondary jungle, wild pig had come into the estate and the Chinese killed them for their meat by slinging a wire over the overhead high-tension cables, leaving one end trailing on the ground across a path that was being used by the pigs. With luck, two or three pigs would brush against the wire each night and be killed. Instant roast pork.

When I got back to my office I telephoned Perak Hydro Electric and was told that the current had been switched off for line repairs at 8 am – 15 minutes before I had grabbed the wire. The engineer was most apologetic and hoped that I had not been too greatly inconvenienced. I assured him that I had not been. Murray-Duncan's company of Gurkhas was camped in the grounds of the estate hospital and I reported the matter to their OC. He was furious because, following the death of one of his officers, he had expressly forbidden the local Chinese to use this method of trapping pigs. A few of his younger officers hatched a plan in my bungalow to take out some riflemen, lie in wait for the Chinese responsible, and to drive them on to the live wire. I was still very angry about my own experience and agreed to accompany them. But the OC got to hear about their intentions and, quite rightly, forbade it. However, I called in all the Chinese contractors and told them to pass the word around that this practice was to cease forthwith and that, because I was not subject to army discipline, I would most certainly put the subalterns' plan into effect if ever it happened again.

I had not been back on the estate for more than a couple of weeks when one middle of the night I heard footsteps mounting the steps to the verandah. I switched on the light and waited. I was not unduly worried as, whoever it was, they were making no attempt to be quiet. My bedroom door was flung open and there was Reid Tweedie. He had travelled up from Singapore on the night train, got off at Sungei Siput and walked up from the station. This was a wonderful surprise, and immediately called for a few celebratory stengahs, no matter the hour. We made up a bed in the spare room, and he lived with me until shortly before Jean's return. I was very pleased to have Reid's company and we had lots to catch up on. Furthermore, he was the first ex-POW that I had had the opportunity to talk to at length about life in a Jap prison. Actually, being a civilian, Reid had spent most of the War in the Sime Road internment camp in Singapore before being transferred to Changi, and to some degree had escaped the terrible hardships and atrocities suffered by servicemen. Of course his professional skills had been much in demand, and he had many stories to tell of bribing guards to bring him drugs and medicines, and of witnessing savage beatings and other atrocious behaviour on prisoners by the Japanese guards. Reid's only possessions were the Persian rug mentioned before, which he carried rolled up under his arm, and a doctor's bag with his instruments.

As the weeks went by the estate gradually took on a more cared-for appearance, and more and more trees came under the knife. The undergrowth was being controlled, the roads cleared and the factory machinery and equipment overhauled and repaired. Charles Ross and my other European assistants, having recuperated in Britain, were returning, and Uncle Hannay was getting the tin mines back into operation. At the same time my building contractor, Yap Tong, was repairing the senior assistant's bungalow, where I was living, and making it suitable for the manager of one of the major Guthrie estates. We used as much material from the demolished manager's bungalow as we could reclaim, especially the marble paving and the beautiful hardwood floor from the verandah.

Inevitably there was much lawlessness about. Savage Japanese reprisals were a thing of the past, so gangs of murderous thugs had been able to roam the towns and kampongs doing as they wished, getting away, quite literally, with murder. The three weeks between the Japanese surrender and the arrival of British troops at the beginning of September 1945 saw a spate of crimes committed against person and property. Personal scores were settled. Anyone under the slightest suspicion of having assisted the Jap was murdered. There was wholesale looting of factories, godowns and houses. With the arrival of the British Army and the Colonial Police the crimes decreased dramatically, but Malaya was never really the same again. Nearly four years of merciless Japanese military rule had almost completely destroyed the peace-loving, kindly and honest Asian way of life. But not quite. The elderly Malay, Indian and Chinese soon returned to their well-mannered, easy-going ways, but the youngsters, brought up in the inhuman days of the occupation, when it was every man for himself, could not readily adapt to a more civilised new way of life.

I was in my office one afternoon when an Indian, scarcely out of his teens, walked in unannounced, sat himself down uninvited, and introduced himself as the secretary of the local branch of the Tamil Estate Workers Union. I recognised him as the office peon (postman). I told him to get the hell out of there, and to make an appointment to see me through the chief clerk. He started to argue, but beat a hurried retreat when I rose from my chair with a threatening look. I allowed him in again about an hour later as I was curious to learn what it was all about, for this was the first I had heard of an estates trades union.

He opened the discussion with the words 'Jai Hind' – Freedom for India. I told him that if he had come here to spout political slogans he had better bugger off, and that, so far as I was concerned, he was the office peon. Having cleared the air I was ready to hear what he had to say. He recited a whole lot of trades union claptrap of the sort brought to Malaya by John Brazier, a trade unionist sent out within a month or so of the surrender by the new Labour government in Britain, to organise union representation. When he realised that he could not bamboozle me we got on well enough, especially as he had been unable to recruit many members. Most of the estate labour seemed only too pleased to be earning a good living again, and to be free from the fear of summary execution or deportation to the Siam Railway for some minor infringement of Japanese martial law.

Many old friends were returning to Ipoh and district, having recovered from the privations of imprisonment or internment. European women were appearing as well, and my thoughts were constantly of Jean's return. This was governed by John's school holidays – he had been at Milner Court, the prep school for King's Canterbury, since May – the availability of a sea passage, and the completion of the renovations to the bungalow.

In the early days I had to use the estate lorry to get into Ipoh or Kuala Kangsar and I had no compunction in using it in the evenings. Reid Tweedie and I sat in front with the driver, and quite often we carried staff and estate workers in the back, acting as a private bus service. The put-down and pick-up point was Ipoh railway station. In June I went down to Singapore to collect my new car, a Morris Ten saloon, which was to do excellent service until it was written off, bullet-ridden, following an ambush by terrorists on Kamuning in which Paddy Jones, my assistant, was severely wounded and his

Special Constable guard was killed, in April 1950.

The bungalow was fit to receive the mem besar at the end of July, and Jean was expected at the end of August, and I anticipated the actual date with rising excitement. We had enjoyed less than four months together since December 1941. For the first time in her motherhood Jean was to be separated from her only child, and I know that they both felt the parting deeply. In July Jean was advised by Guthrie's London office that they had secured a passage for her on the Dutch liner *Oranje*, sailing at the end of the month and due in Singapore three and a half weeks later. The *Oranje* was a luxury liner, built just before the war, but still converted into a hospital ship and used for ferrying back to the Far East as many Dutch and English passengers at a time as possible, so it was chronically overcrowded. Jean shared a cabin with four other women and two small children.

Eventually the great day arrived. I had set off for Singapore a couple of days beforehand in my Morris, accompanied by my syce Yussof, staying en route in KL. I had to go to the Guthrie office in Singapore first thing to arrange to collect a car for someone else in Ipoh – hence Yussof – to provide the additional space for all the extra luggage that Jean would be bringing, containing replacements for many of the essentials that we had lost in 1941. The office paperwork delayed me and I was a little late in getting to the ship. Jean was naturally rather upset at my apparent lack of enthusiasm for her homecoming.

As soon as the cars were loaded we set off to drive to Tanjong Malim where we stayed the night with Harry Hays and I was able to introduce Jean to my number two for so long in ISLD. Harry was a great curry eater and had laid on an extra hot one for dinner, which appealed to neither of us. Worse still, we had the leftovers for breakfast the following morning, straight from the refrigerator.

We lunched in Ipoh, where Jean did some shopping, and arrived back on Kamuning in time for tea. Jean received the expected emotional greeting from Ayah. I have mentioned her reaction to the Chinese carpet I proudly showed her. It had, of course, been looted from some other European's bungalow, so we made some rather half-hearted enquiries locally in case the rightful owner had returned, but without success.

The custodian of enemy property had taken over large quantities of looted possessions, and people were able to inspect and claim anything they had lost. Unfortunately, the custodian's staff was not particularly good at establishing true provenance, and also there were some rather unscrupulous claimants, so many items were not returned to the true owners. Much more disgraceful was the manner in which one or two senior British generals, whom I could name, sailed home with packing cases full of carpets, silver and other treasured possessions of ex-POWs and internees. All we discovered of ours was a silver egg cup stand, minus the egg cups. The armed forces, being the first to arrive back in the country, had the first choice of anything they could find for their respective messes, and several of our friends managed to claim back the odd piece of silver or furniture they recognised whilst being entertained by the officers. But, other than the sherry glass, the piece of silver and the opium stool, Jean and I lost everything. For several years afterwards we took little interest in material possessions.

After nearly five years for the most part living alone or surrounded by men, it seemed strange at first having Jean run the home, welcome me at meal times, join me in excursions to friends' houses or the club and, above all, to offer encouragement when I sometimes got disheartened at what I considered to be slow progress back to normality. I was happy and contented, but I knew that Jean felt the separation from John terribly.

Soon after Reid Tweedie first returned I began to feel off-colour and he diagnosed shingles. For some reason completely unknown to medical science he decided to inject emetin, a drug then usually prescribed for dysentery. I bared my bottom, lay on the bed, and he started jabbing. After a whole series of jabs, each one more painful than the last, Reid at last managed to penetrate my skin. When I had stopped yelling and cursing I asked him how long he had had the needle. He said it was one of only two he had used throughout his three years in captivity!

Strangely enough, malaria had not flourished over the war years. Without the anti-malarial measures just the opposite would have been expected. But the malaria-carrying mosquito only breeds in shallow water exposed to sunlight, so, with the neglect of the rubber estates, drains becoming blocked and undergrowth covering the streams and water courses, its breeding grounds were lost. In any case, the disease could now be held at bay with the new wonder drugs Mepecrin and Plasmocrin, so much so that I was to suffer from it again only when I went down with German measles whilst on leave in 1947, and with mumps after retirement in 1973.

Jean was free from malaria, too, but she went down with something far more serious. One day, soon after her return, she complained of aches and pains and was obviously running a fever, so Reid treated her for malaria. However, she quickly got far worse, her temperature reached 105, and she became delirious. Reid and I managed to get her wrapped in one of my sarongs and we drove at breakneck speed to Batu Gajah Hospital, me sitting in the back with her in my arms. The hospital was functioning again, just, but the only bed available was in the maternity ward and we were warned that, should a new baby arrive, Jean would have to be moved. All that night and the next day the doctors struggled to get her temperature down, but without success. I was beside myself with worry. I stayed at the nearby Batu Gajah rest house, from where I made frequent visits to the hospital. On the evening of the second day the doctor said that if they could not get the temperature down that night the consequences would be fatal. To my great relief they rang at about midnight to say that the temperature had broken and that Jean was sleeping peacefully. From then on she slowly recovered and I was allowed to take her home after three weeks. I visited her every day, and usually stopped off at the Ipoh Club for a few stengahs on the way home. She had been desperately ill, and the diagnosis was urban typhus.

I learned that there were two types – scrub or river typhus, and urban typhus. The first was spread by the ticks that feed on rats, the second is contracted from rat urine. After nearly five years lying derelict the bungalow had become infested with rats and we saw many running around, even during the day. Kim caught several. It was obvious that they were getting into the built-in cupboards in the servery where our china and cutlery was stored, and contaminating the dishes. I therefore had the estate carpenters construct new, free-standing cupboards lined with tin, and Jean instructed that all china and cutlery was to be washed immediately before being used, and no food of any description was to be left out in any circumstance. At the same time I instituted a drastic rat extermination campaign. We poisoned literally scores. On the very first morning, having put down more than 50 pieces of poisoned bait overnight, we picked up 20 dead rats, at least two as big as a large cat. I continued the campaign for a month, throughout the whole compound, until we were only picking up the odd one or two each night, which I judged to be strays from outside, which we would always get, and I considered the problem to have been overcome. I also instigated a similar regime throughout the estate with equal success although, unfortunately, we also killed quite a few dogs, cats, and wild animals.

Just before Jean's sickness we had paid our first visit to the Kuala Kangsar Club, where the old Chinese head boy embraced us, and we spent a good half an hour swapping stories of our lives since we had last met. The club had only started to function again shortly before. But he seemed rather disconsolate all the same and when I questioned him he complained bitterly about the behaviour of the British Military Administrator acting as district officer and, therefore, ex-officio chairman of the club. The old man's summing up was succinct: 'Tuan DO, dia tida ada gentleman' – Tuan DO, he is not a gentleman. This, of course, had nothing to do with his schooling or his accent, but everything to do with the way he behaved and spoke to the Asian employees.

Several functions were held in the Kuala Kangsar Club. 'Function' was a very popular word with Asians, and covered every gathering of more than a half dozen people. At one such function the Sultans of both Perak and Pahang were present. The former was charming and spoke very good English, whereas the latter seemed rather surly and insisted in speaking only raja, or court, Malay, so that much of his conversation was beyond us. However, towards the end of the evening, and probably due to judicious mixing of gin with his orange juice, he suddenly broke into fluent Oxford English, and told one or two rather risqué jokes.

Also present at that party were two Sikh army officers, tall and handsome, with their immaculate beards and turbans. We got on well, especially when I found out that we had been at the Battle of Donbaik together. We asked them to dinner the following week and had most enjoyable and interesting discussions over supper and lasting well into the small hours. They were both far better educated than either of us, could recite much English poetry and pages of Shakespeare. One's favourite was *Henry V*, as befitted a fighting man, while the other's was *Romeo and Juliet*, and John Donne and Keats. They were very practical men, admitting that, though swearing allegiance to the King Emperor, they were basically mercenaries and would be happy to fight for the best paymaster, all except the Communists. We then analysed the precise meaning of 'best' in this context, and I was pleased to learn that it included things other than just pay, such as regimental traditions and the competence of senior officers.

Then came the New Year and the expectation of home leave. Guthrie's had promised me leave early in 1947 as recompense for my agreeing to take my discharge in Singapore, although I realised that they were hardly being generous on that score. We made plans to sail in the *Oranje* at the end of March. The liner had been restored to her former glory since Jean had travelled out on her, so we looked forward to almost a second honeymoon on what was then the most luxurious liner on the Singapore–East Indies run. We were not disappointed.

I handed over the managership of Kamuning to Ian Murray, who also agreed to look after my old friend Kim, having learned the few essential Japanese words. The estate was well on its way to making reasonable profits, the roads were in good shape, devastated areas were gradually being replanted, the new clearings were now in bearing, and some of the oldest machinery had been replaced. All in all I was satisfied with the progress my staff, European and Asian, had made, and I knew that this would be maintained by the extremely competent in my absence, supported by my equally efficient senior assistant, Charles Ross.

We drove down to Singapore via KL and Linggi Estate, where we stayed the night with Donald and Betty Gray, before going on to Singapore in Donald's car. We embarked the next morning, accompanied by the usual large party of well-wishers and scroungers, who disembarked at the very last moment. We had a very comfortable suite, comprising cabin, day cabin and bathroom. The ship was air-conditioned throughout, so it was no longer necessary to be POSH. The passengers were, naturally, predominantly Dutch, but there were quite a number of British aboard, including a number of old friends with whom we shared a most lively and not altogether alcohol-free table in the saloon.

The trip was restful and enjoyable, calling in at Balawan Deli, Colombo, Suez, Port Said and Genoa, where many passengers disembarked to travel overland to Holland. The ship then continued past Gibraltar and turned northwards into the Atlantic.

We had known that northern Europe was experiencing one of the severest and most prolonged spells of extremely cold and bad weather ever recorded, so we were not particularly surprised when off the coast of Portugal the sea began to get really rough, with the crests of the waves sometimes many feet above us. Jean had met the Captain on his rounds and he had warned her that the *Oranje*'s sister ship, the *Indrapura*, had met gales and seas in the Bay of Biscay of monstrous proportions and had warned us to proceed with the utmost caution. But our captain went on to say that he had received instructions from Rotterdam to reach port before the Easter holidays at all costs, and that he must do his best to obey these instructions. A very high price was to be paid for these orders.

We entered the Bay at over 20 knots, and the deeper we sailed into it the worse it became. The passengers had been warned of the weather ahead and advised to remain below decks. Jean and I, being good sailors, thought that we would view the wonderful sight of these massive breakers from the grandstand – the top deck. The *Oranje* was a large passenger liner, over 27,000 tons, and standing very high out of the water. But still the waves towered above us. It was truly awe-inspiring. After a few minutes Jean decided to go below, leaving a friend and I clinging to the rail and relishing the spectacle. Suddenly along came a truly terrifying wave, at least 60 feet higher than the ship. Before we could retreat it broke over the ship, swept us off our feet, and the next thing I knew I was hanging on to the ship's rail for dear life, with my legs and feet at right angles to the deck, over the side. I was getting very frightened wondering just how long I could hang on; how long it would be before the ship rolled back again in the opposite direction. It did so as suddenly as it had rolled the other way, and I was dumped on the deck with so much force that it split the seat of my trousers. Then the siren sounded signalling 'man overboard'. It could very easily have been me.

The pair of us crawled to the saloon on all fours; it was simply impossible to stand. In the saloon the grand piano, despite having been bolted to the floor, was piled up against a bulkhead with other pieces of furniture, smashed to little more than matchwood. It had come adrift and skidded across the dance floor before pinning two lady passengers against the wall, breaking their legs, and injuring several others. I was most relieved to see Jean huddled up on a settee which had held firm. A ship's officer announced that the mountainous wave that had nearly done for me had broken the main steering and that we were now using the emergency which was situated right aft over the rudder.

The sea anchor was put out, and for the next 24 hours the great liner just wallowed. No meals were served, not that many were in the mood to eat. Every time the ship rolled the crash of glass and crockery could be heard. Until then I had rather scoffed at the Bay's reputation for bad weather, but no longer. It was no myth.

When the *Oranje* finally got under power we made our way slowly through the Bay and the Channel into Southampton more than 36 hours late, to be greeted by the *Daily Mail* headline: 'Dutch Death Ship Arrives'. In all five of the crew had died, either washed overboard or crushed to death on the deck by the sheer weight of water – the fourth officer, an engineer officer, a steward and stewardess and a nurse. Those not washed overboard were buried at sea. We learned later that several quite large ships had been lost without trace, one not many miles from where we had been wallowing.

It was a joy to be home again with a united family, although the weather continued to be bitterly cold. We made our base at the Cuthbertsons' home in Hornchurch.

It was not my intention to buy a car, but I soon realised that for the full enjoyment of my long-awaited leave a car was essential. Through Grandpa Cuthbertson's contacts I got hold of a Standard Fourteen. A really first-class car, I took it back to Malaya with me and eventually sold it to Tim Earl, my senior assistant, in 1950.

The cold spring gave way to one of the hottest and driest summers on record. Compton and Edrich were in their prime and scored many runs. I saw them bat at Lords, Chelmsford and Dover. The South Africans were touring as well and I managed to get tickets for the Lords Test through the East India Club.

One of my first excursions was to drive over to the Guthrie's office at Dorking, to where they had moved from the City to escape the blitz. They had taken over the large country house formerly owned by the Webbs who had founded the socialist Fabian Society. My first meeting was with the Kamuning company secretary Keith Anderson, another son of the man who had put Guthrie's on the planting map in the early days of the century.

The chairman of Guthrie's, throughout my years with the company, was Sir John Hay. He had joined the company in 1904 as a junior bookkeeper and, after a year or so, had transferred to the estates department. By the end of the 1914–18 war he was in charge of the department and had been appointed to his first directorship, and in 1925 had become general manager, at the age of 42. He was knighted in 1939 for his services to the rubber industry.

John George Hay was a great man. He was vain, at times petty and spiteful, and on the whole unpopular within the company, particularly towards the end of his reign when he became almost a total dictator. But he could also be most generous and charming. Jean and I took to him from our first meeting and, throughout the years from 1947 until his death in 1963, we were the best of friends. Sir John had no time for 'yes men'. If one stood up to him the bullying stopped. When we were introduced by Keith Anderson almost Sir John's first words were, 'D'yer know, Hembry, the only thing I have against you?' 'No, Sir John.' 'You are not a Scot.' But this error of judgment on my part did not appear adversely to affect my progress within the company as, in less than four years, I had been appointed to the top position in Guthrie plantation management.

The long leave seemed to pass very quickly. In spite of all the pleasures of seeing family and old friends, and watching first-class cricket and John playing at Milner Court, where he had gained a place in the XI, I looked forward to getting back to Kamuning. Although I was pleased with the results so far, there was still much to do to make Kamuning a jewel, if not *the* jewel in the Guthrie crown. And I missed my old friend Kim. Guthrie's had booked me on the old Cunard liner *Georgic*. She had been burnt out and half sunk at Suez during the war, had recently been refloated, and was being used as a troopship. I had avoided sailing on a trooper hitherto, and was not best pleased to have to now that I was a civilian, and a reasonably senior member of my profession. It was certainly a comedown from the *Oranje*. But passages were still controlled by the Government and in short supply. I refused to allow Jean to accompany me, in spite of our having to be parted from one another yet again, as I knew that conditions on the ship would be fairly awful. Anyway, we thought that it would be good for her to have an extra four months at home so that she could spend Christmas with John and her parents. In the event it was a fortunate decision as it was the last one that Grandpa Cuthbertson was to have. I did not see him again after we said our farewells that September morning.

We sailed from Liverpool. My first glimpse of the sleeping arrangements filled me with dismay. Through the cabin doorways I saw 20 or so double and triple bunks, some, to my horror, occupied by women. The steward, however, showed me to a cabin with just three singles, which I was to share with another planter and the Postmaster General of Malaya. I was put at the captain's table. Captain Gradidge was a most interesting man, and kept us enthralled with his seafaring tales. He was to become Commodore of Cunard, to command the *Queen Elizabeth*, and be knighted. Many a night he made life bearable, particularly in the Red Sea, by inviting me up to the bridge and his quarters which faced forward and so caught what breeze there was. The trip was very uncomfortable, and must have been hell for the several hundreds of service personnel and service wives who were confined between decks for most of the time, only allowed on deck for exercise in strict rota. As the *Georgic* had been burnt out there was scarcely any wood to be seen. The walls, ceilings, stanchions and pillars were all just white-painted steel, which gave off the heat horrifically.

We called in at Suez, Asmara and Colombo before reaching Singapore about 30 days out of Liverpool. I watched my Standard hoisted out of the hold on to the dockside, and saw that it was only slightly damaged, I suspect by a Liverpool docker very obviously having walked over the bonnet in his hobnailed boots. He was probably related to the dockers who stole the monthly cigarette supply which Jean's parents had kindly sent out to me every month throughout the war. I did not receive a single one. A door handle had been wrenched off, too.

I drove over the causeway and up the long weary road to KL where I stayed the night with the Walkers, Trevor now being in charge of the estates side of Guthrie's. The next day I reached Ipoh in time for a late tiffin at the club, before getting back to Kamuning in time for tea.

The handover took only a couple of days, after which the Murrays duly departed, and I was on my own again, the start of a five-year period, which was to be full of interest, excitement, sorrow and anger, and which was to culminate in my first coronary, at age 42.

Bandits

September 1947 – January 1951

I very soon settled back into the familiar routine. Ian Murray had continued the good work on the estate during my absence, and Kamuning was rapidly regaining the air of prosperity it had always had prewar. Alagamah – Ayah – fulfilled her duties as cook/boy most admirably. But the nights were lonely without Jean, and the four months of her absence dragged. I spent a lot of time in the garden as an additional kebun determined that it would be a show place for Jean's return.

Some evenings I spent in Ipoh with friends, some from before the war and others of a later vintage. Among these was Donald Wise, the junior assistant who had been recruited during my absence.

Donald was a character. Tall, bearded, thin and angular, he had arrived on Singapore with the Suffolk Regiment in February 1942 only a few days before the surrender, and had spent the next three and a half years in captivity, both in Changi and on the Railway. On release he had returned to England and resumed his army career, volunteering for the Parachute Regiment. He had also found that, as he had been reported as 'missing, presumed killed' in the final battle for Singapore, his wife had married someone else and had moved to America. Then, after a brief spell at journalism, he had come out to Malaya again. His second wife was delightful – as were to be his third, fourth and fifth.

In 1957, at the time of the EOKA insurgency in Cyprus, Jean and I were watching television when Donald appeared on the screen, arguing with Barbara Castle, a senior and leading left-wing figure in the Labour Party, over the rights and wrongs of the situation on the island. We were particularly interested as John was serving out there in the Army after having taken part in the Suez landings late the previous year. Of course, Donald knew what he was talking about, whereas the lady manifestly did not. Donald by then had become a world-renowned war correspondent. I immediately telephoned the BBC and within moments was speaking to him and arranging to meet at the East India Club the following evening.

Donald told me a story that was connected with Colin Park. After he had left the Army he and Colin had shared a flat, together with their Turkish girlfriend. One of the men worked during the day, the other at night, a Box and Cox arrangement that suited all concerned. However, they became aware that someone seemed to be watching the house, and they began to fear that it might be an irate father or elder brother. Shortly afterwards their young and beautiful Turkish girl was arrested and deported. She was a Russian spy. I met Colin months later, when he was in Ferret Force based in Ipoh, and he confirmed the story.

Donald was transferred to another estate down in Negri Sembilan early in 1948, but planting was not the life for him. The next time we met he too had joined Ferret Force, a unit of former SOE, SAS and other similarly adventurous types, who penetrated deep into the jungle in small patrols in search of communist terrorists, showing the regular army what could be done with proper training and determination. Towards the end of the Emergency, in the late 1950s, such operations were commonplace.

As a correspondent Donald later went on to cover all the world's major conflicts, and most of the minor ones as well, from the Congo to Vietnam, before settling down to a desk job with the *Far Eastern Economic Review* in Hong Kong, with his charming and gracious fifth wife, Daphne.

I spent Christmas with the Reynolds, staying at the E&O Hotel in Penang. It was during a drinks party given by Molly and Freddy that a distinguished-looking elderly lady approached me and expressed pleasure on hearing that I was from Kamuning Estate. Introducing herself as Mrs Crawford, she told me that she had once been there and had taken tea with the manager, 'but it was a long time ago'. I knew the names of most of my predecessors, so started with Humphrey Butler, the manager from 1928 to 1938, then Roy Waugh,

1920 to 1928. Then I suggested Shelton Agar, 1912 to 1920. Still no recognition. So I said triumphantly, 'Then it must be Machardo.' That drew a blank, too. In desperation I said, 'Then it must have been D'Estere Darby.' She cried, 'Yes, that's the name!' 'But,' I said, 'you must have gone there sometime in the 1880s.' She agreed. Her husband, an engineer, was working on the main Singapore to Penang railway line and they were living in Ipoh. She had travelled the 19 miles to Sungei Siput, and back again to Ipoh in pony and trap, along unmetalled roads. I was all agog and plied her with many questions. Here was someone who could remember Kamuning before the turn of the century. She had landed in Penang, taken a local steamer to Port Weld, the port for Taiping, and then travelled by bullock cart to join her fiancé in Ipoh where they were married. In those days, of course, the dirt road would have been cut through virgin jungle.

Jean arrived in Penang at last at the end of January 1948 on the *Canton*, then the newest P&O liner. We stayed her first night back at the E&O, dined at the Penang Club, saw the latest Marx Brothers film, and got back to Kamuning in time for a late tiffin. The Tweedies had just moved into the new house that Reid had built on land that I had leased him for 25 years, situated on a hill on the Sungei Buloh division, with most magnificent views looking over to the Kamuning bukit, the whole of the Sungei Siput area, and the jungles behind. In fact he was to die in the 'White House', as the bungalow came to be known, 40 years later. Reid and Ruth arrived for tea and stayed to nearly midnight; there was much to talk about.

Laurie Brittain had been made manager for Nestlé in northern Malaya, based in Penang. Whilst with ISLD in Australia he had met and married Jean, a journalist. We saw quite a lot of them, as we tried to spend at least one weekend a month in John Treaby's beach house out at Batu Feringgi, and they visited us in Sungei Siput as often. Laurie liked a good 'beat up' at the Ipoh Club. We tended to rely on our Ipoh friends from prewar, as the old Sungei Siputians had been drastically reduced by retirement and death in the war. Apart from the Tweedies, there were only the Ferguson brothers and Jumbo and Helene Morford left.

The first few months of 1948 were uneventful and saw steady

progress on the estate. Most of the area laid waste during the Japanese occupation had been rehabilitated. The price of rubber was reasonable and we were making good profits. But to anyone with an ear to the ground, and an eye capable of gleaning snippets of information from obscure corners of the newspapers, it was obvious that trouble was brewing. The Communists – as they had in Great Britain – had penetrated the Malayan trade unions which had been so enthusiastically promoted by the Labour government, against the advice of the Malayan civil service, the police and employers of labour. There were just not the moderate labour leaders available; there simply had not been the time since the end of the war to train them. By comparison, those now in positions of power in the unions had all been schooled in communism by the MPAJA or had arrived from Mao Tse Tung's cadres in China. I recalled my prognostications in ISLD, and Bob Chrystal's post-war reports to the Malayan authorities, all of which had been ignored. Claude Fenner told me, when we had tiffin together at the Lake Club in KL at about this time, that he doubted whether a quarter of all the weapons that Force 136 had parachuted into the jungle had been returned, so there was a lot of firepower out there somewhere.

Unknown to Guthrie's, I established a small secret fund on Kamuning, from which I paid Chinese contractors to keep me au fait with the local political situation. These men, who were totally reliable, made me aware that trouble had been planned for Kamuning. Being the largest estate in the area it was an obvious target. The size of my resident Tamil labour force was inadequate so we made up the shortage with Chinese contract labour. In addition, I had also engaged a Malay contractor who supplied a score or so Malays from local kampongs. This was Eusoff, my splendid platoon sergeant from the Perak FMSVF, who had turned up looking for work when he had heard that I was back. He was not oversupplied with energy, but he was reliable and had proved himself in battle. He would be a tower of strength in the days to come.

Special Branch, commanded by my old friend John Dalley, had repeatedly warned Sir Edward Gent, the high commissioner, that the former MPAJA were assembling in their jungle camps, and strongly advised that the leaders, who were still out in the open and known to the police, should be arrested. Gent declined, no doubt acting under the orders of the Colonial Secretary in London, James Griffiths. By the time that such action was sanctioned it was too late. The communist leadership had taken to the jungle.

Before the war there was a young Tamil boy on Kamuning named Perumal who showed great intelligence and an appetite for education, and very soon outgrew the small estate school. With Bob Chrystal's agreement I had used some of the profits from the estate toddy shops to subsidise his education at the Sungei Siput village school, as I had thought that he had great potential as a senior office clerk. He was still on Kamuning after the war, but I found him a totally changed man. He was now surly and deliberately offensive in both manner and speech. He was no longer interested in becoming one of the clerical staff but, together with his constant companion Aramugam, joined a tapping gang. Early in May 1948, I happened to visit the factory one morning and found my factory clerk Kandasamy lying on the concrete floor, having very obviously been felled by Perumal and Arumagan, who were standing over him looking very aggressive. I knocked Perumal to the ground with a blow to the head and was ready to do the same to Arumagan when he was grabbed by a kangani who pinioned his arms. I instructed a clerk to telephone the police, and then I lambasted the two miscreants with my tongue, whilst trying to find out exactly what had happened. It seemed that Kandasamy had reprimanded them for being insolent and they had attacked him. When the police arrived I said that I would be laying charges against the two for assault, and they were taken away. I did not realise it then but these two men were avowed communists, Perumal the local commissar. They were fined, and imprisoned for 14 days. On the day of his release Perumal passed by my office and swore that he would kill me. At the time I thought it merely bravado. I was to learn differently. The two men disappeared into the jungle, only to sally forth to commit more than 20 cold-blooded murders in the district.

Our old friend S. E. King would tell me many years later in England that, towards the end of May 1948, John Dalley had told him that 'the balloon will go up in about three weeks' time'. He was not far out. Just prior to this a planter had been killed in Johore, on his way back to his estate with the wages. And about two weeks later a Chinese towkay had been ambushed and murdered a few miles outside Ipoh, the terrorists leaving a note pinned to his body saying: 'So perish all traitors and running dogs!'

After these incidents the Special Branch again advised the high commissioner to order the arrest of all known communists, but as before the Colonial Office would not allow it. Eight years later the casualty toll at the hands of these communists and their terrorist henchmen was in excess of 20,000. Such was the criminal stupidity of British politicians and much of the ruling class. Will they ever learn?

Following the murder outside Ipoh my Chinese informants warned me that we were in for trouble on Kamuning. Sure enough one day a young Chinese woman presented herself at my office and introduced herself as the local representative of the Malayan Chinese Estates Workers Union. She told me that she intended to negotiate better terms for the Chinese tappers. I enquired as to the terms she had in mind, knowing full well that they would in fact be demands, and so outrageously high that she had no intention of reaching any agreement. I bandied words for a little while and then invited her to come to my bungalow at 5 pm when I could have one of my Chinese contractors present to act as interpreter in case her Malay was insufficient. I wanted no misunderstandings.

She duly appeared and, together with Ah Fat, we sat on the lawn. We talked for over two hours. Compromise was impossible. She made no threats, other than that of calling all the labour out on strike, including the Indians if they would 'follow'. She meant, of course, that my Tamil workers would be terrorised into withholding their labour. I broke up the meeting and she departed. I never saw her again, but heard that she had gone into the jungle and joined the communist terrorists – shortly to be known throughout Malaya as 'bandits', and later as 'CTs'.

At the end of the first week in June, and as I had been warned, the Chinese labour struck. I had previously been to see Innes Miller, the British adviser in Ipoh, and had got him to arrange for a company of Gurkhas to be placed on stand-by in case of trouble. Lakri Woods, their colonel, had come out to Kamuning, in plain clothes so as not to warn the Communists whom I, quite rightly, took to have spies everywhere, to recce the area and to discuss what course of action to take should there be insurrection. I had already been made aware that my Indians were being got at, and I had called the Tamil kanganis to a meeting in my office and had assured them that they would have adequate protection if they stood by me.

I also called a meeting of all the other estate managers in the Sungei Siput area, suggesting that, to show solidarity, they should all lock out their Chinese. They refused to a man, stating that (a) the quarrel was a matter between Kamuning and its labour force and nothing to do with them; and (b) their managing agents in KL would not approve.

It was ironic that on the day 'the balloon went up' every European in the district descended on Kamuning. We did not let them down. I even suggested that we parted with some of our Gurkhas, billeted in the Kamuning hospital grounds, so that others could have some protection.

My spies told me that the strike was set for the next day. At 5 am a company of Gurkhas arrived and, amidst much laughing and cheering, escorted my Tamils to work. They did this for a week. To make up for the loss of the Chinese tappers we tapped twice that day and the shortfall in the latex crop was negligible. After a few days the Communists saw that they had lost the first round and the Chinese started to drift back to work. Needless to say, Guthrie's KL was constantly on the telephone, asking for the latest news. In return they could offer little more than sympathy.

There had been a spate of bank robberies throughout the country; hardly a day went by when *The Straits Times* did not report them. The Communists were obtaining funds on a large scale. They were also extracting smaller amounts as 'protection' from estate and mine workers up and down the country. If a tapper refused, he would find his wife and children murdered. Understandably, few refused.

An incident which occurred earlier in the year may have been connected with this communist fundraising. It was the routine for

Ayah to place a tray of tea and fruit on the table on the verandah each morning at about six, before being driven by the syce down to the village for the daily shopping for fresh food. Having got up and had my morning 'cuppa', some fruit and the first cigarette of the day, at about 7 am. I would stroll down to the factory.

On this particular morning Ayah, having set down the tray, noticed that Kim was still asleep on the floor outside the bedroom door and did not greet her as usual. Then, when she went under the house to where the syce was waiting, she saw several empty soda water bottles scattered around. Funny, she thought, what was the tuan up to last night? It was then that she realised that there was still no movement from overhead, and that Kim had not come downstairs with her for his usual constitutional. Earlier she had noticed that the refrigerator door was open, in contravention to Jean's strict instructions concerning the rats. Curiosity aroused, she ran upstairs again shouting, 'Mem, Tuan, Mem, Tuan!' and came into our bedroom to find Jean and I slowly coming to as if with monumental hangovers. Meanwhile, Kim had also woken but was most reluctant to move. I staggered out of bed, reassured Ayah that we were all right, and took stock of the situation. The first thing I saw were foot marks leading from the bathroom to our bedsides, then to the dressing table, and then out by the bathroom door again. I went downstairs and saw the empty soda bottles, and decided that the intruders must have used them to blow a drug up through the gaps in the floor planks into our bedroom and then had walked through Jean's talcum powder on the bathroom floor into our bedroom. They had taken a $10 note that was lying on the dressing table, and some cheap costume jewellery, and then had left. Under my pillow was a loaded Luger and in the lavatory a .30 carbine. It was well that they did not look in there, and that I did not wake up and go for my pistol, as the robbers would have been armed and would most certainly have shot us.

It later transpired that Reid Tweedie, who was then still living in an estate bungalow near the office compound, was also robbed of $100 that night, as was an assistant on Dovenby Estate nearby, and a timber merchant living on the other side of Sungei Siput. The gang was caught through an informer, both found to have been collecting money for the Party, and to have been armed. The police thought that the drug used on us would have been opium.

For the week or so after the strike there was an uneasy peace. It was obvious, however, that something would soon break. Not only had my own informers warned me of trouble ahead, but police agents throughout the country, who had been infiltrating the upper echelons of the unions, reported that there was to be a major insurrection very soon. Unfortunately, the Government still hesitated to accept the advice of Special Branch, and gradually the Communist leaders had quit their posts and disappeared into the ulu.

Tuesday 16 June 1948 began as most other days on Kamuning Estate, Sungei Siput. Down to the office and factory at about seven, back to the bungalow for breakfast at nine; then to the office again at ten. It was Reid Tweedie's official visiting day when he would call in to discuss any health matters. On this particular day he reported that there had been several cases of malaria, which was worrying. We were talking about this when Devadason, my head office clerk, knocked and came in looking very worried, and said, 'I have just heard that Mr Walker has been shot at Elphil Estate.' I asked him how he had heard and he said that the office peon had just returned from the village and had heard it there. I told Reid that he had better get over to Elphil straight away, sent word to Charles Ross to do likewise, telephoned the police station and was informed that Bill Powndell, the OCPD Sungei Siput, was already on the scene. I went back to the bungalow to collect Jean, for I was thinking that Verna, Wally Walker's wife, and now very probably his widow, would need comforting. I grabbed my Luger and followed Reid post-haste down the Lintang Road.

We were still a couple of miles short of Elphil, which lay astride the government road, when we saw heavy palls of black smoke rising ahead. This could only mean that the rubber drying sheds had been set alight. The police and the Gurkhas from Kamuning were already there. Verna was sitting in Reid's car by the bungalow, Reid doing his best to console her. Jean joined them. Bill Powndell then told me that not only had Wally been murdered, but so too had John Allison and his assistant, Ian Christian, on nearby Phin Soon Estate. The labour force was beginning to collect on the estate padang, looking very shocked and some openly weeping.

These first few hours of the Emergency have been described by several authors, none of whom was there at the time, their descriptions vary considerably, and most could not possibly be less accurate. However, I was there, and for the rest of that day, and several afterwards, I was at the centre of events. As far as the civilians were concerned I was in charge, and was consulted by both police and army. As manager of the largest estate in the area, and vice-chairman of the Perak Planters Association, the leadership of the planting community naturally devolved on me.

Charles Ross arrived and I told him to take charge of Elphil and to get the daily work under way, as I was determined that the terrorists would not be successful in closing down the estate. I arranged with the Gurkha company commander for a platoon to be positioned on the estate, and asked Charles if he would stay the night. He bravely readily agreed and dashed back to Kamuning to collect an overnight bag.

The stories of these murders had been pieced together. Wally Walker was sitting in his office at about nine o'clock when three young Chinese cycled up, leaned their bikes against the building, and whilst one went to the office door and bade Wally good morning, the other two slipped round behind the office and shot him in the head, at point-blank range, through the open office window behind his chair. All three then remounted and rode off, leaving a terrified and horrified office clerk witness to the whole affair, too dumbstruck to do anything for several minutes.

Within half an hour, and less than three miles away, a gang of about a dozen terrorists surrounded the Phin Soon office in which John Allison and Ian Christian were sitting, burst in, bound them to their chairs, and shot them dead. They then set light to the drying sheds and rubber stores and departed.

Interrogations of surrendered terrorists, and captured documents subsequently revealed that Charles Ross and I were to have been the main targets, but because of faulty planning – Charles usually came later to the office on the days when Reid reported in – and my good fortune – on this occasion I had left the office almost immediately to return to the factory to inspect a new piece of machinery and so was away from my desk – they missed us. Later, one of the kranis did remember seeing a couple of young Chinese on bicycles hanging around the estate office earlier in the day, but had thought nothing of it at the time. Whether they were terrorists we shall never know. I have my doubts as, surely, if Charles and I had been considered so important there would have been more of them, especially if Perumal had been involved. But the Police were sure they were, and there certainly would have been time for them to have reached Elphil by nine o'clock, picking up the third accomplice on the way.

Fortunately for the rest of us European planters in the Sungei Siput area, Chin Peng's plan, that there should be simultaneous assassinations of all European planters and miners in Perak, misfired. Some of the CTs jumped the gun, thus allowing us time to take protective measures.

When I saw that there was nothing more that I could do at Elphil, Jean and I returned to Kamuning with Verna, the poor girl naturally still in a deep state of shock. My next job was to locate John Haytor, our local padre. It was essential that the funerals were held before the end of the day. As luck would have it John was on his travels around his parish but I eventually tracked him down in Telok Anson. He would return directly to Batu Gajah.

By lunchtime there must have been 15 planters and their wives sitting on our verandah, looking ashen-faced and harassed. And very thirsty. Jean laid on tiffin for everyone. I busied myself in my office with telephone calls to Guthrie's in KL, outlying estates, the police and the British Resident in Ipoh, and receiving incoming calls from the Governor, the Colonial Secretary in Singapore and other senior officials, and my old friend John Dalley of Special Branch. After a hurried lunch I sent Peter Madden off to find Eusoff, who was working out on the estate with his Malay labour gang, with instructions for him to report to me in my office straight away. Peter then went to Ipoh with orders to buy at least a dozen shotguns and a thousand cartridges.

I had quickly realised that the army and police could not indefinitely stand guard over us all, spread out as we were. Also, the sooner we took some kind of offensive, or at least the initiative, the better. When Eusoff turned up I asked him to select a dozen of his best young men to act as guards on the Kamuning bungalows. I would arm them all; the company would pay their wages and look after their families should they come to a sticky end. By nightfall we had 20 good Malays and true standing guard.

This was how HOBA – Hembry's Own Bloody Army – was born. By the end of the month Eusoff had recruited further men and had taught them basic arms drill and fire discipline, so the factory and office could also be guarded. We had bought them khaki uniforms, and Jean had sewn on the HOBA shoulder flashes which she had hurriedly embroidered.

The scene at Elphil has been described by Noel Barber in his book *The War of the Running Dogs*. It gained much credence, almost to the extent of becoming the accepted record of the events of that day. However it, too, contained many inaccuracies, and when I wrote to him pointing them out he replied that he had depended on interviews with Donald Wise, whom he had got to know several years later in the Middle East, and with Bob Thompson, a Chinese protection officer based in Ipoh, who figures most prominently in the book. But Donald had been transferred to Port Dickson Lukut Estate three months previously and so was at least 200 miles away, and for the life of me I cannot remember seeing Bob Thompson there, and neither does Jean. There was no earthly reason why he should, or even could, have been there. He would have had no authority to do anything. It was, after all, a police and army matter, and they were already there, and I had assumed responsibility for the management of Elphil Estate. However, the future Sir Robert was to become prominent in the long struggle, and later served as special adviser to the Americans during their war in Vietnam.

Together with Colonel Lakri Woods, who had now arrived at Elphil, and Bill Powndell I arranged for a section of Gurkhas to be positioned on each estate around Sungei Siput, to protect the planters' bungalows and to show the Indian workforces that armed assistance was at hand. We all had confidence in these little men from Nepal. It was at this meeting that Bill Powndell told me that the local communist top brass had met in Sungei Siput three weeks before, and that the police had known all about it beforehand and were furious that they had not been allowed to arrest everyone present.

The planters and their wives gradually drifted back to their respective estates and lonely homes during the afternoon. We at least were on the main road so did not feel as isolated and out on a limb as many of the others. That evening we drove down to Batu Gajah for the funerals of our friends. John Allison had not been an easy man to get on with. He always seemed to have a chip on his shoulder and rarely entered into the local social life, so it was ironic that as we pall-bearers lowered his coffin into the grave one end slipped and it dropped the last couple of feet, landing with a thud. Someone said, 'Good old John, awkward bugger to the last,' which raised a smile. The only one that day.

John Haytor suggested that Jean cable home to say that we were safe. He pointed out that the newspapers would report that three planters had been murdered in Sungei Siput, and as Kamuning was the only estate with three Europeans, the wrong conclusions might be drawn.

It was very late before Jean and I got to bed. I remember feeling terribly depressed. I could not see how we were going to combat this menace. There was an acute shortage of armed forces, a wishy-washy socialist government at home, some members of which were known to be sympathetic to the communist cause, and many equally wishy-washy recent appointments to high places in Malaya. The enemy was the old MPAJA, armed and trained by us in the arts of subversion and guerrilla warfare. Added to which there was the age-old Chinese propensity for secret societies, now coupled with Mao Tse Tung's brand of fanatical communism. I knew from my ISLD days that Chin Peng's objective was the formation of a communist state in Malaya subservient to China.

In June 1948 the jungle-based ex-MPAJA was about 5,000 strong, but there were probably a good 100,000 sympathisers. Most of us would 'sympathise', would agree to collect money, provide food or hiding places, or report on the movements and routines of our employers, if our families were threatened. These sympathisers were the Min Yuen. The Chinese farmer was a sterling character, independent and very hardworking. He lived at the jungle edges, built himself an atap hut in which he and his family lived, bought a sow and a few hens, tilled the land, and sometimes worked on neighbouring rubber estates or tin mines. Ideal for Chin Peng's purposes.

During the next four or five days murder, arson and other acts of violence were wholesale throughout much of Malaya, but particularly in Perak, Johore, Selangor and parts of Negri Sembilan, where there was a very large proportion of Chinese. Although no part of the country was to be free from terrorism, the states where Malays predominated, such as Kedah, Malacca and those on the east coast, were generally quieter. Particularly gruesome were the atrocities committed on those Chinese who had the courage to stand up to the CTs. Men were hacked to pieces in front of their families, usually with a changkol (a heavy spade-shaped hoe). Sometimes the victim's intestines would be cut out, together with the liver, and the wife made to cook them. On other occasions the poor victim would be left to die in agony in front of his family and fellow villagers pour encourager les autres. Another method of persuasion was to crucify children. I know this from personal experience, having seen the awful remains of just such an obscenity on Kamuning. Everything, however vile and despicable and bestial, apparently could be justified in the name of Marxist Communism. Small wonder that many of us feel towards communism, and its fellow travellers, hatred beyond description.

The terrorists had their camps deep in the jungle, many of them maintained since 1945. In them a few hundred of the most dedicated ex-MPAJA communists had spent the intervening years planning and training for their insurrection, mapping the jungle paths, recovering and storing the arms and ammunition dropped in by Force 136, and recruiting the Min Yuen.

From Sungei Siput a road runs north-east for some 10 miles before it peters out at the River Plus. From here the jungle stretches out for hundreds of square miles over the main mountain range towards Kelantan to the east, Siam to the north, and Pahang to the south. In fact, it is continuous, mountainous jungle from Siam right down to Johore, so that the terrorists could travel, unmolested, by jungle paths from north of the border with Siam southwards to Johore, only a score of miles from Singapore. These were the tracks used by Bob Chrystal, Freddy Spencer Chapman, and others of Force 136 and ISLD.

A mile up the Plus road a secondary road branches off south-east for about five miles, before it too peters out near the Jalong and Korbu rivers. For the first mile or so the Jalong road passed Malay smallholdings and plantations, but thereafter it went through many hundreds of acres of jungle that had been cleared over the years by the Chinese farmers, in fact squatters, who were now in considerable numbers. It was the sons and daughters of these squatters who made up the greater part of the militants in our part of Perak, and, naturally, their parents would offer succour – food, shelter, information and alibis.

Police informers had told us that the bandits had come down from their jungle camps around Korbu Mountain and had been fed and sheltered by the squatters along the Jalong road, both before and after committing their atrocities at Elphil and Phin Soon. The police thought there could still be members of these gangs, or others of the same murderous persuasion, hiding there.

I was asked to chair a meeting of senior planters, police and military, at the Heawood Estate bungalow to discuss the security situation in the area. It was agreed by all to be totally inadequate, and that representations should be made to the British Resident to obtain more troops. I knew that this would be a forlorn hope in the short term, so suggested that we would all have to fall back on our own resources, to follow Kamuning's example and recruit their own 'home guards', to fortify our bungalow compounds, factories and offices, and if necessary to bring our labour forces' houses into defensive areas. I was surprised at the reaction of many of the planters and miners present: they complained about the cost.

But we did agree to mount an operation against the terrorists the following day. Before daybreak a company of Gurkhas, with planters to act as guides and interpreters, would drive hell-for-leather to the

Jalong squatter area to endeavour to surprise any terrorists hiding there, to search the houses for illicit weapons, and generally to show the locals that the security forces were to be reckoned with.

At 0430 hours we assembled at the Kamuning Estate hospital where we climbed aboard the army three-tonners. We were about 60 strong. We had planned to be as quiet as church mice, intending to arrive in the squatter area undetected, to surprise any CTs still abed. Each lorry had a planter on board. The signal to move off was given in the traditional army manner – shouted words of command. The lorries revved up and moved off into the night with the maximum possible noise, warning everyone for miles around that the military were involved on an operation. Half an hour later we reached our destination, debussed, fell in, and moved off in half sections, again with shouted words of command, we planters in rubber-soled shoes, the soldiers in hobnailed boots, marching in step. The thunderous noise when we marched over plank bridges had me in hysterics, whether from laughter or frustrated anger I cannot now remember. It was a classic demonstration of how not to undertake such an operation, and I was disappointed that such an example should have been set by Gurkhas, of all people.

Of course, in a short period of time, the military, and particularly the Gurkhas 'got their act together', and became the best jungle fighters in the world. Who would have imagined, having seen the debacle of January and February 1942, that in only eight short years the British Army, composed to a great extent of two-year National Servicemen, would be operating silently in small patrols, in the deepest jungle, and winning the war against a highly motivated, experienced enemy, on its own ground? I do not believe that the nation has given nearly enough recognition to this fact.

Needless to say, we found absolutely nothing. But it was significant that the only inhabitants were the old and infirm. Of the young there was no sign. Those we interrogated denied all knowledge of the 'Tiga Bintang' – the three stars that uniformed bandits then wore on their caps.

But it was this farcical episode that gave me the germ of an idea that I was to put to Sir Henry Gurney, the high commissioner, not long afterwards when we met at the Ferguson bungalow. By then I was able to propound my theories concerning the squatters and cutting off food supplies from the terrorists in some detail.

We got back to Sungei Siput at about four in the afternoon. A postmortem was called for the following day and I was invited to attend. It was agreed that the previous day's only value was to have shown the enemy that the security forces were responding and prepared to take the offensive deep into enemy territory for, make no mistake, it was enemy territory.

We planters and miners, at that stage of the 'Emergency' – in fact a very real war, but never called one so that the insurance companies, rather than the Government, would be responsible for war damage reparations – were the main targets, and we quickly realised the difficulty in spotting the enemy, for he could well be one of our own estate workers, tapping our trees during the day, tabeking (salaaming) when the tuan passed by, dressed in the normal blue blouse and baggy trousers by day, and after dark would be in jungle green uniform with tiga bintang cap, preparing to ambush one returning from Ipoh, slashing the rubber trees, crucifying a child on a neighbouring estate, or besieging a bungalow. Their plan was quite simply to murder as many planters and tin miners as possible, as quickly as possible, to terrorise the labour forces into submission, and bring the main industries of the country to a standstill. They planned to capture isolated police stations and army posts, and from these take over the control of thus 'liberated' areas. They in fact achieved this at the isolated town of Jerantut, and held it for a few days before being driven out.

I have felt for some time that the eventual outcome could well have been different if, in addition to terrorising the countryside, in the classic Maoist way, the Communists had also resorted to large-scale urban terrorism, as practised latterly by the IRA in Northern Ireland.

Ten days after the outbreak of hostilities Guthrie's asked me to fly down to Kuala Lumpur to discuss the situation, so that they could compile a comprehensive report for Sir John Hay in London. Jean and I flew down by Malayan Airways DC3 and were met by Dan

Wright who drove us back to his house on the outskirts of KL. I spent Saturday morning talking to Charles Thornton and Trevor Walker, respectively the Nos.1 and 2 of Guthrie's KL – Peter Taylor had by this time become managing director and had moved to Singapore.

Charles was well-informed about the general situation, and assured me that every effort by Special Branch and the unofficial members of the Legislative Council was being made to persuade Sir Edward Gent, the high commissioner, to take much tougher measures, not only with the communist terrorists and their trade union sympathisers in Malaya, but also with the Government at home whom, it was considered, were sitting in splendid isolation in their ivory towers in Whitehall, listening to the usual socialist claptrap from their Labour supporters and advisers. Gent was still not persuaded, so John Dalley quietly went to work on Malcolm MacDonald, the commissioner general for South East Asia. Fortunately MacDonald, in spite of being the son of Ramsay MacDonald and himself a supporter of the Labour Party, was far more receptive and perceptive, and flew up to KL to see Gent. Gent was still not convinced that it was not just a 'little local incident' which could easily be contained. It is reported that, as a result of this meeting, MacDonald cabled back to the Colonial Office expressing his opinion of the great seriousness of the situation in Malaya and advising the appointment of a new high commissioner.

Gent was recalled to London early in July and when circling over Heathrow, his aircraft collided with another and he was killed. Gent was a gallant man; a double first at Oxford, a rugger Blue, and winner of the DSO and the MC, but unfortunately blind to the perils building up in Malaya.

My weekend in KL followed very much the usual pattern of such visits – office at eight thirty, brandy and ginger ales at Robinsons at eleven, back to the office until one, adjournment to the 'Dog' (the Royal Selangor Club) for a few beers, home for a late tiffin and lie off, a round of golf or a swim, followed by the first stengahs of the evening, home to bath and change, and then out for dinner and dancing at the Lake Club. Sunday was a day of rest. A round of golf in the morning, followed by several beers and a couple of large pink gins before curry tiffin, home for a long lie off, maybe a gentle walk after tea, a light supper and early to bed. The first flight to Ipoh on the Monday morning would get me back to Kamuning for tiffin.

The evening we got back from KL, Bill Powndell drove up for a chat and a stengah and warned us that he had evidence that the telephone lines were being tapped, even that the Sungei Siput exchange had been infiltrated by the Min Yuen, so that any important discussions, especially concerning movements, routes and timings, must be coded somehow, or spoken in French or German or Latin. I was agreeably surprised as to just how much Latin I still retained from school.

Early in July I received a call from John Barnard, the police chief in Perak, asking me to attend a meeting in his office that same morning. Present were Malcolm MacDonald, Innes Miller, the British resident, Neil, the State legal adviser, J. S. Ferguson, chairman, Perak Planters Association, myself, the vice-chairman, a brigadier, the Gurkhas' commander.

This was the first time that I had met Malcolm MacDonald, and he impressed me from the start. We were to meet many times, and became quite friendly, and Jean and I visited him on several occasions informally at his official residence, Bukit Serene in Johore Bahru.

John Barnard read out an 'appreciation of the situation', which was far bleaker than even I had anticipated. Because of the semi-official censorship that existed, the media had not been informed of half that had occurred. We discussed security in some detail, and I briefly mentioned the necessity of controlling the squatters somehow, but that was deemed impractical, so soon forgotten. I also spoke about HOBA, and suggested that other estates and tin mines might consider establishing their own home guard units, as not only would it relieve the police of static guard duties, for which they lacked the people anyway, but it also showed the CTs that we too meant business. I then suggested that the military might be able to assist in their training, as not many estates would have Kamuning's advantage of a resident experienced platoon sergeant. This was thought a good idea and would be considered.

One decision that was taken at the meeting was that all estates from Ipoh to Kuala Kangsar should arrange to collect their pay from the banks at an agreed day of the month, which could be varied, meet up at the Ipoh Club car park, and return along the main road in convoy, pulling out from it when the convoy reached the entrance to their respective estates. I thought this a daft idea, and pointed out that not only would it mean that the banks were overloaded with cash on one given day each month and would thus present an even more worthwhile target for the terrorists, but that any ambush would far more likely take place on the estate roads, where there was more cover to lay up in wait, and to escape into. I was overruled, but, in the interests of solidarity with my fellow planters, I went along with it. In the event it proved to be a fiasco; the convoy went far too slowly, was too conspicuous, and the last couple of estates on the route received no benefit from the convoy system anyway.

During my absence on leave the estate had been issued with a jeep for the manager's use. It was now decided that this should be armoured. When it was returned from the workshops I drove it around the estate for a day or so, but found it impossible. It was like an oven, and I felt like a sardine. I had the doors removed. I felt that if ever I were ambushed or mined I could disembark far more quickly.

We erected a high barbed-wire fence around all the estate bungalows, and during darkness these were patrolled by our Home Guard. HOBA went from strength to strength. In the early days Eussoff and I used to drill them, and march them up and down the main road in front of the main bungalow, factory and labour lines. Later I installed a searchlight. This was particularly useful when I woke in the middle of the night for, if I did not see the sweep of the light after an interval of about five minutes, I knew that the operator was asleep. One night when, after an interval of about a quarter of an hour, the light failed to come on, I crept downstairs and found my HOBA guard asleep. I removed his rifle – shotguns had been replaced – and went back to bed. The following morning I ordered Eussoff to parade the men for a weapons inspection. One very shamefaced man paraded minus his rifle. The derision of his peers was enough punishment, but I deducted a week's pay having ascertained from Eussoff that the man was unmarried, lived with his parents, and would be spending his money on the local prostitutes.

It was not too long before the idea of a Home Guard became official policy, and all such 'private armies' were incorporated into the Special Constabulary. This was a far better idea; it meant that the 'Specials' were properly equipped and trained, could be drafted to where there was most need, and subject to official police discipline. Sergeant Scarlet, a Coldstream guardsman, was put in charge of training the Specials in our area. When he understood that the Kamuning Estate padang was not Caterham, and that Malays fresh from a kampong had to be treated differently to a Guards recruit, he did well and our Specials took pride in their drill, especially if they were being watched by British soldiers. When Sir Henry Gurney came to Sungei Siput, HOBA mounted the Guard of Honour for the High Commissioner, and was complimented on its smartness. They continued to wear their HOBA shoulder flashes until the newly appointed police officer in charge of the Special Constabulary in Perak insisted they were removed, much to the disappointment of the HOBA members.

At about the same time most estate managers were sworn in as honorary police inspectors, to allow us to issue orders directly to the Specials guarding us. We were also issued with Sten guns. The Sten was not as accurate as my American carbine, but made much more noise, and could loose off 150 rounds a minute if it did not jam. The Sten was also a dangerous weapon, to friend and foe alike, because of its habit of going off at the slightest jolt. On one occasion Bill Powndell was up the Plus road with a young planter, a former soldier who was waving his Sten about in all directions. Bill had told him to take care where he was pointing it. The silly young man took exception to Bill's advice and said that he had been on an army small arms course so there was nothing he could be taught about Sten guns. With which he dropped the gun, whether on purpose or by accident history does not relate, which promptly went off, one bullet ploughing a furrow across Bill's ample backside. I gather that to say the air was blue would be an understatement. When later recounting the incident Bill told me that he'd got back through at least three generations of the young man's family, on both sides, without repeating himself.

Knowing Bill I could well believe it.

One night, shortly before Bill was to go on leave, we had him to dinner. Dan Wright was also staying with us, as VA. We were just settling down to the first after-dinner stengah when the bungalow was splattered with bullets. We followed our drill. Jean turned out the bungalow lights and tried to telephone the police station, but the line had been cut. Then she took refuge in the tiled bathroom. We men ran down the stairs to rally the Specials, and tried to spot where the firing was coming from. I made a dash for the sandbagged redoubt where HOBA was gathered, ready to direct the searchlight on to the enemy position. Spasmodic firing went on for some minutes with Bill and I returning fire with our pistols in the direction of the CTs' muzzle flashes. When the firing had stopped I went back to the bungalow and could not help laughing as I saw the ample bellies and backsides of my friends protruding from each side of the pillars behind which they were taking cover. But I feared that the CTs had only moved on to attack the factory and office, so I ran down the drive, trusting that they did not know of my short cut. At the gateway I ran into cross fire, as the factory Specials opened up on the CTs. I worked my way into the factory compound by a monsoon drain and was both pleased and proud to find that my Specials were all at their posts, returning fire in a disciplined fashion and with no sign of panic. The CTs soon withdrew, and after a few minutes congratulating all those concerned, I returned to the bungalow – quite forgetting to duck under the barbed wire fence, and gashing my forehead. By the time I reached home I was covered with blood, so much so I thought that I had better shout a warning to Jean not to worry when she saw me. I have the scar to this day.

I do not remember whether it was during this episode or one later that a bullet ploughed its way through a nine-inch wooden beam and missed Jean's head by only a couple of inches. It was because of this that I sandbagged the verandah around the whole house, and had a trap door made in the floor of the bedroom so that we could drop down straight into the sandbagged redoubt below where most of the Specials would be.

I was very angry and distressed at about this time over the

treatment of my trusted contractor and undercover agent, Wong Fatt. Wong was subpoenaed to appear as witness for the prosecution in the trial of a captured terrorist. I thought it quite wrong for the prosecuting authorities – not the Sungei Siput Police; they would have known better – to call on this man to appear in open court to give evidence, as it would be sure to attract reprisals. I was overruled by Neil, the State legal advisor in Ipoh, but did receive his promise that Wong Fatt's name would not be published. To my utter disgust and dismay his name and photograph appeared in the local newspaper a few days after the trial. I immediately telephoned Neil and gave him a large piece of my mind. He said it was the law, despite having promised me otherwise. I told him to change the bloody law. 'How the hell do you expect witnesses to come forward if their lives were at risk?' I was told I was exaggerating.

Later that day Wong Fatt came to my bungalow and said that he had already been threatened and what should he do? I told him to stay in our kitchen quarters for as long as he wished and that I would help him get away. After a few weeks I drove him up to Penang where he said he had some distant relatives and would be unknown there. Nearly two years later Wong returned. I was surprised to see him but he assured me that he would have been forgotten by the Communists, so I reappointed him one of my estate contractors, but with grave misgivings.

One morning at about six thirty as I was having my tea and fruit on the verandah I heard shots from behind the bungalow, I estimated about a mile away. I grabbed my Sten, telephoned the police station to tell them roughly where the shooting had come from, yelled for Abdul my syce, went like the clappers northwards on the main road towards Kuala Kangsar, until we reached the turning off for the Sungei Koh division. From there we proceeded more cautiously until, rounding a bend, I saw a body lying in the middle of the road, about 50 yards away. I told Abdul to stop the jeep, got out and took to the trees, and approached the body with extreme caution as I feared an ambush. Sure enough, it was my old friend Wong Fatt, riddled with bullets. Hearing some movement behind me I spotted a half dozen bandits moving off, including Perumal. I decided that discretion was the better part of valour and did not give chase. Perumal obviously decided likewise and did not return to carry out his threat to me, no doubt because he thought that the police or military would soon arrive in considerable numbers. I waited and waited, but still no police. I then shouted to Abdul to turn around and to go and look for the police to guide them in; he would be sure to find them on the main road. More waiting. I was feeling terribly exposed and hoping against hope that Perumal would not have second thoughts and return to finish me off. Eventually Paddy Jones, my Sungei Koh assistant, arrived and, despite my warnings to stay put, immediately set off in pursuit of the bandits. Luckily he failed to spot them and returned to keep me company.

Eventually two lorry loads of police arrived. They had decided to take the long way round, through the estate, in case the CTs had been luring them into an ambush. I suppose that they were right, but I had had an extremely unpleasant and lonely hour. I was very sad at this totally unnecessary killing. To the Malay police, Wong Fatt was just another orang Cina (Chinese man); to me he was a trusted and trusting friend.

I have always considered that the prosecuting authorities in Ipoh were willing accomplices in Wong Fatt's murder.

The RAF dropped millions of leaflets over the countryside designed to explain the situation to the populace in general and the Communists in particular. One evening, and to my intense irritation because it took a day to clear up the mess, an aircraft flew over us and dropped a good few hundred thousand of these leaflets over the Kamuning factory area. I telephoned Innes Miller to complain. His response was: 'But Boris, they were intended for you. You're the biggest bloody Bolshie around here.'

The authorities thought it a good idea to erect trip wires around our bungalows. These consisted of a wire some 18 inches off the ground attached to which were small explosive canisters, some 25 feet apart; the principle being that any night intruder would trip over the wire in the dark and set off the nearest explosive. The first couple of nights we were continually woken by explosions, followed by the searchlight sweeping the ground looking for CTs. All that could be seen were startled animals, fallen branches, night owls, even our own cat out on the prowl. I removed the explosives and replaced them with empty cigarette tins filled with a few pebbles, which had the effect of not waking us but keeping the Specials on their toes, at least for a little while.

Sungei Siput was not, of course, the only hot bed of communist activity; far from it. Nearly everywhere suffered from terrorism. Scarcely a day went by without reports of some fresh disaster. The enemy could strike wherever it pleased with little or no retaliation. For months it seemed that all we could do was to hang on. I was no great authority on this type of warfare but it did seem to me that the Security Forces and civil authorities were going quite the wrong way to defeat the insurrection.

I served on both the Sungei Siput District War Committee (as its chairman) and the Perak State War Committee, and on both these I continually pressed for a more realistic approach by the Security Forces to combating the terrorists. It was an uphill task, as I see from my notes. Even as late as October 1949 I was arguing for smaller and more mobile units of the military and police to get out into the country, to move stealthily, to lay ambushes, to pay large bribes to reliable informers – in fact, to play the CTs at their own game, only better. The Army must not rely on lorried transport, marching down roads in step in hobnailed boots, and operating in platoons or half companies. I was not the only one pressing for a change in tactics, and gradually the powers-that-be came round to our way of thinking. All this time, also, I was thinking about controlling the squatters and the ability of the terrorists to obtain their food supplies, information and assistance.

As the situation worsened, Malaya became news at home, and many London journalists descended on us, the most famous being Patrick O'Donovan of the *Observer*, Lachie McDonald of the *Daily Mail*, and Malcolm Muggeridge of the *Daily Telegraph*. At a lunch given by Guthrie's in London in 1952 I sat next to Muggeridge and was able to congratulate him on the accuracy of his reporting.

Patrick O'Donovan wrote a rather more romantic article about Jean and me, and when we tackled him later about his flights of fancy he replied that it was for home consumption, and the editors liked it that way because it sold newspapers. O'Donovan had a very narrow escape when staying with us on Kamuning. On the morning of his departure, and having an hour to spare, he asked if I would show him around the estate. We set off in the armoured jeep. After a mile or so we came to a fork in the road. I stopped to decide which way to go: the left fork was the quicker way back to the office, and I knew we had a weeding gang working near the roadside which I could make a show of inspecting. The right ran deeper into the estate, and consequently there would be more to see. I chose the right fork. We eventually got back to the office where Patrick's taxi was waiting, and he departed.

No sooner had he left when an out-of-breath and extremely agitated Tamil kangani came running into the office, salaaming furiously, and so relieved to see me he all but threw his arms around me. He was in charge of the weeding gang. It seems that about half an hour before we had nearly visited him, Perumal and six Chinese CTs had suddenly appeared and enquired whether the tuan besar had been there yet. When told no, the CTs had instructed the weeding gang to go on working as normal, threatened death to anyone who raised the alarm, and hid in wait for me. They then heard my jeep approach, stop for a moment or two, and then drive off in the other direction. A few minutes later the bandits left, and the kangani dashed back to the office to report to me.

One morning Perumal and Arumugam appeared on the muster ground and, in front of the best part of 250 workers, stabbed to death one of my conductors. They did not use guns, as the shots would have been heard and they knew that my well-armed Specials would have come running. I was so angry I kept all the workers on the muster ground until the body had been removed and then tore strips off them, calling them all the names I could think of in Tamil, Malay and Anglo-Saxon, pointing out that they outnumbered the two bandits by over 100 to one. They hung their heads in shame, as well they might.

Throughout all this time, Jean, like many other wives, was a tower of strength. I think that if I had suggested that we pack it in she would have poured gallons of scorn on my head. She loathed communism and its creed as much as I, and was not going to give in.

By the end of 1949 Ferret Force had been formed. For some time they were based on Dovenby Estate, the other side of Sungei Siput from Kamuning, so we saw quite a lot of them when they came out of the jungle. By now they had been joined by both Donald Wise and Colin Park. They were operating in the jungles around Gunong Korbu and achieving some success. Equally as important as actually killing bandits was the lift to our morale and the subsequent fall to the enemy's. Until then they had thought that they could operate off the roads with impunity. Ferret Force proved to both the CTs and to the Security Forces that the jungle was neutral, and could be equally home to the Army as to anyone else. Through Ah Kim, my bud-grafting contractor and another undercover agent, I was able to give Ferret Force the information that a gang of CTs was living in the jungle behind my Sungei Buloh division. John Davis, fluent in several dialects of Chinese, and I interrogated Ah Kim behind the ruins of the old manager's bungalow, well out of sight of anyone. As Malay was not the prime language of either Ah Kim or myself, I had felt it better for the conversation to be in his own tongue. I was able to promise Ah Kim $600 should his information prove correct. In the event the Ferrets chalked up two kills and the destruction of the bandit camp. I had endless arguments with police headquarters in Ipoh to get payment of the promised reward and in the end had to threaten to telephone the Chief of Police in KL.

When I handed over the money to Ah Kim I told him that under no circumstances must he go on a spending spree. To my dismay he turned up the very next day on a brand new Norton motorbike, and I feared that he would not last long. But he survived to continue being one of our most reliable informers.

Ah Lieu was another notorious local bandit, with a large sum on his head. Ah Kim told me that Ah Lieu would be in Kanthan village at a certain time on a given day. The police raided the village and arrested a number of suspects. I was anxious to find out whether my information had proved correct, but was told that Ah Lieu was not amongst them and that, after screening, they had all been allowed to go. I called Ah Kim to my office on some other pretext and found him almost speechless with anger and despair. The very first suspect the police had interrogated was Ah Lieu. He lived for another year, committing many murders, before being gunned down in one of the limestone caves near Kanthan.

In addition to managing Kamuning Estate and my work with one or other of the war committees and the Perak Planters Association, it seemed that scarcely a day went by when we were not visited by top brass of one form or another – the Police Commissioner from KL, the British Resident, Guthrie directors, even the Commander-in-Chief on occasions when he came up to Perak, and ministers and Opposition leaders out from England. Jean coped with all and sundry with her usual aplomb.

During the first few months the CTs seemed to have everything going their way. The majority of Chinese, if not actually supporting them, were very sensibly sitting on the fence, waiting to see which side would gain the upper hand. The Malays were definitely opposed to the Chinese attempts to take over the country because, of course, they regarded Malaya as theirs, and if anyone was going to supplant the British it should be them. The Indians were generally with the Malays. But, of course, it is difficult to refuse to co-operate with anyone if the alternative is to have your wife and children murdered, and often in the most brutal way. I know I would have co-operated.

Bill Hillyer arrived as the new police chief for Sungei Siput. Without the gravitas or experience of Bill Powndell, nor the avoirdupois, he was young and very enthusiastic, and did not spare himself or the men under him. We worked closely together and organised several sweeps through the neighbourhood, but with only limited success.

Towards the end of 1948 the Police Commissioner H. B. Langworthy, was replaced by Nicol Gray. The former was a prewar Malayan police officer, had spent three and a half years in Changi, and was just not capable of coping with the situation. Most of his senior officers had also been POWs, and as such had had no experience of warfare other than the few weeks in 1942. To add to the problem there had arisen between those who had escaped in 1942 and those who had been captured feelings of bitterness and animosity: I have even heard one of the latter accusing one of the former of having run away. I could never understand the sense of that accusation, as what use was anyone to the Allied cause in captivity? It was just that many of the older prewar police officers were simply out of their depth.

Gray was an entirely different man from his predecessor; ruthless, obstinate, and determined to get his own way. He had won the DSO as a Royal Marine commando during the D-Day landings. He had been a successful inspector general of police in Palestine. But his appointment to the highest police post in Malaya was most unpopular with the majority of the senior officers in an already divided force. While disagreeing with one or two of his early decisions, what worked in Palestine would not necessarily always work elsewhere, I liked and admired Nicol Gray. He visited us on Kamuning several times, and later, when attending Federal War Council meetings in KL, I sometimes stayed with him. We met in London on several occasions when we had retired, usually at the Special Forces Club, but seldom after he had become clerk of the course at Newmarket.

One of the first things that Gray did was to recruit several hundred ex-Palestine policemen, mostly of sergeant rank. These men were posted as police lieutenants around the rubber estates and tin mines, where they took charge of the Special Constables, and general security on their patch. This freed the regular police for more conventional and important duties, but was not always popular with some of the more hidebound career Malayan Police officers, as many of the more capable ex-Palestinians threatened their promotion chances.

Nicol Gray very quickly made his presence felt. Weapons, radios and other essential items of equipment to carry the fight to the enemy began to arrive. But for some reason he was against the police use of armoured vehicles, almost to the point of it being a phobia. This resulted, in my opinion, in many unnecessary casualties. Acts of terrorism would be committed in outlying areas, and the police, rushing to the scene, would in turn be ambushed in their soft-skinned vehicles. In one ambush alone 24 police were killed. The Army, too, had few armoured vehicles, I suspect because of parsimony by the

Treasury in London, rather than any reluctance by soldiers to use them.

In October and November 1948 two tragedies occurred along the Plus and Jalong roads, within sound of my office on Kamuning Estate. In the first incident 10 Gurkhas were killed and 10 severely wounded, and in the second 17 soldiers of the Fourth Hussars lost their lives. I will refer to these terrorist ambushes later.

In 1952, when I visited Kamuning as VA, Charles Ross and I calculated that upwards of 120 soldiers, policemen and civilians had been murdered by CTs within a radius of only five miles of the Kamuning bungalow. I think Sungei Siput must be considered to have been one of the blackest of spots during the Emergency.

Towards the end of November General Neil Ritchie, commander-in-chief Far East Land Forces (FARELF), with his second-in-command, General Harding, and Brigadier Scone, commander of North Malaya District, visited Sungei Siput, with what appeared to be half the Army as escort. I had invited several planters to meet them at the Kamuning Estate hospital where we were addressed by these top brass. But mainly they were on a fact-finding mission, as it was obvious to all concerned that we were losing the battle. Unfortunately, because of the short notice of their arrival that I had been given, I was unable to correlate all the managers' suggestions and ideas and so present a united overview, which was a pity as we must have appeared a rather wishy-washy crowd, with no single plan of action to propose

We saw Colin Park quite often; whenever he had a few hours to spare he would come up to the bungalow for a hot bath, good food and music. Ferret Force was proving to be the one bright light in our armament, and beginning to have successes deep in the jungle, consisting as they did of intelligent war-experienced officers, highly trained in guerrilla tactics. They operated in parties of only half a dozen men and, I believe, it was these successes that finally brought home to the military the value of small, well-trained and well-armed units, capable of taking on the CTs at their own game and winning, rather than the more usual army formations fighting their traditional way.

One day Colin was in a Ferret Force patrol along the Plus River, where it was known that a substantial party of CTs were harassing the squatter community, and from where they were carrying out atrocities against the local estate labour forces. It seems that Colin and another officer took a canoe on to the river, leaving the rest of the party to trek through the jungle. They came under fire from bandits on the bank, which killed his companion and badly wounded Colin, both falling into the river. The rest, hearing the shooting, rushed to the spot and found nothing but the empty canoe. After a search they found the body of the companion, but no Colin. They camped nearby and during the night the sentries kept hearing groans and choking noises which they put down to wild animals. At first light they found Colin's bullet-ridden body only 20 yards away.

Jean and I were terribly distressed. Colin was cremated and the ashes scattered in New Zealand.

During the exchange of correspondence following this tragedy, Sir Keith Park offered me a job in New Zealand. Bob Chrystal also wrote strongly advising me to chuck it in and to join him in Perth, where I could be a partner in a business he had started, manufacturing a special kind of waterproof cement. There were to be several times over the next few years that I regretted not having taken up one or other of these kind offers. Bob's business prospered, and I would have been a wealthy man.

On 6 October 1948 I sat down in the Kamuning office and wrote the long letter, which I had been formulating in my mind over the previous weeks, to the Central Perak Planters Association, with copies to the United Planters Association of Malaya, Guthrie's KL, Keith Anderson, the Kamuning Estate company secretary in London, and Innes Miller, the British adviser in Ipoh. Shortly afterwards a colonel rang me up from KL and asked if I would provide another copy to Major General Charles Boucher, the director of operations. My letter was headed 'State of Emergency – Sungei Siput Area'. I like to think that it had some beneficial effect.

I started off by listing the Communist outrages in the Sungei Siput area during the first three months of the Emergency:

- murders: 13 (this was shortly before the two major ambushes of the Gurkhas and Hussars mentioned above)

- estates attacked & buildings destroyed: 10
- estimated cost of damage: $500,000
- estimated loss of revenue: $2,000,000.

In addition, the police stations at Lintang and Salak North had been attacked and destroyed, the Penang to KL night mail train had been attacked (this on the section of line that ran through Kamuning), and only narrowly missed derailment, and the Perak Hydro Electric sub-station in Sungei Siput blown up, bringing most industry in the area to a temporary standstill.

I complained about the Army's refusal to provide adequate protection for Jalong Tinggi Estate, which was in an extremely isolated position, and was in fact closed down, with the consequent loss of jobs and revenue. I criticised the reduction of the number of troops during the previous fortnight, despite the increased CT offensive.

I pointed out that the CTs moved mainly at night, in small numbers, seldom above a dozen, and that it was fatuous to billet security forces of company strength or more at the Kamuning Estate hospital, and to send them out by the lorry-load, invariably after the event. I also criticised the abortive sweeps through the estates, kampongs and nearby jungle, all accompanied by the rattle of weaponry, the clanking of mess tins, the crunch of standard issue army boots, and the thunder of heavily laden three-tonners crossing wooden bridges, all of which gave any bandits for miles around ample warning to retire deeper into the jungle, or to don their tapper's clothes and get to work on the trees.

I said it was obvious that the army must have proper equipment – rubber boots, for instance, and a more suitable weapon than their normal .303 Lee Enfield rifle, which was totally unsuitable for jungle work. I suggested that the Army should operate in sections, or even half-sections, to go out and lay their own ambushes on likely routes to and from the squatter areas, that they should garrison certain 'black' areas, if only with a platoon, to provide rapid deployment to an incident – within minutes rather than hours.

I commented on the obvious strained relations between the army and police, particularly noticeable in the higher ranks in KL, but also evident at local level. This problem, I said, must be overcome without delay, because unless there was absolute unanimity of purpose and total trust between the military, the police, and the planters and miners, nothing much would be achieved and we might as well all pack up and go home now.

I suggested the various strategic points around Sungei Siput that I thought should be garrisoned, and that the local commander, whether he be of a platoon or a company, should have a free hand in deciding his dispositions in consultation with local police and planter or miner. I considered it absolutely essential that a substantial force, at least a platoon, should be positioned within the Tikus squatter area. This would serve not only as an ideal base for continual offensive sweeps through this notorious area and up the Korbu valleys, but would keep the area open for government officers to spread the anti-communist gospel, and allow the squatters to go about their lawful business without hindrance.

I also mentioned my hobbyhorse – the need to control the ability of the CTs to obtain food and other essential supplies to sustain their activities. I was able to expand on this particular theme in greater detail at a meeting held at Freddy Ferguson's bungalow on Changkat Kinding Estate with the new High Commissioner Sir Henry Gurney, a few weeks later. I believe that my ideas would eventually form the basis of what was to become known as the Briggs Plan, later to be fully implemented under General Gerald Templer, and which played a great part in the winning of the war in Malaya.

Shortly before delivering my letter personally to the British Adviser in Ipoh I added a postscript: 'Since writing the above, news has just been received of an ambush in broad daylight on the Lintang road resulting in the deaths of 10 Gurkhas and the severe wounding of 10 others.' Consequently, at least two of the wounded also succumbed.

Innes Miller said that I would not be popular with the military or the police. I said that worried me not in the slightest. All I was concerned with was the defeat of the enemy as quickly as possible.

In fact this took nearly 10 years, at a cost of more than 20,000 casualties and many hundreds of millions of dollars.

Guthrie's in London had an wholly unexpected fit of generosity when the Board announced that, with immediate effect, they would grant a monthly allowance of $250 and $100 respectively to their European and Asian staffs, to permit them to take a long weekend away from their estates, once a month. This was most acceptable, as we could all do with a couple of days away from the fear of being murdered. Most Europeans took themselves off to Singapore, KL, Penang or Cameron Highlands. We tended to go to Penang and stay either with the Brittains or at the E&O.

Tommy and Jean Spence were on Sungei Krudda Estate. Of all the planters in the Sungei Siput district they lived in the most dangerous position, about 10 miles up the Plus road, with an ideal spot for an ambush every couple of hundred yards or so. This isolated stretch of road, where the Gurkhas, the Hussars and several civilians had been murdered, was 'no-man's-land' during the daylight hours, and definitely enemy territory after nightfall. Jean and Tommy were marooned in their bungalow compound for days on end and relied very much on the telephone for contact with the outside world. The Hembry and Spence Jeans spoke to each other on most days when the line had not been cut. The Spences were certainly the bravest planting couple that we knew, determined to stick it out and not to let the Communists win. On one occasion, following a particularly harrowing time when Sungei Krudda had experienced a night of siege, Jean and I went over there, escorted by a section of Gurkhas, and spent a day with them. I left Jean there overnight, with some misgivings, to give Jean Spence support. When I collected her the following afternoon Jean told me that the whole bungalow was riddled with bullet holes, and that at least a dozen shots had been fired at it during the previous night, apparently about par for the course. Tommy and Jean Spence stuck it out until their leave was due and then to their surprise, and to the disgust of all who knew this brave couple, Tommy's contract was not renewed. No doubt the London board, whose only contact with any shooting was on the grouse moors, had decided that Sungei Krudda's profits were not quite what it thought they should be.

In December I was appointed to the Review Board, a committee of about six, whose task it was to interview internees, mostly Chinese, who had been picked up as suspects, to decide whether they should (*a*) remain interned; (*b*) be charged with a criminal indictment; (*c*) be deported; or (*d*) be released. I recall releasing just one; most of the rest were deported back to China.

In the following March I was appointed to the Perak State Security Committee, to represent the planting industry.

It had been made a treasonable offence to print, distribute, or even to be found in the possession of communist literature, the penalty for which was arrest and detention without trial. Sometime towards the end of 1949 the then Dean of Canterbury, Dr Hewlett Johnson, known universally as the 'Red Dean' because of his support for all things Russian, passed through Singapore en route for Australia. Within a very short time of arriving in Singapore he had started to distribute communist tracts, in spite of being reminded by the authorities that it was illegal. At the Security Committee meeting the following day I demanded that this stupid old man should be instantly arrested and thrown into Changi, as would be any of the millions of citizens of Malaya, in accordance with the law. But I was overruled by the civil servants, and accused of overreacting. With my Canterbury connections – John by this time was at the King's School – I knew that Johnson was only a mischievous, silly old man, but the majority of educated Asians and Australians thought that he was the *Archbishop* of Canterbury, second only to the Monarch in order of precedence, and therefore a personage of immense importance.

Christmas 1948 was spent at Silver Sands, a beach bungalow out at Batu Feringgi, way beyond Tanjong Bungah on the outskirts of Georgetown, on Penang. It was a great relief to be able to chuck my Sten gun on to the top of the wardrobe – where it promptly went off, half a magazine of bullets ploughing through the wooden wall and disappearing into the ulu. Later that afternoon, when driving to the local kedai for stores, we were stopped at a police roadblock on the beach road. The whole area was seething with police and soldiers looking for the CTs that had been reported to have opened fire earlier in the day. In all innocence I said I would be on my guard.

Half a dozen Labour MPs and one Tory, Walter Fletcher,

came out to Sungei Siput during the first 12 months or so of the Emergency, ostensibly on fact-finding missions. I think they chose Kamuning because it was very definitely in the thick of things, but also on the main road and easy to reach and return from to the safety of Ipoh during half a day. I do not remember any of the socialists, most of whom appeared to be time-serving trades union officials, but Walter Fletcher was a big man, full of Churchillian anecdotes which I remember to this day.

On 11 February 1949, at a formal dinner in KL attended by senior government officials, military brass and planters, the High Commissioner Sir Henry Gurney said: 'The Malayan Government could not contemplate that the Emergency would continue for two years, or any time of that sort.'

It was my duty to propose the toast to the Security Forces, and Major General Charles Boucher to respond. As I write, the newspaper cuttings are in front of me. Only the speeches of Gurney, Boucher and myself were reported.

I told the assembly: 'Without a strong government, planters may never again be able to go about their duties in peace and quiet'. I went on, 'We planters have never ceased to voice our disappointment at the lack of progress to eradicate the communist menace. In fact, it would be wrong to claim, even, that honours were even. But, we must all agree that if it were not for the Security Forces, our homes and livelihoods would have been untenable by now. For this alone our gratitude is due to the Security Forces.'

I recalled that I lived in the notorious district of Sungi Siput, Perak, and so could claim to have been in the forefront of the struggle from the beginning. I acknowledged the disadvantages experienced by the Security Forces in tracking down and bringing to battle an elusive enemy, an enemy that carried a tapping knife at one moment and a gun the next. I emphasised my view that the need to control the supply of food to the terrorists was of paramount importance, and ended by acknowledging that whilst I had never hesitated to criticise the methods of the army and police, for their part they had never presumed to tell me how to perform my job. 'Such forbearance, I think, speaks volumes for the understanding, co-operation and goodwill that exists between planters and the Security Forces.'

Boucher prefaced his reply by saying, 'Any praise from Mr Hembry of Sungei Siput is praise indeed.' He then went on to echo Gurney's optimism by stating, 'It is obvious that neither the planters nor the economy of the country, nor the overstrained Security Forces are prepared or willing to do two more years under the present strain. It is for this very reason that we are determined to end this situation within that time.' He added for good measure, 'I think that by the end of two years, by which time the last militant communist will have been hanged or deported, our enlarged and re-organised police force will have picked the final red plum out of the Malayan pudding'.

My heart sank at the expressed optimism of Gurney and Boucher, and I thought back to my letter of 6 October in which I stated it was apparent that the top brass in KL were out of touch with the actual situation. The two years developed into seven and by then, amongst thousands of others, Sir Henry Gurney and General Boucher were dead, the former murdered, and the latter from sheer exhaustion.

I see in my scrapbook a newspaper cutting dated 18 January 1977 which reads: 'Malaysian army troops have seized a Communist camp in the jungle near Sungei Siput, Perak State, after a running fight in which two soldiers were wounded. About 20 guerrillas occupying the camp escaped.' A very prolonged two years!

There was a sequel to the ambush and murders of the Fourth Hussars. In the middle of 1949 Anthony Eden, as shadow foreign secretary, visited Malaya to see the situation at first hand. He worked his way up from Singapore and eventually reached Ipoh, where the leading lights of the Asian and European communities were invited to meet him over a buffet lunch at the Station Hotel. Jean and I found him a most charming man and, more importantly, well versed in the situation, not sharing the official government view that the Emergency would soon be over. He asked some extremely pertinent questions, and I took the opportunity, yet again, to press for control of the squatters. The British Adviser asked if we could entertain Eden the following day on Kamuning, as Churchill had asked him to visit the scene where so many of his old regiment had died. Winston was colonel-in-chief of the Fourth Hussars. Of course, I said that we would be delighted, but stressed the need for a very strong escort.

The party duly arrived and, after Eden had spoken a few words to Jean and other assembled Sungei Siputians, he and I got into his government limousine and set off for the ambush scene. We had two armoured scout cars at the front and behind, and at least one lorry full of troops following up. Then, at intervals of every quarter of a mile or so there were at least a section of soldiers positioned on both sides of the road. Altogether I had over an hour's talk with the future prime minister with no one else present except the driver. We got out at the ambush scene and a Hussar survivor explained what had happened. We then drove down to the Tikus valley and to the road's end at the river. He saw at first hand the squatters' houses and clearings, and could appreciate how the CTs could receive sustenance. On our return Eden asked if I could have some photos taken of the ambush spot for the Old Man, and send them to him care of the House of Commons.

I returned to the scene the next afternoon to take the snaps, driven by my faithful syce Abdul, completely unescorted, and feeling very exposed. I was pleased to get back to the estate. Jean asked Abdul whether he ever got frightened when out with the tuan. All Abdul said was, 'Where Tuan goes, I go.' I think that Abdul and his wife Puteh were the two people we missed most when we left Kamuning.

The full glare of publicity began to shift away from Sungei Siput, because many other areas throughout Malaya had by now experienced the same high level of terrorist activity, the same atrocities and the same degree of communist beastliness. However, there continued to be incidents every day and night on and around Kamuning and the neighbouring estates, and Chinese and Indians continued to be murdered and security forces ambushed. But the Specials became better trained and armed, and made it difficult for the bandits to attack estate factories without risking death or capture, and planters and miners went about their normal business, rather as one did in England during the blitz, always mindful of the security risks. Our wives, especially, lived under a strain, for they never knew when they said 'Cheerio' in the morning whether they would see us again. By now each bungalow had its Malay Specials, so the men were able to get around their estates moderately confident that their wives and homes were protected. I endeavoured to use my wartime training to advantage. I developed eyes in the back of my head. I never followed a set routine, even varying the time I went the few hundred yards to the office, and rarely returned from anywhere by the way I went. I never took Specials as escort, as we had been strongly advised to do, because I felt safer on my own. I would not have to worry about them if we were ambushed. Unfortunately Abdul was a sitting duck, but he would have been very indignant had I left him at home.

One evening in June 1949 Jean and I were sitting quietly reading in our bungalow when the telephone rang. It was the post office relaying a telegram. 'I send you my warmest congratulations on the well-deserved honour which has been awarded you by His Majesty the King. Signed, High Commissioner.' I thought it was a legpull, and began to think of which of our friends would have been the perpetrator. Then at least another half a dozen telephoned through in quick succession, including from the Commissioner of Police Malcolm MacDonald, and the GOC Malaya. The following morning the confirmations arrived, together the newspaper reporting that I had been awarded the Colonial Police Medal for Meritorious Service, in the King's Birthday Honours List. The citation read:

Mr Hembry is the Manager of Kamuning Estate in the Sungei Siput district. It was in Sungei Siput that the first three planters were murdered at the outset of the present Emergency. Mr Hembry was among the first to volunteer for service in the Auxiliary Police Force, and his courage, initiative and high morale has been an inspiration to other planters in the district. He has played a leading part in raising and training the Special Constabulary in Perak, and has been ready at all times, often at great inconvenience to himself, not only to assist the Police and Military Forces by providing information, but also to take part in offensive patrols against bandits.

His record of voluntary public service is outstanding

and he has made a most valuable contribution to the Government's drive to thwart the expressed intentions of the Communists to paralyse the rubber industry.

Cables of congratulation came from Guthrie's in London, Singapore and KL, together with many letters and telephone calls from friends and acquaintances. Jean and I were astonished that I should have been singled out, but nevertheless most gratified. Three other planters were similarly honoured, and in due course our medals were presented by the High Commissioner Sir Henry Gurney, on the Police Padang in Kuala Lumpur. The medal was engraved, but unfortunately with my name as 'Maurice'. I have recently decided to have this corrected, but after 30-odd years I cannot find it.

Kamuning being on the main road certainly had its advantages. Between Sungei Siput and Ipoh there were very few places that bandits could set up an ambush, and there was constant military or police traffic, so that our visits to Ipoh were hardly restricted, and we were able to lead a more or less normal social life. This was in marked contrast to the majority of planters in Malaya who, at least in the early years of the Emergency, lived very much in a siege situation for most of the time.

The Europeans held annual balls organised by the Societies of St George, St Andrew and St Patrick, usually on the nearest Saturday to the particular Saint's Day, and the Sultan of Perak used to attend at least one of these functions each year. In 1950 it was the turn of St George. The Sultan and his entourage were seated at the top table and, towards the end of the evening, after the various loyal toasts, Yola, the wife of 'Cave' Cave-Penny, the president of the society, became a little worried that the Sultana had not visited the ladies' room all evening, so she passed the word up to her husband to ask the Sultan whether the Sultana would like to do so. The Sultan replied in a loud voice for all to hear, 'When my consort wishes to pass water she will catch the Aide-de-Camp's eye.'

On another occasion, Jean was present when the wives of certain senior government officials, planters and tin miners were being entertained in the Istana, at Kuala Kangsar, when their hostess, the

Sultana, asked the somewhat startled ladies whether they would like to go down to the river to see the Sultan's erection. It turned out that he had built a new gazebo which he was rather proud of.

One morning in 1950 word came that a number of trees in my 1938 clearing had been slashed. This was an obvious trap, for the inclination of any manager or assistant would be to rush out to assess the damage, and the CTs would be waiting. I was too wily an old bird to fall for that one. But when I did eventually go I was shocked at the damage. Rubber trees had only to be ring-barked for them to be taken out of production. The Communists need only to have concentrated on ring-barking the trees to have brought the rubber industry to a standstill. In this instance there was only a little damage, so I was not unduly worried.

Despite my wariness I was guilty of the occasional lapse of good sense. After a certain time living in almost constant danger one inevitably relaxes. Soon after the tree-slashing episode on the Ayer Hitam division I arranged with the Gurkhas to mortar the area to frighten off any bandits who might have returned to the scene to continue where they had left off. That evening, shortly after 5 pm, I drove out with Jean to have a look at the clearing. Round a corner we suddenly came to a tree that had fallen across the road, completely blocking it. My immediate thought was 'ambush!'. The road was far too narrow to turn; on one side was a 10-foot bank, and on the other a precipice. There was no alternative but to clear away the obstruction. Fortunately, I always carried an axe for just such emergencies. While I chopped away, half expecting a fusillade from ambushing bandits, Jean hugged the Sten gun and kept lookout, and an eye on her watch. Remembering the last occasion when I had been shelled by my own side, I prayed that her watch had not stopped. I managed to hack sufficient branches away to enable me to slew the trunk around and push it over the precipice, before jumping back into the jeep and driving away only a few moments before the bombardment began. We could not have been more than a couple of hundred yards away from where the first rounds landed. I was very annoyed with myself for my stupidity.

The RAF from time to time bombed certain areas, usually jungle, where CTs had been reported. On one occasion the target was in the vicinity of Batu Gajah. Afterwards a very irate European woman telephoned the squadron's adjutant on Ipoh airfield to complain bitterly about the noise and general disturbance. 'And, what is more, a valuable piece of porcelain was shattered!' 'Really, madam,' replied the adjutant, 'I do hope you weren't sitting on it at the time.'

The first Kamuning Estate annual report since the start of the Emergency came out in 1949 and I was gratified to see the Chairman's speech at the AGM reported in full in *The Times*. 'Sir John Hay opened his statement with a reference to the dangerous position of Kamuning and a tribute to the local manager, Mr Hembry. He reported that during these very dark days, the Company's staff stood steadfastly to their duty and carried on their normal work. He went on by saying that such quiet and persistent courage in the face of recurring violence evokes great admiration.'

I had the report translated into Malay, Tamil and Chinese and copies pasted up around the estate where it could be seen by my staff, labour force and bandits alike. It was because of the loyalty and support of the vast majority of the estate's employees, of all grades and races, that Kamuning withstood the first onrush of the communist insurrection so well.

Early in 1950 Charles Ross returned as senior assistant, with his charming wife Nancy, Tim Earl his predecessor was transferred, and Peter Madden went on well-earned leave. His place was taken by Paddy Jones, who had had a few years' experience on estates down in Negri Sembilan, so I was able to give him charge of both the Banda Bahru and Sungei Koh divisions and, as the security situation had slightly improved, I felt it safe enough for him to live in the rather isolated Sungei Koh bungalow – with, of course, his Special guards. Paddy was a character, as one would expect of someone with Irish-Welsh parentage who had been a rear gunner in RAF bomber command in the war, but was on occasions somewhat impetuous. Whilst his refusal to yield in any way to the communist bandits was wholly admirable, he did cause me to worry about his occasional risk-taking. Eventually his luck ran out.

Jean and I were staying for the weekend in Penang with Jean

and Laurie Brittain. Sir John was out on one of his periodic trips and I had an appointment on the Monday morning to meet him at the Guthrie office. I had just started talking to Sir John when Charles Ross came on the line to say that Paddy Jones had been ambushed, severely wounded, and was in Batu Gajah hospital. The Malay special constable escort had been killed, as had Paddy's dog. I passed the news to Sir John and left at once to return to Kamuning. The attack had taken place at one of the most obvious sites for an ambush, near the boundary between Main and Sungei Koh divisions.

Paddy was out of danger when I saw him in hospital that evening. He had been very seriously injured – at least four bullets had hit him – but despite this he had managed to stop the car before it plunged over the bank. He had fallen out of the car on the side opposite from where the CTs were shooting, tumbled down the bank and escaped. The car was a complete bullet-ridden write-off. Knowing Paddy I would not have put it past him to have given chase to the bandits – we suspected that it was my old adversary Perumal, as my spies had told me only a few days before that he was in the area again

In February 1950 I wrote another appreciation of the situation concerning the security situation, and took it to the British Adviser, with copies mailed to the Commissioner of Police and the Director of Operations (General Briggs had by now replaced General Boucher) in KL, and a few members of the Federal Legislative Council, in Singapore, whom I knew.

In the preamble I pointed out that it must be clear to everyone that we were no nearer to destroying the forces of communism than we were in June 1948. In fact the situation had considerably deteriorated during the previous three months, in spite of large-scale operations by the Security Forces.

I went on to suggest that Malaya could not continue to rely entirely on the UK for troops and finance and that the time had arrived when Malaya should rescue itself from the near-disastrous position it was in. It had the manpower and the money; all it needed was the will.

My main proposal was that all able-bodied men, of all classes, colours and creeds, should be conscripted into an armed militia, for a period of two months each year. Five to ten thousand at a time would be required to undergo a month of intensive basic training, comprising PT, weapons training and jungle field craft, followed by a month on active service. As soon as the first batch had been trained, the second would be required to report. This way the full 30,000 would be available within six months. The second year of service would only require a week's refresher course before active service.

Where the men were in gainful employment their salaries during their embodiment would be met by their employers, otherwise the State would pay a basic allowance to the unemployed or casual labourers. This way all parts of society would have a stake in the fight against terrorism, and it was fair that the greater their stake in a peaceful, free and prosperous country, the more it should cost that person or his employers.

Included in the necessary legislation would be the legal requirement for employers to re-employ everyone at their old job, on completion of embodiment. Obviously all arms and equipment would be supplied by the Government, and it must be of good quality – not, for example, leftovers from the Great or even Boer wars.

The tasks would be several:

1. Aid to the Civil Power.
2. Active operations against the Communist bandits, in conjunction with and under the command of the regular forces.
3. Consolidation and garrisoning of areas cleared of Communist terrorists.
4. Provision of interpreters and providers of local knowledge for the regular forces.

Finally, I stressed the absolute necessity to form a first-class intelligence service, the Government's own Min Yuen, with information leading to arrests and conviction well paid for. Five hundred dollars to the Government is nothing; $500 to a squatter or labourer, who had vital information to impart, was riches.

In front of me is a cutting from *The Straits Times* dated 20 April 1950, some two months after I wrote the above. It reads as follows: 'Unofficial Members of the Federal Legislative Council today unanimously expressed the opinion that the manpower available in the country should be mobilised, trained and properly equipped to shoulder the responsibility of restoring peace and security.'

Of course I have no means of knowing, but I do know that my paper was circulated fairly extensively and I like to think that my ideas had some influence on the above resolution in the Legislative Council. Despite some improvement in the situation, the scale of CT activity in Perak remained massive. I think only Johore was as bad, although Negri Sembilan and Selangor and parts of Pahang were nearly so. The bandits in the Sungei Siput district were particularly daring one night when they entered the village and under the noses of the police and army relieved the villagers of their identity cards.

Perumal was a constant source of irritation to me. He was in the habit of visiting the outlying divisions and raiding the shops for rice and tinned stores. He also invariably helped himself to a bottle or two of orange crush. I suggested to the police that we should lace a marked bottle with cyanide and reward the shopkeeper who managed to palm it off, but they refused to accept my idea, on the grounds that there could be a mix-up resulting in someone innocent being poisoned. I also suggested that I should act as a decoy, with a section of Gurkhas disguised as tappers standing by, but this, too, was vetoed. Perumal's parting words were always for the shopkeeper to tell the tuan that it would only be a matter of days before he killed me.

In due course the police were relieved of certain guard duties in and around Ipoh, such as the airfield, fuel dumps, electricity substations and telephone exchanges, and replaced by Specials.

One morning I was driving around the Sungei Buloh clearing when someone took a shot at me. The bullet struck the armour plating with a clang, not too many inches from my head. I stopped the jeep 200 yards further on and took to the rubber trees, retracing my path, but saw no one. I could not believe that it was Perumal as he would have mounted a proper ambush, with several accomplices. I concluded that it was most probably a lone bandit on his way home to join a weeding gang, after a night's nefarious activity. Jean later reminded me that I always had at least two dogs cavorting and barking behind my jeep, which I always drove slowly around so that I could inspect the rubber, which would have identified me as the driver.

In June 1950 I received a letter from the secretaries in London, who had been instructed by the board to write direct to me. This was most unusual, if not unique, as it was the cast-iron rule that all communications between the Board and a manager must go through the agents in KL, otherwise it could lead to cross-purposes and misunderstandings. I quote the letter dated 1 June in full:

Dear Mr Hembry,

We have been asked by the Board to write to you direct expressing their regret at learning of the latest outrage on Kamuning Estate, and conveying their best wishes for Mr Jones' speedy recovery. These sentiments were conveyed to you in a private telegram sent through the Agents yesterday, which we hope you received.

The Directors feel the utmost admiration for the courage and devotion to duty shown by the Staff, both European and Asian. As you know, they are prepared to authorise spending the company's money to whatever extent considered necessary and advisable to protect the Staff, both by the institution of precautions and by the provision of insurance against the possibility of the worst happening. Though the Board cannot claim an extensive knowledge of the different districts in Malaya and of the outrages that have occurred there, they are of the opinion that the Sungei Siput district has had more of (sic) its share, and they are writing to the Agents suggesting a suitable letter should be addressed either to Mr Griffiths (Colonial Secretary) or Mr Strachey (War Minister), if they are still in Malaya, or failing them to Mr Hilton Poynton (Permanent Secretary, Colonial Office), listing the outrages, particularly murders, in the Sungei Siput district, emphasising how bad it is, and going on to say that the directors of companies whose estates have suffered so much cannot go on indefinitely asking men to expose themselves by working there in so much danger involved. We shall be grateful if you will co-operate in producing a list of outrages, and in any other way which you may consider advantageous.

With renewed best wishes for the safety of yourself and all others on Kamuning Estate and the speedy and complete recovery of Mr Jones.

Yours faithfully,

London Secretaries

Naturally I did my best to co-operate, and provided the requested list and quite a lot more information which I thought might strengthen the case – as if it needed to be! I also had a long talk with Sir Hilton Poynton when he visited Ipoh and attended a State War Executive committee meeting. I repeated my demand for the arrest of the Red Dean. Sir Hilton replied by saying, 'Hembry, whilst I agree with you, I cannot say so officially.' This latter exchange was while he was alone with me in my car as I was driving him to the club for lunch by a somewhat circuitous route, to give me more time to bend his ear in private.

I then wrote to Sir Hilton summarising the salient points that I had put to him in the car.

The letter from the London secretaries was followed by one from those in KL. They reiterated the sentiments expressed in the London letter, complimented me on my 'forceful' letter to Sir Hilton Poynton, and followed by saying, 'Your routine reports are read with particular interest and concern and you are to be congratulated on your dogged and efficient conduct of affairs in the face of such exceptional, trying and difficult circumstances.'

This again was most gratifying. However, I was aware, through conversations with other planters, that some other companies were not nearly as supportive of their staffs, whether Asian or European, as Guthrie's. It must have been very trying for them to feel that there was not the acknowledgement by those who worked in the safety of KL, Singapore or London of the very great dangers that most of us worked in every day.

Dates for our next home leave were now being discussed and it was tentatively agreed that we should return home in July, when Jean received disturbing news about the health of her father. We therefore decided that she should go at once. We were in KL having her passport renewed when Charles Ross telephoned to say that a cable had been received giving the news that Grandpa Cuthbertson had died on 15 April. He was only 68, and had enjoyed but three years of well-earned retirement. Jean managed to obtain a flight home during the first week of May.

I had persuaded the agents to appoint Charles Ross to act for me during my leave. He knew Kamuning like the back of his hand, and was familiar with my modus operandi and future plans, and more than capable of holding the fort until my return. But towards the end of June, within a matter of weeks of my scheduled departure, Charles became very ill and the X-rays showed inoperable cancer. But Reid Tweedie refused to accept this diagnosis and arranged for him to fly down to Singapore to see a surgeon friend for a second opinion. The latter diagnosed something less sinister, but which requiring an immediate operation. Luckily he was correct; there was no malignancy, and Charles made a complete recovery, convalesced in Australia, eventually succeeded to the Kamuning management and finally retired to Scotland.

Arrangements were hurriedly made for Louis Denholm of Kerling Estate to take Charles' place, and I duly handed over to him. An excellent choice, but it was whilst showing him around the estate that we heard of my old friend Ralph Inder being murdered on the neighbouring Dovenby Estate. Acting as pall-bearer again, to another planter and old friend, was one of my final acts before departing.

I said my fond farewells to Puteh and Abdul, and of course to Kim. Alas, only a month or so later Louis wrote to say that the old boy had fretted away and died. I was so glad that I had been able to give him a good and loving home for the last five years of his life. He certainly repaid me with his love and loyalty.

I stayed the night in Ipoh, flew down to KL, where I was advised by the agents that I was shortly to be offered a more senior appointment, and then on to Singapore before flying home to arrive in London some 30 hours later, full of joy to be with Jean again, flattered that it appeared that a promotion was in the offing, but sad at the prospect of leaving Kamuning.

The first week of leave was truly hectic. We stayed at the Royal Commonwealth Society, as the accommodation in the East India & Sports Club was lamentable, and went to a show every night. After one, accompanied by Freddy and Mollie Reynolds, who were also home on leave, Freddy insisted on taking us on to the Gargoyle Club, which he had joined whilst up at Cambridge some 30 years before, and had not visited since. The entrance was by a tannery and the smell was disgusting. We ascended to the first floor by an old-fashioned lift, one of those which one propelled oneself upwards by pulling on a rope, which opened out to the bar. The first thing we saw was a fat, scruffy, bleary-eyed man in a clinch with a female, on a settee, with another man who was looking decidedly unamused, looking on from the other end of the settee. As the barman said that the latter was the woman's husband, we were interested to see what would happen. When the couple came out of their clinch the unprepossessing lover started to speak in the most beautiful, melodious man's voice I have ever heard. He introduced himself as Dylan Thomas, and would we join him in a drink? I quickly declined, as I thought that if we did we would be in for a very long night. But after a couple of bottles of champagne I became so impressed with the club that Freddy insisted on proposing me for membership there and then, and getting Dylan Thomas to second me. The secretary then discovered that Freddy had not paid his annual subscription for 30 years, and charged him over £100 to get up to date. We both paid our due subscriptions, and none of us ever returned. But Jean and I enjoyed ourselves, dancing to our favourite tunes from prewar. The club had been started by the painter Augustus John, and was the haunt of bohemians and queers.

We based ourselves at Hornchurch. I took delivery of the Humber Hawk that I had ordered in Malaya, and would be taking back with me at the end of my leave, so we were mobile. It was when I had driven up to meet my mother at Euston Station that I bumped into Anthony Eden again. 'I know you, don't I?' he said. 'Malaya. Sungei Siput, isn't it?' I marvelled that this statesman could remember what to him must have been such a trivial occurrence in his long and distinguished life. He quizzed me for a few minutes about the current situation in Malaya, hinted that he hoped that there would be great changes in not too many months time, shook hands and left to catch his train.

Very soon I was summoned to Guthrie's, now back in their headquarters in Gracechurch Street, in the City, to meet Sir John, and to attend a meeting of the Kamuning Board of Directors. Shortly after this Sir John asked me to join him at Lords for the Gentleman vs Players match. This was the game in which Freddy Brown made the quick hundred that ensured his captaincy of the MCC tour to Australia that winter. Sometime during Brown's innings Sir John casually asked me whether I knew anything about oil palms. I replied, 'Damn all.' After about another 30 runs Sir John said that he wanted me to take over at Ulu Remis, the Oil Palms of Malaya estate at Layang Layang, in Johore. I repeated that I knew nothing about oil palms, well aware that Ulu Remis was the largest estate in the whole of Malaya, and the most prestigious and best-paid managership in the Guthrie group. He replied that there was an extremely experienced and capable staff there, quite able to look after the horticultural and manufacturing side of the business. I would be required to administer the enterprise, and to sort out the unhappiness and back-biting (Sir John's words) that seemed to be prevalent amongst the divisional managers. Obviously the man I was to replace, Steve Thorburn, for all his abilities, had allowed this to occur. The plan was for me to act for Thorburn while he was on leave, to gain some experience with oil palms and re-establish good staff relations, before taking over from him after his final, shortened, tour.

I recognised the honour and the confidence Guthrie's were showing in me, that at 41 I was very young for such responsibilities, and that it would give me a chance to earn a large income, even by Malayan standards, for at least 10 years. But I viewed the proposed change with mixed feelings. I sought no better position than Kamuning, which I considered home – or at least home from home. North Perak was a lovely part of Malaya, within easy reach of both Penang and Cameron Highlands for weekends, and where most of our friends lived. Of all the states that I knew, I liked Johore the least. I was happy with my European staff of two, and did not relish the idea of 'sorting out' more than a dozen Europeans, most of whom were older than me and with many years experience of oil palms. In addition, the Layang Layang area of Johore had the reputation of being a terrorist hotbed.

Sir John then said that the police had advised Guthrie's that captured communist terrorist documents had showed me at the head of their 'death list', after only the High Commissioner, the Chief of Police and the Director of Operations. I found this hard to believe as, in spite of my anti-CT activities in Perak, I was after all only an ordinary rubber planter, and no more important than any of the other 800-odd planters in Malaya. But Sir John assured me it was so, and that they had agreed to move me. I did wonder whether my wartime activities had any bearing on this. Chin Peng might have thought that I knew too much about his contacts and plans. If so, he had the wrong man. Bob Chrystal and Freddy Spencer Chapman most certainly did, but they were thousands of miles away. Claude Fenner and John Davis most certainly did, and they were marked men, too. But if it were true, I wondered why it was proposed to move me to somewhere equally as dangerous as Sungei Siput.

Towards the end of our leave, Sir John and I were invited to lunch by Alan Lennox-Boyd, the 'shadow' colonial secretary, at his beautiful house in Mayfair. His wife was a Guinness, and they lived accordingly. Pre-lunch drinks were champagne cocktails, and the exquisite meal, the raw materials for which must have been brought over from their estates in Ireland as there was still food rationing, was served by the butler. Throughout the meal I was closely questioned by our host on many matters concerning the Emergency, and asked for my views on various ideas that he was formulating in the hope of being in government within months.

I pressed the point that, in my opinion, the local government must be given a freer hand to act decisively and robustly, and to be backed to the hilt by the home government. I raised my hobbyhorse about controlling the squatters and their ability to supply the CTs with food and information, the need for our own Min Yuen to supply us with first-class intelligence, and the necessity for much larger sums of money to be made available to reward informers. Asked how I would control the squatters I suggested that they should be gathered into protected areas to make it easier for the police and military to oversee them, and more difficult for the Communists to gain access. I also suggested that it might be possible to use captured CTs in some way to lure their colleagues away from the jungle, although I foresaw difficulties from the legal authorities over the matter of rewarding convicted criminals. Lennox-Boyd appeared to listen attentively and took notes continually.

I do not pretend for one moment unduly to have influenced future events, or to have been the only person thinking along these lines, because to those of us at the 'sharp end' they seemed so much common sense. But the fact is that everything that I had been advocating to those in authority since almost the very beginning of the Emergency, and which Sir John and I had again pressed for over lunch with Alan Lennox-Boyd, had been fully implemented by the time Sir Gerald Templer left Malaya. To be fair to Sir Henry Gurney, who has never been given the recognition he deserves, many of these ideas had been accepted and put in hand before he was murdered. Templer was also lucky in that he had been granted almost unlimited powers, enjoyed direct access to Winston Churchill, the prime minister, and in Oliver Lyttelton had a very strong colonial secretary.

Jean received a letter from Mrs Gibson, Sir John's personal secretary, dated the 22 June 1950. Having passed on both her's and Sir John's condolences, she went on to say that the *Sunday Dispatch* newspaper was chasing Sir John for a piece on the Emergency in Malaya and that he had written back to suggest that an article 'red hot from the field of operations' would be much more interesting for their readers. 'The editor's reply is enclosed, from which you will see that if Boris would agree to give an interview, the ghost writer could do the donkey work. In view of all that has happened around Sungei Siput and Boris's colourful, not to say picturesque, descriptive manner, Sir John thinks we could get some very useful publicity which might stir people at home to a better realisation of the true situation in Malaya.' She concluded, quite rightly, by saying, 'The *Sunday*

Dispatch, of course, is hardly the intelligentsia's cup of tea, but it has an enormous readership composed mainly of what our present masters call the 'working man', whose votes they are most anxious to retain. Sir John thinks it a good idea to build up public opinion about Malaya within that section of the population, and hopes very much that Boris will agree to co-operate.'

With some reluctance, I agreed to the interview. Mrs Gibson wrote again to the editor, Barclay Barr:

> Boris Hembry manages one of our large rubber estates in Malaya, which happens to be situated in about the most bandit-ridden area in the country. He has just returned on leave. His estate has been under constant attack, and we have been advised that he is one of the bandits' marked men. Fortunately he has so far escaped, although a number of his assistants, both Asian and European, have been either killed or wounded. He is a very vigorous personality, has played a prominent part in the work of the Volunteer Forces and has been awarded the Police Medal for leadership and bravery.
>
> Sir John thinks you would find an interview with him, or an article by him, of great interest for your columns, since he has been living and working in a most dangerous district ever since the disturbances began, and will have at his finger tips all the latest possible information. He is also the sort of personality which can vividly convey his impressions to others.

The *Sunday Dispatch* replied:

> The Editor thinks that, with Sir John's approval, the subject would be worth two or three articles rather than one. It is not often that such an authoritative personality as Mr Hembry is accessible to a newspaper.
>
> I will place a skillful ghost-writer at Mr Hembry's disposal.
>
> Yours sincerely,
> Victor Suhr, News Editor

Barclay Barr called on us at Hornchurch, and we talked for nearly three hours, he taking notes all the time. 'My' article appeared in the *Sunday Dispatch* some three weeks later, and made chilling reading. It was entitled 'The (Almost) Forgotten War', and started, 'War in Korea. Banditry in Malaya'. The substance was pretty much as I had described it to my 'ghost', with added information as to the numbers involved. For instance: at the end of 1950 the security forces – British, Gurkha, Malay Regiment, other Commonwealth, and armed constabulary – numbered more then 80,000. In addition, the RAF were flying on average more than 100 sorties a day, bombing and machine-gunning the Communist terrorists over an area of jungle stretching 500 by 200 miles, in addition to the many ops flown to drop supplies to the ground forces. I stated that in July 1950, for example, Lincoln bombers dropped 41 1000-pounders over an area of jungle within five miles of Kamuning, alone. The final paragraph read: 'We have a very real war in Malaya, which is and has been for two years bigger than Korea, and strategically, economically and commercially far more important to the free world than Korea.'

I was paid 30 guineas for 'my' article.

We had another week staying in London, and seeing shows in the evenings, entertaining or attending meetings at Guthrie's during the day.

Strictly speaking my leave was up just before Christmas, but Guthrie's agreed to extend it until after John returned to school in mid-January. Although Jean and I would have much preferred to return to Malaya by sea, I agreed to fly back, as Steve Thorburn, the general manager of Ulu Remis, was overdue his leave and was most anxious to get away. Sir John Hay was travelling out by sea and would be arriving in Singapore at about the same time as us.

After the usual sad partings, we stayed our last night at the Cumberland Hotel. The following morning we left Heathrow by KLM, putting down at Amsterdam, Rome, Cairo, Baghdad, Karachi, Calcutta and finally Bangkok, before being met at Singapore with a Guthrie car. We spent the night with the Taylors, and were collected by Steve Thorburn the next morning and driven over the causeway to Johore Bahru, and Ulu Remis.

Whilst I realised that the challenge and opportunity were there, and that I was extremely lucky to have now reached the pinnacle of my chosen profession, both Jean and I were homesick for Kamuning.

Palm Oil

January 1951 – September 1951

I had heard a lot about Steve Thorburn over the years and little to his credit. Both Jean and I disliked him from the start. During the drive back to the estate he appeared affable enough while he started to brief me about the senior management at Ulu Remis. It was obvious that his principle of management was divide and rule. He told me that he had set up a network of informers amongst some of the more senior Indian staff, so that there was nothing that occurred out in the divisions that he did not know about very quickly. The system seemed to work, but it certainly was not conducive to 'a happy ship', and was one that I had no intention of employing.

Ulu Remis was so large, with over 20,000 acres under cultivation, that each of the divisions was managed by a senior planter of management rank. But it was obvious that he considered them to be little more than mere senior assistants and treated them accordingly. This was, in my opinion, stupid, as there were many fine planters amongst the European staff, and I quickly found, when Steve had departed, that they performed far better, to everyone's benefit, if permitted to use their own initiative, to get on with the jobs that they were undoubtedly more than capable of doing.

Despite Thorburn's many failings – and I was to discover many extremely disquieting things of which I felt ashamed, if only by association – Ulu Remis Estate was a great monument to him, his pioneering spirit, drive and enterprise. In the middle 1920s the State of Johore had granted Guthrie's about 25,000 acres of virgin jungle for development. Steve, with only one or two Asian assistants, had simply stopped the train from Singapore at Layang Layang, made a clearing for a camp, and set to work surveying and planning his oil palm estate. He engaged local Chinese labour and, over the next

25 years, cut down the jungle, built the roads (by 1951, 250 miles of them), the bridges and culverts, the coolie lines, the processing factory, hospital, staff bungalows, schools, the 150 miles of private railway, and planted up 20,000 acres of crop – by anyone's standards, a monumental achievement.

I took over 30 European and senior Asian staff, a labour force of 3,000 and 60 lorries. The large factory was very ably managed by John Twitchen – 'Twitch' – and his assistant Charlton.

In addition to the planted area, there were over 5,000 acres of jungle reserve. The estate was surrounded on three sides by thousands of square miles of jungle, much impenetrable swamp – impenetrable, that is, until the Gurkhas and other regiments penetrated it in pursuit of the enemy.

After a couple of days Brownie Smith-Laing, Guthrie's senior VA, arrived to oversee the handover. It seemed that the agents lacked faith in Thorburn's ability to give the incoming manager a fair deal. It was just as well that Brownie was there for I had not been on the estate for more than a day or so when I went down with flu and took very little part in the proceedings. Of the week put aside for the handover, I spent four days in bed so, Brownie having compiled his detailed report on the state of everything, my actual take-over consisted entirely of counting the petty cash. We were thankful when Steve left and we had the bungalow to ourselves. Our new home was newly built, in the style of a normal two-storey house in England, not the traditional planters' bungalow on piers that I had been used to for the past 20 years.

Ulu Remis was in one of the most isolated and dangerous areas in the whole of Johore and, for that matter, in the whole of Malaya. Layang Layang railway station had been captured and burnt down by the CTs, several planters had been murdered on neighbouring rubber estates, and the Security Forces had suffered many casualties, both from ambush and during their own offensive operations in the jungle and swamps. All the staff bungalows were within high palisades of barbed wire, and had Malay special constables on constant guard, as were the factory, hospital and other estate facilities. In many respects the situation was worse than in Sungei Siput where at least some semblance of law and order had been restored. The drive to the estate, once one had turned off the main road, was through miles of secondary jungle, dark and depressing, every yard presenting good ambushing possibilities for bandits. We were always glad to reach the comparative safety of the estate.

An early visitor was Harry 'Piper' Gray, whom I had dropped in to Johore with Colin Park in 1945, who was in charge of research, and from him I gained much information about my European staff. He confirmed my original impression of Steve's policy of divide and rule. I decided very early on that my subordinates were all competent at their respective jobs, and so could be left, for the most part, to get on with them with minimum interference. However, I was soon made aware that there were several rackets going on, not something that I had ever directly experienced before. I made it very clear to every one of my European and senior Asian staff that I simply would not tolerate corruption of any kind, whatever Thorburn's attitude, which at first I considered merely ambivalent. I found very soon that it was not. Steve was in fact at the centre of most of the rackets.

A few people resented my efforts to stamp out these malpractices, and someone evidently wrote to Steve to advise him what I was up to in this respect, because he wrote to me telling me not to interfere with the existing practices. I did not forward this missive to the agents in KL, as perhaps I should have done, but decided to keep it on file, together with all the other evidence I had gathered, for possible future use. Knowing Steve's methods, he would certainly make it very awkward for both myself and those staff who had obviously supported me, when he returned six months later. In this respect, Twitch and Piper particularly were outstanding in their loyalty to me. Anyway, some of the rackets had been going on for so long that a few more months would not make all that much difference, and I could clean out the Augean stables when I took over permanently. Also, Ulu Remis was extremely profitable, so that the improprieties were not having too great an effect. It merely shocked me that Europeans should be involved in such practices.

Ulu Remis was divided into four divisions, each with a manager, all a good deal older than me, and an experienced assistant. The manager of Hay division was 'Fergie' Ferguson, whose clothes I had helped shoot to shreds 20 years previously. The others were strangers to me, so that the farewell drinks party we gave for Steve, held at midday because of the strict dawn-to-dusk curfew, was the first chance that I had to meet everyone.

I was not overwhelmed by the new job. The problems were pretty much those with which I had to contend on Kamuning, but on a larger scale. The solutions were usually the same. The property was obviously in first-class condition, and the staff very competent. Even my efficient Indian personal clerk knew shorthand and took dictation. We soon settled down. The early days were spent in going around the estate with the divisional managers. Although my natural inclination was to spend as much time as possible out in the field, very soon office work took up most of my working hours and consequently, by the end of my eight months stint at Ulu Remis I still did not know my way around the estate with any degree of certainty.

Communist banditry was bad, and getting worse. Ulu Remis, like Kamuning, being the largest property in the area, automatically became the main target for the CTs. A company of Gurkhas was positioned on the estate, and they gave us much confidence. They patrolled constantly, but as soon as their backs were turned the terrorists returned. Shortly before our arrival they attacked Layang Layang, and killed many of the villagers and guards, although the Specials put up a good fight before succumbing.

Shortly after my arrival the telephone rang and I was advised that one of our lorries had been waylaid. At that time of the morning it could only have been carrying Chinese labour out to work on palm fruit gathering. Not knowing my way around I asked Piper to go with me as guide. As an old ISLD 'jungle wallah' he had my complete confidence. He led me to the scene of the incident, both of us well aware that it might only have been a set-up to ambush us, so we approached the scene with extreme caution. 'Incident' is such a harmless and commonplace word to describe what we found. The lorry burned out, the charred remains of at least four Chinese women, and the others standing around in deep shock, sobbing at the horror of the fate suffered by their friends and companions. This was the face of communism that we knew in Malaya. The military follow-up to this incident found nothing, which led us to believe that the CTs were most probably members of our own work force.

The Emergency was now into its third year, and the acts of terrorism continued unabated. But things were changing; new government strategy was beginning to bear fruit. At the beginning the army acted very definitely as the 'aid to the civil power', and came under the jurisdiction of the Commissioner of Police. When General Briggs was appointed director of operations in 1950 he was able to co-ordinate the activities of all the security forces in the country, a process which was to be further improved by Sir Gerald Templer and which lasted throughout the rest of the war.

At the top, in KL, was the Federal War Council, with similar councils at state and district level. All these councils consisted of the civil, military and police commanders of the appropriate rank, with the addition of representative 'unofficials', such as planters and miners, in mirror image. I served on the Sungei Siput War Council, with the local police OCPD, the company commander of the troops stationed on the estate, the District Officer, and usually the Chinese Protectorate officer, too. Then I was also on the Perak State War Council, together with the British Adviser, the brigadier commanding the army, based in Ipoh, and his brigade intelligence officer, the Chief of Police for Perak State, the Legal Adviser, and one or two other 'unofficials'. Early in 1951 I was appointed to the Federal War Council, which was chaired by the High Commissioner, and consisted of General Briggs as director of operations, Nicol Gray, the Chief of Police, senior members of the MCS (Malayan Civil Service), two unofficials, such as myself, and representatives of the Malay, Chinese and Indian communities. Of the latter I thought there were too many, as all expected to get in their twopennyworth during discussions, and I thought the fewer people privy to the most secret plans for combating the terrorists the better. I considered the wartime principle of 'need to know' a good one. The exception, of course, was to be my old hockey-playing friend from prewar Kedah days, Tunku Abdul Rahman, a man of exceptional wisdom and integrity.

My appointment to the Federal War Council was reported in *The*

Straits Times as 'Ex-Force 136 Colonel on War Council'. In those days anything to do with clandestine operations was always lumped under the general heading of Force 136, which says much for the SOE publicity machine. The report went on:

> Kuala Lumpur, Tuesday.
>
> Former Force 136 Lieutenant Colonel and experienced guerrilla fighter, Mr Boris Hembry, has been appointed Member of the Federal War Council in succession to Mr G.D.Treble.
>
> Mr Hembry, who is at present the general manager of Ulu Remis Estate, Layang Layang, Johore, was formerly of Sungei Siput, Perak, where the murders of three planters in one day started the Emergency.
>
> Last year Mr Hembry was awarded the Colonial Police Medal for meritorious service. Mr Hembry is an honorary officer in the Auxiliary Police.
>
> In the House of Commons recently a Member asked the Secretary of State for the Colonies why the Incorporated Society of Planters had not been consulted on the appointment of Mr Hembry as planters' representative on the Federal War Council. The Minister replied that the High Commissioner who made such appointments did not wish to have nominees of organisations, but to use his own judgement. Mr Hembry came under this category.
>
> *The Straits Times* was told today that the ISP had not been officially consulted on Mr Hembry's appointment, but they were very pleased that he had been chosen as he is an energetic member of ISP, and an experienced planter.

I cannot understand why my appointment should have been discussed in the House of Commons at all, or who could possibly have raised the matter with an MP. But I suppose that it is not every day that the name of a total nonentity is bandied about in Parliament. I did think it might have been Thorburn, tipped off by a friend on Ulu Remis, but decided that even he could not have been quite so influential, surely.

Our closest neighbour on the estate was Piper Gray and, as a birthday present, he gave Jean an adorable English bull terrier puppy, whom we called Pedro, the grandest dog we ever had. I almost wrote 'possessed', but we had the great privilege to have been possessed by him. I think everyone who has dogs loves them all dearly, but over a lifetime has one that is particularly special. Ours was undoubtedly Pedro. As a companion we bought an Alsatian bitch puppy, Greta, from Katie Ferguson, and the two dogs became inseparable companions. We took great care to avoid 'bullsatian' puppies, feeling that such a combination could be difficult to handle, if not lethal. These two friends were to be an essential part of our lives for the rest of our time in Malaya, and it almost broke our hearts to leave them behind when we returned to England in 1956.

Singapore was only 60 miles away and we tended to spend many of our weekends there, staying with friends. But there was a very strict curfew in Johore from 6 pm until 6 am, so it was necessary always to leave sufficient time to get back to the estate by dusk. Many a young planter had to spend the night in a police cell en route to his estate because the Sunday curry tiffin party had gone on too long.

In April I was approached by both Piper Gray and Charlton, the factory assistant manager, telling me that they wished to resign. This was a serious blow to both the company and myself. I was assured by both of them that their reasons had nothing to do with my appointment, which was a relief. In the case of Harry Gray it was very definitely the Emergency, and the consequent wish of his wife to live somewhere free from danger to her husband, her family, and herself. Charlton gave the same reason, but over drinks at his bungalow it emerged that it was really the frustration of his job.

Charlton was a qualified engineer whereas his immediate boss, Twitchen, was not. Twitch, as factory manager, earned a great deal more money, yet relied on Charlton's expertise to retain his post, for without a qualified engineer in the factory the company would be breaking the law. Based on what Charlton told me it also appeared that Twitch had treated him somewhat shabbily over the years, a situation not helped by Thorburn's management principles. Apart from having his bungalow furnished with cast-offs, Charlton's salary had not kept pace with those of similar seniority on the planting side.

Twitch was a man of enormous energy and outstanding ability, but he also had weaknesses – haven't we all? – so there was an obvious need to exercise stricter control over him. As Sir John later very aptly put it, 'The realisation of his dependence on his better-qualified juniors should surely induce a more modest bearing and greater consideration for those upon whom he must rely if he is to continue to occupy his present position.'

As the two men held key positions in the Ulu Remis company, the directors in London were particularly concerned about the resignations, and Sir John Hay took the almost unprecedented step of writing a confidential letter directly to me, the gist of which was whether the reasons given were the truth, or whether there were others undisclosed. Sir John went on:

> The fact that the country is unsettled and labour difficult makes it more incumbent upon us than ever to keep a staff which is experienced, has acquired a knowledge of the country and labour, and has proved its practical competence. Replacement of these men with special qualifications is at present extremely difficult.
>
> I would be glad if you would write to me quite frankly regarding these two resignations and any other matter which has a bearing on the staff situation.
>
> I give you my assurance that whatever you write will be treated as entirely confidential.

Taking him at his word, in addition to the matter of the resignations, I wrote back raising the subject of salaries, retirement and career prospects. I think our exchange of letters makes interesting reading today. I wrote:

> There is widespread feeling, particularly amongst the more senior planters, that despite the higher incomes drawn in Malaya compared to those at Home, the continual fight

to make ends meet, the feeling of insecurity and the constant danger of being killed or maimed, the separation from one's family, and the total inability to save other than through the provident fund, is not worth the candle, and many feel it is better to get out while one is between forty and forty-five and find alternative employment elsewhere than wait until they are over fifty, with so much less chance of getting a job and when one's savings may be of less value than they are today.

On re-reading this, after a period of 30 years, I do not remember any struggle to live on my salary, allowances and commission, at least after the initial years. Also, we all chose to live and work in Malaya and, in spite of the dangers, I for one would not have chosen to be anywhere else.

Sir John, whilst acknowledging the obvious disadvantages of the current situation, pointed out, with complete justification, that our incomes compared most favourably to those in the United Kingdom.

Out of a population of fifty million people, in the years 1948/49 only 86 people enjoyed an annual income of over £8,000 net. If you tot up what a planter receives in the way of housing, allowances, substantive salary and commission, I think you will conclude that, on the whole, the planter does uncommonly well.

Even though he was one of the 86 mentioned I would not quarrel with his sentiments. Whilst there were, of course, many planters in Malaya of outstanding ability and devotion to their chosen calling, there were, as in any profession, just as many useless ones, drawing large salaries, whom I would not have had on my estate as a junior conductor. Nevertheless, I do acknowledge that there was not much advantage to be had in drawing a commission of, say, £4,000 one day, and lying on a mortuary slab the next

I had not been on the estate many weeks before I realised that the resident Special constables, who were stationed on all the bungalows and at the factory and offices, required better supervision and training, if possible by an experienced senior NCO. Compared to HOBA they were shambolic. With Guthrie's permission I recruited just such a man, whose name I regret I cannot now remember, and provided him with an armoured vehicle. He was billeted with one of the assistants on Home division.

The new security officer had not been there long before he was in action. Although there was a nightly curfew, and to ignore it was foolhardy in the extreme, it was somewhat relaxed on the Home division, as the bungalows were fairly close to each other, and after-dark visiting, by prior arrangement, was the rule rather than the exception. A minute before the scheduled time of arrival the Specials would open the perimeter gates, so that the short journey between the respective bungalows could be made at speed.

One night we had Piper Gray to dinner. Shortly after nine o'clock a Special sent word in by the boy that he wished to see me, so I went downstairs to see what it was all about. The Special said that he thought he had seen a cigarette glowing just outside the perimeter fence. I told him to fire at the spot where he had seen it. He fired one round. This was immediately answered by fusillades, including tracer, from several other places. Harry and I dashed around organising the defences and taking potshots at the muzzle flashes outside the fence. All the time our dogs were barking furiously, which added to the confusion. After about 15 minutes, during which time the CTs succeeded in penetrating the perimeter only to be driven back by a very gallant Malay NCO, the shooting stopped and we reviewed the situation. Several of our guards had been wounded, one seriously. Jean's ambulance training came in handy and she carried out first aid on the casualties, warning that the one Special was losing a lot of blood and would have to get to hospital quickly.

The telephone rang – the CTs had forgotten to cut the line – and it was the Security Officer to say that he would be driving over, at speed and with headlights blazing, with welcome reinforcements, and would we open the gates at the very last moment. He had also contacted the military who were on their way.

It was an exciting and anxious quarter of an hour. Fortunately the bungalow was built of brick so afforded good protection, and we were lucky to escape with so few casualties.

Our Malay guards were first class and came through their baptism of fire with flying colours. I was very proud of them, and saw they were rewarded.

I do not know what made the bandits respond in the way they did, to the one rifle shot, but I soon found out the reason for their presence. A week or so later Jean questioned the cook as to why he should need over 40 pounds of flour in a week for the small quantity of bread required by two people. He was unable to offer an explanation, even when I accused him of supplying the CTs. Shortly after that he was arrested for illicit distilling of samsu (rice wine) – in our own kitchen! He pleaded that this was permitted by Tuan Thorburn. When in court he said that he had asked Thorburn whether the new tuan would let him carry on with the distilling and Steve had, so he said, replied that the new manager was a good tuan and would not object. If this were true, and I believe it was, then it shows Thorburn up in even a worse light than even I had come to perceive. Quite apart from a senior manager and respected figure being involved in an illegal racket, he had allowed his own cook to supply succour and sustenance to communist terrorists, bent on destroying the very industry and way of life that provided him with his living. I was quite happy to see my cook go to gaol and was absolutely furious when Twitchen, for reasons that I found frankly incomprehensible, agreed to provide bail. Needless to say, the cook disappeared. I considered reporting the matter to the police but decided not to as, of course, with the cook missing, it would have been impossible to prove a case.

I discovered another racket, and as with most such lucrative rackets it was simplicity itself. The local bus service was fuelled at the estate petrol pump near my office. A bus would draw, say, 30 gallons but only pay for 25, and the difference would be put down to our estate lorries. Thorburn would then take a cut of the bus contractor's savings. I had the pumps removed to the factory compound and placed under Twitchen's direct responsibility. Thorburn was furious when he found out what I had done, although I cannot believe that he missed the extra income.

John flew out for his school summer holidays. There was much to see and do. He spent many hours driving our railway engines while shunting the trucks around the factory compound. I would not allow him to go off around the estate. We swam in the estate swimming pool on most afternoons, joined by Pedro and Greta floating on their tyre inner tubes, and went down to Singapore on several weekends to stay with friends, and for John to play cricket. I foolishly agreed to pay him a dollar a run and a dollar a wicket. He kept wicket. In the first match, Schoolboy Visitors against Schoolboy Singaporites, played on the Padang, he took five dismissals – standing up to the fast bowlers most impressively – and scored 45 not out. I did not make the same mistake the next game, when he was chosen to play for the Civilians against the Services, again on the Padang. He went on to play regularly for MCC, and the St Lawrence Club, whose home ground was the County Ground at Canterbury, where Jean and I were to spend many happy days in later years watching Kent.

In March we had an official visit from Richard Peters, the newly arrived American Consul in Singapore. He stayed for two nights, and I showed him around the estate, heavily escorted by Gurkhas, to acquaint him with life under siege on a Malayan estate. In his letter of thanks to Guthrie's he said, 'the visit to Ulu Remis has evoked tremendous admiration for the calm, courageous and cheerful spirit in which the men and their ladies are carrying on under the trying conditions that prevail. Please be assured that I shall not fail to convey these feelings to my Government.' He wrote to me personally saying, 'I can't resist saying that you and Jean have restored my faith in the British. It had begun to wane in what we found to be a rather supercilious atmosphere prevailing in Singapore.'

The close proximity of Ulu Remis to Singapore meant that we were ideally situated for official visitors to spend the day with us, to get some idea of the situation 'upcountry'. Hardly a week went by when I was not required to entertain and educate someone 'fact finding', such as Sir Robert Wilkinson, chairman of the London Stock Exchange. On that occasion, I was due to meet him somewhere on the main north-south road but, while I waited on the road side for several hours with an armoured escort, he somehow had made his own way quietly and unescorted through bandit-ridden country to arrive in front of a very surprised and worried Jean. After this I wrote to Peter Taylor to stipulate that, henceforth, visiting VIPs would have to be responsible for getting themselves to the estate. In return I was reprimanded by Peter for 'allowing' Sir Robert to take such a risk – as if it were my fault – and he pointed out that it was in the interests of both Guthrie's and the Malayan planting industry that as many VIPs as possible visited estates, to see for themselves the conditions under which we worked. I pointed out that I was general manager of an oil palm plantation, and that what I saw as unnecessary tours of inspection around CT-dominated countryside put not only the visitor's life at risk but, more importantly to me, my own, and that I was not a public relations officer. He replied that, on the contrary, I was expected to be just that, and was paid the necessary allowances. I felt it fruitless to argue further, so agreed with a certain amount of ill grace to continue to play the diplomat.

Sometime in July Guthrie's asked whether I would take over Bukit Asahan Estate, a rubber estate of some 8,000 acres, 20 miles east of Malacca, well run but extremely isolated, at the end of a long and lonely road, overlooked by Mount Ophir, where Malacca, Johore and Negri Sembilan states meet. I had assumed that I would return to Kamuning after acting for Thorburn, for one last spell before taking over Ulu Remis permanently when he retired. But as it had now been decided that he would only be returning for a year, they considered that it would be too unsettling for all concerned if I were to go back to Sungei Siput for such a short period. I accepted this with great misgivings, but realised that a period away from the 'front line' would probably do me good.

I was unaware of it at the time, but I was getting tired and, after four years of a reasonably active war, and now three years of the Emergency, beginning to live on my nerves. Also, unknown to me I was building up to a far more serious illness that was to curtail my career, just when I was about to reach the top of my chosen profession, and at a much earlier age than most who achieved such a well-paid and prestigious position. These problems are insidious and are seldom recognised in time.

In addition to the perennial social round, I was in close, sometimes daily, contact with Sir Henry Gurney, the high commissioner, General Briggs, the director of operations, and Nicol Gray, the commissioner of police, so was very much at the centre of all things concerning the prosecution of the war against the Communists. With my senior managership in Guthrie's, and as confidant and sounding-board of Sir John Hay, the chairman, I had reached the very peak of my career in Malaya.

We were sad to see John off at Singapore airport after his holidays, to return to King's. Shortly after his departure Dick Reid, by now a Guthrie's visiting agent, asked whether we could put him up for the night and show him around the estate as he wished to learn something about oil palms. We were only too pleased to welcome him, and he arrived with John Craig, the secretary in the KL office who dealt with Ulu Remis. We were sitting in my office when the security officer looked in to say that some bandits had surrendered and were at the Kim Foh lines. He was off to collect them, to hold them until the police arrived.

The SO had only been gone a few minutes when I asked the others whether they would like to see some CTs at close quarters. They positively leapt at the chance so I grabbed my carbine and set off to the Kim Foh lines where a somewhat distraught Special told me that the information was incorrect; there had been no surrender, but the SO's armoured vehicle had met with an accident and he and two Specials had been taken to the estate hospital with severe injuries. In addition, Geoff Hackney, one of my junior assistants, had run into a bunch of armed CTs and had been shot. All in all not quite what I had expected to be showing the box wallahs from KL.

I told the Special to remain where he was and wait for the arrival of the military, whilst I would go forward to see what was happening. We proceeded with caution until we reached the armoured jeep lying on its side, in a ditch. It was obvious that, in his haste to get to the 'surrendered' terrorists, the SO had taken the bend too quickly. A Special was standing guard, armed with his Bren gun, bravely holding his ground in the face of several armed bandits. He told us where the enemy was; 100 yards or so ahead, spread out over the summit of a small hill. Somewhere between us and the CTs was a wounded

Geoff Hackney.

I took over the Bren gun, gave the carbine to John Craig as Dick Reid carried the revolver he was issued with when visiting estates, and the three of us set off on foot towards the hill, hoping against hope that we would get to Geoff Hackney before the CTs. We had not gone more than a few paces when we were met by a burst of automatic fire. We took cover, Reid to my left and Craig behind. I found it difficult to fire the Bren from the hip, and the few shots I got off were very inaccurate; I had not used a Bren gun since 1942. I thought at the time that Dick Reid and John Craig were being very brave to follow me without question; they were certainly experiencing what was a fairly common occurrence for many of the planters they controlled. There was a constant buzz around my ears and I shouted to Craig to raise his sights and to be more careful where he aimed. We saw at least eight CTs on the hill, and knew that there would most probably be more. We were completely outnumbered and the situation was becoming somewhat tense, when I spotted Geoff staggering towards us, covered in blood, and obviously in a pretty sorry state, dodging from tree to tree for cover. I handed the Bren gun to Reid, told him to give covering fire, in short bursts, and went forward to meet Geoff. He had blood pouring from his stomach and was trying to staunch the flow with his left hand, whilst holding his revolver with his right. I grabbed him under his shoulders, and dragged him back to the others where I gave the order to withdraw, praying that the CTs would not follow us. To my relief I found that the Special we had left by the jeep had somehow managed to extract it from the ditch and was reversing it towards us. We all tumbled in and I told the Special to drive straight to the estate hospital, pausing for only a moment to tell the subaltern doubling along the road with a platoon of Gurkhas the enemy's position. After handing Geoff over to the hospital dresser we went home to a late breakfast, forgetting in all the excitement that Jean must have been worried stiff. She would have heard the shooting, have realised that we were well over an hour overdue, and have feared the worst. That such a worrying experience was commonplace to most planters' wives throughout the Emergency could not have made it any easier. I remembered in time to stop under the porch and to shout up that, not to worry, the blood that covered me was not mine.

Having showered and changed, and got outside a stiff brandy, I said to John Craig, 'John, you certainly put the wind up me, firing so close to my head like that.' He replied, 'Sorry, I didn't fire a shot. I couldn't find the safety catch!' It was only then that I realised that it had been enemy bullets buzzing like bees so close to my ears.

After breakfast I returned to the hospital to find that Geoff had been transferred to Johore Bahru hospital under army escort. It was a horrible wound, as the bastards had been using dumdums which had blown a large hole in his stomach.

I am glad to say that Geoff made a good recovery, to spend many more years on Ulu Remis, and to attain the acting general managership of the estate. I was particularly pleased that the brave Special Constable who stood by his post, in the full knowledge that he was exposed and heavily outnumbered, received a most deserved Commendation from the Chief of Police, and a bonus from the estate, for his gallantry.

We escorted Craig and Reid down to Rengam, said our goodbyes, and called in to see some friends on their rubber estate, on the main road. We refused lunch, having had a late breakfast, but after the second drink I began to feel very queer, feeling colder and colder. I was not in any pain, but I soon passed out, and came to on a bed some minutes later. I remember to this day the exquisite feeling of the cold, clean sheets and closing my eyes, remaining still until my strength returned. The next thing I recall was Twitch, in response to a telephone call from Jean, and the estate dresser bending over me, the latter giving me an injection which kept me asleep until the next morning. This was a particularly brave effort by Twitch and the dresser, for their journey was over eight miles or so of dangerous roads, with at least one gang of bandits known to be active in the area, and the return journey at night along the same way. I am sorry that the name of the dresser escapes me, as I am equally in his debt. As I have said before, I had more confidence in estate dressers than in many doctors I have known.

Twitch came over the next morning and drove us back to Ulu

Remis, where I was immediately put to bed again and where I stayed for two days before feeling strong enough to get up and resume my normal life. My 'turn' was put down to delayed reaction to the excitement of the morning, but in view of what happened shortly afterwards, and the fact that I had experienced many other close shaves and been under far heavier enemy fire before without similar results, it made me doubt the diagnosis on reflection.

Soon after this John Twitchen and I were visiting Hay division when an excited Malay lorry driver drove up to the Fergusons' bungalow, where we were having tiffin, with the news that he had spotted a gang of heavily-armed CTs at the edge of the jungle reserve that divided Hay and Home divisions, and he said he suspected that they were laying an ambush for Twitch and myself.

We telephoned the military and explained exactly where the bandits had last been seen, and agreed to delay our departure for home long enough for the Gurkhas to investigate. An hour or so later we left to return, passing a full company of the men from Nepal on their sweep through the oil palms and jungle. But the enemy had fled, presumably because their main targets had not materialised. We learned later that there were over 20 CTs in the gang, and that they did indeed intend to murder Twitch and myself and, having done that, to have attacked the factory. The Malay lorry driver undoubtedly saved our lives, and he was suitably rewarded.

My time at Ulu Remis was getting short. Steve Thorburn's return, at the end of September, was typical of the man. He was expected for tiffin. He arrived, considerably the worse for drink, at dusk, beating the curfew by minutes. He had spent the afternoon with the Fergusons and openly boasted to me that there was no need for a formal handover as he had learned all he needed to know, including my moving the petrol pumps. I was furious and made my feelings very plain. I told him it was outrageous that he should not have left the handing over to me rather to my subordinate, and that Guthrie's would certainly hear about it. The subsequent two or three days were tricky and Steve was seldom sober after seven in the evening. Never once did we venture out into the fields as he seemed more intent in questioning the staff, both European and Asian, to discover which of his many rackets I had put a stop to. I was not sorry to leave Ulu Remis, but optimistic about my long term future there, and already planning the changes that I would be making.

Disaster

September 1951 – September 1952

We drove in convoy, my car followed by two estate lorries loaded with our luggage to Malacca, and down the lonely road to our new home. Because of its isolation, Bukit Asahan, I was to learn very quickly, unlike most estates in this predominantly Malay-populated state, had become the focus of attention for bandits based in the jungles around Mount Ophir. Curfew was from 6 pm until 6 am, which meant there could be very little socialising even with the few neighbours there were, and trips to Malacca were confined very much to daytime sorties to the cold storage. Malacca was a small, attractive, seaside town, with 1,000 years of history. In the 16th century it was colonised by the Portuguese, and then by the Dutch before the British. Many of the old buildings remained, and it was interesting to see their various architectural styles. And being mainly Malay it had an easy-going charm that was absent from most other Malayan towns where the Chinese dominated.

We had a company of Green Howards on the estate, and their presence added much to our sense of security. However, we did not see as much of the officers as we had hoped as the curfew applied equally to off-duty soldiers as it did for the rest of us, and anyway they were continuously out on patrol around Mount Ophir, where they had several good kills. We often had a grandstand view of the RAF bombing the mountain, although whether they did so in response to known targets or merely to shake up the enemy, I never discovered. I had meant to ask the senior RAF officer who sometimes attended the Federal War Council meetings, but always forgot. The Royal Artillery also regularly brought 25-pounder field guns on to the estate and fired onto the mountain slopes. They certainly made a lot of noise, but whether they inflicted any casualties again I never knew. I suspect that it was used to keep the gunners' hand in at their gunnery rather than anything else.

When I took over Bukit Asahan I also inherited the overseeing of two Chinese-managed estates which, although adding to my income, involved a great deal of personal danger, because of the inaccessibility and loneliness of the properties. I made a point of varying my monthly visits and never forewarning anyone that I would be coming. Also, I always travelled alone, without an escort. I did not want the worry of the possibility of Specials being wounded and maybe having to be abandoned to savage mutilation by the terrorists. The Green Howards did patrol the area, but, quite rightly, were not prepared to co-ordinate their sweeps with my visits. In the event all my visits went off without incident, although it was certainly nerve-racking and only added to the strain that I was under.

We were deeply shocked to hear the news, on 6 October , that Sir Henry Gurney had been murdered whilst on his way to Fraser's Hill. He was travelling, together with Lady Gurney and his private secretary, with a police escort, and was ambushed on the main Kuala Kubu to Pahang road by a heavily armed gang of CTs, estimated to have numbered at least 40. The first burst of fire killed His Excellency outright, and severely wounded the driver, bringing the car to a halt. Lady Gurney was unhurt, but the escort suffered several casualties in an action that lasted the best part of 20 minutes, before the bandits withdrew.

The High Commissioner's death caused tremendous gloom throughout Malaya. All of us who knew Sir Henry personally felt a great loss. His was not a dynamic personality, but his experience in Palestine brought some much-needed realism about the problems we faced against an armed insurrection. I was summoned to KL for a hastily convened meeting of the Federal War Council. It was chaired by M. J. Hogan, the acting officer administrating the Government, in the absence of Vincent Del Tufoe, the deputy high commissioner, who was on leave.

The first question to be answered was how did the CTs know that the High Commissioner would be travelling on that road and at that time, as it was generally accepted they were lying in wait. Who at Government House was privy to the travel arrangements? I see from the minutes which I retain that we agreed it was most probable that a member of staff at King's House was a member of Min Yuen. I queried how it was that the High Commissioner had been travelling along one of the most dangerous roads in Malaya, with good ambush positions virtually its entire length, without a large military escort, and sections of the army pre-positioned at reasonable intervals along the whole route as had happened during Anthony Eden's visit to Sungei Siput three years previously. I admired Sir Henry's insistence in travelling everywhere openly as the Queen's official representative, in his Rolls Royce, with the minimum of fuss, but the bandits' success gave a tremendous impetus to' their cause, and caused many an ordinary citizen to question the sense of his loyalty to a Government that was unable to protect even its head.

But his untimely death did lead to the appointment of Sir Gerald Templer as the next high commissioner, who was given almost total powers by the new conservative Government in London, to prosecute the war against terrorism in the manner that he and his advisers on the spot thought necessary. It is said that Winston Churchill, whilst on a visit to Canada, ran his finger down the Army List until he reached Templer's name. He was in England and was sent for. After a chat about everything under the sun except Malaya the PM growled, 'Malaya. Total powers. Heady stuff. Use it sparingly.' Sir Gerald returned to England, and in a matter of days arrived in Kuala Lumpur, with more powers than had been bestowed on any soldier since Cromwell. He was lucky, too, to have the backing of a strong government in Britain, and in Oliver Lyttelton (later Lord Chandos) a colonial secretary who was determined to smash the Communists at almost all costs. For the terrorists it was a lethal combination.

In the interim the Government of Malaya was administered by Del Tufoe, who chaired the Federal War Council meetings. One of these was attended by Oliver Lyttelton. I thought him a tremendous man, large in every respect – physically, mentally, breadth of vision, grasp of detail, and sense of humour. I sat next to him and was able to brief him on recent happenings out on the estates before the meeting got under way. At one stage he suggested that we recruit Sakai as agents and spies. I got increasingly irritated as the argument against the idea went on and on, mainly on the grounds of expense and that it would be impossible to recruit and train several thousands. I could hold back no longer and said, 'Mr Chairman, I am quite sure that the Secretary of State had in mind to recruit and train no more than a dozen or so.' Lyttelton turned to me and said, 'Thank you, Hembry.'

That night the Del Tufoes held a dinner at King's House to which Jean and I were invited. Afterwards, when most of the guests were leaving, Lyttelton asked me to stay behind for a talk. In addition to Del Tufoe and the Colonial Secretary, there were General Briggs, Nicol Gray – with whom Jean and I were staying – and only one or two other senior police and army officers. We discussed the whole sorry situation until well after midnight. Someone raised the matter of Gurney's successor, but Lyttelton did not enlighten us, except to say that the rumour in England was that Field Marshal Montgomery was being considered. I had the temerity, as the only 'unofficial' present, to say that I considered him to be unsuitable, as the Emergency here in Malaya, in my opinion, was not Monty's kind of war, and that Bill Slim was the man. Lyttelton, with only the mildest sarcasm, said that he would pass on my recommendation, although Slim had just been made Chief of the Imperial General Staff, so it might be difficult.

Eventually Lyttelton said that he had been working for over 16 hours that day and that his trade union would object. I made him laugh when I said, not to worry, I felt sure that he could get special dispensation from our trade union friend Mr Brazier.

I was to meet Oliver Lyttelton again when on leave in England in 1952. He had asked me to call in to see him at the Colonial Office for a private discussion, before inviting me to the House of Commons for Prime Minister's Question Time. Actually to see and hear the Old Man speaking in the House of Commons was one of my life's great privileges.

Sir John Hay wrote to me on 17 October 1951 'in strictest confidence' saying that he had been asked by 'a senior member of the Government' for his views on certain matters in connection with the Emergency. Whilst I have unaccountably lost Sir John's letter, I have my reply before me as I write. I started by saying that the Federal

War Council meetings I had attended gave me no optimism for an early cessation of hostilities. I stressed that it was not an 'Emergency', but all-out war. I said that in a private conversation I had had with General Briggs he said that he had found the Socialist Government at home uncooperative at times, and appeared unable or unwilling to grasp the enormity of the Malayan problem, and that he 'did not know the answer'. He had also agreed with my criticism that plans made in KL were often inefficiently carried out on the ground, by second-rate officials. I went on to say that I had overheard Sir Henry Gurney tell the Malayan Chinese community leader, Dato Tan Cheng Loc, that only the Chinese could save the country, and that special efforts should be made to convince them that it was in their best interest to support the Government, for they would be the major sufferers in the event of our losing the battle.

I said that danger to life and property was increasing rather than diminishing after more than three years of conflict. I pointed out that, to date, 60 planters had been killed since June 1948. (I did not contemplate at the time that this figure was to reach 100 by 1955. Thus, when this number is added to the number of planters who lost their lives in the war, the total killed in the years 1941 to 1955 exceeded 350, more than one planter in three.)

In answer to Sir John's specific questions, I replied:

1. The combatant Communists appeared to be better trained and, at the start of the Emergency, even better equipped than we were. Even now, after three years, still too few of our troops could operate in the jungle to the same effectiveness as the CTs. The latest intelligence was that they still numbered between four and five thousand, so they were experiencing but little difficulty in replacing casualties. According to captured documents Communists had infiltrated into executive positions in most trade unions (the familiar pattern, even in the United Kingdom) and other sensitive positions (Government House, for example). I suggested that our Mr Brazier had been only too successful.

2. I emphasised the lack of co-operation that still existed, to my certain knowledge and personal experience, between States,

and even Police Circles within States, frustrating plans that were now being put into effect to deprive the bandits of food and information to force them out into the open where they could be dealt with more easily (The Briggs Plan). Eventually this was so all-embracing that estate workers were not permitted to take food to work, and Europeans required a special permit to collect from the local cold storage.

3. Regarding estate costs, I pointed out that, as the labour forces were not allowed to take food to work, they could only work six hours per day instead of eight, but were still paid for the eight – which, according to Brazier's trades unionists, was only entirely fair, but meant that the Communists had effectively raised our tapping and other field costs by twenty-five per cent – this on top of the cost of all the security measures we were required to take. I gave my opinion that, not only was payment for eight hours work unethical, but would inevitably establish the principle of a six hour working day.

4. I suggested that planters' morale was pessimistic, rather than low. It did not appear to the man on the estate that any progress had been made towards victory over the Communists. Added to which, the feelings of frustration caused by the loss of efficiency on the estates, the curfew that confined us to our bungalows night after night, the need for eternal vigilance, and the almost daily news of fellow planters being murdered or wounded, was very morale sapping.

I ended my letter by saying that the major part of government policies now being put into effect had been suggested by myself and, for all I knew, other planters back in 1948, and I added, for good measure 'The appointment of a Governor of the calibre of General Slim would inspire more confidence.'

I was not to know then that just such a man would shortly be arriving in Malaya.

I recall that in 1949, in one of my several memoranda to the powers-that-be, I strongly advocated compulsory service for all able-bodied men, of all nationalities. This was finally made law in December 1951.

One night I awoke sometime after midnight with the most acute indigestion, and pains down my left arm. I sat on the bedside, in agony, chewing Rennie indigestion tablets until the pain eased. I had a repeat performance in my office towards the end of January 1952, but I dismissed it as indigestion, probably caused by an ulcer – 'All the worry of working for Guthrie's, you know'.

We spent that Christmas at the Wittington Bungalow at Frasers Hill, with Len and Vera Cooper from Guthrie's Singapore office, having followed exactly the same route up there as Sir Henry Gurney.

Just before we left to return to Asahan I received a message from Sir John Hay, who was visiting Malaya, asking me to call in at the KL office as he wished to see me urgently. I wondered, like a small boy called to his headmaster's study, what it was all about. Within minutes of our meeting he asked me to take over Ulu Remis as soon as possible, as Steve Thorburn was to go on 'accelerated retirement'. He said that he wanted me to get a few months home leave before taking over, and that arrangements were being made to relieve me on Bukit Asahan. Under no circumstances was Thorburn to know why I was going home again after barely 12 months; it would be put about that I was sick and required treatment at home.

Little did anyone realise, except perhaps Jean, how near the truth this was.

I booked Jean to travel home on the *Oranje* in late January and I would follow by air in February. In due course I drove her down to Singapore where I saw her off in the knowledge that this time the separation would only be a matter of weeks rather than months or years. Sir John was flying to Ceylon and would be joining the ship at Colombo. In the intervening weeks I handed over Bukit Asahan Estate to Ian Murray who had, somewhat reluctantly, agreed to postpone his retirement for one more tour, and attended two further meetings of the Federal War Council in KL. At the end of the second I handed in my resignation, having had the satisfaction of voting for the 'Call up under the Manpower Regulations Bill Regulation', which made the call-up of all able-bodied men law, something I had advocated years before. I also see from the minutes that I expressed myself rather forcibly on the following:

1. Self Government: Law and Order must be permanently restored before any move to granting self-government to Malaya.

2. Police Intelligence: This was still woefully inadequate, and no effort or expense must be spared to building this up. The best candidates for our own Min Yuen would be 'turned' CTs.

3. Special Constabulary: The Specials must be better equipped and led, to provide the general and normal security throughout the country, leaving the military free to operate deep in the jungles.

4. Operation Starvation – the Briggs Plan: This was still only half-hearted in far too many areas, and must be vigorously enforced everywhere.

5. Chinese: More efforts must be made to secure their full co-operation; to persuade them not to assist the bandits. This may require them to be made more frightened of retribution from the security forces than the CTs. [This latter suggestion caused some consternation, as several members of the Council thought that I was advocating we torture or shoot squatters, whereas I had in mind only severe restriction of their movements and generally making life inconvenient.] (See Appendix C)

I received a letter from the Secretary of the Federal War Council, on behalf of General Sir Gerald Templer, the new high commissioner, thanking me for my services, and wishing me a 'pleasant leave and speedy return to good health'. It seemed that news of my 'illness' had spread even to the highest quarters.

My final official duty before departure for England was to attend the formal opening of the new Guthrie headquarters building in Singapore, as one of only two planters invited by Peter Taylor to represent the estates side of the business. My final unofficial duty was to cable Henleys in England to confirm my order for a new Mark VII Jaguar which I intended to collect soon after my arrival for use during my leave, and bring back to Malaya. This Jaguar now looks very cumbersome, almost bus-like, but at the time I thought it the epitome of grace and comfort.

I flew home to an England still very much in mourning for King George VI, who had died on 6 February, and full of hope and enchantment for our new young queen. Jean met me at Heathrow, then still little more than a collection of huts on the old Bath Road, and we spent a few nights at the Royal Commonwealth Society, going to the theatre most evenings before dining out, usually at the Savoy.

Whether as part of the cover story or not, I cannot recall, but early in my leave I went to see Dr Gregg, the company doctor. I must have mentioned my prolonged attacks of indigestion for he examined me for quite a long time and closely cross-questioned Jean, who had accompanied me, about the exact location of my pains, and their duration. I still suspected nothing very untoward when he telephoned Dr Evan Bedford and made an appointment for me to see him, there and then. We walked around to Dr Bedford's Harley Street consulting rooms and, within a very short space of time, I was subjected to more rigorous examination, blood tests, X-rays, and close questioning as to my dietary and smoking habits. The two doctors then went into a huddle after which they said that I should return for a further examination in three months time. Even though by then I had realised that Evan Bedford was a heart specialist, one of the foremost in England, the penny still did not drop.

Shortly afterwards I received a hand-written letter from Sir John, imploring me, in the strongest terms, to give up smoking. Up till then it was nothing for me to smoke 100 cigarettes a day – or, at least, to light up that number; I usually threw them away only half smoked. My working days on the estate in Malaya, during the worst of the Emergency, lasted usually well over 18 hours, sometimes nearer 20, and I found smoking calmed the nerves, allowed me to think on my feet, and kept me going. I would light up the first one of the day with my early morning cuppa, and put the last one out at bedtime.

Early in June, a matter of only three weeks before we were due to fly back to Malaya, and following another merely, or so I thought, follow-up examination by Drs. Evan Bedford and Gregg, I made a routine visit to the Guthrie office in Gracechurch Street to discuss with the secretaries some changes to the senior staff on Ulu Remis that I wanted to make, when Sir John called me into his office, and dropped the bombshell. I had developed arterio-sclerosis, which caused angina, in a reasonably serious way, and the last thing it was felt I needed was to have the stress and strain of the top management post, in one of the most dangerous areas of Malaya. Whilst being most sympathetic to my protests, Sir John said that he was not prepared to go against the medical advice and give me Ulu Remis. Gibby, whose office led into Sir John's, gave me a much-needed and very stiff whisky from her desk drawer, whilst the enormity of the news I had just received sank in.

I paid another visit to Evan Bedford who explained exactly what the problem was. He said that there was nothing much that medical science could do about it, but with care and good sense, which included giving up smoking forthwith, there was no reason why I should not live for many years more. As this all happened over 30 years ago I have sometimes wondered whether the doctors did not in fact exaggerate my condition, and in doing so deprive me of what would have been the most remunerative years of my life. A pointless speculation, but one nevertheless which I found difficult to get out of my mind. Nowadays, I expect, I would have had a heart bypass operation and returned to work as fit as a fiddle within a few months.

Jean and I retired to the Savoy for several drinks and lunch to contemplate the devastating news that I had just received. We were staying the night at the Royal Commonwealth Society, and the following morning I returned to Guthrie's for a further talk with Sir John to discuss my future. He was kind and sympathetic to a degree, but obdurate. As luck would have it, he said, Pennefather, the manager of Kong Moh Seng (KMS) Estate, in Kedah, was about to retire, and I was offered his position. KMS was a medium-sized estate, in a quiet part of the country, with a new bungalow, a couple of miles from Sungei Patani town, and less than 40 miles from Penang. Of course I knew it well from my early days, 20 years before.

I made one last effort to regain Kamuning, but this was vetoed because, even though the security situation had greatly improved, it was very hilly and the medicos had stipulated no hill climbing. And anyway, Sir John said, it would not be fair on Charles Ross to alter his appointment yet again, and at such short notice.

We set out to enjoy what remained of our leave, determined to hide the acute disappointment. I also traded on Sir John's kindness and obtained permission to return to Malaya by sea, getting the office to book our passage by the P&O liner *Carthage*. Meanwhile, I attended the AGMs of both Oil Palms of Malaya (Ulu Remis) and Malacca Rubber Plantations (Bukit Asahan), and was able to answer several questions from shareholders. It was at the MRP luncheon afterwards that I sat next to Malcolm Muggeridge, who was evidently a shareholder.

I was also called to the Colonial Office to see Oliver Lyttelton. Having greeted me somewhat cursorily, he slammed down a copy of *The Times* on his desk, and almost shouted, 'What the hell's the meaning of this?' his finger pointing to the offending paragraph. It read something like 'WHITES BAR SULTAN FROM CLUB'. It went on to say that the Selangor St Andrews Society had omitted to invite the Sultan of Selangor to the Society's annual ball, and that the Malays were showing resentment. The Colonial Secretary appeared to blame me personally for this alleged incident.

I was somewhat taken aback, and all I could say was that I did not believe it as, so far as I knew, all the Sultans were ex-officio presidents or patrons of all the clubs, both European and others, in their respective states, and would have been the very first on the list to be sent an official, formal invitation to such an important function. I said I could not believe such a gaffe was possible. (Unfortunately, I was wrong. The committee of the Dog, the Selangor Club, had indeed taken leave of their senses. General Templer, the new high commissioner, forced the resignation of the entire committee on threat of closing down the club forthwith, under the emergency powers vested in him: he would have done so, too!)

The Secretary of State then asked whether I would like to attend another debate in the House of Commons, and when I said yes please I accompanied him in his official car. Unfortunately, this time all I witnessed was a rather boring debate, with Barbara Castle having plenty to say to only about six other rather somnolent members.

Our departure was scheduled for the day after John's return to King's. We caught the P&O boat train from Waterloo to Southampton and boarded in the late afternoon. The first people we met, at the top of the gangway, were Ronald and Doris Wilshaw, whom we had met occasionally at the Dog and the Selangor Golf Club, in KL, and with whom we were to establish a firm friendship during the voyage.

Having given the necessary instructions for unpacking to the cabin steward, we went back on deck to watch our departure. Ronald and I were leaning on the rail, talking, when the Needles came into view on the port side. 'Good show,' said Ronald, 'the bar will be open in 10 minutes,' as we would be outside the three-mile limit, and carried on talking. To our chagrin we saw the Needles again, this time slipping by on the starboard side, as the tannoy advised us that there was engine trouble and that we were putting back. Horrors. No bar. Fortunately, Ronald had a bottle of whisky in his cabin, to where we repaired with alacrity.

The engine trouble was soon rectified and we proceeded to have one of the most enjoyable of voyages. We were placed to dine at the Captain's table, together with the Wilshaws, and celebrated my 42nd birthday in great style, courtesy of P&O. We called in at Port Said, Suez, Aden, Bombay and Colombo, and eventually disembarked in Penang. I stood on the quayside watching my new Jaguar being unloaded, all the time thinking of what might have been, and wondering how I would feel on a quiet rubber estate, seemingly far from the dangers we had lived with for the past six years, and on far less money than I was expecting only a few weeks previously. Above all, we were longing to be reunited with our beloved dogs Pedro and Greta.

Home

September 1952 – December 1955

We stayed the first night ashore at the E&O, collected the car from the dockside the next morning and took the ferry across to Butterworth, arriving in time for a brandy ginger ale or two at Parry's Bar. Afterwards, Jean loaded up the back seat with stores from Singapore Cold Storage and we set off for Sungei Patani and KMS Estate.

The scenery between Butterworth and Sungei Patani did not appear to have altered much since I had taken the same road with Tuke, back in December 1931. The beauty of the padi fields, with Bukit Metajam in the foreground and Kedah Peak in the distance, was still enchanting. There was noticeably far less military traffic on the road than I had been used to over the previous four years, which I thought was a good omen. But we were aware that the inside of the car was becoming increasingly hot, and I was beginning to doubt my choice of car. Scanning the fascia I noticed that the heating was set full on, and even when I turned the knob to 'off' the heaters continued at full blast – the ambient temperature outside would have been in the mid-90s Farenheit, and the humidity at nearly 100 per cent. We drove as quickly as we could into Sungei Patani with all windows open, but the Chinese garage mechanic who lifted the bonnet took one look at the massive Jaguar engine and slammed it shut, saying that he would not know where to begin. We drove to the Sungei Patani Club and telephoned the Borneo Company garage in Penang to book the car in for the following week to have the heater disconnected. Unfortunately, in those days only American cars and Rolls Royces seemed to have air conditioning, and even then, by today's standards, it was primitive.

We arrived on KMS in time for tiffin. The house seemed just as uninviting as we remembered from our last visit, when Guthrie's had suggested that we might like to build a bungalow of similar design on Kamuning, and, having seen it, I had said not bloody likely. The irony was not lost on me. Even the garden seemed unattractive, but it did have a magnificent and uninterrupted view over padi fields towards Kedah Peak; the classic Malay scene, which was to give us much joy over the next three years.

The takeover was simplicity itself. Pennefather was a senior and respected manager and I was happy to take his word for the condition of the estate. All I did was to go through the books and check the rubber stocks, and that was that. The one assistant was Menon John, a most efficient and personable Asian, who had been the office clerk before the war, and had gained most deserved promotion.

Shortly before they left, the Pennefathers threw a farewell party, and the Malay labour force gave a ronggeng (dance), at which there was much dancing to gamelans (gongs), which I have always found most romantic, and another sound which I will take with me to the grave. We knew a number of the guests, some, like Walter and Betty Northcote-Green, and Jumbo Downes, for over 20 years. However, we did meet Bepi and Elena Reginato, a young Italian couple, for the first time. Bepi was the nephew of Baptista – 'Regi' – Reginato, the inventor of the sheeting battery, whom I had first met at a demonstration in Johore in 1934. Beppi and Elena were our nearest neighbours – we had to drive past their bungalow whenever we left the estate – and we soon were the best of friends and, like everyone else, became captivated by Elena's beauty and sparkling personality. Elena had arrived out in Malaya without a word of English, let alone Malay. She was to be fluent in both in a matter of months, although not totally with English sayings as she reported that Uncle Reggi, now long retired back to Italy, remained a man of many interests, with 'a finger in many tarts'.

Uppermost in our minds was the reunion with Pedro and Greta. We had left them with Matheson on Asahan when we went home on leave, and had arranged for them to be transferred to quarantine kennels in KL for their inoculations against rabies. Having read the Jaguar's owner's manual I discovered that the heater could be isolated merely be removing the appropriate fuse, so there was no need to make a special journey into Penang after all. So, the next weekend we drove the 300 or so miles down to KL, and stayed the night with Jack and Joyce Brown. As soon as we got to their bungalow I telephoned the vet to ask whether we could call in that night to see the dogs, before collecting them the first thing the following morning, and was rather disconcerted to be advised not to, as they were, in his words, in a sorry state, and that it would be better, for our own peace of mind, to wait until tomorrow and then take them away with us. Thank goodness we accepted his advice.

When we arrived at the kennels first thing the next morning Pedro spotted me and threw himself into my arms, crying with joy. Greta could hardly manage more than a tail wag in recognition. They were emaciated, filthy and stinking. Our hearts were nearly broken, and both Jean and I wept at the realisation that we had put our two trusting friends through so much neglect and indignity. They must have often wondered what they had done to us to deserve such treatment.

The stench in the car on the journey back to KMS was quite awful, and took several weeks to dissipate. As soon as we reached home Jean bathed them several times before giving them each a good meal. Mindful of the problems that the POWs had experienced when first released from the Japs, when they had been made sicker and several had even died, from over-eating good wholesome food after such a long interval, we fed them little and often. I swear that there was even a sparkle in Pedro's eye when we bedded them down for their very first night home. In only a few weeks they were back to their old selves, although it was most noticeable that Pedro was extremely loath to let me out of his sight for a moment, even following me and sitting outside the door when I went to the lavatory.

We immediately set about improving the bungalow. Starting with the chicks (bamboo slatted blinds), which were lowered to follow the sun around the house, we built a fine, airy and comfortable bungalow. The bathrooms and kitchen were completely refurbished, a new generator, which started automatically whenever power was required, was installed, and the staff quarters at the back rebuilt. At the same time, Jean was redesigning the garden so that it was to become one of the most beautiful that I have seen in all my time in Malaya. The lawn in front fell away down to the padi fields, which stretched as far as the eye could see towards Kedah Peak in the distance.

After the horticultural, labour and, above all, the terrorist problems I had experienced in the post-war years, KMS was a revelation. I was unused to an estate untouched by war, a settled and contented Indian and Malay labour force, less then 15 minutes from a well found little town with all the amenities, a good club and the usual government offices, not to mention the Gurkhas' training depot, and even a good vet, but frankly I was bored, professionally.

Soon after our arrival on KMS I was elected president of the Kedah State Cricket Association. I was also an honorary member of the Gurkha Depot officers' mess, and went to all their mess nights and cocktail parties, with or without Jean as appropriate. They certainly worked hard and played hard. It was interesting seeing how quickly the young men from Nepal could be turned into disciplined, trained fighting men, surely the best ever. They practised patrolling on the estate and we would see them every day. I gave the company commander permission to ambush me on the estate, at a given time and place one day, and promptly forgot all about it. At the appointed hour, to my initial horror, rounding a bend on the road I was subjected to a fusillade of small-arms fire, and several 'grenades' – thunder flashes – whilst I cursed myself for having left my Luger at home, and for being so careless in travelling along the same road at the same time each day. Then I remembered. The patrol returned to the bungalow where our cook made tea for all the riflemen and NCOs, and the officers sank a few well-earned cold beers in the bungalow.

Menon John had been on the estate for many years. He had been a clerk on Bukit Lembu Division when I had arrived on the neighbouring Sungei Gettah Estate in December 1931. He was now an entrepreneur, with interests in a pawnbroker's and a pharmacy in Sungei Patani. I saw no reason why he should not be able to have outside interests, so long as there was no conflict with his position as my assistant. But I did have a different attitude to Pennefather on several matters of policy, particularly to the standard of living quarters, from my own, to the Asian clerks and conductors, and the resident labour force. Old Penny was a planter of the old school; had been through the Depression years of the early 1930s, and was not inclined to spend more money than strictly absolutely necessary. Consequently, I took over a lot of inferior buildings. I laid down an annual replacement programme for all the old and decrepit buildings, and improved the water supplies, especially necessary on Bukit Lembu Division. I had always believed that a happy workforce had a better chance of being an efficient workforce, and, in those troubled times, a loyal workforce.

KMS had the inestimable advantage of having been managed by Bob Chrystal from 1924 until 1939, when he had been transferred to Kamuning, and all subsequent managers had benefited from his conservative tapping policies, which resulted in first-rate bark reserves and the consequent maintenance of relatively high yields. If I had a criticism it would have been that the older rubber had not been replanted to the extent that it should have been, and that the proportion of older plantings compared to the younger, higher-yielding budgrafts was out of balance. I set about redressing the balance.

Altogether KMS was a first-class estate, easily run, so that I was not extended; on reflection the reason that I was there. After a month or two adjusting to the new situation I stopped being bored and began to enjoy the lack of excitement and challenge. It was almost like a planter's life prewar. Not once did I arm myself or travel in an armoured vehicle. I handed my carbine over to the police for safekeeping, and retained only my Luger, which I hid amongst my socks in my dressing room. This part of Kedah had been declared a 'white area', that is to say free from terrorist activity, mainly because it was predominantly inhabited by Malays which gave little scope to the Chinese Communists to 'spread the word', and made it well nigh impossible for them to obtain succour. But we were well aware that other parts of Kedah, most notably inland, along the mountain range, were still as dangerous as ever.

Only on one occasion did I hear of bandits in the area. Apparently a small party of them had passed through the nearby Sungei Patani

Estate and had questioned some Malay tappers about me. I am sure that it was a gang that operated in Perak, and were either on their way up to Siam for a rest, or on their way back afterwards. But it showed that their intelligence, the Min Yuen, was as good as ever.

John flew out to visit us for his school summer holidays in 1953 by Comet, then the first jet airliner to enter regular airline service in the world, by several years. As so often happens with pioneers, the designers at De Havilland had not fully understood the dangers of metal fatigue, with the result that the planes disintegrated in midair. It so happens that both aircraft that John flew in crashed shortly afterwards, after which they were withdrawn from service. The Americans benefited from the lessons learnt when designing the Boeing 707, which then collared the market that should have been the Comet's.

John enjoyed what was to be his last school summer holidays, playing much cricket, including two matches in the Kedah state side, against Selangor and Perak, driving the Jaguar around the estate roads, cataloguing what was by now our extensive gramophone record collection, and playing with Pedro and Greta. He and Pedro seemed to establish a close affinity.

Soon after John's departure Sir John Hay arrived in Malaya. Guthrie's had arranged for him to take the SOCFIN bungalow at Port Dickson for a couple of weeks during his stay, and he let it be known that he would like Jean to act as his hostess. I was, of course, included in the invitation, in fact a royal command, but I pleaded pressure of work and went down to PD for the second week only. Gibby had retired, so Sir John's new private secretary, Esther McWilliam, was there to handle the business side of things.

Sir John was in great form, and when not visiting estates locally would spend many hours on the beach dictating letters and memoranda to all and sundry. For reasons I cannot recall, Jean was required to inspect the Gurkha guard on several occasions. On reflection, these were most probably retired soldiers who had stayed on in Malaya after being discharged at the end of their service, to act as night watchmen. Whilst not armed with firearms they would all have retained their kukris, so would have been formidable opponents should anyone have been foolish enough to try to get into the bungalow compound. I drove down to PD by way of KL and the Guthrie's office.

During my stay, Jean had to arrange two formal parties. The first, in the evening, was for General Perowne, I think the director of operations who had succeeded General Briggs, his ADC, and Charles Thornton, Guthrie's number one in KL. We had met the General on several occasions on his visits to the Gurkhas at Sungei Patani. The conversation, which mainly concerned the Emergency, where we had gone wrong in the past and how we were now getting things right, went on till the wee hours. The CTs were beginning to surrender in quite large numbers, as the Briggs Plan was working well and they were finding it increasingly difficult to get food and help, and the army had learnt by now to operate deep in the jungle in small patrols, so were getting many good kills.

The second was purely a Guthrie affair. Sir John had expressed a wish to entertain all the Guthrie planters and their wives who could get to PD and return home by curfew time, about 60 guests in total. This was a buffet lunch in the garden, under the trees, and was a great success.

On our way back to Kedah we met Sir John again at the Lake Club in KL when he presented Jean with a pair of Kelantan silver salad servers. It was during this dinner that he let slip that he had just disposed of most of his private investments in Singapore for $3,500,000, no mean sum in those days, so he was full of beans.

Whilst it was a relief to get back to KMS and our dogs and to be living in an area at relative peace, I would have to admit that I missed the excitement and personal satisfaction of being at the centre of things, on the Federal War Council, and general manager of the largest estate in the whole of Malaya. But Guthrie's always treated me as one of their most senior managers, invited me to attend many of their Group policy meetings in KL, and always asked my views on matters of estate security.

From time to time my heart caused problems, but I did not disclose this to Guthrie's. On one occasion I collapsed at the wheel of the Jaguar and only just managed to stop before passing out. This gave both Jean and me a nasty shock, and the problem was further exacerbated by my having forgotten my TNT pills. Thenceforward Jean assumed the responsibility of ensuring that they were always with me.

Early in 1954 we made up a party to spend a long weekend on the island of Langkawi, which I had last visited by submarine in 1944.

We drove up to Perlis from where it had been arranged we would take a government launch over to the island. Unfortunately it had been forgotten that the day we had intended travelling was a Muslim religious festival so that the Malay crew were not available. Rather than delay our crossing we travelled over on the ferry, little more than an outsized fishing boat, very smelly, with no amenities except the usual two planks over the stern. The other travellers, all Malays or Chinese, were not used to seeing Europeans using this ship and eyed us first with suspicion and then with amusement. Before long I was deep in conversation, explaining about my last visit, when one of the Malays listening suddenly jumped up and said that he had been one of the fishermen in the fishing fleet that we had come across, and how the headman had ordered, on pain of death, that no one was to mention having seen the tuans paddling by when they returned to port. The headman had died, but I asked the man to thank, on my behalf, any other survivor of that little episode for their loyalty.

The voyage took only a couple of hours and we were soon ensconced in the government rest house, typically with wide verandahs, clean and comfortable, the large old-fashioned bathrooms complete with Shanghai jars, and excellent food cooked by the Chinese chef. We spent the days walking and picnicking along the beaches and in jungle clearings, the evenings talking about our plans for the future, aspirations, failed hopes and disappointments, and how lucky we all felt we were to live and work in such a wonderful country with such wonderful people, and how, when independence came, we were sure that Malaya would make a go of it. We had taken our own liquid rations, so we were a cheerful party.

I tried hard to identify exactly where I had landed, but having narrowed it down to one of three beaches, was unable to be certain, as they all looked the same. Perhaps I should have approached them from the sea. On the southern side of the main island are several smaller ones, one of which is called Pulau Dayang Bunting – The Island of the Pregnant Princess. We hired a boat to take us over to it, and then walked through the jungle to its centre where there is a freshwater lake rumoured to be the home of a great white crocodile, into which the princess had been changed for getting pregnant out of wedlock. We picnicked nearby, but not too near the water's edge just in case the legend was true. A truly beautiful place, and one that had never been visited by more than a handful of Europeans. We felt privileged. I understand that all these islands have now been 'developed', and are teeming with hotels and tourists from the world over. Progress?

We frequently weekended in Penang, usually staying with Jean and Laurie Brittain, or at Reid Tweedie's beach bungalow out at Batu Feringgi, with the view across the strait to Kedah Peak that I had first seen in 1930. We attended the usual St Andrew's and St George's nights' festivities at the clubs, although my reeling days appeared over as I experienced heart pains after only a little such violent physical activity. Slow waltzes and foxtrots were now all I could manage. The weekly cricket matches became social events in themselves, and, in my capacity as president, we did quite a lot of entertaining of the visiting sides.

The weeks slipped by; the Emergency scarcely concerned us, the war in Korea was many thousands of miles away and increased the price of rubber, and therefore our commissions. Very few of our Kedah friends knew what it was like to live under curfew, under constant threat of being ambushed and killed, with the movement of food strictly controlled, night attacks, staff and labour force being murdered, obscene or threatening telephone calls – all the normal daily experience of the planting community in other parts of Malaya.

Jean and I had now been together since February 1952, the longest spell since November 1941. Unfortunately, this happy state of affairs was not to last much longer as Jean began to feel distinctly off-colour in the latter part of 1953, and I began to have grave doubts as to how much longer she could tolerate the uncomfortably hot and humid climate before another spell at home. She had regular bouts of fever and dripped with perspiration, even in the cool of the bedroom, with the overhead fan, and a portable one aimed straight at her, going full blast. Dr Dunlop, our regular medico, was on leave so we called in the locum, a retired government medical officer. He duly arrived, took her temperature and remarked that she appeared to be sweating profusely, stating the all too obvious. He told me to get Jean into the Georgetown Hospital as quickly as possible, which I did that same afternoon. But they were perplexed, so I telephoned Reid Tweedie, explained the symptoms and asked whom I should consult, and he recommended Dr Allen, a mutual friend. After tests he diagnosed B. coli infection and treated her accordingly, and strongly recommended a trip home as soon as possible.

It so happened that we had recently received a letter from Jean's mother's doctor in England suggesting that Jean should try to get home as soon as convenient, as the old lady was far from well, and that we should be prepared for the worst. We flew down to Singapore, where, without the usual round of socialising, I put Jean on a KLM flight home, at the end of March 1954. Granny Cuthbertson was to live in the best of health for another 22 years, dying peacefully in her sleep in her 93rd year.

Jean had not been home for more than a few days when she found herself in the Hospital for Tropical Diseases, in London, by the express instructions of my old 'friend' Dr Gregg, the Guthrie doctor. The problem was eventually diagnosed as something caused by the hysterectomy she had had in 1944 when, I suppose, that operation was not quite so much a routine procedure as it was to become. She made a complete recovery from both this and the B. coli infection, was able to be with John for the few weeks after his final summer term at King's awaiting to go into the Army for National Service, before flying back to Malaya in September.

Jean's return to Malaya coincided with John's call-up. She left a boy, and when we all met again, a year later, we met a young man about to receive his Commission in the Royal Artillery.

Living alone was not unusual for me, but the older I became the more I realised how much I depended on Jean, not only for the loving companionship, but also for her encouragement and support, let alone for the smooth running of our home.

Pedro and Greta were great companions. Whilst travelling in the jeep Pedro had to be chained up on the back seat to prevent him from jumping out to attack any stray pie dog or goat we happened to pass. He was by now quite notorious throughout the district, both as a character and as a killer. He was very powerful, without an ounce of superfluous flesh, and with the usual bull terrier's jaws that locked on to the prey. It was noticeable that he never attacked any well-bred dog, whether they belonged to friends or strangers, but pie dogs were clearly anathema to him. I once saw him throw a cow, but fortunately I was able to drag him off before he killed it. At about six each evening I would speed off in the jeep along the estate roads, on a fixed route that Pedro came to know, and he would hare along behind, sometimes taking short cuts through the rubber, to meet me further along the way. After a mile or so I would stop and wait for him, before repeating the ritual. He would then hop in next to me, apparently too exhausted to bother about any 'game' we happened to come across on our way home.

But sometimes he would arrive at our rendezvous first, and when this happened he would use my absence as an excuse to dash off into the nearby jungle to chase monkeys. When this happened it would usually be at about nine, some three hours later, when we would see the rascal slinking in, trying not to be noticed, to lie under my chair. He would be covered in slimy mangrove mud, streaked with blood from the razor-sharp mangrove roots, and stinking to high heaven. As soon as he saw me looking at him, he would wag his tail and quite literally give a broad grin. And the more I scolded him, calling him a smelly, horrible bastard, the more he would grin and wag his tail. I would then take him out to the back of the house, hose him down, and rub antiseptic ointment into his wounds. Chasing monkeys could be dangerous, because if a pack had decided to come down from the trees and attack, as they have been known to do, even a bull terrier of Pedro's strength and courage would not have stood much of a chance.

One day, soon after Jean's return, I was driving along the main road to the Bukit Lembu Division, with Pedro and Greta as usual in the back, when as we drove into Sungei Patani I became aware of much shouting and gesticulating from the pedestrians that we passed. I stopped to see what the fuss was about and saw, to my horror, that I had been dragging Pedro along by the chain on his collar, at a good 30 miles per hour, along the metalled road. All four paws had been ripped to pieces and were dripping with blood. He had almost been strangled and was gasping for breath. I picked him up, held him in my arms and wept. He wagged his tail, smiled, and licked the tears from my face. The government veterinary department was only five minutes away and, luckily, the vet was there. After cutting off the loose claws he bandaged all four paws, injected an antibiotic, and sent us home with instructions to carry him out into the garden so that the battered old friend could answer the call of nature. The vet gave little hope for his recovery.

Thank God we were near the town when he had obviously seen a dog and jumped out to give chase. Jean was as shocked and distressed as I was. She nursed him with great tenderness and loving care, changed the blood-soaked dressings many times a day, and applied the antibiotic ointments prescribed by the vet. In a week he was hobbling, but still in pain, in three he was stumbling out into the garden unaided to 'perform', and in five it was almost as if nothing had happened. Jean's constant nursing and his own indomitable spirit had brought him through. And, perhaps, the knowledge that the Chief of Police, the Gurkha Depot Commander, the Mentri Besar, and a host of friends had all telephoned to find out how he was. We were sure that Greta's companionship and obvious concern had also helped. A prince of dogs. And quite the most affectionate and most loyal friend that Jean and I ever had.

In July, while Jean was still at home, I attended a dinner at the Dog, KL, for former members of Force 136, other branches of SOE, and similar clandestine organisations. I was invited in my dual capacity as an early member of SOE (101 STS was a forerunner of Force 136) and head of Malayan Country Section, ISLD. Sir Gerald Templer, the high commissioner, who had served in Military Intelligence and SOE during the war, attended as guest of honour. I travelled down to KL by car the day before, and stayed with Jack and Joyce Brown. Jack had been in SOE, based in Australia. I spent the morning of the dinner with Claude Fenner and Jock Campbell at the Dog discussing the arrangements over several beers – talking is thirsty work – before returning to the Browns' for lunch and a lie off.

General Templer was met at the door by Claude and John Davis and escorted to the top table, and introduced to those of us privileged to be seated there. He had evidently been well briefed as, when shaking my hand, he said, 'Ah, Hembry. Sungei Siput. Where it all began, wasn't it?' He gave an excellent speech, causing amusement by finishing by saying that this 'get together' was a good way to find out where everyone was in case we were ever wanted again. Audrey Sherwood, the wife of a Kedah planter, was also at the dinner. She had been a Force 136 secretary in Colombo where we had had a nodding acquaintance. After the dinner some of us decided to go along to the Lake Club to dance and I suggested to Audrey that she might like to accompany me. When she agreed I asked Jack to please arrange for my car – in fact, his Rolls Royce – to be brought around to the door, where, having first held the rear door open for Audrey and me to get in, he got into the front with the syce. Seated thus we drove in some style to the Lake Club. I never ascertained whether Audrey realised that it was all a charade, or whether she thought that Guthrie planters were paid very much more than those in other companies.

It was good to be reunited with so many friends, some not seen since 1945, with whom one had so many experiences in common.

I flew down to Singapore to meet Jean off the plane, and held a welcome-back lunch party at the Tanglin Club. The next day we boarded the *Carthage* for the short overnight sea trip back to Penang to arrive off Georgetown at about noon. I thought that Jean would enjoy it, and that it would help her get rid of her jet lag (although the term had yet to be invented, as there were only a few jet airliners flying in those days the principle was the same). We took a taxi to the E&O, for a late lunch and a shower, and then were driven back to KMS where Jean had a boisterous welcome from Pedro and Greta, and life resumed its uneventful passage – until Pedro's near-fatal mishap.

Christmas was spent with Reid Tweedie at Boa Fee, his seaside bungalow at Batu Feringgi, together with the Brittains and other friends. We were also planning our next local leave, and had decided to go further afield than the usual hill stations in Malaya. We chose Hong Kong.

We sailed from Penang in the *Carthage* in February 1955, down to Singapore, arriving the next day, once again enjoying the marvellous trip through the islands. We spent the day visiting friends, lunched at the Singapore Cricket Club, overlooking the Padang, dined with the Coopers at the Tanglin Club, before returning on board in time for the midnight sailing. It was a completely different ship after Singapore. Until then, even allowing for those passengers who had disembarked at Penang, the ship appeared full. After Singapore there were fewer than 100, and barely 20 in first class, where the stewards outnumbered their guests. This was luxury indeed. We dined at the captain's table.

The four days in Hong Kong were spent sightseeing during the day, and wining and dining during the night. We slept aboard the ship. We were taken up to the border with Communist China, in the New Territories, by Gurkha officers whom we had met in Sungei Patani. I remember remarking that from where we stood there was nothing but alien territory all the way to Norway, about a third of the way round the world. We hired a car and drove all the way round Victoria Island, calling in at Repulse Bay for lunch, and one of the famous floating fish restaurants at Aberdeen for dinner. We took the funicular railway to the Peak, window shopped, and generally behaved like tourists visiting the Far East for the first time. On our last night we threw a party on board for all our Gurkha friends, some 20 in all, and others whose names I have unfortunately now forgotten.

We sailed just before lunch, which we missed because we wished to stand on the deck and watch Hong Kong disappear from sight; the last to recede from view was the Peak. The return voyage to Singapore was as enjoyable and calm as the outward leg, and we arrived back having experienced quite the most enjoyable and restful local leave in my 26 years in the East.

In May our thoughts began turning towards another home leave, and Guthrie's booked a passage for us on the new Blue Funnel Company cargo/passenger liner *Patroclus* for early September. The ship was relatively fast, had large staterooms, and a reputation for good food.

Life proceeded very much as before, and I was looking forward to another tour on KMS before retirement in 1960, when I would have done exactly 30 years in Malaya. At the age of 50, I would still be young enough, or so I thought, to obtain a reasonable job in England. With the help of my efficient and loyal staff I was firmly in the saddle and enjoying a quiet canter home. The estate prospered, my replantings were proceeding at a pace, as was the refurbishment of staff and labour quarters. Not quite a case of 'God was in his heaven ...', but all seemed well. The Emergency, still raging in many other areas of the country, seemed miles away, and one was only aware that the fight was still going on from newspaper reports.

We had a strike on one of the divisions on Bukit Lembu. The trouble arose over the alleged unfair behaviour of the divisional clerk. I settled the strike with the help of the local trades union official, a moderate-minded Indian who volunteered to get everyone back to work if I would discipline the clerk. I persuaded him to let me do this informally, so that the man would not be required to lose too much face with his fellow staff, but nevertheless I docked his salary because he had been stupid and had cost the company a day's production. I refused to permit the tappers any overtime to make up for their loss of income from their strike.

I would have been happy to leave Menon John in charge of the estate during my leave, but Guthrie's thought otherwise, and brought up an experienced senior assistant from one of their estates in Negri Sembilan, whom I had not met before, but who had a good reputation. We arranged for a dog-loving planter in the neighbourhood to look after Pedro and Greta for the six months we were to be away.

During the last few weeks before departure we were entertained with several 'farewell' parties, as was the custom in Malaya. I was also busy on the estate tying up a few loose ends. Jean spent much time packing, as we had decided to take as many of our chattels home with us as possible this time – premonition? – leaving only the barest of necessities for the last agreement starting six months later. This was made easier by the availability of rubber chests, similar in size and shape to tea chests, and ideal for house moving. I think, also, that we had decided that, when we finally left Malaya, we would return to England via Australia and New Zealand and across the Pacific, and so would not want a lot of barang to have to move from ship to ship. Nor did we want our possessions to arrive in England and merely be dumped in a godown to await our arrival some months later.

I forbade a party to be given by the estate labour force as, after all, we were only going on leave, not into retirement. When the day came, we bade au revoir to our charming Indian mother-and-daughter bungalow staff, Rosa and Mary, and lastly a sad and tearful parting from Pedro and Greta, whom we delivered to their temporary home, with promises to see them again in the not so distant future. To this day I remember the disconsolate look on Pedro's face. I suspect he knew it was goodbye for ever.

We waved our farewells to many estate workers who, knowing the day of our departure, stood at the roadside waving back. Leaving the estate and out on to the main road, we drove through the beautiful padi fields, the same route that I had first travelled 25 years before. We lunched at the Penang Club, handed over the car keys to the local Jaguar agent at the quayside, and boarded the *Patroclus*. That evening we were joined for dinner on board by Uncle Hannay, the last of our friends to say goodbye to us.

The ship sailed in the early hours, and we went on deck just in time to see the top of Kedah Peak disappearing into the haze. We then returned to the saloon, without a backward glance, to eat a hearty breakfast and to plan the day ahead, blissfully unaware that we had seen the last of Malaya, my home for 25 years, and Jean's for 20, and our beloved dogs. Our emotions would have been entirely different if we had known the truth then. On reflection, we were very glad that we were spared that knowledge, although, years later, Jean confessed that she had known in her heart that we would not be returning, and had cried herself to sleep on that first night after sailing, long after I had passed out, in realisation of the fact.

The ship and the voyage were all that we expected. Our stateroom was spacious, there was air conditioning throughout the passenger area, we had pleasant companions, the food was good, the booze cheap, and the ship's officers and crew efficient and polite. We called at Colombo, Bombay, Aden, Suez, Port Said, and finally docked in Liverpool – my point of departure for Malaya over 25 years before – another omen, perhaps, but still unrecognised, at least by me. This voyage had taken 18 days; the first 28.

We decided to base ourselves in Eastbourne, as Jean's mother had moved to a private hotel there and mine was in a hotel nearby, whilst she was deciding where to live. My mother had been living in South Africa for some years and had only returned to England recently. I made my usual visits to Guthrie's in London, and attended a KMS board meeting at which my future plans for the estate were discussed. Dan Wright had been appointed to the board, and soon after the meeting he and I took ourselves off to the Beguinnot for lunch which, as can be imagined, lasted several hours. I declined his invitation to go on to Merrie's Club, off Portman Square, even though I knew it was much frequented by submariners past and present.

One day, returning by train to Eastbourne from London, we were joined in our compartment quite by chance by a woman whom Jean recognised as Brenda Blades, a friend whose parents had lived near Jean's in Hornchurch, although her married name was now Warnant. In those days the train steward could be summoned from the dining car to take orders for drinks, so we had a round or two. During the conversation Brenda enquired whether we would stay in England, given the chance. Without much thought I said, somewhat flippantly, 'Yes, if I could find a job paying a thousand a year,' and thought no more about it. It must be remembered, in 1956 a salary of £1,000 a year was considered handsome.

A few weeks later Brenda telephoned to ask whether I had been serious when I said that I would stay in England for an annual salary of £1,000. I said no, but why do you ask? She replied that she was secretary of the Rotary International Club, in Portman Square, London, and that the general manager there had just been dismissed and the committee were looking for a replacement. The job paid 1,000 a year, a first-class mews flat nearby went with it, and one was permitted free meals in the Club. This put me on a spot. I discussed it with several family and friends and most seemed to be against such a move, my brother Bill particularly so. But I decided that nothing would be lost if I met the committee. I was interviewed and shown round both the clubhouse and the flat. The former was a magnificent building, with all the facilities of a first-class London gentleman's club except, as I was to find out later, its membership, and a drawing room ceiling painted by Angelica Kaufman, which was a showpiece. The flat was spacious and conveniently close.

I was in two minds. I arranged to see Sir John Hay, and, to my surprise, he was most definitely opposed to my taking the job, to my taking early retirement from Malaya. He pointed out in almost vehement terms that in Malaya I was known and respected throughout the country, whereas in London the opposite was so. In Malaya I was at the top of my profession, whereas in London I would be at the bottom. He also said that, quite apart from the difference in salary levels, in his opinion I was unsuited to the pettiness of the 'rat race' in England.

My meeting with Sir John should have been decisive. Alas, it was not. I sat at a desk in the East India Club smoking room and wrote down the pros and cons. So far as I can remember the pros for my taking the London job were: my health was dicey and I felt fitter in a cooler climate and where, presumably, there were more and better heart specialists; it would be easier to get a job at the age of 46 than 50 ; the proposed salary and benefits were adequate to live on and, together with my savings and Planters' Provident Fund, we would be moderately well off; Jean and I both had widowed mothers, now well into their 70s, living in England; Jean was finding the heat and humidity of Malaya increasingly debilitating; most of our oldest and dearest friends from Malaya had either already retired or would soon do so; the position at the Rotary Club was open now and could not be held indefinitely; and, finally, John was at the threshold of his adult life and we felt that we should be able to see something of him.

The cons were: I was an unknown quantity in the United Kingdom;

I had not worked in England before, so would be as new to the scene as the latest immigrant from the West Indies; we would be leaving Pedro and Greta behind, as two large dogs would be impossible in a small London flat with no garden (this weighed heavily on me); I was efficient at my job and could expect a reasonably large salary and commissions until retirement; I was young enough to reach the top again, if my health held up; by resigning at 46 I would miss out on most of the benefits of the new Guthrie pension scheme that had been in force for only three years; I would have a good chance of several estate directorships if I waited; John was now a grown man, in the army and likely to be posted abroad; and, finally, it would be a 'step into the unknown'.

So, against my better judgment, I made possibly the worst decision of my life and resigned from Guthrie's.

I loathed the new job from the very first day, missed the dogs terribly, and whilst being on call for 24 hours a day as manager of a rubber estate was perfectly acceptable, as a manager of what was little more than a working mens' club in London it was not.

What made the matter worse still was that we heard from Malaya that Pedro was pining away for us, and died not long afterwards, I suspect from a broken heart. And the irony of it was that, when I resigned from the Rotary Club, we moved down to our cottage in Suffolk, where there was ample room for both dogs in the large garden, only six weeks after they would have come out of quarantine if we had brought them home. I will have this on my conscience until I die.

It is a fact that, ever since making the decision to leave Malaya I have lacked confidence in every subsequent decision concerning our personal life, welfare and finances.

However, I did manage to carve out for myself two interesting and reasonably successful careers. First, by taking over the managership of a large apple orchard on the Essex-Suffolk border, and then, in 1962, by joining a firm of land agents and surveyors.

Having answered an advertisement in the *Daily Telegraph* I was selected by Drivers Jonas & Company, in London – I think the oldest of such firms in the country, having been started in 1725 – as leader of one of their teams responsible for surveying routes and negotiating easements for a major oil pipeline being laid from Southampton to Liverpool, with branches off to Birmingham and Nottingham. The employment was to last for six months.

I resigned from Drivers Jonas 17 years later, having worked well into my 70th year, the last seven years of which as their resident consultant land agent with the British Gas Corporation, responsible for negotiating the easements of the new North Sea gas mains network throughout the whole of South East England, including London. The very last job that I did was for the Channel Tunnel project, near Folkestone. But, even though it involved only a short journey from Canterbury, I felt it was too much for me.

So, in a sense, my life story has turned full circle. I started out as a surveyor in 1928, and finished as one in 1980. I am aware that had I stayed on in Malaya it is unlikely that this opportunity would have come my way, so perhaps I made the correct decision after all.

My story, or at least as far as I intend to go, is ended. It has taken two years to complete, and is most certainly not for publication. I have been nearly drowned in the flood of memories and could have quite easily succumbed to prolonged bouts of nostalgia. I have omitted many anecdotes, some crude, some unrepeatable, mostly hilarious. There are also episodes from my time with the ISLD which I have not mentioned, which must remain secret (as the law requires), and are anyway best forgotten. No doubt a historian, many years in the future, will unearth some of the details from official documents, but neither I nor any of the other participants will be around to comment on their findings.

I started these memoirs reluctantly, continued with some enthusiasm, and ended with relief. I hope that my family will consider my efforts worthwhile.

Postscript

At a ceremony held at the Soestdijk Palace, near Utrecht in Holland, in October 1983, I had the honour to be invested with the Netherlands Resistance Memorial Cross by HRH Prince Bernhard of the Netherlands, in the presence of Princess, formerly Queen, Juliana, for services to the Netherlands – my trip with Korps Insulinde to Atjeh in the Dutch submarine O24, back in 1943. John drove Jean and me over for a most enjoyable two days, which included a very moving wreath laying ceremony at the nearby Dutch Resistance Memorial, and a very jolly dinner hosted by members of the Dutch resistance organisation.

The British end was organised by my old friend Bernard Hanauer who, as well as having taken part in Operation MATRIARCH, was responsible, with his very tough fitness training, for saving our lives.

Appendix A

Non-appearance of Spencer Chapman at Tanjong Malim rendezvous

On the day before Freddy was due to leave KL to drive up to meet us at the Tanjong Malim rendezvous he went down with malaria. Luckily, it was of the kind known as 'benign tertiary' – not the most serious type, but extremely debilitating all the same. Consequently, his departure was delayed whilst he received medical treatment. He persuaded the doctor – obviously a gullible man – to allow him to set out, even with a temperature of 103 degrees, on condition that he lay up in the jungle for a few days whilst his temperature fell.

During that day, 7 January 1942, the Japs broke through our line at Slim River and the British Army fell back to Tanjong Malim. On learning this, Freddy sent amended orders up to us by motorcycle despatch rider, but the latter could not get through before the Tanjong Malim bridge was blown, so had to return to KL, the message undelivered. Freddy then decided that he would join the other half of his 'stay behind party', consisting of Bill Harvey, Sartin, Sheppard, Shebbeare and the rest, at Sungei Sempan, and having done so would then try to get across the river to Tanjong Malim to join up with us. In the event he was not able to. Then most of his stores, including his wireless, were stolen by some Chinese. After several brushes with Jap patrols, Freddy split up his party again. Bill, leading one party, was subsequently captured and taken to Pudu Gaol, in KL, where he was eventually joined by Frank Vanrenen and Ronald Graham. Freddy, having come across Bob Chrystal and Robbie Robinson, members of another 'stay behind party', at their jungle camp near Sungei Sempan, went on to spend three years in the jungle with the MPAJA and Sakai, before we were able to get him back by submarine to Ceylon in May 1945.

Appendix B

Fate of Frank Vanrenen and Ronald Graham

Having flown back to Singapore in the Tiger Moth from Sumatra, Frank and Ronald reported to 101 STS Headquarters in the Cathay Building where they met John Davis and Richard Broome who, together with Basil Goodfellow, were planning to establish and lay down supplies for an escape route to the Indigari area of Sumatra for the many British Army stragglers known to be wandering around behind the Japanese lines. As Frank and Ronald were to attempt to meet up with Freddy Spencer Chapman, the two parties joined forces in the requisitioned motor junk *Hui Lee* and sailed to Bagan Siapi Api, on the east coast of Sumatra, under the command of Col Warren.

At Bagan Siapiapi my two friends hired a sailing junk to take them across the Strait of Sumatra to the vicinity of Kuala Selangor, setting sail on 12 February. The junk returned to Sumatra towards the end of February to report that Frank and Ronald had not returned. The skipper had stayed near the agreed rendezvous for six days, even though he had been instructed by my friends to wait for only four days.

John Davis, Richard Broome and others were to make their epic escape to Ceylon from Padang on the *Sirdhana Johannes*.

Frank Vanrenen and Ronald Graham were captured by the Japanese and taken to Pudu Gaol in Kuala Lumpur, where they met Bill Harvey who had also been captured after he had split up from Freddy Spencer Chapman. Somehow the three managed to escape from Pudu Gaol, but were recaptured near Bentong trying to get to Bill's old estate, betrayed by kampong Malays, and returned to Pudu.

Tominara, the Jap gaol commandant, who considered them 'truculent and rude' – probably for failing to avert their eyes when in his presence – ordered their execution. Having first been kept in solitary confinement for several days, without food or even water, and made to dig their own graves, my friends Frank, Ronald and Bill were beheaded.

The kampong dwellers who betrayed them cannot be blamed. They knew that the Japs would have rounded up and shot the entire village had they not reported the escapers' presence.

Appendix C

Winning Hearts and Minds

This became one of the twin principles, together with victory in the field, of General Templer's plan to overcome the communist insurgency in Malaya, a phrase which ever since has been constantly used by others in many contexts.

Although many believe the Americans to have coined the phrase in Vietnam (where they singularly failed to implement the concept) I maintain that those words were first used simply as a throw-away remark by Del Tufoe while we were chatting informally prior to a Federal War Council meeting he chaired in November 1951. I see from notes which I retain that I repeated the phrase during the ensuing meeting, voicing my opinion that the Acting High Commissioner's concept was indeed the sine qua non for victory over the Communists. My comment received unanimous agreement.

I have no doubt that Del Tufoe repeated the expression to the new high commissioner, maybe even in the car on the way to King's House KL after the official welcoming ceremony at the airport, and that they were subsequently seized upon by Templer as encapsulating his contention that the war in Malaya could not be won unless the support of the vast majority of the population, of all races, could be won over and retained.

I suspect the phrase was then introduced to the Americans in Vietnam by Sir Robert Thompson.

Glossary

Amah a Chinese maidservant and nanny, see also 'ayah'.

ASDIC now known as SONAR. Used to detect submarines and other underwater obstacles.

Atap roof thatch made from large palm or banana leaves or fronds.

Atjeh old spelling of Aceh, Indonesia.

Ayah an Indian maidservant and nanny, see also 'amah'.

Ayer limo lime and water (now spelled air limau).

Barang luggage, goods, things, stuff.

Basha simple hut or temporary shelter.

Batavia former name for Jakarta, Indonesia.

Blaht small huts built on stilts in quite deep water, and from which they could cast their nets (now more commonly known as 'kelong').

Box wallah slang for a desk-bound or 'armchair' soldier (literally a small-scale travelling merchant peddler in India).

Burra peg double whiskey, see also 'chota peg'.

Bukit hill.

Charpoy a woven bed comprising a wooden frame bordering a set of knotted ropes.

Chaung river (Burmese).

Chota hazri breakfast.

Chota peg slang in British India for a glass of whiskey and water or soda, see also 'burra peg' and 'stengah'.

Dhobi person who washes clothes; also British military slang for 'to wash one's clothes'.

FMSVF Federated Malay States Volunteer Force. Each state had its own battalion in which peoples of all races served. Europeans often held ranks junior to Malays and Indians, as did Boris Hembry.

Force 136 the SOE organisation operating in the S.E. Asia area.

Gunong mountain (also spelled gunung).

ISLD Inter Services Liaison Department. The cover name for the SIS organisation in South East Asia.

Istana palace belonging to Malay royalty.

JB abbreviation for Johor Bahru, Malaysia.

Kampong village or small collection of houses (also spelled kampung).

Kangani foreman.

Kebun short for 'tukang kebun' or gardener.

Kedai provisions shop or, as in 'kedai kopi', a coffee shop.

Kempeitai Japanese secret police – the equivalent of the German GESTAPO.

KL abbreviation for Kuala Lumpur, Malaysia.

Krani clerk

Kuala estuary (hence Kuala Lumpur is Muddy Estuary).

Lalang a kind of long, coarse, weedy grass.

Laut sea.

Makan the Malay verb 'to eat', also a slang form of 'makanan' meaning 'food'.

Malaya the British name for pre-independence Malaysia.

MCS Malayan Civil Service.

Mem the Malayan equivalent of memsahib; madam.

Mentri Besar Chief Minister. During British rule, British-appointed advisors acted as chief ministers in Malayan states with a monarchy.

MPAJA Malayan Peoples Anti Japanese Army. Communist Chinese-led, but trained and equipped by Force 136 to rise up against the Japanese when the Allies invaded Malaya (Operation ZIPPER). It was renamed the Malayan Peoples Anti British Army during the Malayan Emergency.

OCPD Officer Commanding Police District. Responsible for law and order in the district surrounding a town, or large village like Sungei Siput, which had a police station (with administrative offices, armoury, charge room and cells etc.).

Orang person, man.

Orangutan derived from 'orang' (man) and 'hutan' (forest/jungle).

OSPC Officer Supervising Police Circle. In charge of several police districts.

P&O Peninsula & Orient Steam Navigation Company.

Padang literally a field, but also a public square or sports field (especially for cricket).

Padi rice plants.

Parang machete or cleaver-like knife used to cut through thick vegetation and as a weapon.

PD abbreviation for Port Dickson, Malaysia.

Peon office messanger.

POSH Port Out Starboard Home. In the days before air conditioning on ships it was preferable to have a more expensive cabin facing away from the sun. Only the 'posh' could afford such luxury.

Pulau island.

PWD Public Works Department. The government department, so named in all the colonies throughout the Empire, which built and maintained the roads, bridges, and government facilities.

SACSEA Supreme Allied Command South East Asia. Lord Mountbatten was the Supreme Allied Commander and liked being called 'Supremo'.

Sampan generic name for any small boat.

Satu empat jalan Literally 'one *four* road', *satu empat jalan* was a popular expression used by British servicemen and expatriates in Malaya to mean 'one *for* the road', to have a final drink before leaving.

SFC Special Forces Club. A congenial watering-hole in London, for those of all Allied nations who have been, or are involved in clandestine operations and special forces (SAS, SOE, OSS, etc).

Siam the official name of Thailand before it was changed in 1939.

SIS Secret Intelligence Service. The branch of the Foreign Office responsible for acquiring intelligence information concerning foreign (enemy and occasionally Allied) governments, the dispositions and order of battle of their armed forces, and their military, political and industrial intentions and potential. Also known as MI6 (Military Intelligence, Section Six).

SOE Special Operations Executive. Formed originally on Churchill's instructions to 'set Europe ablaze', to organise, equip and train resistance movements in enemy-occupied countries in sabotage and other disruptive activities. 101 STS (Special Training School), established in Singapore in 1941, was part of SOE. SOE operated in the European, Middle East, Mediterranean, Balkans, S.E. Asian and Pacific theatres of war.

Stengah slang in British Malaya for a long whisky and soda or water – see also 'chota peg'.

Sungei river or large stream.

Syce driver (literally Indian groom or stable attendant).

Tanjong spit or promontory (of land or sand) into the sea or river (also spelled tanjung).

'The Railway' the railway line built through the jungle between Thailand and Burma by POWs of all nationalities captured by the Japanese. It was intended to link Singapore with the north of Burma, and ultimately to India.

Tiffin lunch.

Towkay small-time businessman, builder, or contractor, usually Chinese.

Tuan sir.

Tuan besar someone in a senior position, e.g. the manager or director.

Tukang ayer water bearer (now spelled 'tukang air').

Ulu jungle, back of beyond (literally 'upriver' in Malay).

VA Visiting Agent. Rubber companies often employed senior planters as visiting agents to make regular inspections of their estates.

Wayang Malay and Indonesian puppet theatre.

Bibliography

Allan, Charles. Tales from the South China Seas. Deutsch, 1983.

Barber, Noel. The War of the Running Dogs. Collins, 1971

Bartlett, Vernon. Report from Malaya. Derek Verschoyle, 1954.

Brooke, Geoffrey. Singapore's Dunkirk. Leo Cooper, 1989.*

Chapman, F. Spencer. The Jungle is Neutral. Chatto & Windus, 1949.*

Cloake, John. Templer – Tiger of Malaya. Harrap, 1985.

Clutterbuck, Richard. The Emergency in Malaya, 1948-1960. Cassell, 1966.*

Connell, Brian. Return of the Tiger. Evans Bros., 1965.

Cross, John. Red Jungle. Robert Hale, 1957.*

Cruikshank, Charles. SOE in the Far East. OUP, 1983.*

Cunyngham-Brown, Sjovald. The Traders. Newman Neame, 1971.

Foot, MRD. SOE – The Special Operations Executive, 1940-1946. BBC, 1984.

Gough, Richard. Escape from Singapore. William Kimber, 1989.*

Gough, Richard. SOE Singapore. William Kimber, 1985.*

Hobhouse, Henry. Seeds of Wealth. Macmillan, 2003.

Holman, Dennis. Green Torture. Robert Hale, 1962.*

Horton, Dick. Ring of Fire. Leo Cooper, 1989.

Irwin, Anthony. Burma Outpost. Collins, 1945

O'Brien, Terrance. The Moonlight War. William Collins, 1987.*

O'Donovan, Patrick. For Fear of Weeping. MacGibbon & Key, 1950.*

Phillips, C.E. Lucas. The Raiders of Arakan. Heinemann. 1971.

Shennan, Margaret. Our Man in Malaya. Sutton. 2007.*

Shennan, Margaret. Out in the Midday Sun. John Murray, 2000.

Slim, William. Defeat into Victory. Cassel, 1956.

Trenowden, Ian. Operations Most Secret. William Kimber, 1978*

Trenowden, Ian. The Hunting Submarine. William Kimber, 1974.

West, Nigel. Secret War. Hodder & Stoughton, 1992.*

* Boris Hembry is mentioned by name in these books.

Boris Hembry also recorded a two-hour interview for the Imperial War Museum for their archives.

Tiffin party, Kedah, 1933. (STANDING: A.N. Other, Malonie, Jim Davis, Bob Chrystal, Walter Northcote-Green, Jonah Jones, Currie. SITTING: Ralph Inder, Burroughs, Dan Wright, Boris Hembry, Galland.)

Boris and Jean Hembry, England, 1935.

Latex runs down the tapped rubber tree into a collecting cup. Tapping is usually performed in the early morning before the temperature rises so the latex drips for longer before coagulating and sealing the cut.

Waterloo Estate bungalow, 1935. Waterloo was a small estate, under a thousand acres, in Padang Rengas, Perak, some six miles north of the royal town of Kuala Kangsar. This was Boris and Jean's first married home and Boris' first managership.

Gunong Tunjuk (also known as Lion Hill) on Kamuning Estate. On Coronation Day 1937 Paddy Jackson and Boris Hembry climbed to the summit where they planted a Union Flag.

The Assistant Manager's bungalow on Kamuning Estate, 1936. Kamuning Estate, over 8,000 acres in size, was situated astride the main north-south road, about 15 miles from Kuala Kangsar and 19 miles north of Ipoh. Boris and Jean Hembry lived on Kamuning Estate for 14 years.

The Perak Battalion of the Federated Malay States Volunteer Force (FMSVF), Port Dickson, 1938. Boris Hembry initially trained as a Vickers machine gunner with the FMSVF.

2/ Lt Boris Hembry, Perak FMSVF. In early December 1941, Boris Hembry reported to Perak FMSVF B Company headquarters in Kuala Kangsar, where most people were still of the opinion that the embodiment was only a 'dummy run'. Days later the Japanese invaded Malays and Boris Hembry was not to see his wife Jean again until 1944 when sent on a short course to England.

A young John Hembry with Ronald Graham, Kamuning Estate pool, 1940. The following year, Graham escaped from Pudu Gaol in Kuala Lumpur, where he was a prisoner of the Japanese, only to be recaptured in Bentong. Graham was then kept in solitary confinement for several days, without food or water, made to dig his own grave and beheaded.

Boris Hembry, Bob Chrystal and John Hembry, 1940. Bob Chrystal was to survive three years in the Malayan jungle during WWII before coming out of the jungle with Force 136 and Boris Hembry's ISLD following the Japanese surrender.

Desmond E. Wilson with the ISLD Kedah team, 1945.

T-class submarine, like the HMS *Tactician* which carried Boris Hembry from Ceylon to Penang and Langkawi on covert patrols.

Operation EVIDENCE 1, January 1945. Boris Hembry's first operation involved George Brownie, Charles Knaggs, Donald Gray, Chinese agents Ban Ho and Ah Lieu, and the second radio operator Wong Weng Fong.

Operation EVIDENCE 2. Boris Hembry with FANY secretary, Nigel Crompton and Douglas Lee-Hunter.

Air Chief Marshall Sir Keith Park with his son Colin, who Boris Hembry recruited as an ISLD agent. Colin Park survived WWII only to be killed by Communist Terrorists during the Malayan Emergency whilst serving with Ferret Force.

RIGHT Lt Col Boris Hembry, Ceylon, June 1945.

FAR RIGHT Boris and Jean reunited after WWII, Kamuning Estate, 1946.

Boris Hembry (centre) outlines his ideas on squatter control to High Commissioner Sir Henry Gurney (right), Changkat Kinding, October 1948. Hembry's suggesitons were later incorporated in the Briggs Plan.

Hembry's Own Bloody Army (HOBA), Kamuning Estate, June 1948. To protect the estate factory and office during the Malayan Emergency, Hembry's old platoon sergeant from the Perak FMSVF, Eusoff, trained an armed squad of young men from the neighbourhood in basic arms drill and fire discipline. The company payed their wages and Jean Hembry sewed on the HOBA shoulder flashes which she herself embroidered.

Boris Hembry receiving the Colonial Police Medal for Meritorious Service from High Commissioner Sir Henry Gurney. The investiture was held at the Police Padang, Kuala Lumpur, 1949. Hembry received cables of congratulation from Guthrie's in London, Singapore and KL, together with many letters and telephone calls from friends and acquaintances. Unfortunately, the medal was engraved Maurice Hembry instead of Boris Hembry.

Jean and Boris (standing in centre of photograph) talking to Anthony Eden (seated), the future British Prime Minister, Ipoh, 1949.

Boris Hembry travelled by armoured jeep on Kamuning Estate, seen here in 1949.

Paddy Jones, a colleague of Hembry on Kamuning Estate, narrowly survived an ambush by Communist Terrorists in 1952. The car he was driving, pictured here, was a bullet-ridden write-off, his Malay special constable escort and dog were killed and he himself took four bullets.

Payroll drop, Ulu Remis, 1951. At the height of the Emergency, payrolls for employees of isolated plantations were dropped by air to avoid losing the money to bandits in the event of ambushes on the jungle roads. Drop zones were usually clearings near the plantation manager's residence.

Kamuning Estate manager's bungalow, pictured in 1950, following renovation works to make it more secure from attack. The ground level of the house, which normally would be open, was boarded up.

Harry 'Uncle' Hannay, 1954. Harry Hannay served in the Boer Wars and WWI, and was interned for four and a half years in Sime Road Gaol, Singapore, during WWII. He was a mining consultant who called Malaya home and at the time he bade Boris and Jean Hembry farewell on the day of their departure from Malaya, he had not been back to his native Scotland for 40 years.

Special Forces Dinner, KL, 1954. From the left: 'Jock' Campbell; High Commissioner Gen. Sir Gerald Templer; Col. Lloyd Owen; John Davies; Claude Fenner; Richard Broome.

Kim, fully recovered from Japanese brutality, 1946.

Wounded Pedro, Sungei Patani, 1954.

Boris Hembry receiving the Netherlands Resistance Memorial Cross in 1983. Investiture by Prince Bernhard of the Netherlands.

Index